WRITING FOR MASS COMMUNICATION

LONGMAN SERIES IN PUBLIC COMMUNICATION
SERIES EDITOR: RAY ELDON HIEBERT

WRITING FOR MASS COMMUNICATION

EARL R. HUTCHISON, SR.

Longman
New York & London

Executive Editor: Gordon T. R. Anderson
Production Editor: Halley Gatenby
Text Design: Laura Ierardi
Cover Design: Kenny Beck
Text Art: J & R Services, Inc.
Production Supervisor: Judith Stern
Compositor: Maryland Composition Company, Inc.
Printer and Binder: The Murray Printing Company

Writing for Mass Communication

Copyright © 1986 by Longman Inc.

All rights reserved. No part of this publication may be reproduced, stored in a retrieval system, or transmitted in any form or by any means, electronic, mechanical, photocopying, recording, or otherwise, without the prior permission of the publisher.

Longman Inc.
95 Church Street
White Plains, N.Y. 10601

Associated companies:
Longman Group Ltd., London
Longman Cheshire Pty., Melbourne
Longman Paul Pty., Auckland
Copp Clark Pitman, Toronto
Pitman Publishing Inc., Boston

Library of Congress Cataloging-in-Publication Data

Hutchison, Earl.
    Writing for mass communication.

    1. Mass media—Authorship. 2. Journalism—Authorship.
I. Title.
P96.A86H88 1986   808'.066001   85-23194
ISBN 0-582-29033-3

86 87 88 89 9 8 7 6 5 4 3 2 1

CONTENTS

FOREWORD — xiii

PREFACE — xv

PART I
WRITING FOR THE MASS MEDIA — 1

CHAPTER 1
DEVELOPING AS A WRITER — 3
- DIFFERENT STYLES FOR DIFFERENT NEEDS 3
  - Make It Easy for Your Audience 3
- FINE-TUNING YOUR POWERS OF OBSERVATION 5
  - Writing from Imagination 5
  - Writing from Direct Observation as a Participant 6
  - Writing from Indirect Observation 7
- WHEN IS INFORMATION NEWS? 8
  - Some Blind Spots for Beginners 9
  - News Interpretations May Differ 11
- BASIC WRITING PRINCIPLES 12
  - Accuracy 12
  - Objectivity 13
  - Credibility 15
- WRITING FOR THE MEDIA TAKES TEAMWORK 16
  - An Important Team Player: The Editor 18
- SUMMARY 18
- EXERCISES 21

PART II
INFORMATION GATHERING — 35

CHAPTER 2
BACKGROUND RESEARCH — 37
- PUBLIC SOURCES 37
  - Libraries 37
  - Political and Civic Groups 38
  - Government Offices 38
- PRIVATE SOURCES 42
  - Professional Groups 42
  - Research Organizations 43
  - Newspaper Libraries 44
- REFERENCE SOURCES 44
- SUMMARY 45
- EXERCISES 47

Chapter 3
DEVELOPING PRIMARY NEWS SOURCES 51
    THE BEAT ASSIGNMENT 51
        ORGANIZING THE CAMPUS BEAT 52
        ORGANIZING THE CITY BEAT 55
    MAJOR NEWS BEATS 56
        COVERING THE COURTS 56
        COVERING GOVERNMENT AND POLITICS 59
        A COMMENT ABOUT COUNTY GOVERNMENTS 61
        STATE AND FEDERAL GOVERNMENTS 62
        COVERING EDUCATION 64
        NEWS SOURCES IN BUSINESS AND LABOR 66
    VIGILANCE PAYS OFF 67
        THE RELUCTANT NEWS SOURCE 71
        SECRECY IN GOVERNMENT (AND ELSEWHERE) 73
    SUMMARY 76
    EXERCISES 79

Chapter 4
INTERVIEWING 93
    ARRANGING AND CONDUCTING AN INTERVIEW 93
        TELEPHONE INTERVIEWS 94
        HOMEWORK FOR THE INTERVIEW 95
        IN THE BEGINNING, PUT THEM AT EASE 96
        LISTEN TO THE ANSWERS 97
    SUMMARY 98
    EXERCISES 101

Chapter 5
ORGANIZING THE INFORMATION 107
    EVALUATING YOUR RESEARCH 107
        OUTLINING 108
        BRINGING ORDER TO THE OUTLINE 109
        DEVELOPING AN OUTLINE 109
        THE BLOCK METHOD 113
        KEY QUOTES AND KEY WORDS 114
        TO OUTLINE OR NOT TO OUTLINE 115
        ARCHIVING 115
    SUMMARY 116
    EXERCISES 117

Part III
WRITING TO INFORM: THE NEWS 121

Chapter 6
NEWS FOR NEWSPAPERS: LEADS AND BASIC STORIES 123
    KEY INTEREST POINTS 124
        HEADLINES AND SLUGS 124
        SIMPLE LEADS AND THE INVERTED PYRAMID 124
        SOME GOLDEN LEAD RULES FOR BEGINNERS 128
    SUMMARY 129
    EXERCISES 131

Chapter 7
News for Newspapers: Complex Stories — 137

- Expanded Lead and Story Styles 137
  - The Summary Lead 137
  - The Salient-Feature Lead 139
  - The Suspended-Interest Lead 139
  - Follow-up Stories 140
- How to Write a News Interview Story 142
- Different Audiences Can Dictate Different Coverage 144
  - Local News 146
  - Technical News 149
  - Special-Interest News 152
  - Billboard News 160
- Summary 163
- Exercises 165

Chapter 8
News for Newspapers: Writing for Impact — 199

- Sentence Patterns 199
  - Variations 200
  - Attribution 202
- Paragraph Patterns 203
  - The Triadic Structure 203
- Language and Imagery in Newswriting 206
- Summary 208
- Exercises 209

Chapter 9
The New News Technologies — 213
by Helen E. Aller

- The New Technologies 214
  - Videotex: The Electronic Newspaper 214
  - Teletext 215
  - Cabletext 216
  - Newspaper Companies Lead the Way 216
- Skills for Electronic Journalism 217
  - Format 218
  - Editing Is Still Most Important 218
  - Information Management 219
  - Good News Sense Is a Must 219
  - The Importance of Conciseness 220
  - Composing for Videotex 220
  - Composing for Cabletext 222
  - Graphics 223
  - Computer Programming 223
- Summary 223
- Exercises 225

Chapter 10
News for Radio — 233

- The Four Basic Radio News Leads 233
  - The Soft News Lead 233
  - The Hard News Lead 234

The Throwaway Lead 235
The Umbrella Lead 236
RADIO NEWSWRITING: THE CONVERSATIONAL STYLE 238
Radio Writing Checklist 238
REWRITING RADIO WIRE COPY 241
THE RADIO NEWSCAST FORMULA 243
Some Technical Aspects 244
SUMMARY 246
EXERCISES 247

Chapter 11
NEWS FOR TELEVISION
by David G. Clark
269

TELEVISION TECHNIQUE 270
TV Talk 270
Television Scripting 270
SUMMARY 278
EXERCISES 279

Part IV
WRITING TO INFORM: FEATURES
283

Chapter 12
NEWSPAPER FEATURES
285

SOURCES FOR FEATURES 286
STRUCTURE OF A FEATURE 287
Make Each Lead a Sure-fire Hit 288
Setting the Tone 289
Body Paragraphs 290
FEATURE ANALYSIS 291
Valleys and Peaks 292
Style of the Feature 293
The Importance of Details 293
Concluding Paragraphs for the Feature 293
WRITING A FEATURE 294
Assignment 294
Getting the Facts 294
Observation 294
Research 295
Interviewing 295
Outlining 296
First Draft 297
Revision 299
INTERVIEW FEATURES AND SIDEBARS 301
The Question-and-Answer Interview Feature 301
The Sidebar 302
BLUEPRINT FOR IMPACT 305
SUMMARY 308
EXERCISES 311

CHAPTER 13
MAGAZINE ARTICLES — 325

- MAGAZINE ARTICLE LEADS 326
  - THE DRAMATIC LEAD 326
  - THE NOVELTY OR CURIOSITY LEAD 327
  - THE QUESTION LEAD 327
  - THE NO-NONSENSE LEAD 327
  - THE SETTING LEAD 328
  - THE COMBINATION LEAD 328
- TITLES 329
- THE READER-INTEREST PLANE 329
  - THE BUSINESS FEATURE 330
  - TRAVEL AND LEISURE FEATURES 331
  - THE PERSONALITY PROFILE 332
  - CHARTING THE READER-INTEREST PLANE 337
- STEPS FOR DEVELOPING MAGAZINE ARTICLES 342
  - MAGAZINE ARTICLE IDEAS 343
  - MAGAZINE MARKETS 343
- MAGAZINE MANUSCRIPT FORMAT 345
  - REJECTIONS 346
- SUMMARY 347
- EXERCISES 349

PART V
WRITING TO PERSUADE — 357

CHAPTER 14
OPINION — 359

- PREPARATION FOR WRITING COMMENTARY 359
  - IMPORTANCE OF THE OPENING PARAGRAPHS 361
- WRITING TO PERSUADE 361
  - COMPOSING THE COLUMN 365
- THE ESSAY 368
- REVIEWS 375
  - THE REPORTORIAL REVIEW 375
  - THE STANDARD REVIEW FORMAT 375
- SUMMARY 379
- EXERCISES 381

CHAPTER 15
ADVERTISING — 391
BY ROBERT L. BISHOP

- SETTING ADVERTISING OBJECTIVES 392
  - COPYWRITER'S QUIZ 392
- ELEMENTS OF ADVERTISING COPYWRITING 394
  - HEADLINE 394
  - SUBHEADS 395
  - TEXT 395
  - SLOGANS, LOGOTYPES, SIGNATURES 395

ANATOMY OF AN AD 396
    ADS THAT SOLVE PROBLEMS 397
    ADS THAT APPEAL TO COMPETENCE 398
    ADS THAT APPEAL TO STANDARDS OF EXCELLENCE 399
TESTING 401
    CONSUMER RESPONSE 401
SUMMARY 402
EXERCISES 405

CHAPTER 16
PUBLIC RELATIONS AND PROMOTION WRITING   413
by Robert L. Bishop

EXTERNAL PUBLIC RELATIONS 414
    TOOLS 414
    CAMPAIGNS 427
INTERNAL PUBLIC RELATIONS 430
    TOOLS 430
    CAMPAIGNS 432
SUMMARY 433
EXERCISES 435

CHAPTER 17
WRITING FOR THE MASS MEDIA   443

THE *WASHINGTON POST* COVERS THE STRIKE SETTLEMENT 443
THE WALL STREET JOURNAL COVERS THE STRIKE SETTLEMENT 445
ASSOCIATED PRESS COVERS THE STRIKE FOR ITS NEWSPAPERS 447
ASSOCIATED PRESS RADIO SERVICE COVERS THE STRIKE SETTLEMENT 448
CBS EVENING NEWS COVERS THE STRIKE SETTLEMENT 449
PUBLIC RELATIONS TREATMENT OF THE STRIKE SETTLEMENT 450
UNITED AIRLINES' ADVERTISING DEPARTMENT ANNOUNCES THE SETTLEMENT 453
SUMMARY 455

APPENDIXES

APPENDIX A
COPY AND REPORTING RULES   457

APPENDIX B
WORDS COMMONLY USED AND ABUSED:
A LIST TO AID SPELLING AND USAGE   460

APPENDIX C
A COMMONSENSE APPROACH TO PUNCTUATION   **464**

APPENDIX D
COPY-EDITING MARKS   **466**

INDEX   **469**

Foreword

All over the world, mass communication has become an activity essential to modern life. In the past six months, I have visited five European countries, five African countries and three Caribbean countries. Everywhere, people seem to be preoccupied with the news and entertainment and persuasion that they receive from their mass media. And in much of the world, the media are developing rapidly and changing constantly.

In the Caribbean countries of St. Vincent and St. Lucia, people are rushing to buy television sets for the first time, because microwave relay dishes have been set up to bring in TV signals via satellite from Chicago. In the Netherlands, you can now watch television news from a half-dozen different countries, in English, German, Dutch, French and Danish. In France, the government has opened radio frequencies to commercial stations, and you can now listen to dozens of different types of programs and points of view. In Zambia and Zimbabwe, governments have established local news agencies to process all incoming news so that it can be interpreted from each country's own political or cultural perspective. In Kenya and Somalia, communicators are studying the techniques of commercial radio and television advertising so that they can develop similar messages to persuade people to improve their farming techniques, eat proper food for better health and follow simple safety procedures. In South Africa, blacks are working hard to develop their own newspapers in order to keep their people informed of political and social actions that affect their struggle to gain equality.

Never before have the mass media been so important. And never before have they been used so broadly to inform, persuade, interpret, entertain and sell. In industrial societies, agriculture and manufacturing concerns are employing fewer and fewer people as machines and automation undertake more and more tasks. But the information and service industries are employing increasing numbers of people. We have moved from an agricultural age to a manufacturing age to an information age.

Even in the information industries, certain types of activities are being taken over by machines. The manufacture of products can to a large extent be automated. Increasingly, typesetters, printers, engineers and technicians are being replaced by machines. When I first worked for the *Washington Post* in the 1950s, there were more printers than editorial staff, and the printers earned higher pay. Manufacturing the product was more essential than providing the content. Today, there are fewer printers and more reporters and editors, and the printers are paid less. When I worked for NBC News in Washington in the 1960s, there were only one or two dozen members of the news staff, and they were outnumbered by technicians. Now, there are nearly 200 on the news staff in the Washington office alone, far more than their support staff.

The job of gathering, writing, editing and processing information is not only becoming more important, but it cannot be done by machines. Certainly, computers will increasingly aid reporters and editors. But the human mind will always be essential to the tasks of perception and judgment necessary to inform, persuade, interpret, entertain and sell.

So there is a growing need for people with information-gathering, writing and editing skills and talents. Those skills and talents can be developed. And that is what this book is all about.

Learning how to gather information and how to write about it effectively is somewhat like learning how to play a musical instrument. You cannot learn simply by reading a book or listening to a lecture. You must actually do it, over and over again. You must learn certain principles and then apply them. You must start with simple exercises, practice them until they are easy to perform, and then go on to more difficult tasks, learning from your mistakes as you go through the criticism of an experienced teacher or editor. Such a process can make anyone into a polished professional. Some people have better verbal skills than others, just as some are more musical. But almost anyone, with practice and the aid of patient critics, can become a proficient writer.

This book is based on the notion that certain basic principles are common to all effective writing. At the same time, however, those principles must be applied in different ways for various media. Each medium of mass communication has its own "language," and it is as important to learn the language of the medium as it is to perfect the skills of effective writing. The rules for writing news and information, entertainment and interpretation, persuasion and promotion, vary from medium to medium.

This book shows, in theory and through practical exercises, how those basic principles of effective information gathering and writing are applied differently for the various media. This is an introductory text aimed at the first- or second-year college student and providing a broad view of all media. Some students will go on to specialize in particular kinds of writing—news or entertainment or persuasion. Some will go on to specialize in a particular medium—newspapers, magazines, radio or television. The study and practice of writing for all the mass media can help students to discover their own strengths and preferences, aiding that decision to pursue a particular career track.

Yet it is also important for the modern mass communicator to know how all the mass media work—how they are similar and how they are dissimilar. Flexibility in being able to move from one medium to another, or from one kind of writing to another, will be increasingly important to the professional in mass media because the media are all interrelated.

The skills and talents that can be gained from the theory and practical exercises in this book can, indeed, be helpful in all areas of modern life: writing a business report, promoting a small enterprise, organizing material quickly and presenting it effectively in any kind of forum, or becoming a professional journalist with a responsibility for providing thorough and accurate information to readers, listeners and viewers around the world. The results of your time and practice can be well worth it.

RAY ELDON HIEBERT
Professor of Journalism
University of Maryland

PREFACE

Writing for Mass Communication fulfills a vital need in today's information revolution. Written for the first- or second-year journalism student, it provides instruction in all the major areas of media writing, from news and entertainment through opinion and persuasion; from writing for newspapers and television through writing copy for advertising and public relations departments. Not only that, *Writing for Mass Communication* is interesting and easy to read and understand.

If students' writing skills are not what they ought to be, this book will provide the instruction and exercises necessary to improve those skills. We believe that writing skills and basic media writing can be taught simultaneously. And that is what this book does.

Writing for Mass Communication not only treats the skills of information and data gathering prior to putting words on pages and screens, it also treats the art and skills involved in writing those words for greatest impact. Although this is not an English composition text, the reader nevertheless needs to understand the effective use of language, including the perception and thought involved in this use, how grammar affects style, and how substance is wedded to form. In treating the craft of writing, we go beyond the basics to introduce higher levels of writing artistry—preparation necessary for the information revolution students will encounter after graduation.

In this information age, students should be instructed in the writing skills required by *all* the mass media—electronic as well as print. This instruction should cover *all* forms of writing for the mass media—not just news writing, but the kind of persuasive writing, for example, used in advertising and public relations.

Writing for Mass Communication treats three forms of mass media writing: (1) writing to inform, (2) writing to entertain and (3) writing to persuade. More and more journalism graduates find themselves using all these writing forms at one time or another during their professional careers. Indeed, some are required to use more than one form in *one* job. A public relations person, for example, may need to know not only how to write stories or features for newspapers but how to put those stories or features into radio and television form as well. A news reporter for an Associated Press or United Press International bureau may be called upon to write a story for newspaper clients and then to rewrite the same story in radio format for the electronic media. That trend is not likely to be reversed in the future, especially given the advent of the new teletext and videotex technologies and the number of newspapers buying into these different news distribution methods.

The need for this education of journalism students has already been noted in a recent comprehensive study of communications schools by the University of Oregon's School of Journalism. Titled "Planning for Curricular Change in Journalism Education," this study of the future of journalism and mass communication education recommends in part that courses introduce students to this broader view of mass communication education.

In helping to prepare students for this information revolution, *Writing for Mass Communication* creates a whole world. Each chapter builds upon the others to make the learning and teaching experience as easy and enjoyable as possible. Each chapter is also written to be as much of a self-contained unit as possible. Writing principles and patterns are stressed and reemphasized as they appear in the various media forms in different chapters. Chapters are liberally laced with interesting examples of the principles presented therein. Numerous and varied exercises at the end of each chapter are coordinated to present a simulated reality of writing in the media world and to help instructors teach the necessary skills. In essence, this book contains everything needed for a comprehensive media writing course that will lead naturally to more advanced and specialized media courses in newspaper, magazine, radio, television, public relations, advertising and the new technologies.

Finally, *Writing for Mass Communication* can serve the student in the future as a reference book for the greatest course of all—a career in the media world.

This acknowledgment of what I owe to those people who helped me with this book is small tribute indeed. Nevertheless, it shall be a beginning for numerous friends and colleagues.

Among the major contributors are David G. Clark, Robert L. Bishop and Helen E. Aller. All responded unselfishly and on short notice with chapters for this text. Ray Hiebert, advisory editor for Longman Inc., saw the need for a book such as this one, and together we outlined the chapters for it. Tren Anderson, executive editor at Longman, was always there when I called New York for advice, in early morning or late evening. And when the days grew long, Sheila Gibbons brought her editorial skills to shine upon these pages. For their help in the book's production stages, I would be remiss if I failed to mention Halley Gatenby, the production editor, and Martin Billig, assistant editor.

These colleagues responded, again on short notice, to commit their experienced commentary to these pages: H. Carlisle Besuden III, Elise Frederick, William Harwood, W.A. Reed, Ken Renner, Patti L. Smisson and Larry Woody.

How many friends and colleagues I forced to listen to my ideas and words I am fearful of recalling. My colleague Hix Stubblefield was even forced to read some of the chapters. (And did so, I might note, without complaint.) Jay Joyce also read many chapters and cheered me on. The travail inflicted upon my wife, Olivia, in this regard (and which she gracefully endured) has brought me to vow never again to subject her to this ordeal.

Others should be mentioned here, but they are too many—from former professors and other authors who penned the best of the newswriting books to my mentors during my media experience.

Most of all, the students I've been privileged to have in my classrooms should receive plaudits. They have listened. They have heeded. They have questioned. Through all the years, they have endured and have enlightened me. They have been a source of delight during dreary days. They have protected me from cynicism. They have been a constant source of faith. And for those reasons, I dedicate this book to them.

EARL R. HUTCHISON, SR.
Tennessee Technological University

WRITING FOR MASS COMMUNICATION

PART I
WRITING FOR THE MASS MEDIA

Writing is an ever-changing means of communication. With the advent of today's technological explosion, writing, especially media writing, is undergoing spectacular changes. To write with confidence today, to know how to construct the proper relationships between ideas and words and to make the decisions that result in good writing, one must meet the challenges of the information age revolution.

Most people become reporters, editors, broadcasters, and public relations and advertising communicators because of a flair or passion for writing. But there are no shortcuts to becoming a good writer. Although it is only human to want instant success or an instant career—after all, we are products of our age, and our society is rife with instant coffee, fast-food chains and fast tracks—no instant, magic formulas exist for the would-be writer. If you want to write for the media, a rigorous apprenticeship is involved. That apprenticeship not only enables you to write well; it also enables you to think and write quickly, clearly and accurately under pressure. In the world of the newspaper, radio and television reporter and the related spheres of public relations communication and advertising, speed vies with language skill as the most important asset in a writer's ability bank. In this course you will learn, perhaps for the first time, that sooner is better than later and that fewer words can have greater impact. Both of these concepts are basic principles of mass media writing.

The writing style called for by every mass medium requires training. The apprenticeship just mentioned begins in the classrooms at colleges and universities where communication skills are taught. It's on campus that solid information-gathering skills can be learned, then tested through writing exercises that parallel real-world assignments. Joining the campus newspaper or radio station, stringing for a local daily or weekly paper or landing an internship at a TV station, magazine or public relations firm can accelerate your progress and shorten the time you spend as an "apprentice." These experiences will help you move more quickly into the ranks of professionals.

The seasoned professional has a well-developed sense of news and a relentless curiosity. Accuracy is the top priority in the practice of his or her job. Writers are not born with these traits. They are developed through training and experience. It's also important that the beginning writer approach writing with a "professional" attitude. It will help reinforce the ideas presented in this book and in this course.

CHAPTER 1

DEVELOPING AS A WRITER

DIFFERENT STYLES FOR DIFFERENT NEEDS

Make It Easy for Your Audience

A professional writer must have a knowledge of the different media and the different communication characteristics of each. The print media, for example, appeal to the eye. Through typography, headlines and clear writing, they seek to stimulate the reader's desire for details and capture his or her attention. Print media writers also know there is a "sound" to the words they write, and this sound and flow and rhythm should be wedded to the "sense" of what is being communicated. Read this example of a report of a holdup that was over almost as quickly as it began:

> Three bank robbers slipped into the First American Bank this morning, jumped over the counter, herded five employees and customers into a vault, and made off with $20,000.
> "It took less than three minutes," Dr. Jack Ross, a customer, said. "When I saw those criminally close eyes backing up those guns, I ran for the vault."

If that robbery had been more casual, it might have been written like this:

> Three bank robbers walked casually into the First American Bank this morning and robbed it of $20,000. Five bank employees and customers were herded into a vault by one of the robbers while the other two gathered small bills in two pillowcases.
> "They took their time about it," Dr. Jack Ross, a customer, said. "But when I looked into those criminally close eyes, I knew they meant business."

Long, flowing, descriptive sentences, ideal for describing pastoral scenes and leisurely events, don't belong in a story about a fast-paced robbery or a riot in a ghetto.

Writers for the electronic media must be aware of still other considerations. Radio audiences, for example, are listeners. Writers for radio must write primarily for the ear and the imagination rather than for the eye. Radio audiences often listen while engaged in other tasks—driving cars, preparing meals, studying for tests, etc. The audience's attention must first be attracted by a general statement: "A United States senator expressed concern over the growing threat of nuclear warfare today." Once the attention is captured, the details can be given: "Senator Edward Kennedy said that . . ." The listener cannot go back to a paragraph of news copy and reread the details when the newscast is over, so the attention-getting statement to alert the listener is essential.

Compare this story, written by a UPI reporter for the wire service's radio clients, with the story that follows it:

```
    FORMER SECRETARY OF STATE HENRY KISSINGER TOURED
CAPITOL HILL TODAY ... PAYING A STRING OF CALLS
ON CONGRESSIONAL LEADERS. KISSINGER WAS APPOINTED
LAST WEEK BY PRESIDENT REAGAN TO HEAD A SPECIAL
BIPARTISAN STUDY COMISSION ON CENTRAL AMERICA.
    KISSINGER TOLD BROADCAST INTERVIEWERS TODAY (ON
C-B-S) THAT HE TOLD LAWMAKERS NO VIETNAM-TYPE
COMMITMENT OF U-S TROOPS IN THE TROUBLED REGION
WILL BE NECESSARY—QUOTE—"FROM ALL THAT I'VE
SEEN." BUT KISSINGER STRESSED THAT HIS 12-MEMBER
COMMISSION WILL SEEK ONLY LONG-TERM SOLUTIONS TO
THE REGION'S PROBLEMS AND WILL NOT GET INVOLVED IN
THE REAGAN ADMINISTRATION'S IMMEDIATE PLANS. HE
REJECTED SUGGESTIONS THAT THE RAPIDLY DEVELOPING
U-S INVOLVEMENT IN THE REGION MEANS HIS PANEL'S
REPORT—EXPECTED IN ABOUT SIX MONTHS—WILL COME
TOO LATE TO MAKE A DIFFERENCE. IN KISSINGER'S
WORDS ... "THE RECOMMENDATIONS WILL BE RELEVANT."
```

Now read how a different UPI reporter wrote the same story for UPI's newspaper clients. Notice especially the beginning of the story and its length:

WASHINGTON (UPI) — As critics voiced concern about deepening U.S. involvement in Central America, Henry Kissinger said yesterday that the presidential commission he heads will seek to avert a nationally divisive "Vietnam type of crisis."

President Reagan called Kissinger to the Oval Office to discuss how the 12-member commission named last week will come up with recommendations to ease the economic and social ills that underlie troubles in the hemisphere.

But the public stress on non-military solutions to what Reagan has termed "the first real communist aggression on the American mainland" was offset by a growing controversy over military exercises in the area and a new report of plans to step up paramilitary activity against Nicaragua.

The New York Times reported that the administration is planning a massive expansion in CIA-directed operations that would involve "the most extensive covert operations mounted by the United States since the Vietnam War."

The newspaper said the expanded covert activity would include support for a larger force of anti-Sandinista rebels and sabotage directed at Cuban bases in Nicaragua.

At the same time, Navy sources reported that an eight-ship battle group, led by the aircraft carrier Ranger, has arrived 100 miles off the Pacific coasts of Nicaragua, Honduras and El Salvador for the start of military exercises.

The battleship New Jersey and its escorts have left port in Thailand, bound for the same area, the sources said. The voyage would usually take at least two weeks.

Kissinger said the 12-member commission on Central America will deal only with long-range policy and will not be involved with "current operational issues."

He said the commission's report probably won't be completed by the December deadline; he expects that the project will take until February.

The panel may travel to Central America, but it will "look beyond the immediate crisis," he said.

"I think it is imperative that we avoid the bitter debate that characterized the Vietnam period and also that we avoid the same kind of uncertainty about objectives and what was attainable," Kissinger, who served as secretary of state in the Nixon and Ford administrations, told a news conference at the State Department.

The newspaper story actually continued for another six column inches—entirely too long for radio, television or videotex.

The videotex writer composes stories that will be read by persons watching a TV screen or computer screen monitor. Writing for what has come to be known as an "electronic newspaper" requires combining the brevity and immediacy of radio writing with the thoroughness of a newspaper account.

The television writer must not only heed the requirements of the radio writer as far as writing for the ear but must pay particular attention to the sophisticated demands of the eye as well. The visuals (graphics, film, videotape) must be melded with the written words to be spoken by the anchor or the reporter. Being too literal in describing what is being shown on the screen ("Here we see the mayor cutting the ribbon opening the city's shelter for the homeless," as the film of the mayor doing exactly that rolls) will bore the viewer. The writer of television news must develop a script that "dances" with the visuals, as in, "At today's ribbon-cutting ceremony for the city's first shelter for the homeless, the mayor called on the state to assume a greater financial responsibility for indigent citizens." The presence of a visual image can tell part of the story by itself, freeing precious air time for the reporter to provide more of the story.

The most successful media writers may specialize in one medium, but they are familiar with the differing styles of all the others.

FINE-TUNING YOUR POWERS OF OBSERVATION

Though writers adapt their writing formats to suit the particular medium for which they work, the skills that support their writing styles are all the same. The police reporter for the local television station and the police reporter at the city's daily newspaper have both developed the same skills to find the news and report it effectively.

WRITING FROM IMAGINATION

The media writer calls upon imagination as much as memory to help in writing. The imagination reveals the various avenues of story development open to you when you are gathering materials for it. As you track that story, the imagination continually suggests alternatives, branches and development possibilities. When you sit down to write the story, the imagination supplies you with words, phrases and images. Here is an example of the imagination at work in developing materials for a news story:

You read a national wire story that the cost of living has risen so dramatically that citizens on Social Security pensions are buying pet food to eat. How you go about developing the story depends not only on the training you have received but just as much on your imaginative powers.

You check the local Social Security office to determine if the cost of living in University City is affecting pensioners locally as it appears to be nationally. You question the director and various clerks about the matter. How many pensioners live in University City? Some 3,000. Are any eating pet food? The answer is no.

You check utility companies to determine if more bills are going unpaid this year by senior citizens. They are. Anywhere from one to 200. You ask what happens if the utilities are not paid. The answer: They are cut off.

You call the Salvation Army to determine if they are serving more meals to the needy this year compared to last. They are. Are more elderly persons eating there this year? They believe so.

You ask two major grocery chains to check the pet food sales over the past two years. There is a significant increase in canned pet food. Is it cat or dog food? Both. What are the brands? The best-known brands, in cans, constitute the increase. You ask grocery clerks. Have they any knowledge of significant amounts of pet food being bought by the elderly? Two know of such persons for a certainty. You get the names of the senior citizens. You call on those two senior citizens. You ask them if they know people who are purchasing pet food for their own consumption. After some reluctance, they give you names of other persons. You ask them if they themselves have ever eaten pet food. They admit that they have. You guarantee them anonymity and call on three other senior citizens. You get four more names; one woman says you can use her name in your story. Your training, combined with your imagination, have helped you develop an important story for University City.

How you piece all this together, whether for wire or cable service, a newspaper, or a radio or television station, will depend once again on your training, partnered by your imagination.

WRITING FROM DIRECT OBSERVATION AS A PARTICIPANT

Having explored, in cursory fashion, the role of imagination in writing, let us take one step outside of our mind, so to speak, and discuss writing from direct observation as a participant.

At the time of this writing, Tom Baker is mayor of Waitsburg, Wash., a city with a population of 1,035. Not only is he mayor of Waitsburg, he is the chief reporter and publisher of Waitsburg's only newspaper, the *Times*. The only other reporter in Waitsburg is his son. (*His* name is Loyal!) As a direct participant in the city's government and business, Baker can report what happens as no other reporter can. He is there. He is participating. He knows what's going through his mind when decisions affecting the city are made. Perhaps more than anyone else in Waitsburg, he knows first what is happening, when it is happening, and how and why it is happening. A reporter does not have that obvious advantage of knowing the inner feelings of the city official. Even the deep inner workings of city government and business may not be known to the reporter. Unless the reporter has been on the city hall beat for two or three years, that knowledge is usually not available. Those are the advantages that Tom Baker—mayor and reporter—has.

The disadvantages are these: His selection and perception screens are distorted by his role as mayor. His sympathies may be captured by the group he is working with. In this instance, his prejudices and biases are introduced into the reporter's supposedly objective point of view of the city's business transactions. As a participant, Tom Baker is also part of the news. He is something more than a reporter. People who might say something about the way the city's business is being conducted to a regular reporter will be reluctant to mention those things to Mayor-Reporter Tom Baker. As a "reporter," Tom Baker will discover that some events will be "staged" for his benefit.

To be or not to be involved depends on many other factors than those mentioned. Before you would infiltrate the Ku Klux Klan or the police force or a motorcycle gang, you would consider the potential danger to your life. And how would your personal life suffer? Would there be time to infiltrate and engage the trust of those you're observing—would the media budget allow it? Could your reporting be done better through indirect observation? Certainly some indirect observation would be used in the final report in any event. There could be as many drawbacks to infiltrating an organization and reporting on it as a participant-observer as there could be advantages.

WRITING FROM INDIRECT OBSERVATION

If you are assigned a story and you are not going to write it as a direct participant-observer, you will no doubt investigate and report from indirect observation. When you write from indirect observation, reasoning as well as imagination will be brought into play, as the following illustration makes clear.

University City is in a dry county. People used to drink alcohol purchased in cities as far as 50 miles away. One year ago, however, an adjoining county became a wet county. Subsequently, three liquor stores opened up in Virdon, a small town with a population of 3,000 no more than 12 miles from University City. City and civic leaders deplored the opening of these stores. They predicted dire consequences: teen-age drinking, drunken driving and an increase in drinking overall, not to mention the generally accepted evils accompanying that activity. The news director of WUCU-TV tells you to determine the effect on University City of those three liquor stores that were opened one year ago. What do you do?

You check newspapers on file at the library to determine what the citizens feared one year ago. A number of articles verify that civic leaders did predict evil from liquor sales.

You drive to Virdon and ask the liquor store owners what percentage of their liquor sales are made to University City residents. They estimate that more than 40 percent of their liquor is sold to people from University City.

You drive back to the University City police station. Has there been an increase in public drunkenness from last year? No. Has there been an increase in domestic disturbances resulting directly from drinking? No. Has there been an increase in drunken driving arrests? Not significantly. Has there been an increase in drunken driving by under-age drivers? No. The state highway patrol corroborates the police reports: no increase.

You check with garbage collectors. Any noticeable increase in discarded liquor bottles? No.

You check with the dean of men and dean of women at the university. Any discernible increase in drinking noted by their offices? No.

You check with the counseling center. Any increase in the counseling of students with drinking problems? No.

The University Safety and Security Department reports no increase in rowdiness or disorderliness as a result of drinking.

High school principals report an increase in the use of marijuana but not in the use of liquor.

Five of the city's ministers did not note any increase in the use of liquor by members of their congregations.

You have a story.

What you can infer from this series of indirect observations is that University City citizens are buying liquor from Virdon liquor stores. They are saving gas and driving time by buying it there rather than in Carlinville, where they used to buy their liquor. (The change in purchasing site also gives you another item to test: Have liquor sales fallen in Carlinville?) University City citizens and students, despite this shorter driving distance, apparently have not increased their liquor consumption. The city leaders' earlier fears stemming from the prospect of more accessible liquor appear unfounded. When you write your story, you cite your investigation, liberally quoting the people you interviewed.

WHEN IS INFORMATION NEWS?

An ongoing process of evaluating and judging takes place in writers' minds when they are deciding what is, or is not, important information. Both journalists who are news reporters and editors, and public relations writers who work for a company that is making news, engage in this process of evaluating, then communicating, what would be of interest to their audiences. The process involves sifting the routine and the repetitious (those events that represent the cycle of life: births, deaths, anniversaries, etc.) and the non-routine and non-repetitious (fires, business mergers, crime, storms, scientific breakthroughs). The process considers newsworthy characteristics of events, such as:

- ☐ Timeliness (did it just happen?)
- ☐ Proximity (how close is the event, physically and psychologically?)
- ☐ Prominence-eminence (how many people have some knowledge of the person or event?)
- ☐ Significance-consequence (how many people will, or may, be affected?)
- ☐ What will, or may, happen as a result of this?
- ☐ Humor (does it have the comic relief everyone welcomes in this worried world?)

All these thoughts are processed in the writers' minds as they look at an event and attempt to come to a decision about its newsworthiness. During this process, experienced writers keep their own prejudices and biases firmly in mind because they know that their judgment will be influenced by them but that their story must not be. The quilting party in Red Boiling Springs, for example, or the Swan Ball at the Belle Meade Country Club may be two extremes as far as their tastes are concerned. But with prejudices and biases properly harnessed, both can be seen as events worthy of news coverage. Few of you might believe that the news items from "Route 10" would rate coverage in a newspaper, but almost identical stories are printed in small dailies. It's what we call "country correspondence." It's a news staple.

Route 10

Mr. and Mrs. Tom Heneghan visited Mr. and Mrs. Edward Hayes. Hayes has been in the hospital with some heart problems but is home now. He has been home for the last week and he is getting better as of now.

Mr. Charles Dan Ross went deer

hunting last week and came home with a nice deer.

Mr. John Offnutt has been doing fine the last month till last week. Lynn and Bill Hall both came down with this new virus or flu, but they are up and going again. Several people in our community have had the sore throat virus or whatnot.

Mrs. Marge Rios has been stripping tobacco for the last two or three weeks.

There have been a few people in our community who have put their tobacco on the market.

As you can see, the judgments or evaluation of what is or is not news and determining where it ranks on a news value scale are not easy tasks. Some people will never be able to make competent determinations of what constitutes newsworthiness.

You may be certain of one thing, however: If you place 20 news items on a sheet of paper, making certain 10 of them are not of any particular newsworthiness, and then let 20 experienced reporters look at them, the vast majority will point to the 10 most newsworthy events. Not only that, if you ask them to rank them as far as importance is concerned, there will be almost complete uniformity in their ranking—in much the same way that coaches and sports writers are able to agree on the top 10 football teams toward the end of the season.

Some things, of course, are not news. If John K. Sircy is not killed flying his plane from Boulder, Colo., to La Crosse, Wis., that is not news. If Beth Hunter does not visit her mother in Washington at Christmas time, that is not news. "Non-happenings" tend not to be news. But is the obverse true? Are "happenings" news?

Most happenings are not news. Whether they make it into the newspaper or onto television is an indication of the importance of the happenings. What factors determine the importance, or newsworthiness, of the happening? As indicated in preceding paragraphs, these factors determine their newsworthiness: the closeness, or proximity, of the happening; the prominence of the persons involved; the timeliness of the event; the relevance to the audience; and the human interest of the event. The humor of the event also determines newsworthiness, simply because it brings smiles to the faces of worried citizens.

Determining what is news—what should go into a newspaper or over the air and with what emphasis—is a complicated matter. But news events surround and fill our lives daily. And if you're a news writer and you've disciplined yourself to think and observe like a news writer, you'll not only be able to get that story the editor sends you out for, you'll be able to pick up another along the way.

Once you finish your training and are employed as a reporter, you are the major determinant of what is news. If you see something happening, and you go through the news processing procedure with it and determine that it adds up to news, and if you then write the story and it's published, it is, in fact, news.

Some Blind Spots for Beginners

Most people will be able to recognize most news events after a course in newswriting. Blind spots will exist, though, even for those. Here is an example.

At one university, a Luncheon Forum is held every Monday in the University Center almost directly under the office where the university newspaper is put together. Attending the Luncheon Forum are all major administrators, along with 40 or 50 faculty members and 300 to 400 students—among them most of the student leaders. Presiding over the luncheon on an alternating basis are the president of the university and the student body president. About 25 minutes into the luncheon, announcements by various organizations are made. Sometimes awards are presented, and sometimes achievements by various groups or students are recognized. Then the luncheon is thrown open to questions from the floor relative to the functioning and governing of the university. At that time students, irate and otherwise, approach the microphone placed in the center of the room for that purpose and direct their questions and comments to the presiding officer.

"Why are the lights turned out on the tennis courts at 9 p.m.?"

"Why isn't the computer center open on Sunday afternoons?"

"Why have the typing courses been discontinued?"

These questions, directed to the presiding officer, are then referred to the administrator or faculty member in charge of the operation or function under examination.

What is taking place, of course, is an example of democracy in action, a more elaborate form of the presidential press conference. The administration and the faculty, and sometimes other student groups, are called to account for their errors of commission or omission. Leaders are made answerable to their constituents.

The editors of the university newspaper attend the luncheon. (Sometimes they are taken to task for editorials or news stories that do not meet the approval of some of their readers.) If you were to ask these students and other students in the journalism program of the university if that Luncheon Forum should be reported weekly in the newspaper, half of them would say yes, and the other half would say no. Of the half that answered no, however, many would argue that the forum should be used as a source for news stories—that is, questions that go unanswered and are important enough to warrant news coverage should stimulate an inquiry that may result in a news story. For these students, if the important question is answered, a news story would not be warranted.

"Why shouldn't the Luncheon Forum warrant news coverage?" you might ask those students.

"Everyone knows what goes on in the Luncheon Forum," they reply, "so why write a story about it?"

"The president of the United States," you point out, "holds a press conference roughly every month that is covered by all three television networks. Millions of people view it. That conference is covered by the press, so why shouldn't the Luncheon Forum be covered by the university newspaper?"

"That's different," they answer. "That's the president of the United States."

Little things do not mean a lot to them, you say to yourself. You try again.

"The football game at Homecoming is an event attended by more than 10 times the number of students who attend the Luncheon Forum and yet the sports editor covers the story in the newspaper. Why should the editor do that?"

"That's different," they answer. "That's sports."

A blind spot.

In basic training in the infantry, you are instructed to look for the enemy first on the terrain immediately in front of you, because that is where the enemy might very well be. Huge potholes in that recently paved street you drive on to work may mean a contractor skimped on materials. A speed trap may turn into a story on a major crackdown on motorists. A broken window could mean an increase in vandalism because of the economy. When you start looking for news, start at home. Many of the blind spots are there.

When there is no news, sometimes that is news. Here's an example.

Your university is plagued with charges of discrimination of one kind or another. You are given the assignment of checking out one case—one charge. You interview the applicant for the position in question, a tenured position in the English Department. You also interview the faculty chairperson who recommended that the person be granted tenure. You interview the college dean who rejected the recommendation. The university provost, president and chancellor uphold the rejection. You review the procedures for acceptance and rejection.

You determine that there is no reason or basis for the person to claim discrimination.

Is there a news story here? Most beginning news reporters would say no. That is the temptation. But the answer is yes, if the story hasn't been written before. The story is in how one person feels discriminated against and how various regulations and university procedures worked legitimately against that person's claim for tenure.

When there is "no news," look for the angle that might make a "non-happening" into news.

NEWS INTERPRETATIONS MAY DIFFER

It would be wrong to leave you with the impression that every writer will see the same thing in an event or even see the same event in the same way. Different persons perceive different things in different ways. It all has to do with our different experiences, our different lifestyles. As a result of those experiences, our brains have different distortion screens, through which all these perceived events pass.

For example, if you have a friend who handles obituaries for a newspaper, your friend may perceive the man across the street who stoops down to tie a shoelace as having a heart attack. Does that seem a natural reaction to you? It is. Stop at a gas station and ask directions to some location. Chances are the attendant will say, "Drive down the road a couple of miles till you come to an Exxon station. . . ." That's the way it is. Your distortion screen may let you see a Christmas tree as a beautiful decoration, while your environmentalist friend will see it as wanton destruction of nature's resources. So it will be with news interpretations of events. That's why it pays to know your biases. In other words, know what forms your distortion screen.

By now you know that if you are bent on seeing steak and hamburger is flashed on a screen, you may very well see steak. If you are assigned as a reporter to cover a meeting, and if you are bent on seeing that meeting as a confrontation between two factions, you may perceive in any dialogue between those factions animosities and hostilities where perhaps only minor differences exist. Not only that, these differences may actually be ironed out in the dialogue. Look at what happened to two reporters covering the December 1982 meeting of the Organization of Petroleum Exporting Countries in Vienna.

Robert Burns of the Associated Press:

OPEC prices for their oil likely are stuck right where they are for a while, a leading oil minister said yesterday.

Thomas J. Lueck of The New York Times:

The stability of the international oil market is being threatened by mounting dissension among members of the Organization of Petroleum Exporting Countries.

Western experts believe that disputes among the 13 nations could lead to lower prices for consumers, but would pose severe economic problems for several oil producers.

Both stories were published in the same edition of *The Tennessean*.

The moral in all this is that sometimes you can place trust in your sources, but at other times you might better place your trust in still other sources. Both of the reporters at the OPEC meeting would have served their readers better had (1) Burns mentioned what "Western experts" think might happen at the meeting and

(2) Lueck mentioned what the oil ministers of the two countries had to say about the meeting. That would have been more balanced, more responsible reporting.

As the meeting turned out, Lueck was right. And United Press International no doubt took delight in scoring against its Associated Press rival by describing the dissension that ruled the OPEC meeting. UPI Senior Editor Barry James wrote the news story the next day:

> VIENNA — The 66th meeting of OPEC ministers collapsed in shambles yesterday as they failed to agree on the crucial issue of national production quotas.
>
> Experts said there could be a sharp drop in oil prices.

BASIC WRITING PRINCIPLES

The interesting facts gathered by journalists, such as those about impoverished senior citizens forced to eat pet food or the question of change in alcohol consumption by University City residents, would be lost if reporters were unable to present them to their audiences in an interesting way. Having collected the information and drawn their conclusions, writers must now face a typewriter, word processor or editing terminal, and tell the story.

Part III of this book deals extensively with the mechanics of writing for different media. But the objective of this chapter and this section, particularly, is to familiarize beginning writers with the attitude and preparation a professional writer brings to each and every assignment. We look at the writer as a filter of information, an individual who possesses the awesome power to influence the way readers, listeners and viewers of the mass media interpret the world around them.

ACCURACY

Basic, concrete details are the foundation of every story's credibility. Attention to details—or lack of it—will affect a reporter's reputation and, ultimately, his or her career.

What happens, for example, when your writing contains factual errors? When those errors are published on the printed page, on a screen or in a broadcast, a sense of uneasiness is stirred in your audience and in your editors. If those mistakes continue, the uneasiness quickly turns into distrust. How did *you* feel, for example, when you last saw your name misspelled in a letter, in a student directory, in a newspaper, or on a certificate or an award that was presented to you? If you are writing for the media, lack of accuracy will turn off readers, viewers and listeners. They'll simply turn to someone who's more reliable.

In reporting, accuracy is aided by careful direct observation. Attention to detail is extremely important: If you are interviewing a person, for example, how genuine is the greeting? Is the handshake firm? The smile forced? Are the eyes evasive? Listen carefully to the words and how they are spoken. If you are trying to determine how prosperous the business executive is, what type clothing is he or she wearing? Where does the person live? How is the office furnished? Although some details can mislead you, more often than not their total impression gives an accurate picture of the state of things.

OBJECTIVITY

Generally speaking, the more sources you consult, the more sides you'll hear, and the better your chance of presenting an objective view of the event or the issue. Although you will never be *truly* objective, records, documents and other published facts all aid you in your attempt at objectivity.

If you are forced to rely on witnesses—other people's observations to provide you with an accurate estimate of a situation—pay particular attention to their credentials. A political candidate will rarely level with you about the state of a political race if the race is floundering. Rarely will a person fired from a position be able to present you with an unbiased account of the reasons for the dismissal. Knowing the background and credentials of the indirect observer—the witness—enables you more accurately to assess the truthfulness of the picture being conveyed to you. You also have to understand and make allowances for the fact that different people see different things in different ways.

That happens all the time. Read this newspaper account of former Senate Majority Leader Howard Baker's encounter with the law:

Baker Fined for Speeding

JACKSBORO, Tenn. (AP) — Senate Majority Leader Howard Baker ran afoul of the law this week by speeding 16 mph over the limit, but says he declined a traffic officer's offer to let him go without a ticket.

Instead, the Tennessee Republican said he wanted to be "treated like anybody else" and was issued a $55 citation after being clocked by radar going 61 mph in a 45-mph zone on Wednesday.

Baker, who is resigning after his current Senate term expires in 1984, said his wife, Joy, admonished him about the ticket when he returned to his home in nearby Huntsville.

"Joy reminded me of something she has been reminding me of for a year now," he said. "When I leave the Senate, I shall surely perish.

"She said I can't take care of myself. I can't make airline reservations, I can't make hotel reservations, and now I can't even drive myself. She said every time I get out on my own I always get in trouble."

Seems cut and dried, doesn't it? But Sen. Baker's account of the incident may not be correct. The Jacksboro chief of police gave the following version of the incident to United Press International: "Officer Jim Lindsey said that it never entered his mind to turn Baker loose. 'That was a lie,' Lindsey said. 'I did tell him that he knew I wouldn't be doing my job if I didn't give him a ticket.' Lindsey said the senator told him to give him his ticket and let him go."

Different perspectives will provide, many times, conflicting versions of incidents. Baker, expecting to be given an option, interpreted Lindsey's remarks in that light.

To convey the sense of accuracy and objectivity, note the source of all facts that are not common knowledge. That the country is emerging from an economic recession may be common knowledge if, for the past six months, economic indicators such as unemployment figures, housing starts and consumer buying underline the fact and if, for the past six months, various economic experts and market analysts have been making statements to that effect. However, if the indications are less clear, a statement about the degree of economic recovery would require verification from an economic authority. Similarly, the fact that annually a frightful toll of lives is taken on our highways is common knowledge. But if you state that the average weekend toll on the highways is 500, you would be obligated to attribute the figure to an authoritative source, such as a highway safety authority.

In addition, ideas that are not your own should be attributed to their originators. Proper attribution conveys not only that you are striving for accuracy and objectivity but also that you are fair and honest.

Objectivity may be more easily approximated if you understand that absolute objectivity is unattainable. Nonetheless, like Sisyphus, you continually strive to roll that boulder to the top of the mountain. Writers, like everyone else, have biases and prejudices about people and events. More sensitive than the average person, writers also have emotions and feelings that will be stirred more deeply. These emotions and feelings should be understood and removed as much as possible from writing when you are attempting to be accurate and objective.

It's human nature to rearrange and adjust the world of our reality. We persuade ourselves that things are not what we perceive them to be and try to persuade others of the reality of our perceptions. Learning to counter this wish-fulfillment part of our intellectual and emotional makeup is a major part of becoming a mature reporter. If you do not believe that this is a major undertaking, perhaps you should know that most media researchers agree that 50 percent of all news stories contain some type of error. A research report for the American Newspaper Publishers Association indicated that a larger number of psychological factors contribute to these inaccuracies. Among them are these:

1. Fantasies that reporters allow to form in their minds about an event to dispel internal stress or cognitive dissonance
2. Authoritarianism, dogmatism, or open- or closed-mindedness of the reporter covering the event
3. The orientation or predisposition a reporter has about the source and/or the news message

All this means that if you know yourself well, you will be more able to appraise a news event objectively and write about it more accurately.

This is not to say that subjectivity is not permissible. In some reporting, it is encouraged. You can hardly be otherwise when writing about personal experiences in an article titled "Twenty-four Hours in an Emergency Room." Charged with displaying your views on a particular subject to your readers in the form of essays, columns and reviews, subjectivity is permissible. But when you are not engaged in writing such articles, to achieve the utmost objectivity in your writing, you must be aware of how personal feelings muddy the waters.

In the search for truth, for meaning and significance, in the attempt to determine and describe reality, the media writer engages in the same processes that behavioral and social scientists engage in. Through investigation and observation, both journalist and scientist attempt to gather reliable data objectively. Both attempt to report their findings objectively. The major difference between the journalist and the scientist lies not in the attempt to report the truth but in the strength and scope of the investigation. Although the journalist, because of limited time and resources, may at times be guilty of generalizing from a particular set of facts, he or she is compensated by deriving a truth not available to the scientist. The journalist may allow emotion and intuition to enter into various stages of investigation and reporting. Both are valuable in arriving at that approximation of the truth. On the other hand, the scientist, in the attempt to discover the truth, is almost totally limited by the scientific data obtained by observations, investigations and experimentation. In determining the truth, then, the journalist has some of the advantages that the poet has. While the scientist is limited by the most stringent self-imposed restrictions, the journalist may bring intuition as well as common sense and intelligence to the facts discovered by observation and investigation. The whole of the journalist's intellectual, intuitive and imaginative faculties are employed in this search.

CREDIBILITY

To establish credibility with readers and viewers, you should also know the common language and symbols available to you. The medium through which you choose to communicate determines, to a large extent, the kind of language structure you use: Simpler and shorter sentences are used for videotex, cabletext, teletext, and radio and television than for newspapers or magazines. Audiences also affect the language and symbols you use. Different words and phrases are used to address readers of a corporate publication, readers of The Atlantic Monthly, and subscribers to Viewtron videotex.

Also affecting your choice of language will be the subject matter itself. Language used in explaining the near-tragedy of a nuclear meltdown at Three Mile Island will be highly technical compared to the words you will use to describe a day at the St. Lawrence County Fair. But regardless of the subject matter and the publication you are writing for, try not to write down to, or patronize, your audience. Try to be frank and sincere—to write only what you believe to be true.

Your aim, or purpose, in writing will also influence your choice of words and language. Do you want to alert people to the environmental hazards of waste disposal? Your choice of words will be more serious than if your assignment is to describe the operations of a local dating service. Whatever the subject matter, whatever purpose you have in writing, whatever medium you select, whatever audience you address, select language appropriate for the story.

Don't do to your readers what one writer did to thousands who read his account of one of the greatest tennis matches in history. With one story, this reporter established himself as the supreme master of the cliché. The writer took a theme, crafted it into a snappy lead paragraph, then proceeded to overdo the analogy with contrived comparisons. Simply put, it was too much of a good thing:

By WILL GRIMSLEY
AP Special Correspondent
WIMBLEDON, England (AP) — It was the "Thrilla in Manila" all over again but in rubber-soled sneakers on the sacred turf of Wimbledon's Center Court and with tautly strung tennis rackets instead of boxing gloves.

For 3 hours and 53 minutes, the killer Swede, Bjorn Borg, and brash kid from New York, John McEnroe, slugged it out with everything within reach — sabers, sledgehammers, pick axes and cannonballs.

Then, when it was over in the English gloamin', it was the champion, not the challenger, sprawled out on the balding grass and the loser erect, stiff-lipped and unbending.

Borg, the 24-year-old golden-haired Viking and one-time boy wonder whom they say is made of ice and steel, won his fifth consecutive Wimbledon in a titanic struggle 1-6, 7-5, 6-3, 6-7, 8-6, but it wasn't a knockout.

At best it was a TKO with young McEnroe, wearing a red headband of courage, proving himself an unflinching, indefatigable fighter good enough to turn the tide on another day.

For tennis, it was a repeat of boxing's third historic battle between Muhammad Ali and Smokin' Joe Frazier, with striking similarities in the fierceness of the combat, the ebbs and tides and finally the dramatic finish.

Only this month an American tennis magazine published a list of the 20 greatest matches of all time, as selected by an international panel.

Forget it. Call back the editions. Tear up the pages. Order another vote.

Perhaps the greatest of all has just gone into history on July 5, 1980.

Thousands of Wimbledon spectators were left exhausted by the very drama of it. Grayhaired oldtimers conceded they had never seen anything like it.

Mariana Simionescu, the Romanian player Borg is to marry in Bucharest July 24, sat smoking incessantly as she watched. Beside her, Lennert Bergelin, Borg's coach and mentor. The two of them sat intently and hardly spoke a word during the whole match.

McEnroe, 21, a curly haired shotmaking genius, fought off seven match points, repeatedly clawed his way back from the brink of defeat to carry the match to its pulsating conclusion.

Two match points down in the 10th game of the fourth set, he stayed alive by threading a needle down the sideline and stretching to the limit for a do-or-die forehand volley.

These heroics ultimately carried the set into a tiebreaker which goes to the first player to win seven points but who must be two points ahead.

The tiebreaker was unbelievable. The two scratched away at each other like jungle cats, each missing opportunities by fractions of inches. . . .

As you have gathered from the last few paragraphs, you should instruct and entertain your readers—not bore them.

WRITING FOR THE MEDIA TAKES TEAMWORK

The image of a solitary writer, working long hours over a manuscript in hushed surroundings, doesn't fit today's media writers. Quite the contrary: The demands of an information-hungry public require writers to perform at a brisk pace and to stay in constant communication with their colleagues. The business of communication isn't a one-way track from writer to reader or viewer; it's a loop that includes, depending on the size and type of media organization, assignment editors, copy and film editors, bureau chiefs, photographers, artists, stringers, dictationists and circulation directors. The writer must fit effectively into the workings of the group. A life of contemplation and solitude not only isn't a good option for a media writer; it's not available at most companies.

The degree of teamwork involved in writing for the mass media has increased as communication technology has become more sophisticated. For example, television stations with electronic news-gathering (ENG) capabilities can dispatch vans to news locations and, in a matter of moments, be receiving live transmissions at the station that can immediately be put on the air. But the teamwork between editorial and technical staffs, both in the field and in the studio, is essential.

And the possibilities for doing superior work have increased, thanks again to advanced technology. Telex, telecopier and now computer-to-computer communication make it possible for news correspondents to be more responsive to the immediate needs of their publications or networks and for their employers to get instructions and questions to them swiftly. The same technologies enable public relations account executives to share information with out-of-town clients and with offices in other cities and to put their news releases and other important announcements on-line for quick access by journalists and others interested in the clients they represent.

But all the technology in the world would fail without the cooperation of those who use it. It's important for beginning writers to start visualizing themselves as belonging to a professional environment in which, before news can be published or broadcast for an audience, information must be exchanged among team members.

Newspapers, television and radio news operations, and magazines rely on meetings at which editors come together and plan the story "budget." All participants disclose what their staffs have for the next publication or broadcast. Decisions are made about what kind of play stories will get, whether more stories are needed and what they should be. (These meetings may be reconvened during the day in a daily operation if important news breaks and forces editors to shift their plans to accommodate it.) Those editors will go back to their own staffs with instructions, requests for new material and guidelines on treatment and length.

Reporters out covering events check in frequently to get messages and to keep staff in the office apprised of their progress on a story. Newspaper reporters may call in their stories to dictationists back at the paper, then move on to cover another aspect of the story or to another assignment altogether before coming back to the newsroom. Television reporters may go to several locations and cover several stories with a taping crew before coming back to the station. There they'll get together with the tape editor to discuss what's important to keep and what can be left "on the cutting room floor" before writing the script that will accompany the tape on that night's newscast.

Meetings are also vital in public relations agencies and public affairs departments. In agencies, staff members meet with clients to obtain and sustain a mutual understanding of the client's needs and the ways in which they can produce articles, reports and brochures and supply other information to the press and the public that will help them in their coverage of the client. In times of a client's crisis, especially, the public relations contact is a key source of communication. That person remains effective primarily by staying in close touch with the client and with his or her own staff and by being clear and direct in explaining details to the press. The same need for close teamwork prevails in public relations as it does in journalism.

Because media work is teamwork, prima donnas aren't tolerated. PR account executives who become so specialized that they know a great deal about one client and very little about others will become isolated and ineffective. Feature writers who refuse to take any assignments other than ones that interest them personally will soon be looking for work elsewhere. And TV reporters who resent being assigned to stories that are "beneath" them will be told to take a hike. Why? Because media writing requires them to move beyond personal opinions and choices and do whatever it takes to produce a good communication product.

You may not want to rewrite the country correspondence from the small towns in your paper's circulation area or put together obituaries. You may not want to cover social events if you crave a hard-news beat. But you'll do these tasks as well as you can because you are a professional writer.

Even journalists who enjoy successful network careers long for change from time to time, but their employers' decisions prevail. Although ABC's Sam Donaldson protested that he was burned out and wanted to leave the White House beat he'd covered since 1976, ABC thought he was too valuable in that spot.

The consummate professional, Donaldson said, "Everything points in the direction of my staying at the White House. That's what they want me to do. Clearly, I work for ABC. There's no Donaldson Broadcasting Company."

AN IMPORTANT TEAM PLAYER: THE EDITOR

Pride of authorship is an important tenet of the writing profession. There is little that can compare to the excitement of receiving a compliment about an article you've just written, especially if that article has clearly influenced the way people think or behave. But chances are that the article was improved by one or more of the unsung heroes and heroines of the writing world: the copy editors who point their pencils at or set their cursors on words and phrases that keep a story from being brilliant. With a pencil line or a keystroke, they eliminate the offending term or construction and put the story back on track.

Every writer benefits from an editor's eyes. Few writers are so polished that their work can go from typewriter or word processor directly into print without the intervention of the copy editor. That's not to say that writers should depend on their copy editors to do their spelling, punctuation and story organization chores for them. A writer who is careless about his or her work, believing that "the copy editor can always clean it up," will soon have a strained relationship with that editor. A copy editor's role is to play the skeptic, to fine-tune already good work for clarity of thought and correctness of grammar and syntax. If that means cutting your story and rephrasing your thoughts, so be it. If you look at your copy editor as a collaborator and learn to be flexible in your thinking and writing, your writing will mature all the more quickly.

Copy editors handle mountains of material every day. At a newspaper, they may work on articles produced by a dozen or more writers. They know the individual style of their writers, their strong and weak points. Some terrific writers can't spell; others can't remember when to use commas or semicolons. From time to time, even the good ones will turn in a piece with factual errors, with confusing transitions, with complex, rambling sentences. That is where copy editors step in. In partnership with them, writers can find out where their blind spots are and develop ways to work on them. Through the copy editor, the writer can learn detachment and objectivity about his or her own work.

SUMMARY

This chapter was written to help you develop the attitude of a professional writer for the mass media. Before you go on to the following chapters, which will help you learn information-gathering techniques and the different writing styles of various media, you should review the key steps in learning to observe the world and the people in it as a writer would.

The most important principle is this: Mass media writers, be they newspaper reporters, free-lance writers for magazines, TV network correspondents or public information specialists, write not for themselves but for a target audience. The writer's main objective is to fill that audience's information needs with the most current, comprehensive and accurate information available. To accomplish that goal, it's important to develop keen powers of observation, curiosity, even skepticism. The needed skills aren't exclusively intellectual; they also include good instincts, a sensitivity that allows the writer to pick up on more subtle expressions of emotions, and a broad understanding of human nature. This package of abilities helps writers to cultivate sources, expand research skills, and compose articles and news reports with objectivity and credibility.

Mass media writers do not operate in a vacuum. Their work requires them to become involved with others, with people making news of local interest as well as with those making history. To perform effectively, they must combine the methods of the scientist with those of their own profession. They must also be good listeners and reflective thinkers, as receptive to ideas from their co-workers and editors as they are to valuable information from a confidential source.

EXERCISES

1. Select a day during the business week (Monday through Friday) and listen to several radio newscasts and the evening TV news. Make notes on the major stories, paying particular attention to what was said in the lead sentence. Jot down the words that were most descriptive or that had the most impact on you. Make a list of synonyms for these words, and decide which are better for the ear—yours or the newscaster's—and why.

2. Compare the broadcast stories with the way they are written in the next day's newspaper. What details absolutely must go into both print and broadcast versions? Make a list of "common denominator" facts, figures and identifiers.

3. Write a paragraph about a place—a park, a house, a restaurant—in the space provided, for these various audiences:
   a. An entry in your journal
   b. A brief oral presentation to your classmates
   c. A brochure to attract tourists

4. Recall some episode early in your childhood that has made a deep impression on you. Concentrate deeply on each aspect of it and write about the experience. When you are through, when you have relived the episode, read what you have written. Are there things on paper—words and phrases—that you don't recall having written? Were you able to recall little details, such as a crack in a window or a chip off a stone step? If so, you are succeeding in recalling what ordinarily would be lost details.

5. From memory, write a description of the front of the building in which your writing class is being held. (A familiar house or classroom will also do.)

6. Take a pencil and pad and stand in front of the same building. Now write a description of the building while you observe it directly. Compare the two descriptions. In what ways are they different? Why? In what ways are they the same? Why?

7. Interview your friends and classmates about what they see when they look at the front of the building. Write a description based only on their observations. Compare this description, based on "indirect observation," with your "direct observation" description. In what ways are they the same? Why? In what ways are they different? Why? Would you have a better description if you incorporated your friends' descriptions with yours? Why? What does this tell you about the care you should take in gathering information for stories?

8. Write a one-sentence impressionistic description of the building—something like Carl Sandburg's "The fog comes on little cat feet" or Gerard Manley Hopkins's "Moonlight hanging on the treetops like blue cobweb." Compare your description with those of your classmates. Which are most imaginative? Which are the best? Why? Are some better and even more truthful than the direct-observation descriptions? Why?

9. Make an exhaustive list of the characteristics of your pen or pencil as you write with it for 10 minutes. Keep coming back after you think you have exhausted your ability to extend the list. Compare your list with your classmates'.

10. Be especially aware of your surroundings on your way to or from class. List details that had previously escaped your notice.

11. Compare a Page One story from your local paper with an editorial from the same edition. What are the major differences in style? What are the differences in language? How are accuracy, objectivity and credibility achieved in each?

12. Compare a top news story in a television news broadcast with a station editorial that airs the same night. Discuss with your classmates the same elements as in Exercise 2. Make a list of similarities and differences between news and opinion.

13. You are the editor for your university newspaper. Put the following news stories in order of importance for your newspaper readers, according to news values. (Write 1 through 10 to the left of the corresponding letters.) Explain the reasons for your ranking of each.

   _____ a. The School of Nursing receives national accreditation.

   _____ b. The university president is appearing before a congressional committee to testify about federal cuts in educational funds and their effect on higher education.

   _____ c. The university rifle team wins the NCAA championship.

   _____ d. Tuition will be raised 10 percent next year.

   _____ e. Olivia Ann Ross is elected Homecoming Queen.

   _____ f. The College of Business is raising admission standards because only one-third of its graduates can find employment, and it is also swamped with students seeking admission.

   _____ g. The Board of Trustees rules that beer and wine may now be served in the Rathskeller and consumed in dormitory rooms.

   _____ h. Alpha Delta Pi and Delta Gamma sororities are staging protests of the trustees' ruling tomorrow night at the president's home. Invitations to other Greek organizations to participate have been issued.

   _____ i. The University Players are presenting *Much Ado About Nothing* tonight and tomorrow.

   _____ j. The basketball coach has been fired because of back-to-back poor seasons.

14. You are editor for University City's newspaper. Rank these news stories for the citizens of the city, your newspaper readers, according to potential news value. (Write 1 through 8 to the left of the corresponding letters.) Explain the reasons for your ranking of each.

_____ a. The mayor is leaving to go on a trip to Japan to try to entice industry to University City.

_____ b. To facilitate clearing the streets from snow, an alternate-day side-of-the-street parking ordinance has been passed by the city council. It will be implemented in one week.

_____ c. The governor is coming to the city to speak at an economic conference at the university next week.

_____ d. Stanley Ruell, heir to the local cosmetics dynasty, commits suicide beside his swimming pool.

_____ e. Thirty minors in an adjoining state are trapped by a cave-in.

_____ f. Two police officers are suspended while being investigated for receiving money for fixing traffic tickets.

_____ g. Fifty children die in Italy when their school bus slides on icy roads and goes over a precipice.

_____ h. A schoolboy is killed by a 83-year-old woman when she fails to stop her car behind a bus in University City.

15. You are editor of a newspaper in a city of 40,000 in Maine. You can use four of the following stories that come to you over the wire. Which will you use? What order of importance do you place all eight? For what reasons?

_____ a. Buckingham Palace says that the report that Princess Diana is a "bossy little monster" is "rubbish."

_____ b. The remains of a man missing for nine months are found in New Hampshire, right across the border from Maine. He was 85 years old. He collected bottles for extra money; apparently he had gone into a ditch to get a bottle and couldn't get back up.

_____ c. Victims of the economic recession are described as nomads. Anywhere from ½ million to 2 million are homeless, living in cars, vans, buses and tents. The story originates in Denver but embraces the country.

_____ d. Only one battered woman in 10 reports assaults. A case study of a woman and her husband is given.

_____ e. Harold Holden, of Passumsiac, Me., developed a better way to develop film and has sold the rights to Kodak.

_____ f. A spokesperson for OPEC says there's a good possibility that the price of oil will be decreased.

_____ g. Nobel Prize winner Alva Myrdal, a Swede, attacks the United States and Russia, saying in Oslo that they have "created a cult of violence" that threatens global war and breeds urban crime.

_____ h. A 17-year-old was arrested for stealing a herd of goats from a St. Lawrence County farmer in New York. The pickup truck ran off the road when goats stepped on the accelerator. There were no sides on the pickup truck, so the suspect crammed 17 goats into the cab. He had to work the pedals with his hands.

PART II

INFORMATION GATHERING

The first step in writing stories for the mass media is research. Reporters and public relations specialists have to understand the subject they've been assigned to write about before they can determine what the key issues are and what questions will elicit responses that will illuminate those issues. It wouldn't be going too far to say that before a reporter or PR writer can begin writing up an assignment, he or she first has to become a bit of an expert about it. Only by doing thorough research using secondary sources can writers frame questions to ask their primary sources during interviews. Only a mastery of the subject will tell them when they have gathered information of the quantity and the type that they need to bring a fresh perspective to the subject.

Obviously, not every situation will require or even allow for research. A breaking news story, such as a fire in a large center-city office building or a political victory, has to be reported as it is happening. In such cases, research on the "why" of an event follows rather than precedes it.

A step-by-step approach to research, rather than a random gathering of facts, figures and quotes from sources, helps the writer to be accurate, objective and credible. The importance of being thorough in checking into all aspects of the subject one has been assigned to cover can't be overemphasized: People who feel they've been libeled can use evidence of a reporter's negligence in checking facts against that reporter and his or her employer in lawsuits.

Good research is also good armor in a difficult interview. Being well-versed in the subject under discussion gives a writer leverage in interviewing someone who is nervous, who is suspicious of the press or who gives vague answers to questions. A writer can keep the interview on track by supplying some facts to which the person can respond directly and comfortably. A writer's command of the subject also shows the person being interviewed that the writer feels that the subject is important. The result is that many people will respond to questions with enthusiasm and will refer the writer to other people who could become valuable information sources.

The writer for the mass media actually builds a story from the bottom up, just as a contractor builds a house. The writer's finished house would look something like the figure on page 36.

Before you can build the first, second and third floors and attach the roof, you must first build a sturdy foundation. That's the role of background research, using secondary sources. The next step is to begin finding your primary sources—the

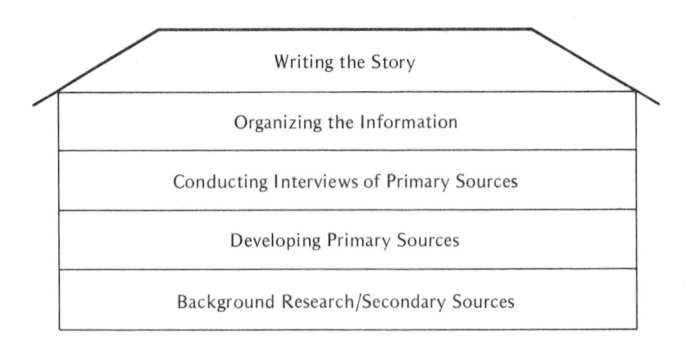

```
          ┌─────────────────────────────────────────┐
         /         Writing the Story                 \
        ├─────────────────────────────────────────────┤
        │       Organizing the Information            │
        ├─────────────────────────────────────────────┤
        │  Conducting Interviews of Primary Sources   │
        ├─────────────────────────────────────────────┤
        │       Developing Primary Sources            │
        ├─────────────────────────────────────────────┤
        │   Background Research/Secondary Sources     │
        └─────────────────────────────────────────────┘
```

persons close to the subject, such as experts, analysts, activists and people with reputations that suggest that they would be knowledgeable contacts on the topic. The third step is to line them up for interviews and to contact others they may suggest you should talk to. At this point, if you feel the interviews have raised key points with which you should be more familiar before you interview anyone else, you can go back to step 1 and do more background research. Once you've familiarized yourself with the information you need, you can pursue more in-depth interviews, perhaps reinterviewing some sources. Now you're at the top floor, ready to pull the information together in anticipation of "putting the roof on the house"—capping your project with an article based on your research materials and interview notes.

How do you know when you're ready to stop researching and interviewing and write the article, report or proposal? When you've found answers to all of these questions:

- ☐ WHAT happened?
- ☐ WHO is involved?
- ☐ WHERE did it happen?
- ☐ WHEN did it happen?
- ☐ WHY did it happen?
- ☐ HOW did it happen?
- ☐ What is the SIGNIFICANCE or consequence of the event?

Who, what, where and *when* are the major facts of the article—the news or interest pegs. *Why* and *how* flesh out the bare facts and, along with the *significance* of the event, give them meaning. Your research can't be considered complete until you have found answers to the "5W+H and Significance" and you're satisfied that the answers are accurate. Only then can the writing process begin.

The chapters in Part II cover the research and reporting process, including development of secondary and primary sources, interviewing protocol and techniques, and tips for organizing research materials and interview notes.

CHAPTER 2

BACKGROUND RESEARCH

Research in the mass media should move from the general to the specific. Writers should first develop a broad background in the area they're investigating and then move in on specific target areas. Although you needn't overresearch a subject—that is, find out everything there is to know about it when what you're really after is a clear understanding of one small aspect—you cannot bring your news writing and interpretive skills into play unless you've developed enough working knowledge of a subject to know what areas are newsworthy and demand closer study.

Take, for example, the 1985 banking crises at savings and loan associations in Ohio and Maryland. In both cases, news broke that one or two institutions were in precarious financial condition because of questionable investment practices. State intervention was necessary to stabilize their assets. That news caused a run on those banks, which led to a panic that caused a run on other S&Ls, including those that were in solid shape financially. For the media to do a balanced, thorough job covering the crises—each of which lasted for several months and caused the Ohio and Maryland legislatures to make sweeping changes in their insurance programs for S&Ls—the writers had to have a good working knowledge of banking practices in general to do an adequate job of reporting on bank problems in the specific. Their general knowledge was supported by additional research on banking and bank regulation and extensive interviewing about the new crises so that they could keep an anxious public informed.

Often news breaks so fast and the facts and figures change so rapidly that sheer lack of time prevents a writer or a public relations spokesperson from doing extensive research on a topic. That's why it's important for writers to know where to go, quickly, to get information that will help them interpret complex details for themselves and, ultimately, for their audiences.

PUBLIC SOURCES

LIBRARIES

Community libraries are fine sources of material for research about local affairs, politics and personalities. They usually carry back issues of community publications and employ a staff that is knowledgeable about community events. A municipal or county library usually has a close relationship with the local government. Its staff can tell inquiring writers where in government or elsewhere to search for the information they need.

Interlibrary loan and computer capabilities have brought greater sophistication to community libraries. In many states, libraries borrow from one another to fill their patrons' requests for material they themselves don't have.

Libraries at public colleges and universities are gold mines for reporters. In addition to having large collections of books and back issues of popular periodicals, they also have special collections, sublibraries devoted to certain academic disciplines (such as medicine, engineering and architecture), interlibrary loan contacts with hundreds of other schools, special-interest magazines and journals, back issues of major newspapers and massive reference resources. Writers can develop almost as many leads looking through the card catalog and talking to librarians as they can developing contacts among experts on their subject. Here, too, librarians are likely to be able to identify additional sources for the writer in search of background information.

Political and Civic Groups

Political groups and civic associations can be counted on for a tremendous amount of information about legislation, zoning, development, schools, highways and traffic, community safety and security, and the costs of these things. Why? Because participants in these groups have a vested interest in who holds the reins of power and how it is exercised. These are politicians, community activists, school board members, city and county council members, members of the state legislature, members of Congress, judges and the leaders of political parties. They range from the homemaker lobbying for expanded after-school programs at her daughter's junior high school to the neighborhood association president, a lawyer, who opposes a shopping center owner's plans to install a video arcade next door to a liquor store. They include the controversial circuit court judge stepping down after 25 years on the bench and the member of Congress who switches political parties to accommodate the swing in party loyalty in his or her district. All of these people and the organizations to which they belong can be excellent sources for the writer with a community beat or the public relations manager looking for ways to focus more attention on his or her company's activities in the community.

These individuals can be very helpful personally because of the knowledge they have by virtue of their community involvement. They are excellent *primary* sources. But they are also excellent for *secondary* source information. These are the people who take opinion polls in their communities, gather information about government plans affecting their neighborhoods, go to public meetings where they demand disclosure of more information, examine and analyze budgets, and score the Democrats' performance against the Republicans'. The documents they produce as a result of their interest in their communities are superb sources for mass media writers because they reveal so much about the expectations and plans of those citizens.

Government Offices

The various jurisdictions of American government—municipal, county, state, federal—possess more data in files and on computer disks than anyone will probably ever read. Our system of government requires so many points of contact with its citizens—through elections, tax filings, license applications, legal actions, jury duty, Social Security, Medicare and Medicaid, government financial assistance and other social services—that virtually no resident of the United States does not appear in one government database or another.

Much of that information, and analyses of it, is, by law, public. It becomes the grist, for example, for news stories on election results, feature articles on population shifts between cities and suburbs, and reports on medical care by PR writers who work in the health field. Local and state governments and the federal government regularly disclose information about commerce, housing, agriculture, monetary policy and other economic indicators. Officeholders, such as mayors, governors, and state and congressional representatives, frequently reveal results of special studies to draw attention to a condition or cause about which they feel strongly. It is, of course, up to the writer to find experts to help interpret the findings of such studies, and the reporter's contacts may strongly disagree with the government's or official's point of view, but the data the government uses in making law and writing regulations are nevertheless extremely important. The different ways in which they are interpreted often make news, especially on the business pages.

Learning which government office to go to for information is a challenge for beginning writers. Even local government can be quite complex. Most media writers find government directories helpful, when they are available. Public affairs officers can point the way initially, but good reporters will do their own checking to make certain they have reached the most knowledgeable person as well as the appropriate office for the information they seek. This is how secondary sources become primary ones, a progression that will be discussed more fully in Chapter 3.

There's no doubt that among the most valuable sources for information available to the reporter are the public records at the city, state and federal levels. Records of births and deaths, annual reports, committee hearings, commission hearings, court cases, property records—all these records and more are valuable sources of information in reporting public events. If you know what you want from the local, state or federal government, chances are that records exist that will not only reveal part of what you want but document it also. If the bureaucrat, law enforcement officer or executive official does not allow you to see the record you want, you can file suit under the appropriate state or federal freedom of information act. The majority of states now have laws based upon the 1974 federal Freedom of Information Act. The Tennessee Public Records Law is one such state law.

As you read the Tennessee Public Records Law, you will see that, like its federal counterpart, so many exceptions to the law exist, justified and otherwise, that self-serving officials can hide their acts and the records under a manifold cloak of secrecy—and they have.

TENNESSEE PUBLIC RECORDS LAW
Tennessee Code Annotated
Title 15
Chapter 3

15-304. Records open to public inspection. All state, county and municipal records shall at all times, during business hours, be open for personal inspection by any citizen of Tennessee, and those in charge of such records shall not refuse such right of inspection to any such citizen, unless otherwise provided by law or regulation made pursuant thereto.

15-305. Confidential records. (1) The medical records of patients in state hospitals and medical facilities, and the medical records of persons receiving medical treatment, in whole or in part, at the expense of the state, shall be open for inspection by members of the public. Additionally, all investigative records of the Tennessee Bureau of Criminal Investigation shall be treated as confidential and shall not be open to inspection by members of the public. The information contained in such records shall be disclosed to the public only in compliance with a subpoena or an order of the court, however, such investigative records of the Tennessee Bureau of Criminal Investigation shall be open to inspection by elected members of the general assembly if such inspection is directed by a duly adopted resolution of either house or of a standing or joint committee of either house. Records shall not be available to any member of the executive branch except those directly involved in the investigation in the Tennessee Bureau of Criminal Investigation itself and the governor himself. The records, documents and papers in the possession of the military department which involve the security of the United States and/or the state of Tennessee, including but not restricted to national guard personnel records, staff studies and investigations, shall be treated as confidential and shall not be open for inspection by members of the public.

(2) The records of students in public educational institutions shall be treated as confidential. Information in such records relating to academic performance, financial status of a student or his parent or guardian, medical or psychological treatment or testing shall not be made available to unauthorized personnel of the institution or to the public or any agency, except those agencies authorized by the educational institution to conduct specific research or otherwise authorized by the governing board of the institution, without the consent of the student involved or the parent or guardian of a minor student, attending any institution of elementary or secondary education, except as otherwise provided by law or regulation pursuant thereto and except in consequence of due legal process or in cases when the safety of persons or property is involved. The governing board of the institution, the state department of education, and the Tennessee Higher Education Commission shall have access on a confidential basis to such records as are required to fulfill their lawful functions. Statistical information not identified with a particular student may be released to any person, agency, or the public; and information relating only to an individual student's name, age, address, dates of attendance, grade levels completed, class placement and academic degrees awarded may likewise be disclosed.

(3) Any record designated "confidential" shall be so treated by agencies in the maintenance, storage and disposition of such confidential records. These records shall be destroyed in such a manner that they cannot be read, interpreted, or reconstructed. The destruction shall be in accordance with an approved records disposition authorization from the public records commission.

(4)(a) The following books, records and other materials in the possession of the office of the attorney general and reporter which relate to any pending or contemplated legal or administrative proceeding in which the office of the attorney general and reporter may be involved shall not be open for public inspection:

(i) Books, records or other materials which are confidential or privileged by state law;

(ii) Books, records or other materials relating to investigations conducted by federal law enforcement or federal regulatory agencies, which are confidential or privileged under federal law;

(iii) The work product of the attorney general and reporter or any attorney working under his supervision and control, or;

(iv) Communications made to or by the attorney general and reporter or any attorney working under his supervision and control in the context of the attorney-client relationship.

(v) Books, records and other materials in the possession of other departments and agencies which are available for public inspection and copying pursuant to sections 15-304 and 15-307. It is the intent of this section to leave subject to public inspection and copying pursuant to sections 15-304 and 15-307 such books, records and other materials in the possession of other departments even though copies of the same books, records and other materials which are also in the possession of the attorney general's office are not subject to inspection or copying in the office of the attorney general, provided such records, books and materials are available for copying and inspection in such other departments.

(b) Books, records and other materials made confidential by this subsection which are in the possession of the attorney general and reporter shall be open to inspection by the elected members of the general assembly if such inspection is directed by a duly adopted resolution of either house or of a standing or joint committee of either house and is required for the conduct of legislative business.

(c) Except for the provisions of subsection (b) hereof, the books, records and materials made confidential or privileged by this subsection shall be disclosed to the public only in the discharge of the duties of the office of the attorney general.

15-306. Violations (1) Any official who shall violate the provisions of 15-304–15-307 shall be deemed guilty of a misdemeanor.

15-307. Right to make copies of public records. In all cases where any person has the right to inspect any such public records, such person shall have the right to take extracts or make copies thereof, and to make photographs or photostats of the same while such records are in the possession, custody and control of the lawful custodian thereof, or his authorized deputy; provided, however, the lawful custodian of such records shall have the right to adopt and enforce reasonable rules governing the making of such extracts, copies, photographs or photostats.

15-308. Records of convictions or traffic and other violations—Availability. Any public official having charge or custody of or control over any public records of convictions of traffic violations or any other state, county or municipal public offenses shall make available to any citizen, upon request, during regular office hours, a copy or copies of any such record requested by such citizen, upon the payment of a reasonable charge or fee therefore. Such official is authorized to fix a charge or fee per copy that would reasonably defray the cost of producing and delivering such copy or copies.

PUBLIC RECORDS DEFINED

15-401. Definitions. 1. "Section" shall mean the records management section of the department of finance and administration.

2. "Public record" or "public records" shall mean all documents, papers, letters, maps, books, photographs, microforms, electronic data processing output, films, sound recordings, or other material regardless of physical form or characteristics made or received pursuant to law or ordinance or in connection with the transaction of official business by any governmental agency.

3. "Permanent records" shall mean those records which have permanent administrative, fiscal, historical or legal value.

4. "Temporary records" shall mean those records which cease to have value immediately after departmental use and need not be retained for any purpose.

5. "Working papers" shall mean those records created to serve as input for final reporting documents, including electronic data processed records, and/or computer output microfilm, and those records which become obsolete immediately after agency use or publication.

6. "Agency" shall mean any department, division, board, bureau, commission, or other separate unit of government created or established by the constitution, by law or pursuant to law.

7. "Disposition" shall mean preservation of the original records in whole or in part, preservation by photographic or other reproduction processes, or outright destruction of the records.

8. "Records creation" shall mean the recording of information on paper, printed forms, punched cards, tape, disk, or any information transmitting media. It shall include preparation of forms, reports, state publications, and correspondence.

9. "Records management" shall mean the application of management techniques to the creation, utilization, maintenance, retention, preservation, and disposal of records in order to reduce costs and improve efficiency of recordkeeping. It shall include records retention schedule development, essential records protection, files management and information retrieval systems, microfilm information systems, correspondence and word processing management, records center, forms management, analysis, and design, and reports and publications management.

10. "Records officer" shall mean an individual designated by an agency head to assume responsibility for implementation of the agency's records management program.

11. "Essential records" shall mean any public records essential to the resumption or continuation of operations, to the re-creation of the legal and financial status of government in the state or to the protection and fulfillment of obligation to citizens of the state.

12. "Records disposition authorization" shall mean the official document utilized by an agency head to request authority for the disposition of records. The public records commission shall determine and order the proper disposition of state records through the approval of records disposition authorizations. (Acts 1974 (Adj. S.), ch. 739, section 1; 1975, ch. 286, section 2; 1978 (Adj. S.), ch. 544, section 3.)

PRIVATE SOURCES

Professional Groups

Trade unions, trade associations and membership groups are mainstays for writers doing research. Many of these groups are wealthy and powerful, able to finance studies and reports about their membership and relevant isues. Because press coverage is important to them, they are usually quite willing to share information with reporters. Those with libraries will usually open them to writers who can demonstrate that they have a bona fide assignment for a newspaper, magazine, broadcast station or other medium.

Most of these groups have lobbying functions that thrust them into the limelight when state legislatures and Congress are meeting. Representatives of unions, trade associations and membership groups are regular witnesses when congressional committees hear testimony. They are heard from regularly during periods of budget cutting and during labor crises. During the United Airlines pilot strike in the spring of 1985, people quoted by reporters read like a *Who's Who* of professional associations. Each day during the strike, news stories would carry comments of spokesmen for the Air Line Pilots Association, United Airlines management, the Air Transport Association, unions who had to cross pilots' picket lines to go to work (such as flight attendants, baggage handlers and machinists), plus federal agencies such as the Federal Aviation Administration and the National Labor Relations Board and airline industry analysts on Wall Street. Keeping tabs on the positions of all these authoritative sources was absolutely essential to telling the whole story and telling it with accuracy, objectivity and credibility.

Another type of organization, composed of persons with a strong personal (as opposed to employment-related) interest, is the special-interest group. These groups are formed by people who feel a formal organization is necessary to accomplish specific goals to improve society. These groups also know that organizing formally will improve their chances of having the press recognize them as authorities and use their comments and reports in the media.

Some of the best-known of these groups include the National Association for the Advancement of Colored People, the National Organization for Women, the 4-H Club, the Anti-Defamation League of B'nai B'rith, the American Civil Liberties Union and the Eagle Forum. They all have local chapters eager to be tapped for information about their activities.

Not all special-interest groups are national in scope; many have interests that are purely local. The Committee to Save Rhodes Tavern, for example, was a Washington, D.C., group that rallied to prevent the demolition of a historic building near the White House. Its members ultimately failed, and the decrepit little building fell to the wrecker's ball. But the group had received much press coverage over several years, usually portrayed as the little David fighting the huge Goliath of urban development.

There are few "special interests" that don't have a formal organization to promote them. The major organizations can usually be found by looking in the phone book; the smaller ones, by obtaining the name of the chief spokesperson or an officer. If that person is difficult to find, call the organization with which they compete or whose goals they oppose. The one taking the heat is certain to know who is keeping it on!

RESEARCH ORGANIZATIONS

Evaluating and quantifying our beliefs, feelings, attitudes and morals is being done somewhere every minute of every business day. Behavioral research is important to anyone concerned with future planning, whether he or she is in marketing, sales, communication, banking, national defense or many other professions. These statistics can greatly help a writer interpret events because they can show what people have done in the past, what they seem to be doing now, and what can be expected of them in the future.

This type of research is done by opinion pollsters, such as Louis Harris and Associates and the Roper and Gallup polls. Some pollsters are specialists, such as Cambridge Survey Research, which specializes in political polling. If you're working on a story on voting traditions in Vermont or a report on people's attitudes toward abortion, polls previously published by these groups on those subjects can give added depth to your final version.

Arbitron and Nielsen are most famous for their broadcasting ratings, during which they "sweep" the nation to find out who is watching or listening to which programs. The results of their surveys can make or break a program. These companies also do other types of consumer research that can be helpful to writers.

The federal government frequently releases reports about its survey research and will provide information about specific topics on request. The U.S. Census Bureau is divided into divisions, each of which is responsible for certain types of demographic information, such as the annual numbers of live births, marriages and divorces, and much, much more. The Justice Department's Bureau of Justice

Statistics keeps records on crime, prisons, criminal behavior and sentencing. These are important sources for the media because they are repositories of statistical information not readily available elsewhere, and the information can be manipulated to cover exactly the geographic area or time frame with which the reporter is concerned.

Major universities generally house a research center or several small ones. Units such as the University of Maryland's Center on Aging, the Texas Real Estate Center at Texas A&M University, and the Center for the Study of Women in Government at the State University of New York at Albany take academic expertise and apply it to practical concerns. The Gannett Co. sponsors the Center for Media Studies at Columbia University, whose fellows conduct research about journalism and media behavior. Chances are you're only a few steps from a university research center. If you're not, make it a point to find out where the university research units are located in your state and what their research specialties are.

Newspaper Libraries

Newspaper libraries are important places to do research, although usually they are open only to their own staffs. Known as the "morgue," the newspaper library is an archive of the paper's own stories and photographs, plus a reference center for writers. If you are newly assigned to a beat at a paper, it's a good idea to review the stories in the morgue written by others who've had the beat, to see what the issues and who the chief contacts have been.

The staff of a newspaper library can save reporters and editors a tremendous amount of time. They are trained to find information fast, and they're well-versed in the many sources from which information is available. The special training offered by library science programs gives librarians skills that a writer on deadline can truly appreciate. Writers can learn a lot from the library staff and should make a point of familiarizing themselves with librarians' information-finding techniques.

Many newspaper libraries will furnish copies of articles in their morgues to writers on the newspaper. These libraries will charge a copying fee; some charge a flat fee based on the circulation of the periodical for which the writer is working.

REFERENCE SOURCES

The standard library reference books you were taught to use in high school remain among the best guides for doing background research on different subjects. You will still find the *Readers' Guide to Periodical Literature* in the reference section of every library. But reference books have multiplied, and tomorrow's journalist and public relations specialist needs to be well-acquainted with the newest generation of reference guides.

Chris Wells, director of *USA Today*'s library, says the importance of knowing what you can find in reference books can't be underestimated. Ironically, there is plenty of room for improvement in the way journalists do research. "Even some older journalists don't really know how to do the most elemental things in terms of finding information, which is supposed to be a journalist's job," Wells says. "So the first thing I would tell a beginning writer to do would be to go to the library and familiarize yourself with just the basic things, like encyclopedias and telephone books. Telephone books are extremely valuable. At the *USA Today* library, the amount of reporters' questions we answer simply by looking in the phone book is amazing."

For leads on how to find books that deal with the subject a reporter is writing about, Wells says the subject guide to *Books in Print* is "invaluable." For finding subject experts, she suggests universities. *USA Today* has media contacts at all the major universities who are specialists in their fields.

Wells suggests *Gale's Guide to Organizations* as a critically important resource for media writers. Why? "It can lead you to sources and point you in other directions," she says. But if writers aren't certain which organization has the information they need, they should start with the *Readers' Guide*, the *Business Periodical Index* or any of the major newspaper indexes to find articles on their subject that will contain clues about the groups and individuals to contact.

Wells believes that media writers must learn more about electronic databases to do really effective research. "In this day and age, you really have to have at least a superficial knowledge of on-line databases," she says. "For journalists, I'd say the three most important ones would be NEXIS, Dialog and VuText. Even if you don't know how to access them, if you know what's in them, you can then find someone to pull up the information for you." These databases store articles from major publications on a broad spectrum of subjects and are especially powerful sources of information because they contain data that, for most writers, would be difficult to obtain without doing a lot of legwork.

Here is Chris Wells's "fundamental 15," her recommendation of reference books that media writers should know and use often, and the companies that publish them:

Almanac of American Politics (National Journal)

Almanacs (*Information Please* or *World Almanac*)

Ayer Directory of Publications (Ayer Press)

Chase's Calendar of Annual Events (Apple Tree Press)

Contemporary Authors (Gale Research Co.)

Current Biography (H. W. Wilson Co.)

Editor and Publisher International Yearbook (Editor and Publisher)

Encyclopedia of Associations (Gale Research Co.)

Facts on File: A Weekly World News Digest with Cumulative Index (Facts on File)

Standard and Poor's Register of Corporations, Directors and Executives (Standard and Poor)

Standard Directory of Advertisers (National Register Publishing Co.)

Standard Periodical Directory (Oxbridge Communications)

Statistical Abstract of the United States (U.S. Government Printing Office)

United States Government Manual (U.S. Government Printing Office)

Who's Who (regional, subject, international editions, etc.) (Marquis Publishing Co.)

SUMMARY

By now, the message should be clear: The way to construct your story's house is to build a deep, sturdy foundation of solid research that prepares you to ask probing questions and develop the freshest angle possible for your article. You will accomplish this by taking as much care to refine your research skills as you do to improve your writing.

Because the amount of information available through private and public sources is increasing and is being made available in new formats, such as computer-accessed databases, today's media writer must develop greater research and reporting skills to do justice to journalism, public relations and advertising.

EXERCISES

1. List 10 federal government local and regional offices located in your area. How did you get this information?

2. Select three of those federal agencies and describe their functions and services.

3. What are the tax rates for your city? How did you find this information?

4. What major lobbyists have offices in your city? How did you get this information?

5. List three local special-interest groups in your area. How did you get this information?

6. Does your state have a public records law? If so, how does it compare to the Tennessee law in this chapter? Ask a city editor, news director or a member of Sigma Delta Chi if your state law is effective in prying information loose from the government.

CHAPTER 3

DEVELOPING PRIMARY NEWS SOURCES

Once a writer has learned how to do background research on an article, the next step is to develop contacts among knowledgeable people whose expertise can be drawn on for articles. Research alone will not add the important human interest element; careful selection of primary sources will.

THE BEAT ASSIGNMENT

To simplify the management of a news staff, editors divide reporters' responsibilities into specific areas. Each person is expected to become an expert in the assigned area and to generate stories about that area for the paper or broadcast station. This system of organization has two purposes: to ensure that the paper has reporters assigned to all important areas and to keep reporters from tripping over one another in pursuit of a story.

Editors devise a beat system by looking at charts that show the organization of city government, at lists that detail important community groups, and at key topics that are of interest to their readers, such as health, sports, and food and nutrition. The readership demographics of the paper help to determine in what areas readers' interests are likely to lie. For example, a newspaper serving a large retired population will be very likely to have someone who has a beat consisting of retirees' issues, whereas that beat would probably be much less important in a community where a new automobile plant was being built. Why? Because the plant would attract much younger workers with families, and their numbers would likely dwarf those of the older population. In such a community, the school beat would be very important.

Usually, when you are hired by a news organization, you are assigned a beat. (The beat system is a systematic and effective plan to ensure that media reporters of an organization cover all the important events taking place in the circulation or audience area.) The beat may be city hall, the legislature, the courthouse, the police or the fire department, to name a few. Or you may be given special assignments in such areas as education or labor. You may even be given the responsibility of covering a combination of these beats and areas of interest. It all depends on the size of the news-gathering organization. On a weekly newspaper or a small radio or television station, you could be covering them all. On a small daily, you may be assigned four or five. On a larger daily or television station, you may be assigned one.

You could also come onto a daily as a general-assignment reporter, handling unforeseen events not encompassed by regular beats: visiting dignitaries, major floods, catastrophes, organization meetings of one kind or another. If you are a free-lance writer, you should develop your own area of expertise, depending on your interests, educational background and experience. To acquaint you with how to go about developing a beat, let's start with familiar turf—your campus.

ORGANIZING THE CAMPUS BEAT

If your university newspaper editor is efficient, the campus will be organized into beats. Organizational charts, directories, handbooks and the like are consulted by the editor to determine who the major news sources are. Those sources, or beats, will be assigned to various reporters according to their interests and experience. Let's say you have been assigned by the editor to cover the alumni and placement office. How do you go about developing the news sources on that beat?

First of all, if the reporter who formerly covered the office is still on campus, you'd talk to that person and be briefed on getting news from the office. If the reporter is no longer on campus and your editor is really efficient, a "beat card" on the alumni and placement office will be on file in the newspaper morgue. You pull the card and read what the last two reporters have to say about the beat: the major source, minor sources, best time to reach the sources, annual special events and ways of approaching various sources.

You read that the office is headed by Peggy Mahaney. You walk into the office: "I'm (your name), a reporter for the *University News*. This semester I'll be covering the alumni and placement office. Would it be possible for me to meet with you at 11 a.m. Mondays in your office? What I'd like to do at that time is discuss the events that will be taking place during the week that might make good news stories."

You arrange a satisfactory time. You find out that the president of the university alumni is Kenneth Adcox and the vice president is Ernest M. Fleenor. You ask to be introduced to the secretary, Cynthia F. Kelley. She will be one of the best news sources.

The assistant director of the office, Jay A. Joyce, briefs you on the operation of the alumni and placement office while Mahaney takes a phone call. You introduce yourself to Deborah Bowman and Edith Sullivan, administrative assistants. You tell them you are counting on them to keep you in mind when something occurs that might be newsworthy—either straight news events or feature story material. You give everyone a card with your name, address, newspaper and home phone number so that they will be able to reach you when news breaks.

You begin meeting with Peggy Mahaney every Monday. You always have a series of questions on cards to ask her. Although there may be slight variations in the line of questioning, depending on what you might have heard about possible news stories from other sources, the staple questions are these:

"Are the alumni chapters meeting this week? What is on the agenda for the meetings?"

"What special projects are the alumni chapters engaged in? Are any scheduled for the future?"

"Are they also engaging in fund raising?"

"What are you, yourself, doing with the alumni this week?"

"What else should I know about alumni activities?"

Having exhausted your questions about the alumni part of the operation, you address yourself to placement activities:

"What companies are coming to the campus this week to conduct job interviews?"

"What is the outlook for jobs for the present? For next year?"

"Who is hiring at this time of the year? What are they looking for?"

"What advice would you want passed on to the student body about job hunting? Do you have any tips on what to wear, how to act, and so on?"

"What else should I know about placement?"

"What's happening with the office staff? Have there been any promotions or new positions?"

You conclude the beat interview by asking, "What questions should I have asked that I didn't?" Mahaney says that the office is getting a computer that will hook into the university computer center and streamline her operations. You've got a major story for the *University News*.

You do not meet with a news source without adequate preparation. Don't, for example, call on the phone and ask, "Is there any news this week?" In the first place, you should physically present yourself at the meeting time in the office. In the second place, *you* are the reporter. *You* determine what's news and what isn't. Most news sources have enough to do taking care of their own duties without worrying about yours. They will resent being forced to reflect on the coming week, over the phone, to help you fulfill your job responsibilities.

And most news sources aren't concerned with news. They don't know what is or is not newsworthy. They just have some vague ideas about what might go on the air or into a newspaper. You must educate them. With your regular meetings and questions you will teach them to keep you in mind when something that seems like news will be happening.

At all times you should be pleasant and courteous with the director and the staff, under even the most trying circumstances. Cultivate the administrative assistants and secretaries. Eventually, your behavior will pay off. They will call your attention to events that may slip the director's mind. They may also tip you off to things that the director may not want to bring to your attention.

Regardless of the beat assigned, this is the basic routine of a reporter covering a beat.

The campus beat prepares the reporter for the city beat. With this in mind, we list the different beats a medium-sized university newspaper covers. This particular publication employs more than 50 student reporters to cover the beats. The title, "Here's Looking at You, Tennessee Tech," is a takeoff on Humphrey Bogart. The listing serves as a promotion piece for the newspaper and gives students the recognition they deserve for covering university beats.

Here's Looking at You, Tennessee Tech*

Do you see your name or an organization you belong to below? We hope so. That's the beat system we use in covering the campus for THE ORACLE. There are an awful lot of stops for our reporters to make, and

* Reprinted by permission of *The Oracle*.

sometimes they aren't all covered. We apologize for that. If you don't have someone from THE ORACLE looking in on you each week and you have something you think warrants publishing in THE ORACLE, give us a call at 528-3031. We'll take down the information and see if we can't do something about it.

STUDENT OFFICES & COMMITTEES
1. ASB officers—Susan McGregor
2. Supreme Court—David Lusk
3. Senate—Rita White
4. RHA—Heyward Dixon
5. Special Meetings on Campus (State Board of Regents, etc.)—Binney Stumpf
6. Academic Council meetings—Teri Fosbinder
7. Student Affairs Committee—Donna Shedlarski
8. Chapter 606—Tom Harris
9. Tech Village Town Council—Michelle Gaps
10. University Programming Council—Tom Heneghan
11. Faculty Senate—Karen Yoakum

ADMINISTRATIVE OFFICES & OFFICIALS
12. President Arliss Roaden—Ken Sircy
13. Dr. Joe Middlebrooks, Provost and Vice President for Academic Affairs—Karen Puckett
14. Dr. David Larimore, Dir/Exec. Assistant to the President—Al Carr
15. Dr. William H. Baker, Assistant to the President for Special Activities—Julie Lawrence
16. Dr. Joseph L. Ledbetter, Vice President for University Development & Alumni Affairs—Sue Grissom
17. Dr. Anna B. Wynn, Vice President for Student Services—Edie Sullivan Admissions and Records
18. Director of Student Organizations and Conduct—Ron Sampley
19. Director of Student Activities and Campus Life—Lillian Ridley
20. Dr. Roy Ruffner, Vice Pres., Office of Business and Fiscal Affairs—Al Carr
21. Physical Plant & Planning—Dawn Rowe
22. Charles Groce, Safety & Security—Karen Puckett
23. William Goodwin, Research—Michael Samford

STUDENT MEDIA
24. Eagle—Paul Dombert
25. Homespun—Mike McClanahan
26. THE ORACLE—Pam Dombert
27. WTTU-FM—Pamela Bingham
28. Photographic Services—Heyward Dixon
29. Library and Media Center—Kenny Boehms
30. News Services—Cindy Webster

COLLEGES & SCHOOLS
31. Dean, College of Business Administration—Betsi Hoey
   a. Accounting and Finance—Buddy Crawford
   b. Management—Wayne McKinney
   c. Marketing & Economics—John Ross
   Marketing Club—Cindy Lou Harkleroad
32. Dean, College of Engineering—Michael Fleenor
   Eng. Joint Council
   a. Chemical—Tony Anderson
   b. Civil—Heidi Hewitt
   c. Electrical—Karen Carr
   d. Mechanical—Gena Rowland
   e. Industrial Technology—Eric Wampler
   f. Industrial Engineering—Ed Heyward
33. Dean, School of Agriculture and Home Economics—Steve Padgett
   Aggie Contact publication—Kim Prince
   a. Animal Science—Charles Fannin
   b. General Agriculture—Edward W. Johnson
   c. University Shipley Farm—Steve Boots
   d. Plant & Soil Science—Jim Herrin
34. Dean, College of Education—Dana Harris
   a. Educational Psychology & Counselor Education—Kenney Boehms
   b. Elementary Education—Greg Leffew
   c. Health and Physical Education—Sue Grissom
   d. Secondary Education—James Ross
35. Dean, School of Nursing—Carol Verble
36. Dean, College of Arts & Sciences—Lisa Snell
   a. Biology—John D. Brummett
   b. Tech Aqua Biological Station—Julie Martin
   c. Chemistry—Beth Hunter
   d. Earth Sciences—Bonnie A. Irons
   Geo Club—Kathy R. Van Winkle
   e. English—Ann Gamble
   f. Foreign Languages—Samuel Watson
   g. History—Charles Scudder
   h. Math and Computer Science—Gary Quinn
   i. Computer Center—Dawn Rowe
   j. Physics—Ann Collette
   k. Political Science—Tonia Duncan
   l. Sociology—Lisa K. Thompson
   m. Philosophy—Ann Gamble
37. Graduate School—Pamela Bingham
38. Dean of Extended Services—Tom Harris

FRATERNITIES & SORORITIES—See the Student Handbook
39. Social groups—Judy Geary
    a. Sororities: there are five, for example: Delta Gamma, Zeta Tau Alpha, etc.—William Patterson
    b. Fraternities: there are 14, for example: Lambda Chi Alpha, Beta Theta Pi, etc.—Danny Dotson
    c. Interfraternity Council—
    d. Panhellenic—Dean Carrothers
40. Professional and Service Fraternities and Sororities—Student Handbook—Robin Greenwood
    For example: Alpha Gamma Sigma, Mu Phi Epsilon, etc.

RELIGIOUS ORGANIZATIONS—(there are 14) See the Student Handbook. For example: Baptist Student Union, Wesley Foundation—Betsi Hoey and Michael Fleenor

OTHER ORGANIZATIONS
    a. Amateur Radio Society—Sharla Perkins
    b. Black Student Organization—Kelly Thompson
    c. Chess Club—Anna Harwood
    d. Circle K International—Donna Bilbrey
    e. Honor Society Council—Bill Sanders
    f. Mortar Board—Leah Helen Hochanadel
    g. Phi Kappa Phi—Jamie Linder
    h. Young Republicans—Brian Donath

UNIVERSITY CENTER
41. University Stores, director Charles Dearman—Beverly A. Marsh
    Bookstore—Ron Sampley
    Post Office—Jennifer Thompson
42. Food Services, director Martha Shanks—Charles Scudder
    Cafeteria—Lannie Ross
    Tech Grill—Mary Frances Lusk
43. Information Center—Kim Allison
44. Placement Office—Trish Griffin
45. Campus employment—Bronson Casey
46. Financial Aid—Sandra L. Cupp
47. Counseling Center—Sherry Monday
48. Health Services—Janet Garey
49. Housing Office (news except for Tech Village)—Betty M. Dowdy
50. International Students—Heyward Dixon
    International Relations Club—Monica Samford

ARTS
51. Tech Players—Tracy Eldridge
52. Community area drama—Janet Garey
53. Music Department—Gena Rowland
    Bands, ensembles, choruses, etc.—Marvin Lamb
54. Art Gallery—Brooke Crain
55. Appalachian Center for Crafts—Lisa Dennis
56. Speech Activities—
57. WCTE-TV—Tonia Duncan

SPORTS
58. Cheerleaders—Al Carr
59. Golden Stars—Samuel Watson II
60. Athletic Director David Coffey—Craig Flagg
    a. Varsity sports—John Geary
        1. Football—
        2. Basketball—Craig Flagg, Rick Arrington, Rhonda Delk, Michelle Crain
        3. Baseball—
        4. Tennis—Alice Jenkins
        5. Cross Country—Sean Heneghan
        6. Golf—John Walton Ross
        7. Riflery—
        8. Soccer—Hedy Russo
        9. Volleyball—Susan DeBoldt
        10. Wrestling—Judy Geary
    b. Intramural sports—Ran Harris
    c. Intramural Council—Susan C. Claeys
    d. Rugby Club—Perry Traw
61. Luncheon Forum—Patti Fosbinder
62. Military Science, ROTC—Esther Cooley
63. Editorial Staff: Steve Doremus and Jeff Johnson

ORGANIZING THE CITY BEAT

If you were to accept an assignment as city editor of a daily newspaper or news director of a radio or television station, you would organize the city into beats to cover it effectively, the same way the *University News* editor organized the campus beats. Consult the various organization charts and directories and the city telephone book, decide what beats must be covered, and divide them up among your staff members.

Let's say that you are a reporter and your city editor has assigned you the police beat. What do you do? You organize the police beat the same way you organized your campus beat. (That's why you should work on the university newspaper every semester covering different beats.) On the campus beat, you learn how to meet people, how to encourage them to confide in you. You learn some of the problems encountered on a beat and how to overcome those problems.

Before you walk into the police station, you talk with the city editor about the police chief, the personnel, and what problems exist internally or with the newspaper. You find out that the police chief, Leon Gillentine, is married, that his wife's name is Mary, and that they have two sons, Mike, 19, and Jeff, 9.

Once you've given yourself this briefing, you walk into the station and introduce yourself to Gillentine in much the same way you introduced yourself to Mahaney in the alumni and placement office. You let him know that you will stop by every day, that your reporting will be fair and honest, and that you are sympathetic to law enforcement problems in society today—exacting, dangerous duties, low pay, little recognition. You discuss problems that may have arisen in the past with reporters who covered the police beat. You ask to be introduced to the rest of the key staff members. Once again, you are pleasant and courteous to everyone you meet, especially to the secretaries and the dispatcher. On this beat, you need all the tips you can get.

If you are to do anything more than read the police blotter (a log of events that have occurred in the past 24 hours), your car will be equipped with a radio on the same frequency as the police department's so that you will be alerted when a robbery is in progress or some other criminal act is being investigated. But checking the police blotter will be a major part of your beat. You will see what events have occurred and make arrangements to interview the officers involved. You may be required to let the city editor know what stories on crime trends could be developed, based on what you find on the police blotter.

The description of the police beat and the organization of it are typical of the approach you will have to take on almost any beat. But each beat is different; each will have different features, and you have to make different organizational efforts.

MAJOR NEWS BEATS

Covering the Courts

A study by the Bureau of Justice Statistics in 1983 revealed that more than 81 million cases were filed in courts. Among the kinds of cases filed in the 46 states and District of Columbia that participated in the study were these:

> *Seattle attorney Murray Ledford Jones, who has been placed on "mental disability status" by the Washington Supreme Court, faces hearings on four new criminal charges next month.*

> *Two assistant vice presidents of the Bank of Cheyenne County were sentenced in Federal Court in Jackson Hole today to one year's probation for failure to file federal current transaction reports.*

> *A Contra Costa man is free on bond today under warning to stay away from another man who says he bit off part of his ear in "a fit of anger."*

The prospect of covering the courts may be overwhelming and even disquieting to you. But like most unknowns, once you've steeled yourself and been on the beat for a week or two, things begin to fall into place, and the court beat won't seem so formidable at all. Elise Frederick, who covers the courts for the *Nashville Banner*, stresses these things that beginning writers should know:

Just as you would on general beats, on the courts beat cultivate your prime sources of news. Be a friend to the secretaries and clerks. The court clerks especially will know which cases on the docket are most important. With the multitude of cases being tried, you can't sit in on all of them. Unless they involve

FIGURE 3.1. Elise Frederick and Managing Editor Joe Worley of the *Nashville Banner* check over a court trial story. Reprinted with permission of the *Nashville Banner*.

celebrities or are of a sensational nature, divorce cases, shoplifting cases or burglary cases are rarely reported in a large city. They are usually relegated to a column of decisions rendered in court. The court clerk will know which trial or hearing will be postponed. Judges and prosecuting attorneys are especially important to be friendly with. Although jurists may not be "on the record" sources, they can provide you with interesting ideas from their particular perspectives.

Although you don't have to be a lawyer to cover the courts, Elise Frederick notes that after six months on the beat you feel like you should be licensed to practice. Your most basic objective in covering the courts is honing your ability to cut through the legalese and write a story an eighth-grader can understand and *still* find interesting.

For Frederick, the courts beat starts when a person is indicted by the grand jury and ends when the person is convicted or acquitted. (The police reporter covers a case until indictment, and state reporters cover the appellate process.) She describes the process, before, during and after:

If the police officer has found probable cause that an individual committed a crime, that person is taken downtown, booked and set for hearing before a city or county judge. If the lower court judge decides there's enough proof, the case will be sent to the grand jury. (The grand jury is an independent group of 13 average citizens. The 13th juror is the foreman.) The defendant may not feel like he or she gets a fair shake before the grand jury since only the prosecution is allowed to testify about the case:

By MERRILL HARTSON
AP Labor Writer

WASHINGTON — Labor Secretary Raymond J. Donovan was indicted yesterday by a county grand jury in Bronx, N.Y., in connection with his past business dealings as a construction executive.

Donovan charged that the indictment was "not worth the paper it is written on" but said he was granted a leave of absence by President Reagan pending the outcome of the case.

"I am outraged and disgusted by the actions and the obviously partisan timing of the Bronx district attorney," Donovan said.

The defendant has no representation before the grand jury. The grand jury either indicts (issues a true bill) or dismisses (issues a no-true bill). If police or prosecutors fear the defendant will skip town, the grand jurors "seal" the indictment until the suspect is caught.

The defendant then appears in Criminal Court and is arraigned. That's a fairly routine affair with the defendant and lawyer receiving a copy of the indictment, pleading not guilty and setting up a schedule of pretrial hearings. (Remember, a hearing is not a trial, even though both involve a lot of legal argument. Even so, when you trim away all the complicated motions, you may find yourself a story.)

When you finally get to the trial stage, here is the process:

First there's a jury selection (*voir dire*, in legalese). Depending on the publicity surrounding the case, the judge will decide whether prospective jurors can be questioned as a group or individually. During the questioning, lawyers tell prospective jurors that while they don't mean to pry into their personal affairs, they have to have a fair trial and pick a jury without prejudice to either side. Although this can become tedious, if you *have* to have a story, you can pick up some pretty good quotes from attorneys. And you really never know when a jury might be selected and the trial begun. (It's usually when the reporter can't stand it anymore and takes a break.)

Once the jury is seated, each side gets to offer an opening argument in which the evidence is interpreted in the best interest of the lawyer speaking. Then testimony is presented. The state goes first, then the defendant. The state is then allowed rebuttal testimony. The case winds up with closing arguments from each side and the judge's charges to the jury. (It's a good idea to slip out of the courtroom during the charge since the judge can spend up to an hour monotonously reading things you already know.)

When that's over, the jury goes to their chambers and begins deliberations. Never try to predict what it's going to do and when it's going to return. You'll almost always be wrong. It's a waiting game. But while you're waiting, take down the names, addresses and phone numbers of the jurors. You do this for three reasons: (1) Nobody knows who the jury foreman (the one who reads the verdict) is until the final moment. You'll have the data you need. (2) If another reporter is covering the trial and the verdict comes in just in time for the opposition's deadline and not yours, you can call up some of the jurors and ask them about the deliberation. Whether they talk is up to them, but if they do, you'll have something your competitor doesn't have for your deadline, or at least material for a good second-day story. (3) It gives you something to do and keeps you close to the courtroom. (As in jury selection, verdicts like to come down while reporters are away from the scene.)

Then, for posterity, when the verdict is rendered, you talk to the lawyers. The defense, if it loses, will usually tell you it plans to file a motion for a new trial within 30 days and then appeal to the state level after that.

Frederick lists additional instructions: Be organized. When a person of news value is indicted, begin a file. Check with the Criminal Court clerk's office for hearing dates on the defendant and mark them on your calendar and in your file. Call the prosecutor and defense attorney periodically about the case. If and when it comes to trial, you'll probably feel like an expert witness.

Always check with prosecutors to see if a defendant is going to settle the case before trial by pleading guilty. Those stories can often sneak right past you.

Be careful when writing lawsuit stories on the civil side of the justice system.

While it's true they are on the public record, printing reckless allegations without checking them out can get your name in Circuit Court as a defendant in a libel suit. One way to get around that is always to make the effort of calling the defendant and giving him or her the opportunity to comment. Many times the response will be "no comment," but those two words can save you.

Be sure to follow up on a lawsuit after it's been filed. Often these cases are settled out of court, and usually the terms of the settlement are not disclosed because they are not filed with the court. Use the power of persuasion to find out the settlement. Only a small percentage of civil cases actually make it to trial, and then it can be two to three years later, depending on the case backlog of the judge.

Don't allow yourself to be used, either by attorneys or parties in the lawsuit. Present both sides of the story.

And last—or perhaps first—of all, pick up a legal dictionary or pocket-sized lawyer's handbook. You'll use them.

An important thing for you to remember in all this is that court reporting can be the most interesting of beats. And it's valuable reporting that continually assures the public that justice is being rendered.

Covering Government and Politics

The prospect of covering that abstract and nebulous thing called government and that even more nebulous thing called politics can send cold chills down the spine of any beginning reporter. At the city level, for example, there are many different forms the government can take. The most common is the mayor-council form. The mayor may share legislative and executive duties with the council. Or the mayor may not share administrative and executive responsibilities with the council, while the council acts as a legislative branch of government. Some cities have a commission form of government without a mayor, with citizens or commissioners performing legislative and executive duties:

> Keokuk city commissioners unanimously approved yesterday an 11-cent increase in the city's property tax rate, while also giving final acceptance to the city's 1986-87 budget.
>
> The previous $1.22 tax rate will be hiked to $1.33 to fund the city's $5 million general fund. Revenue in the general fund provides money for the police, fire, street and sanitation departments.
>
> "The utility portion of the budget funding the gas, water, electric and personnel operations, has been allotted $4.8 million," Commissioner Anthony Anderson said, "but will not receive monies from the property tax increase."

There may also be commissioner-manager or council-manager forms of government wherein the mayor lacks power and a city manager wields power. A mayor-manager form, on the other hand, maintains a mayor with power, appointing most department and agency heads, while the city manager is in charge of the daily operation. A city organization chart might take the form of Figure 3.2.

The city may have a mayor-alderman form of government:

> The Rock Island Board of Mayor and Aldermen have voted 5-0 to change the collection-system design of portions of a federally funded sewer project from a pressure to a small-diameter design.

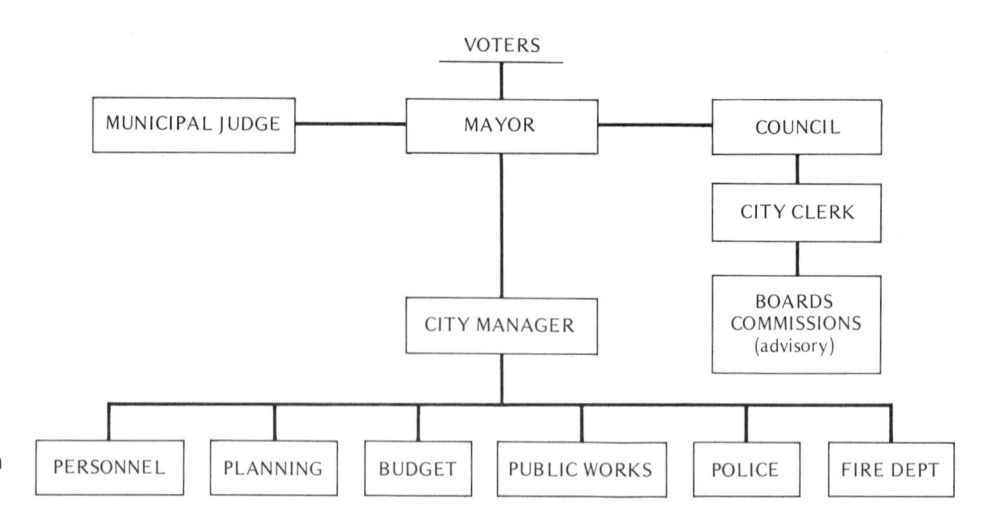

Figure 3.2. City organization chart.

These seemingly chameleonic forms of government create different forms of power in the various offices. But even when you get a chart of the government from the city clerk, the source of power may be off the chart—it may reside in the power hierarchy of the city or, especially on some particular issue, even in a group of concerned influential citizens:

> More than 75 persons attended the city council meeting last night to insist that Highway 77 be widened to four lanes between Thayer and Auburn.
>
> "My primary concern is to do all I can to get this project finished and improve our access to Interstate 80," Wanda Peterson, president of the Christian-Warren County Chamber of Commerce, said.

To understand city and governmental functions, ask the clerks for organizational and flow charts. The flow chart in Figure 3.3, for example, enables you to understand how ordinances become law at the city level. Readings are held

Figure 3.3. City ordinance flow chart.

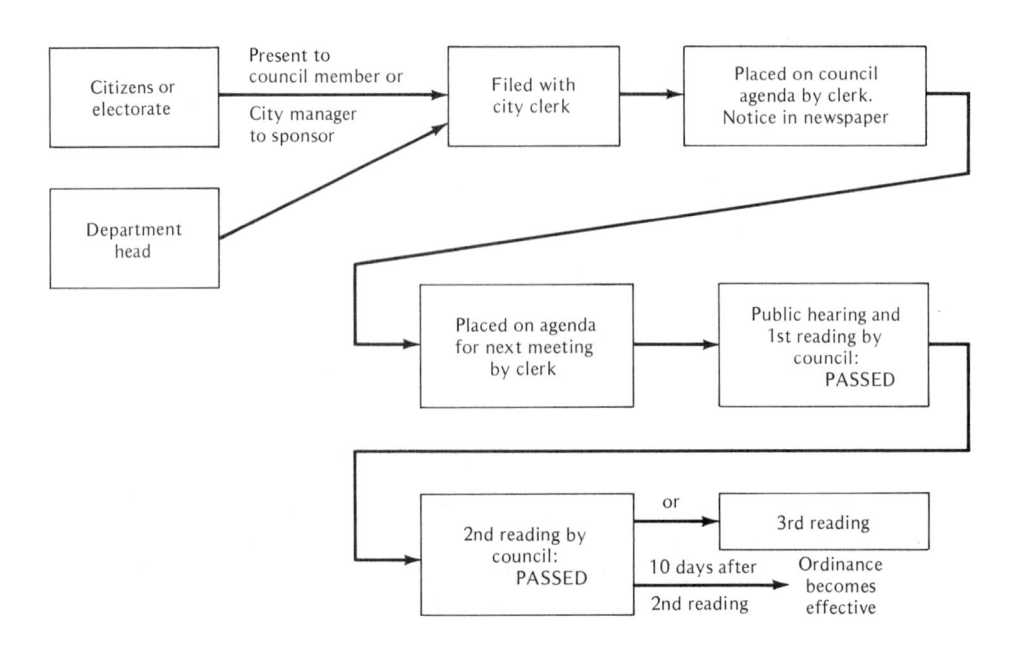

for citizen reactions to the ordinances. Resolutions to amend minor budgets or congratulate the local high school basketball team require only one reading.

A Comment about County Governments

The city governmental functions delegated to it by the state may overlap with county governmental functions, leading to a perpetual state of feuding between the two:

> Providence County commissioners voted last night to pay a $13,000 debt due Tovey for construction of a bridge begun prior to that city's incorporation in 1983.
> "We're morally obligated to Tovey," Commissioner Roger Reed said. "If they hadn't incorporated, we would have had to pay the whole thing. They're just asking us to pay half the cost."
> In other action, William Grant was elected chairman of the County Commission and Jack Bart was elected chairman pro tempore.

In addition, the rural and urban populations, with their diverse interests and needs, constantly engage in a tug-of-war that keeps the reporter provided with issues to report on.

The county form of government may be called anything from a county commission to a board of chosen freeholders. More than 25 different names are currently being used.

Counties are led by an executive who functions much like a city manager:

> By BOB McMILLAN
> Herald-Citizen Staff
>
> John Gentry thinks of Putnam's county government as big business — operating 40 facilities, 200 vehicles and more than 900 employees this year on a $20 million budget.
> But while Putnam County is ahead of many others in efficiency and planning, the county executive says he wants to take a good thing a few steps further. In his annual state-of-the-county address to the County Commission, Gentry proposed:
> A full-time planner. A full-time safety director. A job classification system. A centralized purchasing system. An expanded county maintenance department. A comprehensive building program for county facilities. More use of computers in county records and bookkeeping.

County government *is* big business, with agencies and authorities complicating the governing scene for the reporter:

> Officials from Grantland County have decided to form a central water authority to deal with water distribution.
> Plans to create the authority were drafted during a joint meeting of the Grantland County Commissioner's water and sewer committee and the Grantland County Water Association — an organization of three municipal and six rural water utility districts.

On a higher level, agencies like the New York Port Authority and the Tennessee Valley Authority are almost powers unto themselves. When they run amok, as the TVA has done on more than one occasion, your responsibility is to provide a check by letting your readers know.

If a cloud of despair is settling over you now while contemplating the prospect of this bleak reporting terrain, dispel it by remembering that with each form of government there will be the equivalent of the city clerk or executive secretary who will help you see what the important issues and events are until you're able to do so on your own. And remember that all of this involves politics, and you, as a media reporter, are seen as a very valuable person and possible ally in the eyes of all politicians.

STATE AND FEDERAL GOVERNMENTS

State and federal government forms may be more uniform compared to city and county government, but tracking down the real power still calls for detective skills on the part of the reporter.

Ken Renner of *The Knoxville Journal* covers Capitol Hill in Nashville, Tenn. What he says about state government and politics may be applied to government on the local and federal levels.

Covering government and politics is similar in most respects to covering any other news story or beat. You may have to have the who, what, when, where, why and how in any news story. But why an event occurs in the political arena usually takes on more significance in government and political news.

Government is politics. Every governmental decision is made in a political context. Former Governor Ray Blanton was criticized when he said, "Everything I do is political." But he was telling the truth. Even if a decision is reached on an issue without regard to political impact, that decision is going to have political consequences.

A corollary to that rule is the fact that politics, reduced to its simplest level, means money. Politics and government are the means we use to apportion and redistribute wealth. It's easy to see this when you talk about budgets and taxes. When governors announce their budgets each year, what they really are saying is who they are going to take money from through taxation and who will get that money through salaries, welfare benefits, state contracts and services. The budget is a statement of priorities, and the rankings are easily discerned by looking for the bottom-line expenditures allocated for each program or service.

These linkages, however, are sometimes less easy to see when you cover complicated battles in the state legislature. Every year the legions of lobbyists representing business and industrial groups troop to Capitol Hill, hats in hand, seeking some special favors, protection or advantageous changes in regulations governing their clients. When optometrists and ophthalmologists square off over which will have the legal authority to dispense prescription drugs, what they're really battling over is shares of the market for eye care. Ophthalmologists don't want optometrists to keep their monopoly over all patients who require some drug therapy in their eye care. Optometrists don't want to give it up. The General Assembly must arbitrate the dispute, and the stakes are almost purely financial.

To tell the story of what is happening in state government, a reporter has to understand those connections. Developing reliable sources of information is crucial, as in other forms of reporting. Prejudices should not be allowed to get the best of you. For example, most people think of lobbyists as shadowy characters handing out payoffs or engaging in other dirty dealings. The fact is that lobbyists are consistently the most reliable source of information on issues. They know the ins and outs of issues better than most legislators, who may be only peripherally concerned with any given topic. The lobbyists' job is to push their clients' interests, but lobbyists must be prepared to back their statements with facts. Since all that lobbyists have going for them is their credibility, whether with lawmakers, administration officials or media persons, they'll seldom lie. As long as you

FIGURE 3.4. Ken Renner of *The Knoxville Journal* covers Nashville's Capitol Hill. Reprinted with permission of *The Knoxville Journal*.

remember that there's more than one side to a story, lobbyists can be a valuable shortcut to understanding complex topics.

Friendships frequently win out over facts when legislators make up their minds on how to vote on bills. Most lobbyists understand this, but many reporters are politically naive in this regard. Those friendships can be built up in a variety of ways: Taking legislators out to dinner, contributing to their campaigns, doing them favors, or simply having longstanding relationships with them can often make a difference when a controversial bill hits the floor for a vote. Understanding those friendships is important for a reporter who wants to understand how and why things happen the way they do.

The Administrative Side of Government. When you're covering the administrative side of state government—the various departments and agencies that have a daily impact on citizens' lives—digging out the news can be tough. Administrations vary in their willingness to be forthcoming with news. Some administrations will announce both good and bad news. Others will announce only the positive, non-controversial things they do. All administrations, Renner says, try to put the news in the best possible light. The reporter's job is to report everything that's important, whether it's handed out in the form of a press release or whether it has to be dug out of the bureaucracy with a pick and shovel.

When news is not forthcoming, a reporter has to know where to look for it. Developing friendships and source relationships with middle-level people in the bureaucracy is frequently the key: The people at the top of most agencies are usually too busy to know the minute details of what their entire department is doing. Those at the bottom never knew much to begin with. The mid-level managers, however, are often most familiar with the nuts and bolts of how programs work, what the problems are, and how they can be fixed.

Pack Journalism. There's too much "pack journalism" in government and politics coverage. Reporters don't learn much when they just cover what everyone else is covering, talking mostly among themselves about stories and measuring their coverage by what shows up in other papers or broadcasts. Sometimes it's impossible to break away from the pack when a major issue is brewing, when big events occur, or when your editors are asking you to top your competitor's lead on a story last night. Yet it's important to try. When the pack heads in one direction, try going in another. Ask the different question, pursue the neglected angle. You'll certainly come up with a different story. Frequently you'll come up with a better one.

Records. It's crucial to know what records are kept and where. You *can* cover government by just rewriting news releases and attending press conferences—the staged news of the day. Or you can try, when time and priorities allow, to dig behind the media events. Detailed records of tax collections, candidate financial disclosures, prison records, travel vouchers, quarterly bank reports, purchasing documents, business permits and registrations, and even personnel files can provide valuable information if you're patient enough to go through them. They can flesh out stories with pertinent information or lead to new story ideas and issues.

When you report a story, tell readers how it affects them. If you weren't a reporter, would you be interested if a candidate made a small shift in his stand on an issue? Tell readers why it's important and what the result would be if the candidate's latest position results in a law being enacted. Too often, particularly in government and political reporting, reporters tend to share the insulated world of government. There is a tendency to start believing that our readers and listeners share our detailed interest in the subjects we're reporting. Events have to be made relevant. What does a $200 million tax increase mean? We see big numbers like that all the time in stories. But the woman who glances at the paper before rushing off to work isn't going to have time to figure out the meaning of the increase. If you have explained that it will cost the average taxpayer $40 next year, you're dealing in terms that make sense to her. If you don't tell readers why they should be interested in your story, they'll ignore it.

COVERING EDUCATION

Education in our society touches everyone, from children to parents to taxpayers. Its importance in preparing children to enter our society as responsible citizens and weaving the fabric of that society by passing on our values and goals and heritage cannot be denied. In addition, no other institution uses local funds on the scale of educational institutions. Your job in covering education, then, is an important one. You represent the public. You are responsible for seeing that the system is functioning properly, that monies are spent wisely, and that problems are solved in acceptable ways. All those responsibilities are not easy to accomplish, especially when you encounter administrators and educators who are not performing well. Always keep in mind that our society pays people more to handle bricks (not to mention footballs) than to handle children. Although you should not tolerate the inefficiency you may encounter, you should be able to understand it.

More and more media are employing or designating reporters to cover the education beat. Some are called education editors. You need not have teacher or education administration training to be assigned the education beat. If you follow the procedures we prescribe in covering your beat, you should have few difficulties. As always, you should be fair as well as skeptical, tactful as well as persistent and firm.

The responsibility for educational services is most often delegated by the state to independent school districts, usually following city boundary lines. School boards, generally of five to seven members, are either elected or appointed by the mayor. The board may then hire a superintendent to carry out its policymaking decisions, or the superintendent may be elected. An elected superintendent may wield more power than a hired superintendent because the elected person may feel more independent than the hired person. (The situation of course varies with the personalities involved. An overpowering hired superintendent may simply overwhelm a school board; an elected superintendent who lacks confidence may be whiplashed by a strong school board.)

The composition of the board and the way it is selected may be changed by the electorate:

> Incumbent Samuel J. Watson II and attendance supervisor Pamela L. Bingham are vying for the position of Taneytown County school superintendent in the Nov. 6 general election.
>
> The popular election for the superintendent post is the first in the county's history. Mandated by a referendum passed last August, another item on the same ballot expanded the seven-member appointed school board to a 12-member body elected by the voters.

The regularly scheduled meetings of the school board will occupy a prominent place in your future date book, along with commencement ceremonies, budgets, and policy, curriculum and personnel changes. Budgets, invariably too low, usually provide news copy and a familiarization with the problems in schools:

A shortfall of nearly $1 million in the Dade County school budget will be the result if all obligations are fulfilled for next year, according to Superintendent Holly J. Hewitt.

"We're in real budget trouble," the newly elected superintendent said. "It's something I inherited with the job."

An overestimation of the school enrollment was a key factor in the deficit. More than $350,000 was lost in state revenues because of lower average daily attendance, Hewitt said.

"We're going to be 700 students short of a projected increase of 1,945. We also included $345,000 too much in the budget when we estimated what the county would be sharing with us.

"As if all this weren't bad enough," Hewitt added, "the school board voted four months ago for an additional 2.3 percent pay increase for teachers. The county commission accepted the proposal. That contract agreement will cost us an additional $240,000."

The school system may also be required to settle a federal court discrimination suit for $172,000.

U.S. District Judge Robert Whitman ruled that a black teacher, Rodney Drupp, had been discriminated against by the school board seven years ago when it failed to offer him a position as principal at Dalton Senior High School. Attorneys will receive $76,000, while Drupp will receive $96,000. The $96,000 represents the difference between a teacher and a principal salary.

Hewitt said that her predecessor, John Offutt, had told the board that a county insurance policy would pay the sum.

"The insurance policy didn't cover the suit," Hewitt explained. "But I'm going to recommend as a cost-cutting move at the board meeting tonight that we not fund a newly created job of supervising principal — a position once offered to Drupp to settle the discrimination suit."

This rather long story acquaints you with the kind of complex problems the education reporter can run into on the education beat.

Other non-cyclical stories may involve strikes:

Nearly 5,000 teachers in seven states spent Labor Day on strike, and more strikes are predicted elsewhere. The state hit hardest was Illinois, where 3,274 teachers are on strike. Other states threatened with teachers' strikes are Indiana, Louisiana, Michigan, Pennsylvania, Rhode Island and Washington.

Still other stories may deal with school bond issues, lunch programs and federal aid to education. So prevalent is crime and unrest in the schools today that this could qualify as cyclical news:

By JOEY LEDFORD

WASHINGTON (UPI) — One of four eighth graders expects to smoke marijuana this year, and nearly 20% predict they will use cocaine or heroin. A Florida study revealed yesterday that more than half the students said they plan to drink alcohol.

Firings and transfers provide other news for the education reporter:

A Waltham High School teacher has been fired from her position as a seventh-grade teacher on charges of incompetence.

> Charlotte Wills is charged with giving out final exam questions three days before the date of the final.
>
> The Waltham City School Board also transferred the Waltham High School principal, Jerome Konrad, to a teaching position at Girard High School.
>
> The transfer was made after several teachers testified that Konrad had encouraged such actions to improve the academic profile of Waltham High School.
>
> The American Civil Liberties Union has entered the case, stating that "comparable worth" for women employed also should include "comparable treatment." Their position is that if Jerome Konrad is not fired, neither should Charlotte Wills be fired.

Like most organizations sensitive to their public image, the Waltham County School Board would have liked to keep the story out of the newspapers—especially in light of the fact that a woman teacher was fired for doing as instructed by her male principal, who was demoted and transferred to another school. Had they attempted to keep the meeting closed, you would have mentioned sunshine laws and the board's responsibility to conduct the public's business in public.

In addition to the usual organizations engaging in censorship of library books and textbooks, some states have textbook committees that will occasionally make news:

> The Texas Education Association has been asked to review the textbook selection process for the state's public schools to ensure that books have the latest information and are relevant to students' studies.

In any education meetings or events you attend, follow the usual reporting procedures: Try to find out what's going to take place in advance. Get there early and go over the agenda. Check with the person in charge to determine what are the most important items due to come up and get whatever background you can. Use a tape recorder, take notes and, after everyone else is through asking questions, ask your questions.

NEWS SOURCES IN BUSINESS AND LABOR

The obvious sources in labor and management disputes will be the rank and file of the union and union leaders and the management of the business. But interviews with the workers and lower-echelon members of management should be conducted. You will be surprised at the diverse information given you. At a Teledyne Still-Man factory being picketed, the union version was that Teledyne wanted concessions in terms of benefits and hourly wages from the workers. Management's version was that the union simply wanted a strike. The union presented its demands for a new contract. Management thought it over for a few days, met with the union leaders and agreed to their terms, only to be met with an escalation of union demands. Management refused to meet the escalation demands, and the union struck the plant. Whenever possible, of course, you would try to obtain copies of written statements made by both parties in the negotiating meetings.

Covering private corporations presents problems for the writer that are not present in covering public organizations. Although corporations are owned by investors—the public—they are basically private. They want to make money for their employees and stockholders. And they want to avoid unpleasant news. So when losses occur or the stock goes down, you will usually have difficulty getting statements and comments from management. Chris Welles, director of a fellowship program at Columbia University's graduate journalism school, has outlined some sources you can use to get that needed information.

The Securities and Exchange Commission, for example, will give you three valuable documents:

1. *The 10-K annual report* describes the company and its financial status.
2. The *annual report* is "a kind of public relations version of the 10-K." Although not required by the SEC, the annual report undergoes the scrutiny of the New York Stock Exchange. Financial statements in it must be audited by a reputable accounting firm.
3. *Proxy statements* include salaries and stock holdings of executives and details on transactions between the company and its management and the company and its directors.

Other sources of information about big business are Form 990, which nonprofit organizations must file with the Internal Revenue Service and which you may examine. Congressional hearings and their records can yield information about unethical business practices. Investment publications like Value Line, Standard & Poor's and Moody's encapsulate the financial data you may need for a proper perspective on the company and its holdings and transactions.

VIGILANCE PAYS OFF

If you're going to be a media writer, you will have to be eternally vigilant. What that can mean is explained by Chekhov in *The Sea Gull*. A writer, Trigorin, describes his life, his passion:

Day and night one thought obsesses me: I must be writing, I must be writing, I must be . . . I write incessantly, and always at a breakneck speed. . . . Why, now even, I'm here talking to you, I'm excited, but every minute I remember that the story I haven't finished is there waiting for me. I see that cloud up there, it's shaped like a grand piano . . . instantly a mental note . . . I must remember to put that in my story. . . . A whiff of heliotrope. Quickly I make note of it: cloying smell, widow's color . . . put that in next time I describe a summer evening. Every sentence, every word I say and you say, I lie in wait for it, snap it up for my literary storeroom . . . it might come in handy.

If you are a writer, you must pay the price and always be alert to what is news or what will be news.

Combined with this eternal vigilance, you must employ tact and aggressiveness to ferret out facts for a news story. Knowing when to employ tact and when to resort to more aggressive behavior may determine whether you get the information you need or whether you come away from a source with blank note cards. Always employ tact first. If that doesn't work, you have nothing to lose by being aggressive. Sometimes aggressiveness earns you the respect of the person you're interviewing.

No matter who it is you are talking to—a policeman, a district attorney, a president of a large business or a labor leader—use tact. The higher the officials, the more they have been subjected to aggressiveness, and the more likely they have been repulsed by it. Tact and gentle persuasion work best with almost everyone. However, if you're attending a press conference or pursuing a lead based on a news handout, or if someone comes to you and wants to present his or her side of a story, aggressive questioning may be employed immediately. Dan Rather didn't get to where he is today by being tactful at presidential news conferences. When the presidents he questioned attempted evasion, he called them to task for it. Most often, however, save aggressive questioning for when you've exhausted all available tactful approaches.

"Miss Peach" by Mell Lazarus. © by and permission of News America Syndicate.

Information sources are varied and virtually inexhaustible, depending on the imagination of the person seeking them. Your job as a reporter is to discover what sources are available and then to develop them. That is not always easy. Let's say you are covering city hall for a newspaper in a city of 25,000. You get the organization chart of the city in Figure 3.5 from the city manager. (The solid lines indicate administrative supervision and control; the dotted lines indicate appointing authority.)

You are responsible for the mayor's office and all offices except the city judge and court clerk. (Those are covered by the city and county court reporter.) That's a lot of names and faces to keep track of on the upper level, to say nothing of the secretaries and assistants on the lower level. You'll be calling on the mayor every day and covering the city council meetings once a week. Various departmental meetings will be held throughout the week. You'll also have to become acquainted with the five to 10 council members representing the various city districts.

That's the way it goes. And the larger the city, the more complex the city government. This particular city organization chart indicates a city manager type of government. Besides the mayor, the city manager and the city clerk will be the key news sources to cultivate. The annual budget will disclose the departments with the largest budgets and personnel and the breadth of services. These are indicators of power and influence. However, others besides the city officials might have power and influence in the city government hierarchy. Your job is to discover the power structure in the city. Who influences city officials from behind the scenes? Your city editor and publisher should know who those persons are. Ask them to tell you.

Different cities have different forms of government: the city manager form, the mayor-council form, the commission plan, and consolidated city and county

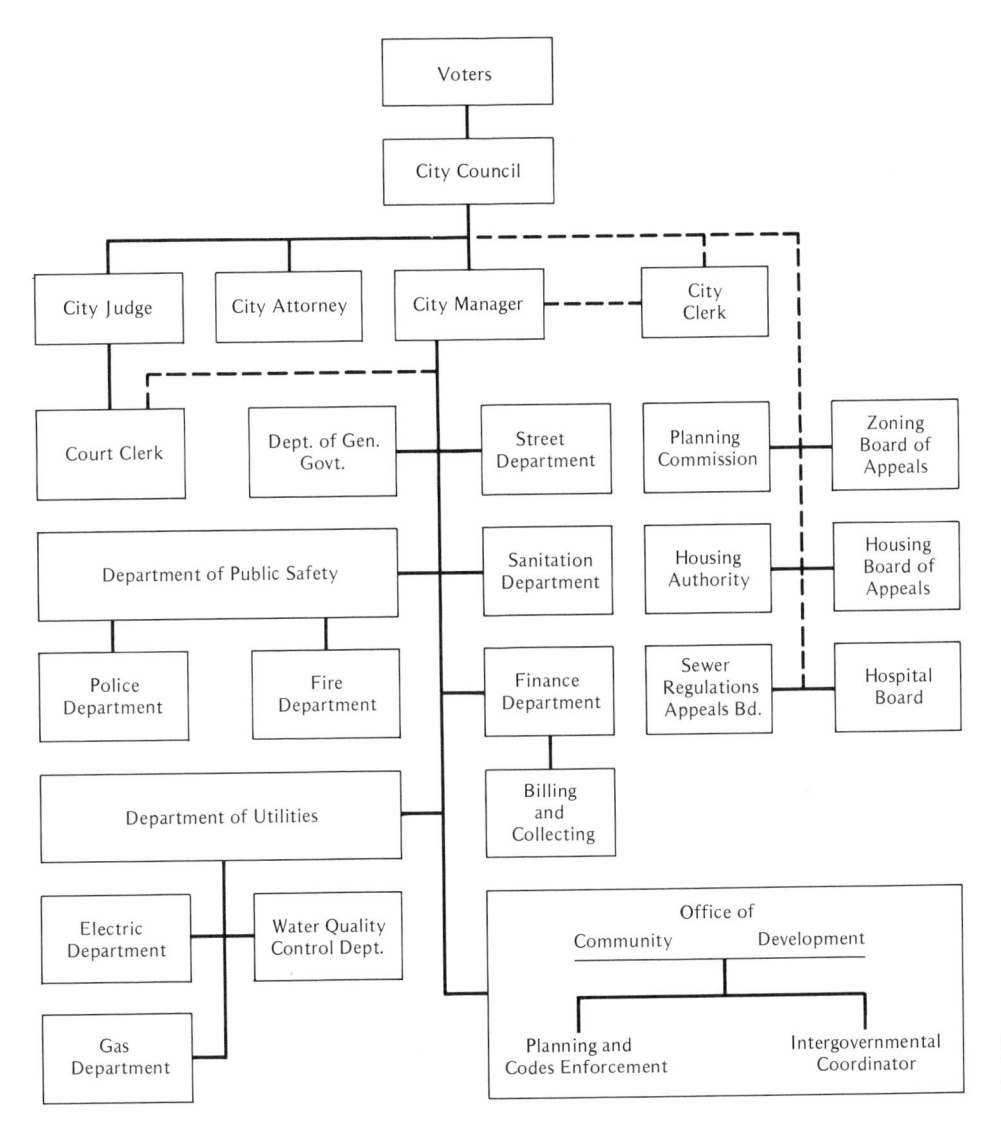

FIGURE 3.5. Municipal organization chart.

governments. The *Municipal Yearbook* spells out the various forms of government in cities throughout the country. Considerable study of city, county and state governments will be necessary to become familiar with the sources available to you. (That is one of the reasons political science courses are recommended in some journalism programs.)

The development of those sources depends fully on the amount of time and effort you spend cultivating them. You can be assured, however, that the time will be well-spent. If your relationship with that city clerk, the court clerk or the clerk who draws up the bills in the state legislature is properly nurtured, you will always be aware of important ordinances, cases or bills circulating in the corridors and in the chambers.

The relationships with these sources, of course, should be on a friendly but professional level. Those sources should know that you are honest and fair and that they can expect that kind of treatment from you in fair weather or foul. You can have lunch with the city attorney and play tennis with a council member if you like, but there should be an implicit understanding that your first obligation is to your profession. That may curtail some of your social engagements, or it may not. John Seigenthaler, publisher of *The Tennessean* and editorial director of *USA Today*, refuses to join the Belle Meade Country Club in Nashville because of the kind of biases such an association might bring in *The Tennessean's* coverage of the city. Other journalists feel that as long as you are objective, any association with a news source is all right, and the higher the person in government, the better. But Franklin D. Roosevelt and John F. Kennedy were great charmers—they caused many a reporter to waver between loyalty to the president and objectivity in his or her work.

What course you follow may depend on the newspaper's policy or your feelings on the matter. When the editor and publisher of the Madison, Wis., *Capital Times* tried to enforce a policy against "freebies" for the staff—tickets to events, cruises, cocktail parties, etc.—the staff sued. They held that freebies should be considered fringe benefits of the job. They lost the suit. But they believed they could accept such largesse and still maintain their integrity. Perhaps they could have, but their credibility to their readers might have been damaged.

Every source you cultivate should be assured of confidentiality if you can ensure it at all. Many of the tips you receive will involve wrongdoing in high places and, not uncommonly, in the organization the tipster is working for. The identity should be protected to save that person's job and vertical and horizontal job mobility. To assure this confidentiality, document the illegal practices either by checking through public records or by actually checking the practice itself. If you receive word that funds from a toll bridge are being skimmed, an actual accounting of the traffic compared with the receipts may determine that a scam is taking place.

At this writing, 26 states help the reporter protect sources through shield laws. The California shield law is typical of most absolute shield laws.

CALIFORNIA CONSTITUTION
Article I
Section 2

a. Every person may freely speak, write and publish his or her sentiments on all subjects, being responsible for the abuse of this right. A law may not restrain or abridge liberty of speech or press.

b. A publisher, editor, reporter, or other person connected with or employed upon a newspaper, magazine, or other periodical publication, or by press association or wire service, or any person who has been so connected or employed, shall not be adjudged in contempt by a judicial, legislative, or administrative body, or any other body having the power to issue subpoenas, for refusing to disclose the source of any information procured while so connected or employed for publication in a newspaper, magazine or other periodical publication, or for refusing to disclose any unpublished information obtained or prepared in gathering, receiving or processing of information for communication to the public.

Nor shall a radio or television news reporter or other person connected with or employed by a radio or television station, or any person who has been so connected or employed, be so adjudged in contempt for refusing to disclose the source of any information procured while so connected or employed for news or news commentary purposes on radio or television, or for refusing to disclose any unpublished information obtained or prepared in gathering, receiving or processing of information for communication to the public.

As used in this subdivision, "unpublished information" includes information not disseminated to the public by the person from whom disclosure is sought, whether or not related information has been disseminated and includes, but is not limited to, all notes, outtakes, photographs, tapes or other data of whatever sort not itself disseminated to the public through a medium of communication, whether or not published information based upon or related to such material has been disseminated.

The New Jersey Supreme Court has ruled that its shield protection law is absolute. Most shield laws, however, provide limited protection. Only if the judges respect the legislature that passed the law and if their interpretations are as intended do absolute shield laws provide absolute protection.

Jails are not the friendliest places. If a news story has ramifications that might involve you with the law, you might consider destroying your story notes before you are subpoenaed—preferably after the story goes to press. (Destroying them *after* you receive the subpoena may subject you to contempt of court charges.) Even so, of course, if the judge so rules, you'll go to prison if you refuse to reveal your sources. For your own protection, try documenting all information your sources gave you through records and investigative reporting.

Reporter Fined for Shielding*

A circuit judge cited a television reporter with contempt of court yesterday and fined him $500 a day until he reveals the names of sources in a police assault case.

Circuit Judge Randall Thomas issued the civil contempt order against Don Phelps of WSAF-TV in Montgomery. He imposed the fine after saying he intended to disregard Alabama's "shield law," which protects reporters from testifying about confidential information.

Phelps's attorney, Tabor R. Novak Jr., said he would ask a state appeals court to set aside the contempt order.

The judge raised the issue at a hearing for four blacks from Michigan and Ohio indicted on charges including attempted murder in an assault on two white plainclothes police officers last Feb. 27.

Defense motions under review at the hearing including a request to throw out the charges on grounds that some of the blacks were beaten by police after their arrest and were intimidated into giving statements.

The two white officers were assaulted and one of them was shot in the melee at a house full of black funeral mourners, most from Warren, Ohio, and Pontiac, Mich.

THE RELUCTANT NEWS SOURCE

Not all people are willing sources of information. Because of past experiences, many are wary, unwilling to talk, even hostile. The degree to which your news story will adversely affect their reputation or livelihood usually determines the degree of reluctance not only to divulge information but to allow you an interview. A stubborn streak of self-preservation is inherent in all but the most perverse human beings. Loyalty to superiors or an organization also creates a reluctance to release revealing information. To do your job as a reporter, you will have to be ready to counter these negative reactions and be prepared to use methods to overcome them.

A more detailed discussion on interviewing and how to question reluctant sources will be presented in Chapter 4. At this time, however, we want to stress three things:

Always Be Courteous and Pleasant. A courteous and pleasant approach will disarm reluctant sources. Always attempt to put the persons being interviewed at ease at every opportunity, especially in the beginning of the interview. Mention

---

* Reprinted with permission of *The Tennessean*.

the weather, the persons' hobbies, office arrangements. When persons demur about answering questions, be pleasant. When they say they can't answer a specific question, be pleasant. When, after a half-hour, they still haven't answered one question, be pleasant. After all, you may be asking them to incriminate themselves or their superiors. Why should they answer your questions? If you were in their place, would you answer them?

Always Be Persistent. A corollary to being pleasant and courteous is being persistent. You are being paid to be persistent. You must, as part of your job, at times discover things that persons do not want to have revealed. If you do not discover those things, you will not be doing your job. If you are not persistent and do not fulfill your responsibilities, you will have to face (1) a disappointed, disgusted or irate editor; (2) disappointed, disgusted or irate colleagues; and (3) yourself in the mirror the next morning. None of these is pleasant. So be persistent.

You will talk to persons who will say they don't want to comment and who will then comment. If they don't answer your questions and if you find in your persistence that an edge is developing in your voice when you ask those questions, do not stop. And if, toward the end of the interview, you find your questioning a little more aggressive than toward the beginning, that, too, is not a bad thing to let the persons being interviewed experience. The combination of these things might move them to answer.

Throughout a trying and exhausting interview, while you are being pleasant and courteous and, finally, when you think that nothing and no one on this earth will move the persons you are questioning to answer, always remember the compulsion to confess. When you think the skies are so cloudy and gray that no ray can possibly break through, you may hear the persons you are questioning let loose a small sigh. You may see their eyes widen. They may start digging around in a desk drawer. When that happens, or something like it, be considerate. Ask them if perhaps it wouldn't be better to answer one or two of the questions. Ask them if perhaps they haven't kept things to themselves too long. Chances are the little boy or girl in them will lead them into confession. When that happens, continue being considerate and pleasant and write everything down. Don't change your expression regardless of what they say. Give them tea and sympathy.

But what would you do if the mayor calls to discuss some things a committee has discovered but the mayor wants to preface the comments with some "backgrounding" so that you will understand the full implications of the situation? The comments, of course, are "off the record."

Your course of action depends on whether the background information will be forthcoming if you *don't* want to honor the off-the-record backgrounding. If that is the condition for the backgrounding comments—they are not to be published—try to persuade the mayor otherwise. If you are unable to persuade the mayor to put them on the record, say that although you would rather not, you will comply with the request. But also tell the mayor that if you discover you can get the gist of the backgrounding comments in your ordinary investigative procedures, you will not feel honor-bound not to publish them.

After receiving the background material and taking notes on it, try to convince the mayor that you should be free to publish it. The mayor may have second thoughts about the restrictions.

In the middle of a line of questioning, someone may say, "That's off the record." Reply that your understanding is that everything you are talking about is on the record. And just what was so important about what was said, anyway? If the interviewee persists, say, "All right, but that from this point on, everything will be on the record." If the person later says, "This is off the record," stop and say, "Just a minute. We had an understanding that everything being discussed is on the record." Be adamant. The person will probably want to make the comment regardless of whether you keep it off the record. If not, ask again later on. The interviewee may then relinquish and reply.

SECRECY IN GOVERNMENT (AND ELSEWHERE)

Since World War II, many books have been written about secrecy in government. Starting with the Cold War, secrecy has proliferated alarmingly at all levels. Because a major part of reporting involves a surveillance of the environment and watching the government, secrecy keeps you from doing your job. The following item about the Cookeville General Hospital meeting illustrates this.

> By MARY JO DENTON
> Herald-Citizen Staff
>
> Cookeville General Hospital's board of trustees held a record short meeting last night, conducting very little business and doing little more than eating their usual steak dinner and telling some funny jokes.
>
> But they denied they had met secretly at the hospital last week, though some employees reported having seen the board members gathering there.
>
> Last night's meeting began at 7 o'clock, just after the seven-member board finished eating, and ended 30 minutes later, making it a meeting held in "record time," as one member remarked.

What is to be done about secrecy? Whenever and wherever it surfaces, fight it. Especially when it occurs in public institutions and public places. You will discover you have powerful allies. More and more state legislatures, instructed in the belief that public business is indeed the public's business, have enacted legislation known as sunshine laws. The laws attempt to bring the public's business out from the shadows of legislative chambers into the public sunshine. The laws decree that unless there is some overriding reason to the contrary, all public business should be conducted in public. Furthermore, the public should be forewarned when public business is going to be conducted so that citizens can be heard or witness the deliberations and transactions of public officials. The New York sunshine law, with its exemptions, is a typical state law. It identifies which meetings are public; it specifies the notification that must take place, the record of the meeting that should be made available to the public, and the nullification of acts and the penalties involved when business is conducted behind closed chamber doors. The majority of states now have sunshine laws.

NEW YORK PUBLIC OFFICERS LAW
ARTICLE 7
Open Meetings Law

§100. Legislative declaration. It is essential to the maintenance of a democratic society that the public business be performed in an open and public manner and that the citizens of this state be fully aware of and able to observe the performance of public officials and attend and listen to the deliberations and decisions that go into the making of public policy. The people must be able to remain informed if they are to retain control over those who are their public servants. It is the only climate under which the commonweal will prosper and enable the governmental process to operate for the benefit of those who created it.

§101. Short Title. This article shall be known and may be cited as "Open Meetings Law".

§102. Definitions. As used in this article. 1. "Meeting" means the official convening of a public body for the purpose of conducting public business.

2. "Public body" means any entity, for which a quorum is required in order to conduct public business and which consists of two or more members, performing a governmental function for the state or for an agency or department thereof, or for a public corporation as defined in section sixty-six of the general construction law, or committee or subcommittee or other similar body of such public body.

3. "Executive session" means that portion of a meeting not open to the general public.

§103. Open meetings and executive sessions.

(a) Every meeting of a public body shall be open to the general public, except that an executive session of such body may be called and business transacted thereat in accordance with section one hundred of this article.

(b) Public bodies shall make or cause to be made all reasonable efforts to ensure that meetings are held in facilities that permit barrier-free physical access to the physically handicapped, as defined in subdivision five of section fifty of the public buildings law.

§104. Public notice. 1. Public notice of the time and place of a meeting scheduled at least one week prior thereto shall be given to the news media and shall be conspicuously posted in one or more designated public locations at least seventy-two hours before each meeting.

2. Public notice of the time and place of every other meeting shall be given, to the extent practicable, to the news media and shall be conspicuously posted in one or more designated public locations at a reasonable time prior thereto.

3. The public notice provided for by this section shall not be construed to require publication as a legal notice.

§105. Conduct of executive sessions. 1. Upon a majority vote of its total membership, taken in an open meeting pursuant to a motion identifying the general area or areas of the subject or subjects to be considered, a public body may conduct an executive session for the below enumerated purposes only, provided, however, that no action by formal vote shall be taken to appropriate public moneys:

a. matters which will imperil the public safety if disclosed;

b. any matter which may disclose the identity of a law enforcement agent or informer;

c. information relating to current or future investigation or prosecution of a criminal offense which would imperil effective law enforcement if disclosed;

d. discussions regarding proposed, pending or current litigation;

e. collective negotiations pursuant to article fourteen of the civil service law;

f. the medical, financial, credit or employment history of a particular person or corporation, or matters leading to the appointment, employment, promotion, demotion, discipline, suspension, dismissal or removal of a particular person or corporation;

g. the preparation, grading or administration of examinations; and

h. the proposed acquisition, sale or lease of real property or the proposed acquisition of securities, or sale or exchange of securities held by such public body, but only when publicity would substantially affect the value thereof.

2. Attendance at an executive session shall be permitted to any member of the public body and any other persons authorized by the public body.

§106. Minutes. 1. Minutes shall be taken at all open meetings of a public body which shall consist of a record or summary of all motions, proposals, resolutions and any other matter formally voted upon and the vote thereon.

2. Minutes shall be taken at executive sessions of any action that is taken by formal vote which shall consist of a record or summary of the final determination of such action, and the date and vote thereon; provided, however, that such summary need not include any matter which is not required to be made public by the freedom of information law as added by article six of this chapter.

3. Minutes of meetings of all public bodies shall be available to the public in accordance with the provisions of the freedom of information law within two weeks from the date of such meeting except that minutes taken pursuant to subdivision two hereof shall be available to the public within one week from the date of the executive session.

§107. Enforcement. 1. Any aggrieved person shall have standing to enforce the provisions of this article against a public body by the commencement of a proceeding pursuant to article seventy-eight of the civil practice law and rules, and/or an action for declaratory judgment and injunctive relief. In any such action or proceeding, the court shall have the power, in its discretion, upon good cause shown, to declare any action or part thereof taken in violation of this article void in whole or in part.

An unintentional failure to fully comply with the notice provisions required by this article shall not alone be grounds for invalidating any action taken at a meeting of a public body. The provisions of this article shall not affect the validity of the authorization, acquisition, execution or disposition of a bond issue or notes.

2. In any proceeding brought pursuant to this section, costs and reasonable attorney fees may be awarded by the court, in its discretion, to the successful party.

3. The statute of limitations in an article seventy-eight proceeding with respect to an action taken at executive session shall commence to run from the date the minutes of such executive session have been made available to the public.

§108. Exemptions. Nothing contained in this article shall be construed as extending the provisions hereof to:

1. judicial or quasi-judicial proceedings, except proceedings of the public service commission and zoning boards of appeals;

2. *a.* deliberations of political committees, conferences and caucuses. *b. for purposes of this section, the deliberations of political committees, conferences and caucuses means a private meeting of members of the senate or assembly of the state of New York, or of the legislative body of a county, city, town or village, who are members or adherents of the same political party, without regard to (i) the subject matter under discussion, including discussions of public business, (ii) the majority or minority status of such political committees, conferences and caucuses or (iii) whether such political committees, conferences and caucuses invite staff or guests to participate in their deliberations*; and

3. any matter made confidential by federal or state law.

§109. Committee on open government. The committee on open government, created by paragraph (a) of subdivision one of section eighty-nine of this chapter, shall issue advisory opinions from time to time as, in its discretion, may be required to inform public bodies and persons of the interpretations of the provisions of the open meetings law.

§110. Construction with other laws. 1. Any provision of a charter, administrative code, local law, ordinance, or rule or regulation affecting a public body which is more restrictive with respect to public access than this article shall be deemed superseded hereby to the extent that such provision is more restrictive than this article.

2. Any provision of general, special or local law or charter, administrative code, ordinance, or rule or regulation less restrictive with respect to public access than this article shall not be deemed superseded hereby.

3. Notwithstanding any provision of this article to the contrary, a public body may adopt provisions less restrictive with respect to public access than this article.

§111. Severability. If any provision of this article or the application thereof to any person or circumstances is adjudged invalid by a court of competent jurisdiction, such judgment shall not affect or impair the validity of the other provisions of the article or the application thereof to other persons and circumstances.

If you have the idea that secrecy exists primarily at the state and federal levels, you are mistaken. Police chiefs will want to keep the police blotter in the desk drawer and the officer to be interviewed in the patrol car. School boards and village boards will go into "executive session," asking citizens and reporters to leave while they discuss "sensitive matters." Committee, board and council members will have "informal" or "casual" coffee breaks to discuss the actions to be taken in the coming meeting. The reasons for and against taking those actions are discussed at these clandestine meetings; when the actual meeting is convened, votes are cast without discussion. When this happens, public business, for whatever reason, is being conducted in private. Democracy is being subverted.

When you discover this subversion, your role as a reporter and as a representative of the people obliges you to protest. In so doing, you can educate your school boards and city council members about what is involved in a democratic government and in the democratic process. Your role and your actions, when this subversion occurs, will no doubt be spelled out for you by the city editor before you take over your beat. If they aren't, ask to be briefed on the courses of action to be taken should these events occur.

One last encouraging word: Covering a beat is not always pleasant. But it is interesting and challenging. Developing sources not only means cultivating them but also educating them and keeping them available for your questions. Not only will this bring out the best in you, but it will inspire you and bring out intestinal fortitude you didn't realize was there.

SUMMARY

News sources who are public officials, industry experts or other authoritative individuals are best cultivated through the beat system. Beats are excellent ways for editors to use their staff resources to ensure coverage of key community politics and business, and they provide a clear pathway between reporters and potential sources. Beats establish customs and ground rules for writers and their sources. Sources come to expect calls and queries from the same writer each time, and they come to know one another's strengths and weaknesses. Writers on a beat become familiar with the ambitions and abilities of the sources they use and learn how to get the most out of the relationship with them. Over time, writers and the sources they've developed learn what to expect from one another and what not to.

It's critical that writers know what their rights to information are. Sometimes a usually cooperative source may be evasive because of pressure caused by controversy. The reporter must decide how to bring potentially damaging information to light in a way that will not destroy the good relationship he or she has developed with the source. Reporters can call on sunshine laws to gain access to meetings and use the Freedom of Information Act to force disclosure of information. But such petitions take considerable time to be processed, and meetings can be delayed or postponed to stall a reporter, so the relationship with reliable sources is most important. It can provide a steady stream of information about important issues and events, and it helps educate the writer about the beat's principal figures and most important issues.

EXERCISES

1. List three subject-matter areas in which you would like to develop an expertise as a reporter or free-lance writer. After each, list the reasons for your choices.

    a.

Reasons:

    b.

Reasons:

    c.

Reasons:

2. What three campus beats would assist you in helping you to develop your expertise as a reporter or free-lance writer? List them below, with your reasons. If you are serious about developing your skills and knowledge in these areas, offer yourself as a reporter to the campus newspaper editor.

3. As news editor for your campus newspaper, you have five reporters at your disposal for news gathering. After consulting the faculty and student directories, the college catalog and whatever organizational charts you are able to find, assign beats for the five. (Attach any organizational charts you use.)

   a. Campus beats:

   (1)

   (2)

   (3)

   (4)

   (5)

   b. What rationale did you use in composing this beat system?

4. Assume that you are the city editor for your city newspaper. You have five reporters working for you. Organize the city into five beats. List the publications or sources you consulted before doing so.

    a. Sources consulted in drawing up the beat system:

    b. City beats:

       (1)

       (2)

       (3)

       (4)

       (5)

    c. What rationale did you use in composing this beat system?

5. Does your state have a sunshine law? (Keep all the information gathered for this exercise for possible use in Chapter 5, Exercise 3.)

    a. If the answer is yes, how do you think it compares with the one printed in this chapter? List major differences.

    b. Interview a reporter or editor about their feelings on the usefulness of the law, and report your findings below.
       Person interviewed: Date:
       Place: Time:
       Findings:

c. If the answer is no, interview a reporter or editor to discover why there is no sunshine law. What is used by reporters in lieu of the sunshine law to keep meetings open?
   Person interviewed: Date:
   Place: Time:
   Findings:

d. Interview a court official or lawyer to determine views on sunshine laws in general and your state law in particular (if you have one).
   Person interviewed: Date:
   Place: Time:
   Findings:

6. Does your state have a shield law or free flow of information law similar to the one published in this chapter? (Keep all the information gathered for this exercise for possible use in Chapter 5, Exercise 3.)

    a. If the answer is yes, is it absolute or qualified? How does it compare with the one printed in this chapter?

    b. If the answer is no, ask a knowledgeable person to discover why there is no shield law.

        Person interviewed: Date:

        Place: Time:

        Findings:

c. If the answer is yes, ask a reporter or editor about the effectiveness of the law.
   Person interviewed:					Date:
   Place:							Time:
   Findings:

d. Contact a court official or lawyer to determine views on shield laws in general and your state law in particular (if you have one).
   Person interviewed:					Date:
   Place:							Time:
   Findings:

7. Does your state have a public records law or a freedom of information law? (Keep all the information gathered for this exercise for possible use in Chapter 5, Exercise 3.)

    a. If the answer is yes, how does this public disclosure law differ from the one printed in this chapter?

    b. If the answer is no, ask a knowledgeable person to discover why there is not a public disclosure law.

       Person interviewed: Date:

       Place: Time:

       Findings:

c. If the answer is yes, ask a reporter or editor about the effectiveness of the law.
   Person interviewed: Date:
   Place: Time:
   Findings:

d. Interview a court official or lawyer to determine views on public disclosure laws in general and your state law in particular (if you have one).
   Person interviewed: Date:
   Place: Time:
   Findings:

8. Fill out this questionnaire on municipal and county government. (*Note to the instructor:* You may want to divide the class into three groups to share responsibilities in gathering the information in exercises 8, 9 and 10.)

   a. Who is the mayor of your city?

      What is the term of office?

   b. What form of government does your city have?

   c. Who is the superintendent of schools?

      What is the salary?

   d. Bring an organizational chart of the city to class.

   e. Who is head of the sanitation department?

      What are his or her duties?

   f. Who is the city clerk?

      What are his or her duties?

   g. Who is on the board of education?

      How did they get on the board?

   h. Who is head of the Social Security office in your city?

   i. Who is head of the employment office?

      How did that person get to be head?

      What is his or her salary?

   j. Bring a copy of the city's budget to class.

   k. Discuss in class how to determine a power hierarchy. Who are the powers behind the power? In other words, who comprises the power hierarchy of your city? Who are the influential people? (They may or may not be city officials.) Go out on interviews to obtain answers to these questions.

9. Answer these questions about your city.

   a. How many members are on the city council?

   b. What parts of city government are they connected with? For example, who is associated with the police department? The fire department? The street department? What are their general duties?

   c. How many persons are on the police force?

   What is their average salary?

   d. How many armed robberies have occurred thus far this year?

   Compared to last year, is this an increase?

   e. How many firefighters are there on the fire department?

   What is their average salary?

   f. Bring samples of various report forms used by the police department to class.

   g. Bring a sample subpoena to class.

   h. Bring a sample of an arrest warrant to class.

   i. Bring sample reports of fires from the fire department to class.

   j. Who is the police chief?

   Whom does the chief report to?

   What is the chief's salary?

   k. Who is the fire chief?

   Whom does the chief report to?

   What is the chief's salary?

   l. Bring the organizational chart of the police department to class.

10. Answer these questions about the judicial system.
    a. Who is the city court clerk?

    Who is the county court clerk?

    b. What are their duties?

    c. Who is the city attorney?

    d. Who is the county district attorney?

    e. Who is the General Sessions judge?

    f. What type of cases does this court handle?

    g. Who is the Criminal Court judge?

    h. What cases does this court handle?

    i. Who is the Circuit Court clerk?

    What are the duties?

    j. What cases does the Circuit Court handle?

    k. Who is the city judge?

    What cases does the judge handle?

    l. Who is the county coroner?

    What are the duties?

m. Bring a sample of a coroner's report to class.

n. Bring to class a flow chart from a court clerk that illustrates the procedures for conducting a civil lawsuit and a criminal lawsuit.

CHAPTER 4

INTERVIEWING

Interviewing is central to all media writing. No matter what your career aspirations—newspaper reporter, magazine writer, business publications reporter, freelance writer, radio or television reporter, public relations practitioner—knowing how to conduct an interview is important. If you want to gather news, rather than edit it, learn the art of interviewing.

Almost without exception, gathering news involves interviewing of some sort. A reporter simply cannot avoid asking people questions. At the accident scene, at human-interest events, at press conferences, at celebrity visitations, at city council meetings, questions must be asked by someone. And that someone is the reporter. When all is said and done, the more you encourage people to talk about themselves, the more you enhance your understanding of people. Remember the anecdote about the woman who had occasion to talk with two of England's great prime ministers: After meeting with Prime Minister William Gladstone, the woman left his office exclaiming that the prime minister was the most brilliant man she had ever met. After meeting Prime Minister Benjamin Disraeli, however, she remarked, "He made me feel as if I were one of the most brilliant women he had ever met!" Disraeli did not dominate their conversation—he conducted an "interview."

ARRANGING AND CONDUCTING AN INTERVIEW

Assume that your editor has told you to interview Mayor Donna Dunlap of University City. Does that mean that the mayor is hanging around a phone waiting to be interviewed by a member of the press? Is *any* person you have been assigned to interview going to want to be interviewed by you? You can't tell for sure. Some politicians welcome the opportunity. Mayor Dunlap, however, may be too involved in doing her job to spare the time. Other reporters, perhaps from your own news organization, may have had trouble seeing her. That's why you, a new reporter, have been assigned to the interview. How do you approach the task of arranging that interview? With supreme confidence.

Approach any interview with an air of assurance. After all, you are a representative of the press—that is of no small importance to the person you are going to interview, especially if that person is a politician. You represent power. The mayor's political life may depend on the image the press projects, and you are part of that projection apparatus.

So when you pick up the phone, you say briskly, "Mayor Dunlap, I'm (your name), a reporter for the *University News*. I have an assignment to talk to you about your plans for the urban renewal project. Would it be possible to get together for about 15 minutes sometime today or tomorrow?"

"I'm sorry," Dunlap replies, "much as I would love to talk with you about it,

I have a very busy schedule through the rest of the week. Perhaps you can call me early next week."

You should sympathize with her. "I'm certain you do have a busy schedule, Mayor Dunlap. I don't believe I could keep up with it the way you do. That's why I'm not planning on taking up more than 15 to 20 minutes of your time. I'm thoroughly familiar with the proposed urban renewal—I just need to clear up a few points on some of the planning of it. As a matter of fact, I only have six questions I want to ask you."

Most politicians welcome press coverage. So if the mayor, as in this instance, still says, "No, I *really* can't spare the time," be persistent. "Mayor Dunlap, it's really important for your program that the public be informed about it. That's exactly what my editor and I are prepared to do."

"I'm terribly sorry, and I know you're right," Mayor Dunlap replies, "but I just can't see how I can spare the time right now."

What do you do in response to this? Capitulate? Of course not. "Well, I'm sorry too, Mayor Dunlap," you reply. "I've got to do this story, and I'd much rather get a balanced picture of the renewal program. I've already arranged an interview with Councilman Rick Arrington for his comments, but you are the authority in this matter, and I'd like to have your thoughts on some of the questions I'm going to pose."

A moment of silence ensues. Then Dunlap says,

"Well, look, if you really need me, I can arrange to see you just before lunch tomorrow in my office. Would that be convenient?"

What happened here? Did you make the mayor feel important? Possibly. But the major factors were that you were persistent and you threw in the magic words "Rick Arrington"—the councilman from the opposition party. The mayor just couldn't stand the idea of Arrington's comments standing alone in the press. It wouldn't be smart politics.

However, it also wouldn't be smart to push for a personal interview if you feel you could accomplish the same goals in a telephone interview. In this case, the issue seems to warrant a face-to-face interview, because it's fairly complex and politically sensitive. A face-to-face interview with the mayor might accomplish more. However, had Mayor Dunlap stuck to her guns and refused the interview, you would have gone for a telephone interview. After all, the mayor had already been reached, and that in itself can be difficult enough!

Telephone Interviews

The telephone is the most valuable piece of equipment a media writer possesses. Throw out the notebook, the typewriter, the editing terminal, the tape recorder, and the reporter or public relations writer could still function if he or she has a telephone. With today's highly competitive media, always pressing to shave minutes off deadlines to beat their opponents, the telephone has come to be the preferred form of making contact, conducting interviews and confirming facts, particularly if a hard news story is at stake. The rush to wrap up features is usually not quite so frenetic, but hard news stories (and speeches and information for public relations professionals' press conferences and media campaigns) usually require immediate handling. The telephone is the most convenient way to do it.

The telephone interview is somewhat different from the face-to-face interview. It has the advantage of saving time. However, it also is much easier for a source to sidestep a telephone call than a prearranged appointment for a personal interview. One can seem to be "out" without really being out at all.

Use this checklist to prepare for and conduct a telephone interview:

1. Introduce yourself and your publication, firm or broadcast station with confidence. State your name clearly, and briefly describe the story or project you're working on. Then explain briefly why it's important that you have the comments of the person you want to interview.
2. Have a list of questions in front of you. Without face-to-face contact, rapport takes a little longer to establish. Having a list of prepared questions can keep the conversation moving. However, if the opportunity presents itself, depart from your prepared list and follow the train of thought your source introduces.
3. When you feel you've covered all you need to cover, thank the person you've been speaking to. Say that you may call back to double-check comments or to double-check your notes. Most people will be receptive to such callbacks, during which you can ask new questions as well as clarify information given to you previously.

HOMEWORK FOR THE INTERVIEW

Preparation for the interview begins with the assignment. Your homework should include research into the project or program that warrants an interview or the accomplishments of the person you are scheduled to interview. Although the newspaper library should be the first stop, if the project is a local one or the person is a hometown celebrity, the city editor or other reporters may suggest background sources for you to check. If the person to be interviewed has written articles or books, the public library or a local bookstore may have copies of those books or the magazines in which the articles appeared. You should read as much as you can prior to the interview so that you can ask fresh and intelligent questions. Record important details on 3-by-5-inch cards.

After gathering the background material, you should write your questions at the top of 3-by-5 cards or slips of paper. Record the answers on the same cards. When the interview is through and you've outlined your story, you'll be able to shuffle the answers around until they reflect the order in which they'll be appearing in the story. This does not take any more time than it would take to record the answers in a notebook. And when it comes time to write up your interview, you'll be thankful you organized your materials in such an efficient fashion.

Organize questions around subject-matter areas. Make certain the 5W + H and Significance questions will be asked, along with the significance of the topic being explored. Start with the easy questions first, and work your way into the more complex questions. Save questions that might create hostility until the very end. It makes little sense to antagonize a person until it's absolutely necessary to do so. Hostile questions can bring an interview to a close quickly, so get the answers to all the other questions first.

Make certain that your tape recorder has good batteries in it and that you have an extra tape in case the interview lasts more than an hour. Whether you're reporting for the print or the electronic media, try to tape your interviews. It's added protection for you in libel cases or if a person denies making comments that appear in print.

During the interview, if the tape recorder inhibits the interviewee, place the microphone off to one side. If the recorder still inhibits the person, turn it off. Tape recorders sometimes have strange effects even on sophisticated persons. If yours does, put it away. If the sight of you taking notes on cards causes distress, write below the desk top, out of sight, on your knee. If the person is still disturbed, say that you want to be certain to get everything down the way it's said. If the person still shows signs of distress and is hesitant to answer your questions fully and fluently, put the pencil and cards away. After the interview, however, write down the answers immediately; otherwise you are likely to forget key words and phrases.

Even if you use a tape recorder, you should write those answers down on your 3-by-5 cards. Newspaper reporters use tape recorders mostly for the record and to check some statements that warrant it once the interview is over.

IN THE BEGINNING, PUT THEM AT EASE

The importance of starting off the interview correctly can't be overemphasized. Put the person at ease. You might want to comment about what happened on the way over to the interview. Ask the person about a memento on the desk or on the wall. Start out with the easy questions, progress to the more complex questions, and end with questions that might antagonize. All the while you are questioning, "read" the person you are interviewing. Are those arms folded over tightly in front? You'll have to open up that person by smiling and asking friendly questions. Does the person perspire? Is the face pale? Does the person have trouble looking at you? Does the person look at the floor when answering some questions? Those things may mean a great deal. When they happen, your job as an interviewer is to determine what is happening and to ask questions that will probe the subject matter that stirred those reactions and emotions. Your audience will be interested in those reactions, so note them all. You may want to use some of these details when you write the interview story.

Reprinted with special permission from King Features Syndicate, Inc.

If the person you are interviewing does not want to answer your questions, be gentle but persistent. Assure the person that there is nothing to worry about: "Senator Flagg, I can't imagine much being wrong with any answer that you give to the question about the survey."

If Flagg still refuses, say that, once again, a balanced view of the situation is better than a one-sided view—which is what will be given if the senator refuses to comment. You will be going to the opposition, you tell him, for answers to the same questions. If Flagg still refuses, say, "Senator Flagg, whatever you say about the survey will be better than my writing, 'The senator refused to comment.' You know how active the voters' imaginations are."

If the senator still refuses, say, with a trace of weariness in your voice for the first time, "Senator Flagg, it will all come out sooner or later anyway. Won't it be better if your side is presented first, and by you?" If Flagg still refuses comment, don't give up. Continue with the interview and then ask again at the end of the interview, "Senator Flagg, all during this interview I've been thinking things over, and for the life of me I can't think of one reason why you shouldn't give your side of the survey. Now what is it that you really think is so bad about the survey?"

If you still receive a refusal to comment, tell him that you feel certain that he's making a mistake. Give him your telephone number and ask him to call you if he changes his mind. Tell him your deadline for the story. If you follow this line of questioning, you will have done all that is possible to get the answers to your questions.

Control your emotional responses to the answers. Nothing will conclude a line of questioning or an interview quicker than a look of surprise or a sharply drawn breath to a sensational answer. And do not ever let the person being interviewed feel as though you are passing judgment on what is being said.

Nod encouragingly every once in a while during the interview. And encourage still more revelations by such comments as these:

"I didn't know that" (stated in a matter-of-fact manner).

"Tell me more about that, please" (again, stated in a matter-of-fact manner so that there is no possibility that the person will not continue elaborating).

"I'm not sure I understand what you meant when you said . . ."

"So what you're saying is . . ." (when you don't understand or, more important, when you want a reiteration or confirmation of a controversial statement).

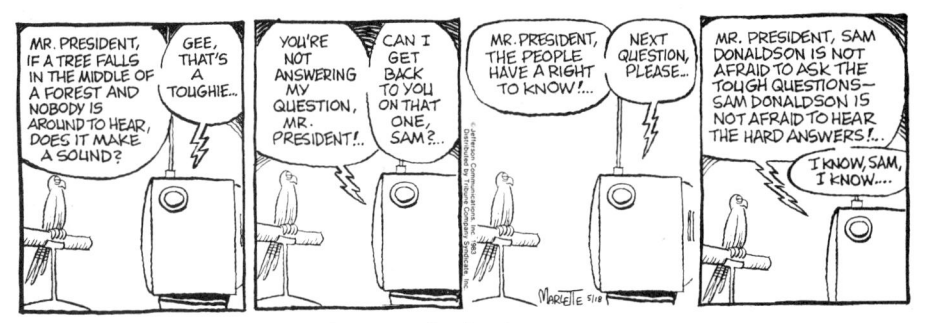

Reprinted by permission of Tribune Media Services

LISTEN TO THE ANSWERS

Listen to the answers to your questions carefully. In one televised presidential news conference, President Reagan revealed that if Russia attempted any move in the Persian Gulf, war would be imminent. More than 100 reporters listened to the answers to eight more questions before one of them questioned the president about the policy implications of his statement.

Mark Fox, a first-string All America Rifle Team member eight times, was asked on television what went through his mind when he squeezed off those championship shots. "I hum a little tune in my mind," he replied. Some years ago, when John McEnroe devastated Ivan Lendl in the U.S. Open tennis championship match, the network interviewer asked him how he felt during the match. "I felt really good about my play. And I kept this tune going over and over in my mind, and things just fell into place," McEnroe said. Neither of the interviewers listened to the answers carefully enough to ask what the name of the tune was at the moment of their great triumphs.

So don't just write the answers down. Think about the significance and ramifications of what has been said. More than one skillful interviewer has been able to uncover a story (other than the assigned one) by following up on an answer that looked promising. If Mayor Dunlap is answering a question on urban renewal, for example, and mentions a small snag or two that has to be eliminated, ask what those snags are. Ask who or what is behind the snag; then check on the facts and the persons mentioned. You may discover that an ethnic group has retained the best lawyer in town to file a suit to halt the renewal—a suit that might delay the construction for at least a year. Politicians like to slip in a hint of what may be big trouble so that later on they cannot be accused of hiding anything in the interview.

Some persons may stray from the question you've asked. If they are trying to evade the question, bring them back, courteously, at the first convenient pause: "Yes, that is interesting. But about the snag you mentioned just a minute ago—what exactly is that snag?"

Some persons may stray from the question simply because their speech patterns or thinking processes work that way. When that happens, listen for a minute or so to determine if anything newsworthy is being said. Stray comments may lead to something important. If there appears to be nothing newsworthy in the comments, once again, at a convenient pause, bring them back to the question: "Hmmmm, very interesting. However, I wonder if we might pursue the question about those snags you mentioned earlier."

Before the interview is concluded, if you haven't done so before, take notes on the setting and on the person being interviewed. Let your reader *see* what you have seen as well as *hear* what you have heard.

What is the dominant impression of the room? Is it cramped or spacious? What was on the desk—a thesaurus, a book of quotations, a letter opener with bright copper pennies embedded in the handle? What was the atmosphere of the room, apartment or home? What presence did the person exude? Could you smell cologne? Was the person neat and well-groomed? What kind of clothing did the interviewee wear? How did he or she shake hands?

Just before concluding the interview, always ask this question: "What else should I have asked you about that I didn't?" That allows comment on things you failed to touch upon. More than one interview concluded in this fashion has been greeted with a laugh and then something like this: "Why don't you ask me about the incident that took place right after the meeting in the lobby of the hotel?"

Reply immediately, without smiling, "OK. What happened in the hotel lobby after the meeting was adjourned?"

When you've explored that aspect of the interview and have it all down in your notes, conclude the interview in this way: "I think I've got everything I need, but in case I've forgotten something, I'll call you. Will that be all right?" When the person agrees, it's your entree past the secretary or the agent.

To make certain your interviews with celebrities are distinctive, once you've completed your interview background research, think of the climb that person had to make to reach the celebrity pinnacle. Visualize that person at the foot of the mountain that had to be climbed. What *preparations* were necessary in the beginning? Why were they necessary? How were they made? What *obstacles* had to be overcome? How were they overcome? How is it at *the top*? Anticlimactic? Disappointing? *What now*? How long does the celebrity anticipate being at the top? On the basis of what? Formulate your celebrity questions around these major points: Preparations, Obstacles, The Top, and What Now?

SUMMARY

The interview is an age-old technique for eliciting information that will help fill the public's need to understand personal points of view and the background behind newsworthy events. The practice of journalism wouldn't exist without the interview.

An interview will be successful if the reporter has conducted the background research necessary to ask the right questions and is confident in his or her approach. Chances are a source has something to gain by granting an interview, but many people also fear they may have something to lose and thus avoid dealing with the reporter. The latter circumstances will require a writer to muster up his or her entire arsenal of human relations experience to persuade a reluctant source to cooperate. In any event, the way in which a source responds depends on the writer's persistence, preparation and professionalism.

The way in which a writer will compose a story based on the interview may be suggested by something he or she noticed while conducting the interview. Sometimes the personal traits and habits of sources or the way in which their offices or homes are furnished provides a peg on which many of the source's answers can be arranged. Such use of detail gives a story a certain mood and gives the reader the feeling of being an insider. These touches of detail can enhance a story, but the writer should be careful not to overdo the technique for fear of filtering the story with an overdose of the reporter's own reactions to the source. The goal of every interview is to bring a source closer to the public. The reporter's skill is necessary to do this—but he or she should be invisible to the reader.

EXERCISES

1. Clip a news-related interview from a local newspaper and paste it below on the left-hand side of the page. To the right, critique it paragraph by paragraph.

2. Write answers to these comments made to you by the person you are interviewing.

   a. "I really don't have time for you right now."

   b. "I don't want to talk about myself."

   c. "I don't want all this publicity."

   d. "Why should I talk to *you* about this?"

   e. "I really have to go now."

   f. "I'd rather not go into that aspect of the episode."

   g. "Why don't you ask me about my business partner's role in this whole thing?"

   h. "I don't have to put up with this kind of questioning."

   i. "That's an insulting question!"

   j. "That's none of your damn business!"

   k. "Your paper never reports anything accurately."

3. Select one person from the class to engage in mutual interviewing. Interview each other for a feature in the *University News*. Write a characterization of the person you interviewed in 25 words or less. Concentrate on one central impression or characteristic (for example, he or she chewed on a pencil while answering the toughies).

4. Your U.S. senator is coming on campus to speak at an economic conference. You draw the interview assignment. Gather information about the senator, and write a memo to the editor about what you propose to cover in the interview and why.

5. The newspaper editor has elected you to do the interview on the senator. Write the questions you will ask.

6. Watch the television programs *60 Minutes* and *The McNeil/Lehrer NewsHour*. Compare the aggressiveness of the various reporters in questioning their sources.

CHAPTER 5

ORGANIZING THE INFORMATION

After researching and interviewing have been completed, writers find themselves at a critical point in the writing experience: organizing the material they've so painstakingly gathered. By this time, your fingers are fairly itching to get to the keyboard and begin writing, but there's one step still to take—pulling the information together in a way that will enable you to write quickly and comprehensively. Learning how to organize notes and research into easy-to-use information blocks can make writing the joy it deserves to be and prevent slow starts, false starts and hesitation about the main statement an article should make.

No two writers organize their materials in the same way. Each one of us has tried-and-true methods that work for us but might fail for someone else. This chapter suggests a sequence of steps that can be adapted by writers to fit their needs. In-depth, investigative pieces that will fill an inside newspaper page on Sunday obviously require more levels of organization than a 10-inch news story slated for Page One of the city section, but the organizational approaches can be similar. The main purpose in following a specific method of organization is so that the writer will always know where he or she is heading with the story and so that each decision on what to report, what to emphasize and what to give brief treatment to will be justified by the research material in the writer's possession.

EVALUATING YOUR RESEARCH

Often writers will have material stored in several forms: on tape, on 3-by-5 cards, in notebooks, and perhaps on an editing terminal (often used during a phone interview). They're also likely to have collected reports and other publications containing background information. How do writers review all that material? How do they sort it into piles? How can they remember what's in each pile? What if someone *moves* the piles? How can they blend all of these different kinds of source materials into a cohesive whole from which to draw the ideas, assertions and facts for the article?

The trick to managing the flow of information you gather is to manage it as you collect it. Don't wait until the bitter end to assess what you have; organize it as you gather it. Make mental or tape-recorded notes on how an interviewee's logic might be used in your report as you're driving away from the interview, and write down your thoughts as soon as you return to your desk. If you've collected statistical data on Wednesday, compare it with the figures you picked up on Monday. Note similarities and differences, if there are any. You may later decide to leave out most of the material from that interview, and the statistics you discovered might be less helpful than figures that become available a week later. No matter; you will have spared yourself a complete review of the interview to decide how every single aspect of it compares with information you now have. Because you analyzed and made notes as you went along, you can make a judgment about the material at the prewriting stage. If you wait until very late in the research and reporting process to review what you've gathered, you may be so overwhelmed by the sheer volume of data you've collected that you will have to research your own research just to figure out what you've got. That can be so exhausting that the actual writing of the article will seem like an impossible chore.

Outlining

Let's start at the beginning of the research and writing experience and look at how some writers manage their materials. Most writing experiences follow this particular pattern: Something happens that stirs your emotions or intellect. (It may be a simple interview for a news story or a feeling that overwhelmed you while viewing a rocket's ascent.) You want to recount that experience, and perhaps your reactions to it, to someone else. Whether your imagination is primarily auditive (stimulated by the ear) or visual (stimulated by the eye), these lively sparks ignite emotions, memories and thoughts that move you into a state of meditation that is a preliminary to the writing stage.

In this meditation—a groping full of false starts and glimmerings of inspiration and a searching for relationships between thoughts—your ideas may be expanded by more incidents, illustrations and examples. There may even be revelations that explore the significance of your initial experience more fully. While this is going on, you are also forming a sketchy outline of how all this could be written.

The meditation may occur at any time or place—while you're bathing, putting on makeup, shaving, or driving an automobile. James Thurber, for example, never quite knew when he *wasn't* "writing" in this fashion:

> Sometimes my wife comes up to me at a dinner party and says, "Dammit, Thurber, stop writing." She usually catches me in the middle of a paragraph. Or my daughter will look up from the dinner table and ask, "Is he sick?" "No," my wife says, "he's writing." I have to do it that way on account of my eyes.

Before Thurber's eyes failed him, he, like many writers, meditated at the typewriter. "The labor of composition begins," Thomas De Quincey wrote, "when you have to put your separate threads of thought into the loom, to weave them into a continuous whole; to connect, to introduce them; to blow them out or expand them; to carry them to a close."

During this meditation, as indicated earlier, a vague outline usually forms in your mind of how that experience is going to be written. You will also consider the audience you'll be writing it for, the reason you're going to write it, and how you're going to treat the experience. You must consider all these things when you compose the outline for writing about the experience.

Some writers write from a vague or sketchy outline they conjured during this meditation (or incubation) period. They may never even commit the outline to paper. Their reasons for this vary. Some have never written outlines. Others may have written them down and felt that they hindered the free flow of thoughts and creativity while writing. But it's certainly safer for beginning writers to use outlines.

BRINGING ORDER TO THE OUTLINE

But how do you actually go about ordering the subject matter within an outline? If the subject matter is a news event, you've already been given guidelines on composing your outline. You use a simple lead story form for a single news event and summary or salient-feature lead story forms for news stories with multiple events or incidents. The outline of the story is dictated by the lead you use. If the subject matter is material for a feature story or a magazine article, you've been given similar guidelines in constructing an outline. The reader-interest plane provides guidelines for outlining materials for articles that call for a climactic order.

How you go about arranging your subject matter is dictated by your audience, the medium for which you're writing, your purpose in writing it, and the treatment you will be giving it—sometimes called your attitude or tone. You may be deadly serious or hilariously funny when writing.

If your event takes place chronologically, it is a simple matter to arrange things in the time sequence in which they happened. If your experience is one that calls for a statement—for example, "Crime is an everyday thing for people living in the ghettos"—your subject matter will be events that support such a statement. You will use the reader-interest plane for an order of climactic effect, but you must also organize your materials to support your statement—an "order of support." You may want to organize them from some of the lesser crimes to some of the more heinous crimes taking place in the ghettos. Whatever the case may be, you will be imposing your patterns of thought on the subject matter and creating your outline according to what you conceive is the best for the medium, the audience and the subject.

DEVELOPING AN OUTLINE

For purposes of instruction, let's look at a series of items you obtained by interviewing an unpublished poet for a newspaper feature or magazine article. Judging by the order in which they are presented, either you have been brainstorming in preparation for writing the article or you allowed your poet to talk freely during the interview. The notes constitute topic headings. Condensed in this fashion, they make outlining easier. All they need now is to be arranged in the order you'll be writing about them.

As you read through this list, notice that a symbol appears before each item. The symbols indicate that certain items fall naturally into different blocks of information. If there are enough of them in a particular block, that block may form a major section of an outline. An outline may have three to five major sections, in addition to the introduction and the conclusion. (It is difficult to develop a subject thoroughly with fewer than three major sections; more than five or six run the risk of overstating the case.)

Interview of Unsuccessful Poet

    * rejections of poems (first, etc.)

    * present-day efforts

    # nursery rhymes

\# miners' strike
   = serious efforts & poem examples
   & Prufrock motif
   ˜ wife's view of his poetry
   ˆ poet's muse
   * triumphs
   + army troop train
   \# "Village Blacksmith"
   * poem to wife
   = humorous poems & examples
   ˆ writing rituals—place, pen, time, etc.
   & Hymen Ensor Xmas letter
   ˜ last rejection
   + high school explications
   * writing workshops
   ˜ friends' views of his poetry writing

After sorting the free-form data into blocks, an outline for the article might look like this:

"The Life and Times of a Rejected Poet"
   I. Introduction
   Lead reflecting the fact that no matter how he tries, no matter how trivial the market or poetry contest, the poet is rejected. And at times totally dejected. How did he get started in this life of rejection?
   II. The Early Years
      A. Nursery rhymes
      B. Coal miners' strike—was taught haunting poetic lines
      C. Elementary school—recitation of "The Village Blacksmith"
   III. Later Years
      A. High school poetry explications
      B. WWII troop train efforts
      C. Present-day efforts
         1. Muse
         2. Rituals
   IV. Triumphs
      A. Friends' views of efforts—"that's what friends are for"
      B. Writing workshops—needed the money
      C. Prufrock motif in prose sermon—a semipoetic effort
      D. Poem to wife—a poetic proposal she accepted
   V. Rejections
      A. First rejection & others
      B. Last rejection
      C. What gets rejected
         1. Humorous poem example
            "On the highway
               of our love
                  she littered."

  2. Serious poem example
   "Umbrellas of love
    furl and unfurl
   In life's
    wintry storms."
VI. Conclusion
 Feelings on getting rejections. How he bears up under them. Statement to the effect that he will keep on writing poetry, knowing he will never achieve fame.

This outline is acceptable. The chronology of the events determines much of the outline. One item has been omitted (Hymen Ensor's Xmas letter); you will discover when you outline this way that some items just cannot be fitted comfortably into the article. When that happens, omit them. You'll probably have a better article.

Suppose you interviewed a woman whose hobby is traveling. She's been all over the world. She's an administrative assistant to a university president and has more time off than most people. She's made the most of it by traveling. Here are the headings of the information you've been able to gather in an interview. Again we've keyed most of them with symbols. We've even keyed the reasons for traveling with the countries the woman has visited.

An outline for this list of topics will require an arrangement that is not chronological—although you could start with the first country she visited and move inexorably through them all, one by one. Before looking at *our* outline, try outlining this yourself.

Interview of a World Traveler

Description of woman traveler and her home—with keepsakes.

Reasons for Traveling
 # History—archaeology
 ^ Restlessness—nomadic spirit
 ^ Relatives and friends
 ^ Provincial background
 + Romance
 ¯ Exotic places
 ^ Curiosity
 * Olympics—sports interest

Places Visited in This Country
 # Mt. Rushmore
 * Lake Placid—Olympics
 * Aspen, Colo.—skiing
 ¯ Grand Canyon
 ¯ Las Vegas—gambling
 ^ New Orleans—Mardi Gras
 * Lincoln, Neb.—Nebraska-Oklahoma football game
 ¯ Alaska
 ¯ Hawaii

Countries Visited
- ^ Japan
- \# Mexico—digs
- Canada
- ^ Russia
- ^ England
- \# Greece—Athens
- ^ China
- \+ Philippines—South Sea islands cruise
- \# Italy—Rome
- \+ Mediterranean cruise
- \# Colombia
- ¯ New Zealand
- \+ Caribbean cruise
- \# Peru

Highlights

Disappointments

Exciting Adventure? Hijacking?

Mode of Travel
- Best-liked
- Least-liked

Traveling Companions
- College roommate
- Sister
- \+ Fiancé
- Alone

We've outlined it this way:

"The World Is Her Home Away from Home"

  I. Introduction
     Lead: She's traveled for so long and so far she's really a world traveler, at home away from home
 II. Jessie Deckens: At Home with Keepsakes
     A. Keepsakes and some memories that flood her when she touches them
     B. First trip abroad
III. Most Exciting Adventure Abroad
 IV. Reasons for Visiting
     A. Restlessness? Curiosity? Feeling of provincialism?
        1. Grand Canyon, New Orleans, Las Vegas
        2. Japan, China, Russia, England
     B. History—archaeology
        1. Mt. Rushmore
        2. Mexico—digs, Colombia, Peru
        3. Greece—Athens; Italy—Rome
     C. Romance
        1. Caribbean cruise
        2. Mediterranean cruise

3. Philippines—South Sea islands cruise
     4. Hawaii
  D. Olympics—sports interest
     1. Lake Placid—Olympics
     2. Aspen, Colo.—skiing
     3. Lincoln, Neb.—Nebraska-Oklahoma football rivalry
V. Mode of Travel
  A. Plane, train, etc.
  B. Companions
     1. Sister
     2. College roommate
     3. Fiancé (didn't work out)
     4. Now alone—likes it better (meets more people)
VI. Highlights & Disappointments
  A. Highlights
  B. Disappointments
VII. Conclusion
   Statement to the effect that despite disappointments, the whole scene has been electric. Planning on trekking to see a guru in Tibet next year, etc.

That is one way to organize this group of topics: according to similar subject matter and on a rising climactic plane. Your outline may be entirely different, however, and still be a good outline. What we want to impress upon you is how to go about organizing your materials and what an asset an outline is. From this last example, you can see how, without an outline, you would be adrift when writing, wandering on the currents of your impulses.

THE BLOCK METHOD

Another method of organization that works for many writers is to visualize material as blocks of information, each block being a subtopic or different angle of a story. The writer can then sort through the various types of material and make a list of which interview, report or position paper contains information that will help explain the topic in that block. In many cases, one interview will support more than one block and will turn up on the list of sources needed to write up that block.

Afterward, the blocks can be put in order and written into a unified, integrated piece.

Let's say you are employed by a public relations firm. The firm has been retained by a nearby private college to develop a program for the school to help reverse declining enrollment there. A major portion of the contract consists of doing a report on why enrollment is falling and how the public perceives the school these days.

You have been researching the issue for two months. You've interviewed students, high school counselors, educators and accrediting boards. You're surrounded by stacks of notes, tapes and studies of similar situations at other schools. The survey people at the firm for which you work have conducted an opinion poll about the college and have given you a printout of the responses with their brief analysis of the raw data. Your client is anxious to see what your sources have said; your boss is anxious to have the report so the firm can get on with a campaign that will boost the school's image and, consequently, its enrollment. Your report must look at the past, the present and the future. It will help decide what that campaign will address.

You dive in. You think you can get the historical block out of the way the most quickly, so you pull out your file of historical material and look at it first. You have information about the college itself, old clippings that detail its image and style of activities over a period of 30 years, its annual endowments for the same 30-year span. You also have material from a national college association that shows enrollment and endowment trends for similar-sized schools over the last 20 years. The materials in this file also contain valuable notes from you to yourself, commenting on impressions made by some of the alumni and reminding yourself to check back with the college association to see if they can get figures for 30 years so you could make a stronger comparison between your client college and national trends. You jot down another reminder to yourself on your note pad, make a brief list of the file's contents, and put it inside the file. You now have a "table of contents" for that file, making quick reference possible.

You decide to build an alumni block next. The school provided you with raw data about number of graduates, their majors, the most popular majors each year and their financial support of their alma mater. You talked to a number of them, and you have notes of those interviews in your files. Many alumni recall their undergraduate years with affection, but few are sending their children to the school. They are vague about the reasons why. One or two have said the school is old-fashioned, conservative; most said they thought the educational quality was competitive with that of the schools their children attend. Your firm's opinion poll, however, shows that among alumni surveyed, a slim majority of those responding said they felt the school's small-town atmosphere and rural location were drawbacks for today's college students. You make a list of the contents and their chief points, add a sheet outlining the survey's main revelations, put the sheet inside and go to the next file, the school's recruitment strategy.

You continue until your myriad piles of material have been merged into story blocks, each of which should consist of material cross-referenced with other files. Each file carries a list of its contents and the main points made by those contents, so you not only have reviewed what your source materials are but also the important things each one contains. You now know where key materials are and in what sections of the story they will have the greatest usefulness.

A big project was selected as an example here so that the process of building blocks could be described in some detail. This cataloging process can be simplified for more simple assignments. The 5W+H and Significance questions are the elements against which your organizational method should be tested. As you organize the different blocks of a story, mentally tick off which of the 5W+H and Significance questions your block will satisfy. When you have finished organizing your material, the final pattern should spell out who, what, when, where, why and how and, what elements are the most significant.

Key Quotes and Key Words

In the course of doing a number of interviews or sifting through stacks of reports for a story, certain key quotes and phrases that stand out at the time they're uttered or read can be forgotten by the time you begin to write the story. Sometimes the sheer volume of research can cause you to lose track of the quotes that make a story sparkle. They simply get buried. So the best way to make certain those stunning quotes and descriptive phrases make it into the story is to make a master list of them and check it as you write to make sure you've put the most important, most compelling, most useful ones into your article or report.

Making a list of key quotes and key phrases serves several important functions. First, it makes for good storytelling. Second, it helps the reader or listener to quickly grasp the gist of the news. Third, it's a check on the writer's objectivity.

A review of key quotes and phrases can help writers decide if they've been balanced in their reporting. The key quote and key phrase list can help them answer these questions:

- ☐ Have I given substantially more space to comments and terms used by one side in a story than to the other? If so, am I justified in doing so?
- ☐ Are the quotes inflammatory? Do I need to add more perspective to the article to help readers or listeners interpret the comments?
- ☐ Are the key words and key phrases as clear to the reader as they are to me and my sources? Have I lapsed into jargon?

If the article you're writing is brief, it isn't necessary to make a separate list of key quotes and key words. Just run a highlighter through key quotes and phrases in your written notes so they'll stand out. If you took some of your notes on an editing terminal, you can recast important quotes and phrases in boldface so you'll be sure to notice them. If you favor tape recorders, be sure to note the counter number on the machine at the moment a source comes through with a pithy quote so you can go back to that point on the tape when you need to. The main point is to keep quotable quotes and descriptive phrases accessible when you begin writing your story.

To Outline or Not to Outline

It's difficult to say how many media writers use formal outlines as a basis for writing their stories. Probably not many do. Deadline pressures at daily newspapers and radio and television stations preclude extensive preplanning. News and feature writers who are working on long stories or writing for a magazine have a tremendous amount of material to juggle and usually a generous amount of time to work on the article, so they are more likely to benefit from a formal outline. Again, the type of detail required of an outline depends on the amount of material the writer has to work with; obviously, planning the execution of a book that will be written over a year's time calls for a more detailed, integrated outline than does a 16-inch news story based on information and interviews conducted over a few days. Beginners should start out with at least a rudimentary outline to make sure they include all the important points and key quotes. As they acquire more and more practice writing news and features, they will need less and less detail in their outlines. Their finely developed news instincts and greater writing speed will enable them to organize more elements of the story mentally, needing only a skeleton outline to remind them of key material.

Archiving

After the story is written, what should you do with your notes and research materials? That depends on the circumstances. The important thing to remember is not to consider the production of an article or report an end in itself. The research and the contacts made in the course of doing the research will have a shelf life far beyond that of the piece that is published or broadcast. Much of that material can be referred to again and again, and the contacts can be reinterviewed for other articles.

For a beat reporter covering a running story, such as a trial that continues for several months, taking good care of one's notes is important. Notes jotted down at the beginning of that trial could be illuminating at its conclusion. That's why it's so important that your notes be intelligible—if you have to consult them months later to check facts or refresh your memory, you'll want them to be clear and precise. If you are ready to file your notes away, make sure they're in good condition in case you need to use them later.

Names, addresses and phone numbers of contacts you made in the course of covering a story should go straight into your Rolodex or card file. Discard material that will become outdated or that is easily replaced.

SUMMARY

Organizing material as you collect it is the most efficient way to approach the writing process. Even if you rearrange the flow of the story a half-dozen times, if your research materials and interview notes are sorted into blocks, you can rearrange them as well. The most important thing for beginning writers to do is to devise a system that enables them to pull up the needed background information when they want it.

Clear organization of research materials and interviewing notes will ensure a story that flows logically, sparkles with good quotes and significant phrases, and satisfies the reader's or listener's need for information.

EXERCISES

1. You're assigned to gather information about the freshman class at your university. List the blocks of information you would attempt to gather information for each of the following purposes:

   a. A news story for the city newspaper about the incoming freshman class

   b. A public relations firm hired by your university to determine the enrollment trend by doing a profile of the freshman class

c. An advertising agency hired by a marketing firm to discover the tastes and buying power of the freshman class

2. You're assigned to determine the organization and functioning of *one* of the following:

   A city newspaper
   A city radio station
   A city television station
   A city public relations firm
   A city advertising agency

What are the blocks of information you would attempt to gather?

3. Using the information you gathered for either one or all of exercises 5, 6 and 7 in Chapter 3, make a detailed outline for a brief presentation to a civic club luncheon. Choose whichever exercise best lends itself to a full outline.

PART III

WRITING TO INFORM: THE NEWS

Newswriting and editing are the basic means of providing information in the mass media. Although public relations releases and advertising display and copy use a large percentage of the space in the mass media, the basic means of providing information is the writing of news. And that news, based as it is on the needs and interests of the audience, is relative: What is of interest to citizens in Buffalo as far as local civic affairs are concerned is usually not of interest to citizens in San Diego. New snow removal procedures for the coming winter, for example, will be of utmost concern in Buffalo but will cause a San Diego native to turn the page or the dial. All of what goes into deciding what is news and the processing of news pertains to the chapters on news and the following chapters on broadcast news and news for the new technologies. Let's review briefly those criteria and the news-determining process before discussing the variety of news and the problems involved in covering those events.

Determining what is news, what should go into the mass media, and with what emphasis is, as you now know, a complicated matter. The basic roles and functions of the mass media must be considered. A continual judging process takes place as writers conduct research, develop sources and complete interviews. As they gather information from different sources, using methods described in Part II, they test what they've gathered for significance.

As a reporter, you will find yourself in a sea of events. Once you've disciplined yourself to think and observe like a reporter, you will be a major determinant of what is news. As stated in Chapter 1, if you see something happening, and you go through the news processing procedure and determine that it adds up to news, and you then write the story and it's published, it is, in fact, news.

What is news for the print media may not be news for the electronic media. Although their roles and functions are basically the same, immediate and basic format requirements dictate different treatment of news. Although some radio stations may have a morning program that tolls the deaths of the citizens in a small city, usually such fare is not broadcast news. Nor are such things as births, weddings or sermons—although there is such a thing as electronic religious programming. With the time constraints placed on the broadcast news programs, such news simply does not win out over more important events, unless, of course, it has to do with prominent persons—mayors, stars, presidents' daughters, and the like. News differs from medium to medium, and there are substantial differences in content in those media, depending on the audience. The chapters in Part III will explain how newswriting, although it is undergoing changes that incorporate the characteristics of all media, is nonetheless still performed with media differences in mind.

CHAPTER 6
NEWS FOR NEWSPAPERS: LEADS AND BASIC STORIES

Our highly formalized style of newswriting, in evolution for more than 200 years, is rapidly changing. New styles of presenting news were established early by the tabloid newspapers and by the weekly news magazines, especially *Time*. Radio and television news now heavily influence that news style. Print reporters have to write with the broadcast media in mind, if for no other reason than that most of the news of great importance has already been broadcast by the time they sit down at the typewriter or video display terminal.

This continuing and now rapidly developing newswriting evolution frees reporters to write more interestingly and entertainingly. And to hold the interest and attention of the audience today, reporters must write more imaginatively and creatively. The founder of *USA Today* realizes this: "We simply stole the best ideas and concepts from television, from news magazines and newspapers across the USA," Allen H. Neuharth admitted, "gave them a national perspective, and added a few different twists and innovations for a unique *USA Today* sparkle."

The competition is fierce. So when a major news story is written for a newspaper, it should have a feel or a mood about it that dictates the tone of the story, whether it should be treated lightly or seriously. Each major news story is unified by the rhythm or flow derived from the facts, the imagery and the tone the writer elects to use.

In a newspaper, a headline will arrest the reader's attention and guide him or her to the story. The first paragraph, or first several paragraphs—known as the "lead"—comprises the next decision point for a reader. If the reader reads the lead, chances are excellent that he or she will stay with the rest of the story, provided the writer makes it easy enough and interesting enough.

KEY INTEREST POINTS

HEADLINES AND SLUGS

News stories are named twice as they make their way from the reporter's desk to the copy editor's. First they get a slug; then they are crowned with a headline. When reporters begin writing, they give their stories one-word names that will tip the editor off to what the story is about. That's a *slug*. Wire services slug their stories with one- or two-word titles when they send them out electronically. The slug has to be specific enough to pinpoint the story's content and angle but not so esoteric that the editor can't figure out what it's about.

For example, an article on acquired immune deficiency syndrome would be slugged AIDS. The slug DISEASE simply wouldn't do. But if a newspaper is doing several stories that day on AIDS, the word *AIDS* won't suffice, either. Instead, you'd see slugs like AIDSSYMPTOMS and AIDSDEATHS.

Slugs should be simple, clear and obvious. They can't duplicate other slugs. A slug is the identifier for every story—its social security number, its fingerprint. It stays with the story right up until a copy editor writes a headline for it. Even then, in the newsroom, it will continue to be known by its slug. (Some editors, however, require their reporters to write headlines rather than slugs to identify their stories. Depending on the space limitations and content of the story identification headline, the copy editor may or may not use the same headline.)

Writing a slug doesn't take a lot of brainpower. Writing a headline, on the other hand, calls for a good memory, a keen understanding of current events, and creativity and economy with words. The headline writer is like a salesman for the article. The headline writer has to get the writer into the story the way a salesman has to get the customer into the store.

Editors of various newspaper sections—news, business, lifestyle, sports—meet during the day to determine how much space a story should get and on which pages of their section it will begin. That decision is generally made as the story is being written, often even before it is written. As the article develops, editors may expand or shrink the space originally planned for the article, depending on its newsworthiness. The space for a headline expands and shrinks, too, but not quite as much. If a story runs twice as long as originally planned, that doesn't mean the headline can be twice as big as it was planned to be!

Headline writers must use colorful words that neither exaggerate nor overdramatize the facts described in the story. They must use as few words as possible, some of which may be a long proper name such as *Gorbachev* or *Union Carbide*. Newspaper headlines should contain a verb. They should not be mere labels on articles. For example, "Miami Area Leads USA in Homicides" is stronger and clearer than a label-type head such as "Most Murders in Miami."

Sluglines help news staffs keep track of stories, and headlines help newspaper readers to make some initial choices of what they will read in that day's edition. But the real work will be done by the story itself.

SIMPLE LEADS AND THE INVERTED PYRAMID

What makes a good lead? An interesting and clear account of what has happened. That account starts by answering the important questions the reporter has asked when he or she gathered the facts for the story: What happened? Who is involved? Where did it happen? When did it happen? Why did it happen? How did it happen? What is the significance of the event? Here is a good example:

> A convicted killer, armed with a sharpened screwdriver, took a woman counselor at a state prison hostage for 10 hours today before freeing her.

In a good lead, the important things come first. They provide the umbrella under which all the details of the story will fit comfortably. The lead prepares the audience for the rest of the news story. But a good lead also does more than that. A good lead whets the audience's appetite for the details to follow and sets the tone for the story. The details usually flow from the lead in an order of descending importance into the succeeding paragraphs. A simple news story about a minor traffic accident or a minor house fire would look like an inverted pyramid (Figure 6.1).

The succeeding paragraphs of a news story should fill in the details *in the order in which they were revealed in the lead*. That's why the construction of the lead is so important. It acts as a blueprint from which the writer pulls out details and explains them further. In addition, a direct quote should be used in one of the first three paragraphs, if possible. Look at the inverted pyramid sketch (Figure 6.2) of the story about the woman counselor taken hostage at the state prison. Each detail in the lead is explained, one by one, in the paragraphs that follow.

When you write simple news stories, keep this graphic representation in mind. Fit your facts into it. No matter what the subject matter of the story, whether it's about a convict holding a hostage or one motorist ramming another, the pyramid structure will provide you with direction.

Using the inverted pyramid as a guide, the reporter places the important details first. The less important details follow. A concluding paragraph ends the well-constructed news story.

Using the 5W + H and Significance questions as a checklist will not only help make certain you cover all angles of the story when you are gathering the facts; they'll also assist you in writing the correct lead and the final story to ensure that the questions have been properly answered and emphasized. But don't try to answer *all* the questions in the lead. When that happens, the first sentence runs on and on and becomes what is called a "clothesline lead"—it is cluttered with answers that belong in the second sentence or paragraph. Let's look at some leads, culled primarily from wire stories and newspapers. Though not clothesline leads, they are too long and complex or emphasize the wrong details. Read the original lead first and then the revision below it. Determine what changes were made before you read the comments about them.

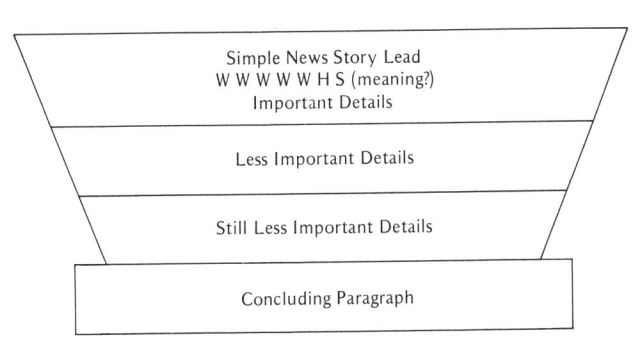

FIGURE 6.1. Schematic representation of a simple news story forms an inverted pyramid.

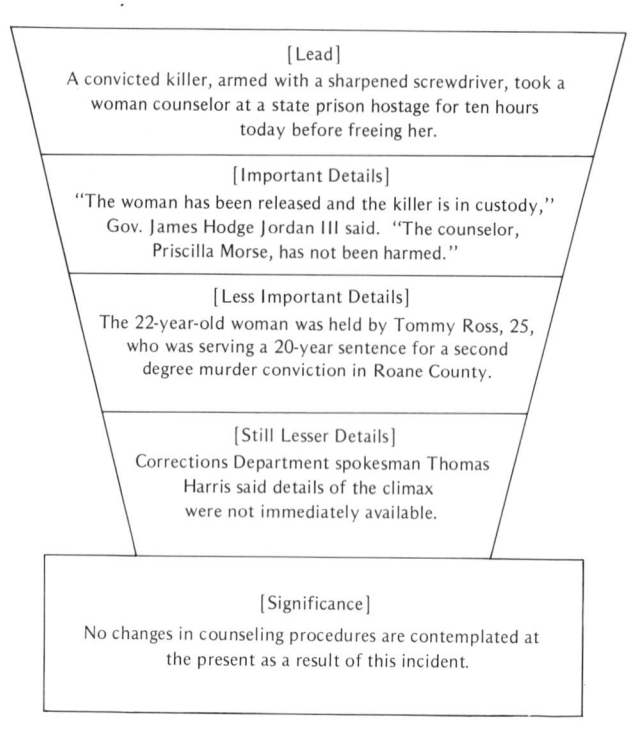

```
                    [Lead]
    A convicted killer, armed with a sharpened screwdriver, took a
     woman counselor at a state prison hostage for ten hours
                  today before freeing her.

              [Important Details]
  "The woman has been released and the killer is in custody,"
     Gov. James Hodge Jordan III said. "The counselor,
           Priscilla Morse, has not been harmed."

            [Less Important Details]
    The 22-year-old woman was held by Tommy Ross, 25,
     who was serving a 20-year sentence for a second
             degree murder conviction in Roane County.

              [Still Lesser Details]
      Corrections Department spokesman Thomas
           Harris said details of the climax
              were not immediately available.

                  [Significance]
  No changes in counseling procedures are contemplated at
       the present as a result of this incident.
```

FIGURE 6.2. A story fits into the inverted pyramid schema.

Original

   The United Auto Workers and Ford Motor Company
   tentatively agreed last night on a contract that aims to
   cut company costs, save union jobs and help revive the
   flagging auto industry.

Revised

   A tentative contract by the United Auto Workers and
   Ford Motor Company may save jobs, cut costs and help
   revive the flagging auto industry.

You no doubt noted in the revision the answer to the most important question—*What happened?*—comes first. Because the revision leads off answering this question, it is called a "what" lead. In the revision, the time of the contract is left for the second paragraph. The original lead is a "who" lead. It starts off by answering the question *Who is involved?* Most "who" leads should be scrapped in favor of "what" leads. But let's look at another example:

Original

   Councilman Wayne Zenner, a candidate for mayor of
   Springfield in the April election, said yesterday that
   the city government must revamp procedures for making
   its appointments to its 13 committees and boards.

Revised

   Current appointment methods prevent maximum citizen
   participation in Springfield's government, according
   to mayoral candidate Wayne Zenner.

> "The city government must revamp procedures for
> making appointments to its 13 committees and boards,"
> Zenner told the League of Women Voters yesterday.

Once again, the original lead is a "who" lead. The revision lead is a "what" lead—it starts immediately with the point of the story, clearly and succinctly. Unless there is an overriding reason not to do so, use "what" leads to start your stories.

In the revision, notice also that a direct quote starts off the second paragraph. Direct quotes create more audience interest in both the print and electronic media. They should be used within the first three paragraphs of a story and profusely throughout the story.

You must either come straight to the point in your leads or create such suspense that your audience is content to listen to, or read, what is unfolding because you've persuaded them that it's worth waiting for.

Sometimes this can be accomplished with the "why" lead. As a suspense lead, the "why" lead serves rather well. If the radio and television broadcasts have been featuring the story all day long, an afternoon paper (or later radio and television newscasts) might want to play the story up in this particular "why"-lead way.

"Why" Lead

> For no particular reason that anyone can think of,
> Stanley Ruell, cosmetics heir, last night shot himself.

A "how" lead in the same story would look like this:

"How" Lead

> Standing next to his swimming pool last night, with a
> .38 special pressed to his temple so that the force of
> the bullet would knock him into the pool, cosmetics heir
> Stanley Ruell pulled the trigger and killed himself.

This "how" lead has turned into a dramatic or suspense lead. Though not bad, at 39 words it may be too long. Leads should be short—25 words or less. If it takes an effort for the audience to carry all that information with them to the end, the lead should be shortened. This particular "how" lead reads rather well. Broken as it is into small "takes," the audience can digest each of them easily, assimilate them, and carry the information with them to the end of the sentence without too much difficulty. But the beginning reporter should stick to the 25-word rule.

You could write an acceptable 25-word lead by cutting out the clause starting with "so that" and including it in the next paragraph, like this:

> Standing next to his swimming pool last night, with a
> .38 special pressed to his temple, cosmetics heir
> Stanley Ruell pulled the trigger and killed himself.
> The force of the bullet knocked him into the pool—
> exactly as he had apparently planned for it to do.

You cannot escape the fact that this shortened lead is better than the original. Good things happen when you revise. Chances are you will create a more interesting, forceful or emphatic lead.

In the "why" lead and in the "how" lead, the audience's imagination is stirred: "Why," the audience asks, "would an heir commit suicide?"

The suspense and drama in the "why" lead is nurtured to the very end of the lead. The audience does not know what has happened until the very last word. You have written what is also known as a periodic sentence—the full meaning is withheld until the very end of the sentence. This device can be used to create suspense, drama or emphasis.

Can you really create suspense by writing a periodic sentence? Of course you can. We will read the lead again as your audience would read it, exaggerating their thoughts a little (indicated in parentheses) to emphasize our point:

> For no particular reason [the audience says, "Yes, yes, let's go on"] that anyone can think of ["Come on, come on"], Stanley Ruell, cosmetics heir ["Finally! I know who's involved"], last night ["For God's sake, man, what happened last night anyway?"] shot himself ["At last"].

Is that the way it really happens for the audience? Yes. Subconsciously, that is exactly what is taking place in the audience's mind.

To impress upon you how important a suspense lead or periodic sentence is in creating audience interest, let's read the Ruell "how" lead in the same fashion:

> Standing next to his swimming pool ["Just who are you talking about?"] last night ["I'm still waiting," drumming fingers on the paper], with a .38 special pressed to his temple ["Are you *ever* going to tell me who is involved and what is going on?"], cosmetics heir Stanley Ruell ["Finally!"] pulled the trigger ["Yes, yes, go on"] and killed himself ["Sigh"—the suspense is over].

SOME GOLDEN LEAD RULES FOR BEGINNERS

1. Stick primarily with "what" leads.
2. Use "who" leads sparingly.
3. Avoid "when" and "where" leads.
4. Once you've mastered the rudimentary arts of writing news stories, "why" and "how" leads may be useful in "featurizing" news and creating drama and suspense in the audience.

We now present some good leads and some bad leads. Determine what makes them good or bad before you read the critique of each. First, the good leads:

> The worst economic crisis since the Great Depression is facing Warren County.
> The county produces and exports more nursery stock than any county in the nation, and people aren't buying these days.

In just 11 words, the first sentence spells out what's happening in Warren County.

> A struggle in the cockpit of a Japan Air Lines DC-8 occurred moments before it plunged into Tokyo Bay.
> Investigators said 24 persons died in the crash.

How can a reader of these few lines resist reading the rest of the story?

> If it takes rioting in the streets to focus attention on joblessness, "that's what we'll do," the nation's top labor leader said today.

The phrase "rioting in the streets" naturally arouses the attention of the reader. That's why it comes first in the lead.

The subject matter for the good leads came from newspaper stories. Now we'll show the original leads of those stories as examples of poor leads. Such leads are published or broadcast every day. You should be able to discern why the leads are poor.

> Warren County, which produces and exports more nursery stock than any other county in the nation, is facing its worst economic crisis since the leanest years of the Great Depression.

The audience would have to be caught up in the demographics of Warren County to continue with the news story with this lead on it. The crisis is buried in the middle of the lead—the least important place in a paragraph.

> Investigators into the crash of a Japan Air Lines DC-8 have said there was a struggle in the cockpit moments before it plunged into Tokyo Bay, killing 24 people.

This lead borders on a "who" lead as far as emphasis is concerned. What boring details the audience has to wade through before they get to the dramatic element in the lead, the struggle in the cockpit. That element, once again, is buried in the middle of the paragraph.

> Prime Minister Felipe Gonzales of Spain told Secretary of State George P. Shultz yesterday that the new socialist government would remain a loyal and trusted ally.

The audience reading this lead is no doubt saying subconsciously, "How long, how long, O Lord, before we get to find out what is happening?" How much easier it would have been to start out: "Spain's new Socialist government will remain a loyal and trusted ally of the United States."

> Riots Suggested to Aid Jobless
>
> The nation's top labor leader says if it takes "riots in the streets" to focus attention on joblessness in the United States, "perhaps we have to go out and organize some turmoil."

Although the headline of this story is "Riots Suggested to Aid Jobless," that interesting element is buried, once again, in the middle of the paragraph. (It's a good idea to compose a headline for your story, even though it probably won't make it into the paper. Writing headlines before or after you write your stories helps you to identify the most important element in the story and suggests to you that you start your lead with it. Had the writer of this lead been forced to write such an identifying headline, perhaps the lead would have been better.)

All the leads in this section were taken from fine newspapers and a wire service. How could all these poor leads have been allowed?

SUMMARY

Newspaper readers "shop" the paper for the stories that interest them. Editors position reporters' stories on pages according to their importance and write headlines that will draw maximum reader interest. The headline's handful of words can influence a reader about whether or not to read the first few paragraphs of the article. The headline is the first key decision point for the newspaper reader.

The lead of the story is the next key decision point. In a simple news story, the first paragraph must be compelling enough to pull the reader into the story, to make the reader want to learn more. That single paragraph bears the burden of communicating the importance of the information contained in the body of the story. It also serves as the blueprint for the article, establishing the order in which details will be described and interpreted in succeeding paragraphs.

A good lead gives an interesting, clear account of what happened, usually in a single-sentence paragraph. The best leads are "what" leads. Of the 5W+H and Significance questions, *what* is the best peg for leads.

EXERCISES

1. Paste five poor examples of leads from a commercial newspaper in the space provided below. To the right of each lead, briefly state what is wrong with the lead. Underneath this statement, rewrite the lead as it should be. (If you need another sheet of paper, use it.)

   a.

   b.

   c.

d.

e.

2. These paragraphs can be rearranged to produce a simple news story. Snip the paragraphs and then rearrange them in their proper order. Underline paragraph transitions. Write a headline for the story.

Although Wonton and two other members of the group were sleeping in the bus when the single-engine Cessna's wing ripped through it, none of them was injured.

He first took two members of the group for a ride, then landed and picked up King and Stringfellow.

Killed were Kevin King, 32, a guitarist; Jack Stringfellow, 33, the group's hairdresser and general aide; and tour bus driver Olen D. Miller, 25, who was flying the plane.

Two other members of the entourage standing near the bus taking pictures of the plane as it buzzed the Blue Heron Airport in Biloxi also escaped injury.

Wonton and the other survivors immediately went into seclusion at a motel and declined to talk to reporters.

A light plane taken for a joy ride Monday by three members of rock star Reggie Wonton's entourage crashed into a bus where Wonton was sleeping and then into a house. All people aboard the plane were killed.

Libby Horton of Dayton, who represents the group, said she was told the tour bus was heading for Baltimore when Miller, a licensed pilot, decided to take a spin.

PASTE EXERCISE 2 HERE.

3. In the space below, write a simple news story from this set of facts:

   Decrease in local crime in Maryville, Mass. (your newspaper's home base)
   Decrease of some 16 percent
   Police chief makes the statement in speech
   His name is Kevin Donaldson
   Made the statement at the local Kiwanis Club luncheon yesterday
   Received standing ovation from some 50 Kiwanis members and guests
   "Next year I promise to reduce the crime rate by 20 percent," says the police chief

CHAPTER 7
NEWS FOR NEWSPAPERS: COMPLEX STORIES

Complex news stories that interpret or develop understanding of events reported in simple news stories call for a different organizational pattern. While the lead form still dictates the order in which ideas will be developed, leads for complex stories will be themselves more intricate. When several aspects of a story vie for prominence in the telling of that story, more careful planning is required if the writer is to do justice to the various elements that will make the story complete and balanced.

There are a number of techniques writers can use to get a handle on complex stories and sustain reader interest from start to finish.

EXPANDED LEAD AND STORY STYLES

THE SUMMARY LEAD

So far our focus has been on various simple news stories—stories with one major element. What do you do if you have more than one element of importance? What if you're interviewing a mayor or covering one of his speeches and he stresses three equally important points? How do you write that story?

You use a summary story form. The summary lead summarizes, briefly, what happens in the news event. In the summary lead, the barest of details of each major event are noted. More details are presented in later paragraphs *in the order of their appearance in the lead*.

The summary-style graphic representation shows you exactly what a summary lead and news story form look like. Each symbol represents one paragraph, and each symbol represents a major element in the news story.

Summary Lead

　　The City Council last night considered raising the sales tax △, building a waste disposal plant ○, and hiring a city manager □.

△ sales tax details
○ waste plant details
□ city manager details
△ sales tax more details
○ waste plant more details
□ city manager more details
▱ concluding paragraph

That is why, in the written summary lead example, a triangle comes after *sales tax* △, a circle after *waste plant* ○, and a square after *city manager* □. Note how, in the graphic representation, each major item is taken up in succeeding paragraphs in the order of its appearance in the summary lead. As you write the story, you may run out of details for one of the events, or you may later in the story want to wrap up discussion on one of the events in two succeeding paragraphs, and you will consequently vary the alternating paragraphs about those events. The concluding paragraph, however, attempts to wrap up the whole story.

Another summary news story might be a weather round-up story or one about three or four automobile accidents in a particular region of the state:

　　Three midstate accidents in a span of seven hours killed three persons yesterday. All the wrecks occurred during the night. All were unrelated to the snowy driving conditions.

　　The traffic accident victims are:

　　Rebecca Allen, 45, of Payne, Ohio, an employee of the Plainfield Nuclear Plant. She was killed instantly near the plant when her automobile was crushed by a tractor-trailer rig hauling 40,000 pounds of steel.

　　Maurice Deckens, 50, of Tucson, Ariz., visiting his parents over the holidays. He was killed when a cattle truck veered out of control, running a red light and smashing into his car at an intersection in Palmyra, Ohio.

　　Melva Hutchison, 68, of Tovey, Ohio, who was dead on arrival at Kincaid General Hospital, after the car she was driving ran off Montchanin Road in Old Hickory, Ohio, and struck a utility pole.

　　The Plainfield area accident occurred shortly after 5 p.m. Wednesday on Highway 45 six miles west of Plainfield when the rear wheels of the tractor broke loose and hit the trailer. The rig flipped onto its side and spilled its steel cargo onto Allen's car.

　　The driver of the truck, Eddy Lass of Cleveland, remained in Kincaid General Hospital in "stable condition." A truck passenger, Howard Murphy, also of Cleveland, was treated for minor injuries and released.

By this time, it should become quite apparent that basic knowledge of an organizational pattern for a story will solve innumerable problems when you start putting the facts of a news story together.

The graphic representations for the summary lead and salient-feature lead stories are modifications of diagrams appearing in the first edition of Julian Harris and Stanley Johnson, *The Complete Reporter* (New York: Macmillan, 1942). Those diagrams also appear in the fourth edition of that book, by Julian Harris, Kelly Leiter, and Stanley Johnson.

THE SALIENT-FEATURE LEAD

What would you do if the city council, instead of engaging in three equally important acts, engaged in only one important action, as is frequently the case, and two or three less important acts? What if the council, for example, voted to charge the mayor with improper conduct of office and also voted to refurbish a troublesome waste disposal plant and replace a city manager who had taken another job? Certainly the action taken against the mayor overshadows the other two actions. How would you write *this* news story? You would use the salient feature lead and news story form. That involves a two-paragraph lead: one paragraph for the most important event, another for the two events of lesser importance.

Having written the salient-feature lead, as in the following column, you would take up the news elements in the lead in the succeeding paragraphs in the order in which they were presented first to the reader, just as you would in the summary lead story. A graphic representation of a salient-feature lead and news story looks like this:

Salient-Feature Lead

   The City Council last night voted to charge Mayor Charles Warden with improper conduct of his office △.
   In other action, the Council agreed to refurbish a waste disposal plant ○ and hire a new city manager □.

△
○ □

- △ mayor charged details
- ○ waste plant details
- □ city manager details
- △ mayor charged more details
- ○ waste plant more details
- □ city manager more details
- □ concluding paragraph

In the salient-feature news story, the third and fourth paragraphs might be devoted to details of the action against the mayor. The facts of the story itself will dictate the final story form. Once again, you have an outline to follow in writing more complex news stories. (Note that the salient-feature lead is not usually a feature lead, and the story itself is not a feature. "Salient feature" designates the major news item in the story.)

THE SUSPENDED-INTEREST LEAD

The suspended-interest news story lead used to be used primarily in human-interest or feature stories. With the competition of news magazines and TV, however, it is being used more and more in news stories that lend themselves to what we call "featurizing" the news.

   As the name implies, the suspended-interest lead captures audience interest and holds (suspends) it, then releases it later in the story. Sometimes the interest is held to the very end of the story. Here are two examples:

Suspended-Interest Lead

```
     You wouldn't think that Huntington Civic Center
officials would have to worry about anyone biting off
heads of bats as part of their jobs. But having booked
rock performer Ozzy Osbourne for Feb. 15, that is now one
of their major concerns.
```

Suspended-Interest Lead

```
     Larry Longerbeam was fishing the Harpeth River
yesterday afternoon when he unaccountably began nodding
and nearly fell into the river. Something, he knew, was
dreadfully wrong. He rowed desperately to keep awake
and, as he later discovered, to save his life.
```

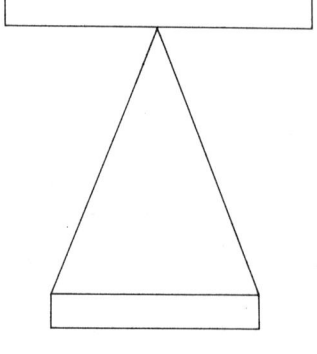

A graphic representation of the suspended-interest news story is shown in Figure 7.1. Most of the time, the very last line or final paragraph of the story releases audience interest. For that reason, the graphic representation has a separate rectangle symbolizing the conclusion of the story.

Rectangles signifying the concluding paragraphs in all the graphic representations in these pages indicate the importance of the conclusion of a news story. Allowing a news story to trail off into nothingness is acceptable, but it is not the mark of a good news writer.

If you master the simple news lead story, the summary news lead story, the salient-feature news lead story and, finally, the suspended-interest lead news story, you will have made enormous strides in learning how to organize and write news events.

FIGURE 7.1. Graphic representation of the suspended-interest news story.

FOLLOW-UP STORIES

Some news stories, having been "put to bed" in newspapers or news programs, refuse to stay there. The next day something else happens that puts a different complexion on the story. Or perhaps it's the next week or even next month that the news break occurs. An airline pilot strike, a long trial, an area devastated by a flood—all have later developments, and those developments require you to rewrite the original news story, bringing it up to date. How do you write about such news events? How do you update a story? You write a follow-up story.

The follow-up story plays up the latest development in the story in the lead and in the story itself. The summation of what transpired before—the original news event—usually comes in the second or third paragraph. In the following example, part of the summation is in the lead itself. Most of the summation, however, comes in the second paragraph.

> The director of the Canyon Ridge School for Boys has been reinstated by State Corrections Commissioner John Ross.
>
> Eileen MacKanee had been placed on administrative leave July 11, the day after Canyon Ridge police used tear gas to subdue a disturbance by the students at the reformatory.
>
> "The results of the investigation by the department into the uprising were discussed with MacKanee by Assistant Commissioner Lynn Hall Monday night," Ross said. "The decision for reinstatement was made today. We believe she acted properly in the matter."
>
> Ten boys have been charged with participating in a riot. Five are being held at the Canyon Ridge jail. The boys barricaded themselves in a recreation room in one of the school's dormitories.
>
> New policies are being studied in an attempt to prevent similar incidents at the school.

In follow-up story after follow-up story, the form seems predictable. In the TVA story that follows, the latest development is the rate reduction. The next paragraph sums up the previous rate reduction.

> KNOXVILLE (UPI) — The TVA staff recommended yesterday that the utility use a $125 million windfall to reduce electric rates by 5.8 percent from April through September.
>
> The recommendation comes two weeks after the TVA board gave consumers a one-time rate cut of 10 percent for March electric bills. The reduction followed more than a decade of spiraling increases that tripled the cost of power.
>
> TVA Chairman Charles "Chili" Dean said the board would vote on the staff recommendation at a March 2 meeting.

More than every once in a while, however, you discover an exception to the rule. The following story on women dominating fiction might be considered a follow-up. But it's more a news story of this year's awards. Some enterprising reporter checked back through the records and discovered that this year, for the first time, women dominated the scene:

> NEW YORK (AP) — Women won four out of five nominations for the best new fiction in this year's American Book Awards competition, awards officials announced yesterday.
>
> In hardcover fiction, the nominated books are *A Mother and Two Daughters* by Gail Godwin, *Shiloh and Other Stories* by Bobbie Ann Mason, *Dinner at the Homesick Restaurant* by Anne Tyler, *The Color Purple* by Alice Walker, and *The Mosquito Coast* by Paul Theroux.
>
> Since the American Book Awards competition began in 1980, 13 of the previous 15 nominees for hardcover fiction have been men.

And in this story about a tax protester who is suspected of killing two U.S. marshals, the follow-up material comes in the last paragraph. But the story does not suffer as a result.

> HEATON, N.D. (AP) — About 100 police officers, using a National Guard armored vehicle and firing tear gas, stormed a farmhouse yesterday in a futile search for a "fanatic" tax protester suspected of killing two U.S. marshals.
>
> "We have searched the house and there is no evidence of the fugitive in there," said FBI agent Richard H. Blay. He declined to say whether authorities found evidence that Gordon Kahl, 63, had spent any time in the house. Kahl, described as a member of a paramilitary group called Posse Comitatus, had vowed to friends and acquaintances not to be taken alive.
>
> In Fargo, U.S. Attorney Rodney Webb said some weapons and ammunition were found in the home, although he refused to elaborate.
>
> Webb also declined to say what direction the search might take and whether he thought Kahl is still in North Dakota.
>
> Authorities had surrounded the farm for 25 hours since Monday, using a bullhorn to plead for Kahl to surrender, but there was no reply.

Usually, however, you can count on a summation of what has previously happened in the second or third paragraph of a follow-up news story. So until you have good reason to do otherwise, follow the graphic representation of the follow-up news story shown in Figure 7.2.

```
                (Latest Development)
  The director of the Canyon Ridge School for Boys has been reinstated
         by State Corrections Commissioner John Ross.
             (Summation of Earlier Story)
  Eileen MacKanee had been placed on administrative leave July 11,
   the day after Canyon Ridge police used tear gas to subdue a
         disturbance by the students at the reformatory.
            (Details of Latest Development)
  "The results of the investigation by the department into the
    uprising were discussed with MacKanee by Assistant
   Commissioner Lynn Hall Monday night," Ross said. "The
    decision for reinstatement was made today. We believe
           she acted properly in the matter."
           (More Details of Latest Developments)
     Ten boys have been charged with participating
      in a riot. Five are being held at the Canyon
      Ridge jail. The boys barricaded themselves in
      a recreation room in one of the school's
                  dormitories.
              (Concluding Paragraph)
  New policies are being studied in an attempt to prevent similar
                 incidents at the school.
```

FIGURE 7.2. A follow-up news story fits into an inverted pyramid schema.

HOW TO WRITE A NEWS INTERVIEW STORY

Although every interview is different and every interview story requires a slightly different treatment, interview stories fall into three major categories: news, question and answer, and feature. We will leave discussion of the last two for Chapter 12, "Newspaper Features." Here we will cover writing an interview based on a news event.

When satirist Richard Armour talked to the elite Civics Club in Madison, Wis., the speech was scheduled for a noon luncheon. The deadline was 12 o'clock for the *Capital Times*. Cedric Parker, the city editor, called in a general-assignment reporter.

"Find out what Armour's going to be saying," Parker told him, "and write it up. Let the readers know early on that it's an interview. Armour's waiting for you at the Downtowner Motor Inn."

Starting at 10 o'clock, while Armour ate breakfast, the reporter interviewed him. At 11 o'clock, with a pack of 3-by-5 cards full of notes—not only about the speech but seemingly about everything else that had crossed Armour's mind on the plane from California—the reporter ended the interview while the satirist was still talking. (Armour, with some perverse pleasure, reversed the roles; usually the reporter seeks to prolong the interview and the interviewee wants to cut it short.)

The interview story that follows incorporates the aspects of the news event—the luncheon address—into the interview, just as Cedric Parker had directed the reporter to write it. The lead is a simple news lead and includes the attendees, what was said, by whom and with what effect.

```
More than 550 Madison Civics Club members enjoyed
instruction in the art of satire by master satirist
```

Richard Armour at the season opening meeting today at the Park Motor Inn.

Armour discussed the comments he would be making in his speech and elaborated upon them in this pre-speech interview.

"Someone once said that today in America we have become too tense to take satire," he said, "especially in touchy areas such as race, religion and politics. I believe this is only true when satire is not done in good taste—when humor does not outweigh the bitterness, when the elements of preaching and reform are not subordinated to humor and entertainment."

The satirist first distinguished between humor and satire, illustrating the latter with witty examples that touched on the future of the human race, the political scene, history, literature and the battle of the sexes.

"Humor entertains. Satire entertains and instructs," Armour said. "It has a target and may bring about reform. Satire is more cerebral and more subtle.

"In satire you simultaneously massage the funny bone and the cerebellum. More intellectual effort goes into satire, and more intellectual effort is necessary to get the nuances of meaning."

The satirist, Armour added, has to look absurdly at the serious, and seriously at the absurd.

"E.B. White, the *New Yorker* writer, is one of the most sophisticated," Armour stated. "But the most outstanding satirist of our day was James Thurber."

This story follows the precepts of good news-interview writing. A direct quote should come within the first three paragraphs. Although reporters frequently believe that readers want to read the reporters' version, in fact, readers invariably prefer the words "straight from the horse's mouth." Furthermore, direct quotes enliven the story.

The fourth paragraph is soon enough to chart the course the speech will follow. The fifth paragraph uses direct quotes again. The attribution is buried in the middle of the paragraph, rather than taking up the important spot at the beginning of the paragraph or at the end of it. No attribution is needed in the next paragraph. That's taken care of by not closing the quotes in the preceding paragraph and by mentioning quickly in the succeeding paragraph, "Armour added."

Most interview or speech stories should be interlaced with direct quotes and paraphrasing, as illustrated in this example.

Attribution should be used sparingly, at the most only once per paragraph. The reader knows who's speaking, so why clutter the story with attributions?

The final quote makes an excellent ending for the interview story.

To fill out the news story about the Civics Club luncheon, names of special guests conclude the story:

Special guests at the speaker's table were Dr. Roy Ruffner, Civics Club chairman; Thomas Holloway, Nitin Chikkannaiah, Diane Dean, Virginia Verble, Donna Wilder, Georgia Reynolds, Priscilla Gaps and Ronald Sampley, students at the university; and Scott Jared, former secretary of the club.

A note of caution: When writing in advance about an event, using details that are anticipated, make certain that things actually went as planned. For example, if Ruffner does not attend the luncheon, delete his name. Stop the presses—or the cameras—if an event changes in some way from the way you report it.

DIFFERENT AUDIENCES CAN DICTATE DIFFERENT COVERAGE

We have often commented on how perceptions influence the writer of news events and, consequently, the way facts are organized and presented. If you are reporting for *The Wall Street Journal*, you will pay particular attention to news events of interest to business people. If you are reporting for the *Miami Herald*, you will write for an entirely different audience, and your news stories will differ accordingly. Different leads and news stories are affected by factors other than personal biases and prejudices. Most often the audience dictates the subject matter in the lead and the organization of the story. That's what happened when Senator Edward Kennedy spoke during the 1980 presidential campaign at Georgetown University after suffering defeats on the campaign trail in Iowa and Maine. The speech was extremely important—it marked a turning point in the Kennedy strategy to win the Democratic nomination for the presidency. Let's look at how some prestigious publications led off their stories:

UPI covers Kennedy at Georgetown:

Sen. Edward Kennedy, seeking to revitalize his slumping presidential campaign with a dramatic speech, today called for immediate gasoline rationing and mandatory wage and price controls to halt inflation.

The emphasis is where it ought to be in this story. Rationing and price controls were moved from where they were mentioned, at the end of the speech, and placed in the lead. Reporting for its wide constituency, UPI played it straight. Now let's look at what *The New York Times* did in reporting the speech.

The New York Times *covers Kennedy at Georgetown:*

Senator Edward M. Kennedy criticized the new Carter doctrine today and called for a "measured response" that would "prove less hazardous and more effective than a unilateral and unlimited American commitment" in the Persian Gulf.

The Massachusetts Democrat, struggling to revive his lagging presidential candidacy, made an attack on the president's foreign policy in a speech in which he also proposed these steps: . . .

For whatever reason, the *Times* perceived the foreign policy aspect more suitable for the lead. (Perhaps because the *Times* perceives its audience as having a more international outlook?)

The Wall Street Journal *covers Kennedy at Georgetown:*

Vowing he has only begun to fight, Sen. Edward Kennedy tacked sharply to port and fired the whole battery at President Carter.

In a speech at Georgetown University, Sen. Kennedy suggested President Carter's economic policies were more Republican than Democratic and that his foreign policy threatens to begin "Cold War II."

This is the most colorful lead of all, a feature summary lead. But notice the mention of Carter's economic policies first off. The *Journal's* readers would be attracted by that lead because, by and large, its readers are concerned with the country's business and economic health.

The Los Angeles Times *covers Kennedy at Georgetown:*

Trying urgently to shore up his sagging presidential campaign, Sen. Edward M. Kennedy Monday called for gasoline rationing and government controls on wages, prices, profits and rents.

Although this lead is essentially the same as the UPI lead, the next two paragraphs stress inflation. After that, four paragraphs are devoted to gasoline rationing, reflecting California's continuing love affair with the automobile.

The Chicago Tribune *covers Kennedy at Georgetown:*

In a scathing attack on President Carter's policies, Sen. Edward M. Kennedy (D.-Mass.) called Monday for mandatory wage-price controls and immediate gasoline rationing.

The *Tribune* sees the speech as "a scathing attack." That's a little different from the *Los Angeles Time's* "Trying urgently to shore up his sagging presidential campaign." Two different reporters, two different reporting perspectives.

The Washington Post *covers Kennedy at Georgetown:*

Sen. Edward M. Kennedy (D.-Mass.) launched the effort to salvage this presidential campaign with a combative and comprehensive attack on the Carter administration.

The *Post* used an all-inclusive lead that stresses all the elements of the speech. What would the London *Times* do with a news event like this?

The London Times *covers Kennedy at Georgetown:*

Senator Edward Kennedy today sought to inject fresh momentum into his faltering presidential campaign with a forceful attack on President Carter's foreign and domestic policies.

Not much different from some of the U.S. newspaper leads. It's altogether acceptable, with the predictable accent on Kennedy's foreign policy attack in the first paragraph. The foreign policy attack, you will recall, was not mentioned in the *Los Angeles Times*, the *Chicago Tribune*, or the UPI story.

The TV networks cover Kennedy at Georgetown:

ABC spent one minute on the speech and one minute and 40 seconds on the reaction to it from the White House. There were no live shots from Georgetown. Frank Reynolds led off with a comment about a sharply worded attack by Kennedy on Carter policies.

NBC spent 2½ minutes on the speech with enthusiastic crowd shots. Reaction from the White House took one minute and 50 seconds. The story started off with how poorly the campaign was going and how Kennedy came out swinging at Georgetown.

CBS devoted three minutes and 20 seconds to the speech and one minute and 20 seconds to the reaction. Walter Cronkite lead off the evening news *with Kennedy's call for wage and price controls and gas rationing. Crowd shots were interspersed throughout the speech coverage.*

What all this probably means is that from seasoned reporters you will get acceptable stories about an event, with an occasional nod of recognition to the audience the reporter is writing for.

Experienced reporters discover that writing for different audiences calls for different decisions about what to lead with and how to organize the body of a story. In addition, they're aware that different writing specialties have their own styles, patterns and conventions. The organizational style of a business writer is quite distinct from that of the sports writer; so is the choice of words each uses to tell their stories. The differences have evolved over time and are useful both to the writer and to the reader or listener. Why? Because it is easy for us to process information that is presented in a style with which we are familiar. Using a similar approach to write about the stock market each day enables the business writer to put together the story more quickly and helps the reader unravel a complex subject more easily.

The different ways in which specialists put the leads and bodies of stories together is outlined here. All have one thing in common: They rely on the 5W + H and Significance questions to write the lead and flesh out details in the first few paragraphs.

LOCAL NEWS

Accidents. About 50,000 persons a year are killed in automobile accidents. That's almost as many as the number of U.S. soldiers killed during the whole Vietnam War. Hundreds of thousands are also injured in those accidents. You would think that with all those accidents, people would grow tired of reading about them, but that is not the case. Perhaps it's because almost everybody drives or rides in a vehicle and can more easily visualize what's being described. Whatever the case may be, almost all accidents, except for those minor "fender benders," are reported. If there are fatalities, that will be highlighted in the lead. If an accident causes major damage—perhaps a warehouse catches on fire—that will be the lead. Chances are you'll almost always use a "what" lead unless a freak accident is being reported. Most will go like this:

```
Five University of Illinois students remain in
serious condition today from injuries suffered when the
car they were in careened out of control and into the
front wall of the Utopia night club just before
midnight.
    The crash ended a 15-minute chase through Urbana-
Champaign, according to Sgt. Louis Crescenzo. The
students' car was observed by Crescenzo running a red
light at Green and Oregon streets.
    The students in University Hospital are Mary and
Robert C. Schumm, Louis Vercellotti, Arthur Cook and Art
Orr. All are listed as engineering majors.
```

Just observe the rules of good newswriting. In the follow-up story, if necessary, you would include facts not available in time for this news story: latest conditions of the injured and their injuries, what the students are being charged with, quotes from the sergeant and perhaps patrons of the Utopia or the owner of the club, an estimate of the damage. If a student dies, give the funeral arrangements and relevant details.

Deaths and injuries are usually always stressed more than property damage in accident stories.

Fires. What has been pointed out about reporting accidents may also apply to reporting fires. Almost as many fires occur as automobile accidents, and you will be called upon to write stories about most of them. The smaller the city you're reporting in, the smaller the fires you'll report. If there's a fire in your neighborhood, you can count on your neighbors' being there—in housecoats and pajamas if it's at night.

Generally, the more units the fire department dispatches to the fire, the bigger the fire. But in some cities, a specified number of units automatically answer alarms in congested downtown areas regardless of the size of the fire. So a five-alarm fire may actually be merely a restaurant oven grease fire that's generating a lot of smoke. A call to a firehouse dispatcher will usually give you the information you need to decide whether to cover the fire personally.

The variety and severity of fires occurring daily ensure a variety of leads and stories, all the way from brushfires to dormitory fires:

```
Forest fires continue breaking out near Helena,
Mont., as droughtlike conditions and electrical storms
with winds up to 30 miles per hour combine to wreak
destruction.
    For the fourth straight day, firefighters are trying
to control fires that have consumed more than 150,000
acres of forests. More than 30 homes have been destroyed
by the flames. . . .

    The third fire in as many days broke out in the men's
dormitories at Princeton University early this morning.
No injuries were reported, though smoke billowed from a
room on the first floor of Joseph Ripley Hall, forcing
the evacuation of more than 300 students.
    "The room was unoccupied," Fire Chief William Vail
said. "It looks like a cigarette in a pack of matches
under a mattress started the blaze."
    Princeton officials said damages amounted to about
$5,000, but that . . .
```

Because ours is supposed to be a society more concerned with human life and suffering than material wealth, a lead on a fire story will feature the number of persons killed or injured. If no one is injured, the amount of damage is a lead highlight. How you write your story depends, of course, on what has happened. If it's one of a string of fires, you'll probably start off the same way as the example just given.

Always include why or how a fire started:

```
    A Christmas Day fire sparked by burning present
wrappings killed two people yesterday and caused an
estimated $75,000 in damage to an apartment house in
Framingham.
    "I don't know how many people were in the two-story
building when it broke out at midnight," Dale Ballenger,
```

watch commander of the Framingham Fire Department, said. "But there are 20 to 22 apartments."

The two victims were Mary Ann Summerlin, 17, and Stewart Frazer, 49.

"It started at the back of the building. Someone must have thrown a lighted cigarette into one of the boxes of trash around the back door. We put it out in about 15 minutes," Ballenger said, "but that was too long for the girl and the man."

If the cause is freakish enough, you will probably feature it in the lead and write a feature lead:

A tiny kitten, attracted by the flame from a hurricane lamp, pawed at the lamp, knocking it over and setting a fire that caused more than $10,000 damage to the Edward C. Sampson home in Oneonta last night.

The Sampsons' three daughters were upstairs in a bedroom cutting paper valentines when . . .

Sometimes a rescue or the escape of persons endangered takes precedence over all, and you would use a feature lead similar to that in the kitten story:

Although John Robert Jumbock grumbled under his breath yesterday at having to pay $100 for a toy poodle for his daughter's birthday present, today he's thanking providence, and his wife, for leading him to the Precocious Pet Shop in Philadelphia.

What that toy poodle did last night was bark and jump on his bed to alert him to the smoke curling up the staircase and into the upstairs bedrooms.

"No telling what might of happened if it weren't for that dog," Jumbock said. "Embers from the fireplace had popped out onto the rug, and that rug was smoldering something awful." . . .

Crimes. Unfortunately, most crime stories are serious, from crimes against property—such as burglary and larceny—to violent crimes—aggravated assault, robbery, rape and murder. Once on the beat, you'll quickly learn the difference between a misdemeanor and a felony as well as the different degrees of murder and the various kinds of assault. When you write your story, however, lead with specifics. If a man is arrested for kicking a police officer, that should be in the lead rather than that the man was arrested for assault and battery.

Except in smaller towns or cities, most crimes go unreported. As a police reporter, you will have to determine what crimes are the most serious and most significant out of a host of crimes and write your stories on them. Some small city newspapers will run a crime column that lists crimes entered on the police blotter, the log of calls police investigated. You may be called upon to report the bare facts for the column and write news stories about the more serious crimes. Develop a good working relationship with the police chief, and cultivate friendships with the radio dispatcher and the desk sergeant at the police station. This will pay off in tips and information. Once you establish yourself as a reporter who is fair and responsible, the rest of the police force should accept you on the crime site without hesitation. And a radio in your car will enable you to pick up the police band. That will get you to most crimes in time to interview victims or relatives of the victims, the police and witnesses:

> A 19-year-old man, charged with shooting his wife's boyfriend to death yesterday, has been bound over to the Dayton County grand jury on charges of murder.
> "I know he shot him," Doris Timko, wife of J. O. Timko, said. "I was right here."

When you write your story, be certain you have the complete identification of the victim, the nature of the crime (if violent, the official cause of death or injury, weapon used, motivation, etc.; if a property crime, the loss and value, modus operandi, etc.), your information source and other essential details. Make certain that all the names and facts are accurate. Inaccuracies bring about libel suits.

> Lesley Roan, 44, of 134 N. Fifth St., Presque Isle, was arrested Friday night on an indictment charging that he is a habitual criminal.
> A conviction on the charge could result in a sentence for Roan of life in the state penitentiary.
> Roan was booked into jail and held under $250,000 bond.

If there are two Lesley Roans in the telephone book, better make sure you have the right address.

Crime stories are read by everyone—the more serious the crime, the more readers. We presume that's because readers have been touched in one way or another by criminal acts, they fear them, or they have a native curiosity about the evil that people do. Your responsibility as a police reporter is to report the crimes as fully and accurately as possible, thereby alerting society to the dangers in the community. When possible, the causes of the crime should be explored—*Why did it happen?*—so that citizens, if they so desire, can insist on those causes being eliminated:

> A task force subcommittee investigating conditions at Carson City Youth Center adjourned a meeting today rather than allow a reporter to hear a witness's testimony.
> "If you insist on being present, we'll adjourn the meeting," Ormsby County Judge Carol Soloman said.
> The task force, headed by Juvenile Court Judge Shirley Ruffner, was formed in July because of the many reports of sexual misconduct and other allegations at the juvenile center.

While the police beat may be an exciting beat for some reporters, it may also be depressing for others. But certainly good and responsible reporters interested in a better society can feel that they are contributing fully to that cause by working the police beat.

TECHNICAL NEWS

The amount of scientific and technical knowledge that has accumulated in the past 25 years is staggering. Take, for example, the Department of Energy Technological Information Center in Oak Ridge, Tenn., the world depository for all abstracts of articles and experiments treating energy, from coal to fission. The block-square depository is fully computerized. So fully automated is the information center that a request for information about coal gases can result in a printed and bound two-inch-thick volume measuring 8 by 10 inches of abstracts of articles, books and experiments. Similar information centers on other technology with the same storage and retrieval capabilities are located throughout the world.

If you are interested in writing technical news, the challenge will be to understand and to keep abreast of the latest developments in your area of expertise. Craven Crowell reported in the Aug. 2, 1984, *Tennessean* that this information is increasing at a rate of 13 percent a year and will soon be increasing at a rate of 40 percent a year. In 1975 the number of technical communication programs in universities stood at 10; today approximately 30 such programs exist (*Directory of Majors*). But these programs are turning out primarily technical writers and editors. You will be the person primarily responsible for writing the news. How will you go about doing it?

Science and Technology. Writing scientific and technical news requires the same kind of writing and reporting that general news requires, according to UPI science editor of the Southeast William Harwood. Accuracy, clarity and concision are essential for both.

Scientific news also embraces the medical field:

> CHICAGO (AP) — The healing touch is a powerful agent that has helped people get well since "the mists of antiquity," but modern medical schools are virtually ignoring it.
>
> "From the first handshake to heart massage, healers touch their patients, and patients expect to have hands laid on them in one form or another," says Jules Older of Otago Medical School in Dunedin, New Zealand. . . .

And stories such as this are scientific news:

> By WARREN E. LEARY
> AP Science Writer
>
> WASHINGTON — Almost one-fifth of all adult Americans have mental problems, and men, contrary to previous belief, have as many emotional disorders as women.
>
> The most comprehensive survey of mental disorders ever conducted in the United States found that about 19 percent of all people over age 18 suffer with at least one psychiatric disorder but that fewer than 20 percent of them seek professional help.

As you might expect, covering the science and technology beat requires different handling than other beats. Unlike general reporting that is aimed at the non-technical reader, Harwood points out that the science writer must be prepared to provide enough detail and interpretation to satisfy the more sophisticated science reader as well as the layperson, without discouraging the latter. This story does that:

> AIKEN, S.C. (UPI) — A mile-wide cloud of radioactive tritium oxide gas released in an accident at the Energy Department's top-secret Savannah River Plant dissipated harmlessly yesterday into the atmosphere.
>
> Plant officials said the gas — a key ingredient of hydrogen bombs —

escaped Sunday night and drifted northward over the South Carolina Piedmont. Neither the 300-square-mile reservation surrounding the plant nor the nearby city of Aiken was evacuated.

Only trace amounts of radiation reached the ground, according to SRP spokesman Cliff Webb.

Although the writer of this story did an excellent job of traversing the line between the technical and general reader, the reporting is less successful. What was the accident that allowed the gas to escape? Were the citizens of Aiken alerted? What about the persons on the site of the accident? Who measured the "trace amounts" that reached the ground?

The following story lead treads that fine technological line:

By ED GREGORY*

Northern Telecom Inc. unveiled yesterday an advanced version of its Displayphone, an integrated voice/data computer terminal whose marketing will, in part, ride the coattails of IBM's successful microcomputers.

As you can see, the writer's role in this area is to interpret the subject matter—to break it down into understandable segments so that a non-expert will be able to read it profitably. Harwood adds that you should always be on the alert for photographs or graphic designs that will help you to interpret your findings.

Business and Labor. Business and labor news may not seem very captivating for most beginning writers, but news interest in this category is at an all-time high. And fortunately for you, if you like business and labor news, the number of capable writers available cannot meet the demand.

Until you know what you're doing in this area, Patti L. Smisson, editor of *Tennessee Business*, suggests that you stick to facts and figures:

Rosser Airlines will purchase four used 747-200 aircraft from Boeing Equipment Holding Co. for $106 million. Rosser currently operates four 747 jumbos. Two jumbos will be delivered in the second quarter of 1985. The others are scheduled for delivery during the second quarter of 1986.

This knowledgeable writer slipped into analysis:

Avon Products has sold Tiffany and Co. to an investor group led by Tiffany's chairman for $135.5 million in cash. The ownership shift may mark a change in the internationally known jewelry's firm effort in the last decade to reach out to a broader range of consumers.

A type of analysis is possible using information, of course, but even then you are merely reporting the facts:

Employment by county governments rebounded last year after two years of declines. The Census Bureau reported that the nation's counties had 1,811,000 workers as of last October, up about 7,000 from the same month a year earlier.

Chances are that the Census Bureau, under the prodding of the incumbent administration, will make such analyses for you.

* Reprinted with permission of *The Tennessean*.

Compared to average readers, business readers are very critical. You should hook them on dollars. Rather than writing about a company celebrating its third anniversary, perhaps you should stress the explosive growth that made it a $10 million company in three years. The profit-making (or -losing) nature of a business is what business readers want to read about. If you're writing about a company going bankrupt, Smisson stresses uncovering the amount of money it has lost, even if you have to hound their lawyer or take one of the junior accountants to lunch. The hard facts may be hard to get, so be persistent.

Stories should be brief. Concentrate again on facts and figures:

> Three El Paso businessmen broke ground today in Lewisburg for Co-Ex Plastics Inc., a new company that will produce polyethylene stretch film.
>
> The 15,000-square-foot plant will be built for about $1.5 million dollars by Harwood's Woodesigns Inc.
>
> "We plan to complete the construction by January 1987 and go into production by July of that year," said President Gerry Clinton. "We'll employ about 60 local people."
>
> The stretch film is used for wrapping products in food operations and factories, Clinton said.
>
> The project is being financed through the First Farmers & Merchants National Bank of Columbia.

Quantify, quantify, and then quantify some more.

If you are called upon to cover labor disputes, you should be even more wary of your sources' statements. The general rule of news gathering applies: Get both sides of the story.

> A strong movement to unionize the Dalton Textile Mill has been generated by the firing of George S. MacIntosh.
>
> "MacIntosh was fired for failing to meet a new quota," union organizer Myles Suede said. "The parent company, South Carolina Mills, told MacIntosh he had to sew the ends onto 250 blankets each day. When he failed to do it, they fired him."
>
> South Carolina Mills president Hershey Williams said in a prepared statement that the plant was failing to make a profit and unless it was turned around, the mill would be closed.
>
> "I don't care what that president says," Suede said in responding to the statement. "I've never seen so many things done wrong in such a short period of time by this management."

In events like this and in labor strikes, sources on both sides are usually more than willing to talk.

SPECIAL-INTEREST NEWS

Special-interest news such as religion, agriculture, sports, consumer news and leisure-time activities takes no more preparation or education than technical news—and sometimes less. But the self-education process of the reporter on the job is, of course, a necessity. If you find yourself assigned to write special-interest news and think initially that the job's not for you, give yourself at least three months to make a final decision. You may find yourself liking the assignment more and more. You could even develop into an authoritative writer in the area. More and more these days, specialists are being sought by editors and directors, at higher wages, to satisfy this burgeoning audience interest.

Religion. Several decades ago, religion reporters or editors on secular media (if there were positions for them) were taken far less seriously than they now are. According to W. A. Reed, a former president of the Religion Newswriters Association of the United States and Canada, that organization helped convince editors and publishers in the 1960s and 1970s that religion is as important as any other beat on the daily newspaper. The religion beat acknowledges the dominant role religion plays in American culture.

Reed makes the point that church news is not religion news. But you may be called upon to write church news or even to put together a weekly Friday or Saturday religion page or program. Your sources will be wire services, ministers, publicity releases and chairpersons of publicity committees, among others. Your newspaper, radio or television station may have a "City Churches" or "Area Churches" column or program where the various meetings and activities will be briefly noted. As a religion reporter, you may attend a different church each Sunday and write a report on the sermon. You will be reporting church news such as this:

FIGURE 7.3. W. A. Reed, former president of the Religion Newswriters Association of the United States and Canada. Reprinted with permission of *The Tennessean*.

> An annual Homecoming Service will be observed Sunday at Clear Branch Baptist Church, Route 2, Klamath Falls. Rev. Fred Garman, a former pastor of the church now living in Grand Forks, N.D., will bring the homecoming message at the 11 a.m. worship service.
>
> A covered-dish dinner will be served in the Fellowship Hall following the service. The Gospel Harmoneers Quartet from Weaverville will sing.
>
> A special song and fellowship service will be held at 2 p.m. All former pastors, members and friends are invited.

The journalistic Golden Rule that John Long of *The Courier-Journal* in Louisville, Ky., would have you follow in writing about religion is as follows: "Write about the beliefs of others as you would have them write about your own." That is especially important when you write about something other than church news:

> Eight churches functioned as political action committees when they contributed money to an anti-liquor campaign, the state attorney general says. Now they must file financial disclosure statements.
>
> "All I can say is we're shocked," the Rev. Lyle Lipke said. His church, the Woodmont Christian Church, gave the Citizens Against Liquor group $1,000.
>
> More than $5,000 was given by the churches to defeat a liquor-by-the-drink referendum in Piedmont in the Aug. 10 election.

"The art and business of writing religion stories," according to Reed, "is that of noting the business activities and changes of national state and local denominations as well as their changes in doctrine or policy. And it is the art of determining whether these church bodies are slanting to the right or to the left and whether their moves are historic or positions dictated by necessity."

One RNA president, Russell Chandler of the *Los Angeles Times*, warned religion writers about the job-related stress and burnout that afflicts one out of every five clergy. He said the proportion of burnout among religion writers was probably just as high. He noted the importance of maintaining investigative instincts. That is what Reed did after thinking about the problems the Catholic Church is now facing as a result of its rule on celibacy, which forbids marriage for priests.

Reed checked out the problem on the local level and wrote a series of articles for *The Tennessean* titled "The Catholic Crisis." Here is the beginning of the first article:

The Nashville Catholic diocese faces a major crisis because many of its priests are resigning — most of them to marry — and there is a growing shortage of seminary students to replace them.

Catholic church leaders have not publicly acknowledged the depth of the crisis. Privately, they admit real concern.

"I fear it will get worse as time goes on," said one veteran pastor who has known several of the priests who recently resigned. "Everybody in the church is distressed."

A partial list of 20 priests who have resigned and the problems they faced was published. The next article covered the measures the Nashville diocese took to deal with the financial problems created by the resignations—including requiring seminarians to sign for bank loans to pay for their education rather than making a token repayment as in the past and curtailing the amount of study they received. A third article reported on the jobs that ex-priests took and their satisfaction or dissatisfaction with them. The fourth article reported on three ex-priests and their wives and their lifestyles. (Priests who attended their weddings were threatened with excommunication.) The concluding article dealt with the laity's changing view of the priest's role.

As you can see, religion news can be high drama. When Reed and Tom Mulgrew covered a seminar for Southern Baptists, the assignment was all that any reporter could ask for:

Area Southern Baptists are forming the nucleus of a nationwide movement aimed at overturning the Southern Baptist Convention's resolution against ordaining women ministers. . . .

More than 50 Southern Baptists from four states are expected to attend an all-day seminar Sept. 29 at the First Baptist Church in Chattanooga to speak out against the resolution, described by some church members as "abominable."

"We're not militant, but we're not going to be passive either," said June McEwen, a member of Chattanooga's First Baptist Church and organizer of the gathering.

"The resolution has galvanized us into action. It looks like we're going to have to rock the boat to change their minds."

The Southern Baptist Convention passed a non-binding resolution July 13 in Kansas City asking local Baptist churches to cease ordaining women ministers since "the Bible excludes women from pastoral leadership because the man was first in creation and the woman was first in Edenic fall."

The resolution says that "scriptures teach that women are not in public worship to assume a role of authority over men lest confusion reign in the local church." . . .

The following stand was taken by a group of activist nuns in defiance of the Roman Catholic Church:

By DAVID E. ANDERSON
UPI Religion Writer

WASHINGTON — The National Coalition of American Nuns urged resistance yesterday to the Roman Catholic hierarchy's campaign to make abortion illegal, rejecting "the claim that to be pro-choice is to be pro-abortion. . . .

"We reject any solution which would re-impose the criminalization of abortion, inasmuch as such a situation in no way does away with abortion but results in making safe abortions available only to the rich, leaving the poor women at the mercy of amateurs."

When you write religion stories, use all that you have learned in writing regular news and feature stories—from news criteria to writing. Bring to the assignment a critical sense of what's being asked of you and an understanding of the event and the religion you're reporting on. If you don't understand what's happening or the significance of it, gather, like any good reporter, a lot of answers from a lot of different people. If you do that, you'll not only write good religion stories, but you'll enjoy writing them.

Agriculture. The third-highest average of financial holdings in this country—$42,118—belongs to the "farmer or farm manager," according to the Federal Reserve. (The largest total of financial holdings was claimed by those in the category of "self-employed manager," at an average of $125,983.) When you consider that doctors and lawyers fell into the *fourth*-highest category of investment holdings, at $32,226, you have a better idea of what is meant when we say that farming has been taken over by the big business entrepreneur. We can add to that examples of farms that milk 3,000 cows three times a day and feed lots that accommodate 100,000 head of cattle at one time.

Medium-sized farms, the heart of American agriculture, are declining, often being absorbed by the big farm operations. Nationally, the total value of farms is down $63 billion from a peak of $825 billion in 1981. The U.S. Department of Agriculture reported that thousands of farmers are burdened with huge loans, secured in part by their land and buildings. Requests for new crop loans are being rejected, and many creditors are calling for repayment of the old loans.

Someone has to keep a surveillance on the agricultural scene and keep its economic troubles and problems before the public. That someone is the agriculture editor or reporter.

While problems for the farmer may be mounting, the amount of coverage devoted to those problems in the press is decreasing. H. Carlisle Besuden III, Lexington (Ky.) *Herald-Leader* farm editor and 1981 president of the Newspaper Farm Editors of America, writes of his experience. It is typical of newspaper and broadcast farm news: "I started as farm editor in 1969. I wrote nearly all copy

FIGURE 7.4. H. Carlisle Besuden III of the *Lexington Herald-Leader*, former president of the Newspaper Farm Editors of America. Reprinted courtesy of the *Lexington Herald-Leader*.

on the farm page that ran Sunday, Monday, Wednesday and Friday during the first six or eight years. Now I'm down to a farm page on Sunday that includes my column. But I also write daily stories pertaining to farming and other agriculture topics as they develop."

The present president of NFEA, Bill Kilby, advises farm writers to broaden their perspectives and write rural-related stories during slack times.

But there are plenty of agricultural stories to be written:

> The Agriculture Department will provide $5 million to help finance some of the most critical soil and water conservation projects across the country.

> The practice of adding antibiotics to the feed of healthy animals is controversial because of the chance that killing off most bacteria will allow a population explosion among germs immune to the medicines.
> And now, for the first time, doctors have traced a serious outbreak of human food poisoning to drug-resistant germs that spread from beef cattle routinely fed antibiotics to promote growth.

> A new class of plant-killing substances—laser herbicides—causes weeds to commit suicide while leaving many crops unharmed.

> The muggy lowlands of Memphis have been invaded by stubborn fleas that have built up a resistance to ordinary pesticides.

> Grocery prices will continue falling if a bounty harvest takes place in the next few months. A good harvest of corn and soybeans will tend to lower prices for meat and other foods, according to economist Pat Nichols.

Feature stories during all seasons can be a staple for the farm writer. They can range all the way from harvesting honey, pumpkins and sugar-maple sap to rounding up cattle for the fall market and cutting firewood for winter and evergreen trees for Christmas. You'll probably excel in this because most of the older farm editors, conscripted from the ranks of farmers, will not write feature stories as polished as yours.

As Besuden says, as a media reporter covering the agriculture beat, you have to keep abreast of all facets of agriculture and, above all, be timely in your reporting.

Sports. Covering sporting events for the media involves something more than just a reporting of the score, an important play-by-play account and statistics. Members of the print media audience, for example, have either seen, in person or on television, the events they're going to read about or already know the results from broadcasts.

Good sports stories for all media generally follow this paragraph pattern:

Typical Sports Story Form and Elements

PARAGRAPH 1

Lead
1. Turning point in game, *or*
2. Anecdote or incident, *or*
3. Effect of win or loss

PARAGRAPH 2
1. Elaboration upon paragraph 1, *and/or*
2. Key plays or strategy
3. (Possibly, game score)

PARAGRAPH 3

Body
1. Significant quote from coach or player (could be in paragraph 2)
2. Game score and effect of win or loss (if not presented in other paragraphs)

PARAGRAPHS 4–8
1. Size of crowd; where played
2. Game highlights

SUCCEEDING PARAGRAPHS
1. Injuries
2. Star players
3. Change in standings
4. Length of game
5. Post-game interview quotes

CONCLUSION

STATISTICS

No one can anticipate all game events or incidents, but the outlined sequence will serve as a general organizational pattern until you become more familiar with sports reporting. If something unforeseen occurs—lightning shuts down the electric power but the game is continued—that, of course may be your lead.

There is one thing you *can* rely on, however: The outline can serve as your checklist for sports coverage of most sporting events. If you don't include the items in the paragraphs indicated, you should probably include them in succeeding paragraphs.

Let's look at some football story leads:

> By PATRICIA PAQUETTE
> KNOXVILLE, Tenn. (AP) — Tennessee football coach Johnny Majors had won only one season opener in his seven years with the Volunteers before his team defeated Washington State 34-27 Saturday night.
>
> "It's good to win a first game after having some hard-fought losses our last two years," Majors said.

Another Associated Press story started this way:

> PITTSBURGH (AP) — Robbie Bosco, the latest in a long line of Brigham Young's prolific passers, led a 50-yard touchdown pass to Adam Haysbert with 1:37 left in the game Saturday as the Cougars rallied from an 11-point deficit to shock third-ranked Pittsburgh 20-14.

There's much too much in that lead. It would have been better if the writer had left "as the Cougars rallied from an 11-point deficit" for the next paragraph. Still, that lead is not as bad as this one:

Bryan Stewart took Oklahoma 72 yards in 29 seconds and lobbed a 12-yard touchdown pass to Cameron Hess with seven seconds left and Jahlal Linn returned an interception 59 yards on the final play as the defending national champion pulled out an incredible 21-13 victory over 15th-ranked Florida Saturday night.

Not content with leaving his readers breathless with this paragraph and its seven numbers, this sports writer then writes another with eight numbers for readers to juggle:

The 10th-ranked Raiders, who upset the No. 1 Knights 20-16 six nights earlier, were 41 seconds away from having the nation's longest winning streak snapped at 12 games when they took a 20-19 lead on a five-yard scoring pass from freshman walk-on quarterback Cedric Anderson to Eddie Heyward.

The following lead does more of what it ought to do:

NEW ORLEANS (AP) — Getting his first college start, sophomore quarterback Don Smith ran for two touchdowns and threw for another to lead Mississippi State to a 30-3 victory over Tulane in a college football season opener.

Sports writer Larry Woody does it even better with this lead:

AUSTIN, Texas — Texas buried Auburn, along with the Tiger's hopes for a national championship, on the Lone Prairie last night.
The final score was 35-27, and, in the final analysis, it was apparent the Tigers succumbed to self-inflicted wounds.

Sports writers, like other reporters, should observe the 25-word-or-less rule that we suggested earlier.

Most of the more interesting sports stories are not written under the simple straight news story formula. It is a combination of straight news writing and feature writing.

FIGURE 7.5. Some of sports writer Larry Woody's best copy featured New York Yankees powerhouse Yogi Berra. Reprinted with permission of *The Tennessean*.

"Writing a sports story under a straight news format is the most simple task in the world," Larry Woody, sports writer for *The Tennessean,* said. "It's also the most boring. You can tune in the 10:30 sports on TV to find out what the final game score is. Since sports are supposed to be played for fun, generally speaking, sports should be written—and read—for fun. So I try to spice up my stories with humor and/or unique twists whenever possible. The quicker and snappier the leads, the better."

By LARRY WOODY

ATHENS, Ga. — Georgia did in No. 2-ranked Clemson yesterday, 26-23. And while the stunned visitors were wondering what happened, there was really no mystery.

The Butler did it.

Kevin Butler booted an SEC record-tying 60-yard field goal with 11 seconds showing on the clock to give his underdawgs the upset victory.

There's no rule that says a story can't be entertaining as well as informative, Woody says. Sports lend themselves especially well to feature writing because they are played by people, and people provide the best feature material.

By DAVID CLIMER*

KNOXVILLE, Tenn. — Around Gibbs Hall, the University of Tennessee athletic dorm, Tony Robinson is recognized as one of the better backgammon players.

In explaining both his prowess and love for the game, Robinson says simply, "I like rolling the dice."

In a sense, rolling the dice is exactly what this confident yet untested quarterback will be doing tonight when Tennessee opens its football season against Washington State.

When you finally "arrive" on a sports staff, you'll be allowed to write your own column. When that happens, you'll really be able to display your creativity. Read what Ben Byrd of *The Knoxville Journal* wrote, in part, for his football predictions in his "Byrd's Eye View" column:

Byrd's Free Thought Association football predictions:

KANSAS AT VANDERBILT— ... Vanderbilt people are very conscious of their superiority to those beneath them on the social ladder, and having to watch Commodore teams play against teams from ordinary, state-supported schools in the Southeastern Conference is quite an ordeal. "We're trying to be as tolerant as we can," said a Vanderbilt official. "But players from Tennessee and those other SEC schools sweat so much. I mean, really, there is a limit, you know." The official vigorously denied that Commodore players are much like athletes elsewhere. "Vanderbilt players do not sweat," he said. "On rare occasion they do perspire, very lightly, but they never sweat." VANDERBILT.

The sports section also includes stories other than basketball, baseball, golf, etc., that most broadcasters don't have time for:

The Camulet Run, featuring a 10-kilometer and a one-mile fun run will be held Sept. 15 in Hermitage.

---

* Reprinted with permission of *The Tennessean.*

By LARRY TAFT*

There'll be a new kid on the block tonight when the 46th annual Tennessee Walking Horse draws to a close with the crowning of the World Grand Championship.

Runners from seven states will compete Saturday in the fourth annual "Idiots' Run"—a 115-mile race over country roads in Houston County.

The Carl Sandburg Tennis Tournament will be held at Fisher Park in Hamilton Sept. 3-5.

West View School will conduct sign-ups for the seventh- and eighth-grade chess team at 10 a.m. Wednesday.

Curling, bowling, stock car races—they're all important to the sports reader. If you report them in a straightforward news fashion, they will be read. If you report them in writing tinged with imagination, however, they will be relished.

Billboard News

Sometimes, because of media time and space constraints, you may be called upon to write according to formulas. That is especially true with billboard news.

Billboard news involves the events that remind us of life's inevitable cycles: birth, engagements, weddings, deaths and weather. Forms for the first four events are usually given to family members to fill in. The stories are then written according to formulas for births, engagements, weddings or obituaries. Some media will insist that you do exactly that. If a prominent family is involved, you would take cognizance of the formulas provided here as well as the newswriting instruction given earlier. Let's look at some formulas for writing news events.

Births. Although babies are a joy to hold and behold, the announcements of their arrivals are cut and dried. Some newspapers even carry them in the same column as realty transfers, lawsuits, and the like:

Poughkeepsie Births

January 28

Matthew E. Wilhelm, son of Dr. Albert E. and Patricia Wilhelm, 77 Womack Ave.; 7 pounds, 5 ounces; 20 inches.

Another way of handling the birth notice is in a short paragraph:

Dr. and Mrs. Albert E. Wilhelm, 77 Womack Ave., are parents of a boy, Matthew, born Jan. 28 in St. Thomas Hospital.

Other pertinent information may be added in small towns, such as whom the baby was named after and how the mother is doing. Country correspondents may even use such words as "proud parents," "blessed event," and "bouncing baby boy," but professional reporters are forbidden that language.

Engagements and Weddings. You may live to see the day when *all* media charge money to publish engagement and wedding announcements. Those that do charge think of the announcements as being in the same category as legal

* Reprinted courtesy of *The Knoxville Journal*.

notices. Most newspapers give forms to parents to fill out and then write formula stories from them:

> Mr. and Mrs. William A. Morse, 35 Halsted Place, Rye, N.Y., announce the engagement of their daughter, Janet, to Mr. Paul Craighead, son of Mr. and Mrs. Robert Craighead of Syracuse.
>
> The bride-elect is a graduate of the University of Colorado with a master's degree in elementary guidance. She is presently employed by the St. Lawrence County Board of Education in Canton, N.Y.
>
> The future groom is a graduate of St. Lawrence University with an advanced degree in counseling. He is employed by the county school system as a guidance counselor.

Marriage announcements read the same way. Sometimes parents are no longer married or are living apart, and that may be noted. Still, all are formula stories:

> Patricia Sue Grimes and Richard M. Hanna were married Saturday at the LaPorte Christ Episcopal Church with the Rev. Richard B. Alfred officiating.
>
> The bride is the daughter of Mr. and Mrs. Donald Williams of Joliet, Ill. The bridegroom is the son of Mrs. Nancy H. Hanna of Lansing, Mich., and Marvin L. Hanna of Joliet.
>
> The bride was attended by Anne Schinbeckler of Brockport, N.Y.; Beth Null of Kings Mountain, N.C.; Marilyn Goss of Austin, Texas; Eleanor Mitchell, Donna Watson, Jeanne Watson, Brenda Johnson and Susan Sampson, flower girls, all of Joliet.
>
> The bridegroom's attendants were Gerald Burnham, Larry Peterson, Harry Frain, Allen Oleson, William Ross, Larry Burnham and John Martin Johnson, all of Lansing.
>
> A reception at the Woodruff Hotel was given by the bride's parents.
>
> The couple will live in Rock Island, Ill., after a wedding trip to Jekyll Island, Ga.

Monotonous though all these stories may be, remember that they are read with avid interest by readers who know the persons involved.

Obituaries. Most obituaries tend to be formula stories. Blanks are given to undertakers and reporters to help gather information about deaths, and stories are written from them. Some take this form:

> KLAMATH FALLS — Kenneth G. Dugger, 87, of Black Diamond, died Wednesday in Harton Regional Hospital, Hartsville. Services 2 p.m. tomorrow at Blood and Grant Funeral Home.

Others appear this way:

> OMAHA — Funeral services for Sarah T. Henly, 86, of Franklin, were held at 3:30 p.m. yesterday at Harris Funeral Home with the Rev. Tom Hubbard officiating. Burial was in Maryland Cemetery.
>
> Mrs. Henly died June 21 at her daughter's home in Franklin.
>
> Mrs. Henly was born April 12, 1898, in Jackson County. The widow of James T. Henly, who died Feb. 24, 1983, she was a homemaker and a member of the Amanda Park Church of God.
>
> Her family includes two sons, Forrest Guy Henly of Mink Creek,

Idaho, and Wyatt T. Henly of Brush Prairie; a daughter, Juanita Rudd, of La Junta, Colo.; and six grandchildren.

The Harris Funeral Home was in charge of the arrangements.

When you are assigned to obits, all you have to do is place copies of previous obits in front of you—obits for people who have just died, who have yet to be buried, or who have been buried. Then plug in the names of the dead and the living. When a prominent citizen or personage dies, however, you're allowed to be creative:

> Truman Capote, 59, the bluntly opinionated author of such best-selling books as *Breakfast at Tiffany's* and *In Cold Blood*, died yesterday.
> Capote was found dead at the mansion of close friend Joanne Carson.

> Jim Fixx, the man who brought jogging to millions of Americans, died of a heart attack this morning while jogging in northern Vermont. He wrote the best seller *The Complete Book of Running*.

If it's a prominent citizen, you'll go to the newspaper morgue and write your lead based on the most prominent accomplishment of that person:

> Archibald Scott III, mayor of Junction City from 1952 to 1964, died today at Baptist General Hospital.
> While Scott was mayor, Junction City enjoyed its greatest industrial and tourist growth ever.

When you write obituaries, above all be accurate and respectful. Newspaper obits are clipped out, laminated, and placed in family Bibles as records.

Weather. The National Weather Service provides weather reports for wire services, and most major newspapers carry the reports on the inside pages. You may be asked to call up the weather service nearest you for a report on local conditions and write a story about the report. If the National Weather Service, located in the major cities, is too distant, you would call the Department of Transportation, which provides local weather information for airline pilots.

Weather stories are usually one or two paragraphs long. Although they may be tedious to write, everyone wants to know something about the weather—if only to talk about it. Radio broadcasters repeat the forecast at least once an hour. Television reporters will find the weather report one of the most watched portions of the broadcast. A brief paragraph can take care of most audience needs:

```
Today's forecast calls for partly cloudy skies with a
30 percent chance of afternoon thundershowers and highs
in the mid-80s. Humidity will be in the 50s. Lows tonight
in the mid-70s. Winds southeast at 5 to 15 mph. Mostly
sunny tomorrow with highs in the mid-80s. Winds east at 5
to 8 mph. Yesterday's high was 85. Last night's low was
60.
```

But when Mother Nature breaks loose on a record-breaking high or low or when a major storm hits, you will be called upon to do something more than write a paragraph. You may have to write about the destructive nature of the storm or its effects. You may write about how people are beating a heat or cold wave. There will be endless varieties of leads and stories for you to write, depending on the weather.

SUMMARY

Newswriting matures and gains polish through the experience of writing complex news stories. Juggling the facts that shape summary and salient-feature or suspended-interest leads and structuring a story that fleshes out those leads requires creativity and an understanding of how readers process information. These more unusual leads help to set a story apart from all the others competing for the readers' attention and pack more of a punch than most simple news leads. Why? Because they sit astride stories that contain more facts, more detail, and bigger webs in need of untangling. They "sell" the story.

Other techniques, such as those suggested for interview articles, help to keep readers' interest high.

Today's jam-packed information pipeline has spawned a considerable amount of specialty writing, from science and business to religion and sports. Each specialty has its own styles and patterns. Writers who develop a specialty learn to mix the conventions of that particular segment of journalism with the skills they've honed during doing other types of writing. Such writers have usually learned the key principle of mass media writing: Vary style and structure with the subject matter and the audience to be reached.

EXERCISES

1. The paragraphs below come from a news story with a summary lead. The news story has been scrambled, as you can see. Your assignment is to cut out the paragraphs and assemble them in a proper, logical order. Start assembling the story by determining the summary lead and continuing from there.

Weinberger aroused Riegle's ire when he appeared before the Senate Budget Committee to defend Reagan's fiscal 1984 budget request for $238.6 billion in defense outlays, an increase of 10 percent after inflation.

Mrs. Kassebaum went after Enders at a hearing on the administration's policy of military aid to the Salvadoran government in its battle against leftist guerrillas.

It was the members of Congress, though, who had the initiative.

Other lawmakers questioned Reagan's sincerity in saying he wants arms control and a bipartisan budget.

It was a far cry from the administration's honeymoon days of two years ago—and not all the strong words came from Democrats.

"I believe that you are damaging our national security," Sen. Donald M. Riegle, D-Mich., told Defense Secretary Caspar W. Weinberger.

Some of the lawmakers' targets gave as good as they got. Weinberger, for instance, told Riegle, "Everything you have said is both insulting and wrong."

At a hearing on Reagan's nomination of Kenneth L. Adelman, now at the United Nations, to be arms control chief, Sen. Joseph Biden, D-Del., did not mince words.

"How do we get off the dime we're on?" Sen. Nancy Landon Kassebaum, R-Kan., asked Assistant Secretary of State Thomas O. Enders in a hearing on El Salvador.

"There's a military stalemate; there seems to be a political stalemate," she said. "How do we get off the dime we're on?"

For President Reagan's emissaries to Capitol Hill last week, it was a little like walking into a buzz saw. Clearly, the honeymoon is over.

"You give every appearance of being an inflexible ideologue when it comes to assessing the defense needs of our country," Riegle said. "By your truly fanatical insistence on defense increases that are larger than needed, larger than we can afford, I believe that you are damaging our national security."

"Some of us, like me, just don't believe that he (Reagan) believes in arms control," Biden said. "I do not think there is serious negotiation under way."

That was the way it went last week. Some of the president's top lieutenants ran into unusually harsh criticism from Congress on both domestic and foreign issues.

"Now that we're coming in for a crash, we're being invited into the cockpit," said Sen. James Sasser, D-Tenn.

At a Senate Budget Committee hearing Democrats questioned the president's sincerity in wanting a bipartisan spending plan.

PASTE EXERCISE 1 HERE.

2. Write a summary news lead story from the following set of facts. (Remember the graphic configuration for summary news stories.)

False alarm sounded three times at Joliet Senior High School today.

Disgruntled students appear to have been ones to set off alarms.

Ten students suspended for one week.

They had been wearing black armbands.

In protest against other students being suspended.

The three students, smoking marijuana at a football game, suspended for one week also.

Food fight started but quickly quelled in cafeteria.

Principal Richard Vibelius commented that there was general unrest.

"Not so much unrest because of suspensions but because of spring being just around the corner."

Sees no continuation of "incidents" in the near future.

3. The paragraphs below have been scrambled. Properly assembled, they will compose a summary lead news story.* Cut out each of the paragraphs and paste them in their proper order.

Patterson's Office has issued 5,138 pistol permits in the last 12 months, but he said it is hard to determine the number of handguns in this city of 143,000.

None of the patrols carry guns, but Stevenson said the time between burglaries in the area is now counted in months, not days.

The district attorney has concluded William Shelton of Huntsville acted within the law in shooting Quincy Adam Teague, 21, as Teague stood over him Dec. 30 with a gun demanding money.

Not all Huntsville residents are using guns to respond to crime. Fred and Chris Stevenson have organized their neighbors to fight back without guns.

"In these three incidents the criminals were the victims and rightfully so. It will make the next armed robber or rapist think before he does something here in Huntsville," Vizzini said.

Cramer said Agnes Goodman, a store owner who killed Robert E. Rice, 18, while the man was robbing her business Jan. 4, also appears to have acted within the law.

"We had a lot of vandalism down here several years ago—10 acts of crime within a few houses over a period of several days—and four of us got together and began asking ourselves if there isn't something we can do about this," Stevenson said.

"I think it was a coincidence that those three shootings happened so close together, but they have had the effect of sending a message to the general public that, yes, burglaries and robberies are a problem, and to the criminal element that they should think twice about committing a crime," said Madison County District Attorney Robert Cramer.

The couple formed the city's first Community Watch program in 1979. Now there are nine such groups of residents who report suspicious people and suspicious activity to the city police.

"Yes, I would shoot to kill if someone broke into my house," said County Sheriff Joe Patterson. "Every home should have a weapon of some type; there's too much meanness in the world. Everyone should be trained and know how to operate a gun."

Property owners who killed three intruders in separate incidents during a six-day period were within the law and may have performed a public service, the county district attorney says.

Their organization, known as Jones Valley Community Watch, includes 265 volunteer members who patrol a 10-mile area in two-person teams with mobile radios connected to a volunteer-operated base station.

"The public is sick and tired of being the victim of a crime, and they want the criminals to be the victims," Huntsville Police Chief Sal Vizzini said Friday.

* Reprinted with permission of *The Tennessean*.

PASTE EXERCISE 3 HERE.

4. Write a news story for your paper based on these facts from public records at University City Criminal Justice Complex.

General Sessions Court Results

KELLEY AVIS, Route 19, Britton Springs Road, charged with assault with the intent to commit murder. Dismissed due to the failure of the victim to appear as a prosecution witness.

TRACY HARDY, L-88 Hillview Heights, charged with receiving stolen property. Fined $50 and court costs and given six-month suspended sentence.

RANDY MALLARD, 501st Signal Battalion, charged with writing a bad check. Dismissed with the defendant to pay court costs.

ALVIN SMITH, 1128 Chickasaw, Paris, charged with driving while intoxicated. Fined $250 and court costs and sentenced to serve two days of an 11-month, 29-day suspended sentence. He also was ordered to attend an alcohol abuse program, and his driver's license was revoked for 11 months and 29 days.

BARBARA CLARKE, Route 3, Dover, charged with writing a bad check. Fined $75 and court costs and given an 11-month, 29-day suspended sentence.

ROLLY WHITWORTH, E-80 Chateau Apartments, charged with possession of marijuana. Fined $250 and court costs and given an 11-month, 29-day suspended sentence.

JOY WATKINS, E-80 Chateau Apartments, charged with possession of marijuana. Dismissed in a settlement.

SABRINA SANFORD, 2207 Stokes Road, charged with writing a bad check. Dismissed in a state's motion.

ANTHONY LEWIS, 606 W. Thompkins Lane, charged with driving while intoxicated and possession of marijuana. Both charges were dismissed as a result of state motions.

GEORGE SMITH, Route 1, Box 55, Adams, charged with writing a bad check. Fined court costs.

LINDA ROLLINS, 2204 Trenton Road, charged with two counts of writing a bad check. One count was dismissed on a prosecution motion; she was fined court costs on the second count.

RAYMOND TOLLIVER, Route 5, Ashland City, charged with driving while intoxicated. Fined $250 and court costs and sentenced to serve two days of an 11-month, 29-day suspended sentence. He was also ordered to attend an alcohol abuse program, and his driver's license was revoked for 11 months and 29 days.

5. The paragraphs below have been scrambled. Properly assembled, they will compose a follow-up story. As a matter of fact, there are *two* follow-up stories loosely strung together with this phrase: "In other court action. . . ." Cut out each of the paragraphs and paste them in proper order.

Merriman is incarcerated at the Joliet State Penitentiary, where he is serving sentences for joy riding and burglary.

Juvenile Court Judge Paul Isbell previously ruled that Estes should stand trial as an adult. He remained in Westchester County Jail, with bond set at $10,000.

Case's ruling came Monday afternoon, less than two weeks after Newark attorneys Russell Brami and Kelley Sweeney argued that pre-trial publicity could prevent Merriman from receiving a fair trial in Westchester County.

In other court action yesterday, Case took under advisement the matter of whether William Estes, 18, of Thayer, should be tried as a juvenile or an adult on charges in the November slaying of his mother. Case withheld a decision following a lengthy hearing in Criminal Court.

Criminal Court Judge Raymond Case has denied a request to move out of Westchester County the trial of Harold Merriman, charged in the 1985 slaying of Nora Kirkwood.

Merriman, 24, of New Paltz, is charged with kidnapping and then killing Kirkwood the night of July 16, 1985. Her skeletal remains were found in Erie County last September.

Estes, 17 at the time, is charged with fatally shooting his mother, Edna Mae Estes, 35, at their Cottonwood Road home.

"After hearing the proof, the arguments of counsel and reviewing briefs submitted, the court is not satisfied that the defendant would be unable to obtain a fair and impartial trial in this county," Case wrote.

PASTE EXERCISE 5 HERE.

6. Write a salient-feature news lead story from the following sets of facts. (Remember the graphic configurations for salient-feature news stories.)

   a. Checking at the local fire station at Alexandria, you find these things on the log:

   Cat in tree at 10 Woodview St.

   Calico cat belonging to Suzanne and Samantha Decker.

   Twins belonging to Charlie and Kim Decker.

   Fireman Bob Harwood climbs 50 feet in oak tree for cat.

   Drops the last 10 feet coming down the tree when dead limb breaks; Harwood breaks left leg.

   Doing "just fine" at General Hospital.

   Cat's doing fine also—cat landed on top of Harwood.

b. Texaco gasoline truck overturned on outskirts of town, one mile west on I-40. Gas floods sewer lines for two blocks around.

Also on highway and in ditches.

Cars rerouted from Interstate Highway 40 through side streets.

Serious for about two hours until gas flushed away.

Four families evacuated because of sewer-line gas.

Fire Chief Charles Hochanadel says, "The firemen followed regular catastrophe procedures set up beforehand for just such a happening."

7. Write a news story for your paper based on the facts in the police department offense report in Figure 7.6.

FIGURE 7.6. Police department offense report. Reprinted with permission of the Cookeville Police Department, Cookeville, Tennessee.

1. Offense: Larceny	2. Classification: of Auto	TN 0710100	84	01	27	0745
3. Location of Incident: 473 South Bowfield		4. Zone: 8	5. Date/Time Occurred: 01-26-84/2130 to		6. Date/Time Police Arrived: 01-27-84/0750	

7. Victim: Mark Wilkerson	Sex: M	Race: W	D.O.B.: 06-17-56	8. Home Address: 473 South Bowfield 01-27-84/0745	9. Phone: 526-3365
10. Business Address: Dale Industries		11. Business Phone: 528-0696		12. Person Arrested: None at time of report	Sex / Race / D.O.B.
13. Complainant: Victim	Sex: M	Race: W	D.O.B.: 06-17-56	14. Home Address: #8	15. Phone: #9
16. Witnesses' Name: a. None known	Sex	Race	D.O.B.	17. Home Address	18. Phone

19. VEHICLE	a. License No. (LIC): 22-6B45	b. State: TN	c. Year: 1984	d. Type: PC	e. Vehicle Identification No. (VIN): F3F84G536235F	f. Year: 1983	g. Make: Ford	h. Model: LTD
	i. Style: 4Dr.	j. Color: Black	k. Other Description or Damage: None					

20. WEAPON	Gen. Description: None	Serial # (SN)	Make	Caliber	Type

21. PROPERTY	Description: Above described vehicle	22. Total Value: $9,000.00

23. Reporting Officer: Tom Smith	Badge: 191	Unit: P-21	24. Approving Supervisor: Sgt. John Thomas

24. NARRATIVE: Give All Information Necessary, Tell Who, What, When, Where, Why And How The Incident Occured. Give Detailed Descriptions Of Any Suspects. All Witnesses' Names, Sex, Race, D.O.B., Addresses And Phone Numbers Should Be Recorded. If A Juvenile Is Involved In Any Way In This Offense, List His Parents' Or Guardians' Names, Addresses And Phone Numbers As Well As The School He Attends.

On January 27, 1984 at about 0745 hours, writer answered a call to 473 South Bowfield in reference to a stolen vehicle. Mr. Mark Wilkerson told writer that he parked the above described vehicle in his driveway at about 2130 hours on 01-26-84. He discovered the vehicle was missing at 0745 hours on this date.

Mr. Wilkerson said that the vehicle was locked. He heard nothing suspicious during the night.

STATUS	Active ☒	Pending ☐	Inactive ☐	Closed ☐	Assigned To: Detective Becker	Authority: CPD	Date: 01-27-84
NCIC/TIES Entries Have Been Made By: V272439146 G.Jackson				Date: 01-27-84	All Items Have Been Cleared From NCIC/TIES By:		Date

TDS-BLER 2-C (7/76) – SF-0567   RECORD COPY

8. Write a follow-up story to the one you wrote in Exercise 7, based on the police department supplementary report in Figure 7.7.

1. Offense: Recovered	2. Classification: Stolen Vehicle	TN 0710100 ORI	84 YEAR	01 MONTH	27 DAY 0745
3. Location of Incident: Mayton's Gap Road		4. Zone: NA	5. Date/Time Occurred: 01-27-84/1535		6. Date/Time This Supplement: 01-27-84/1655
7. Victim: Mark Wilkerson	Sex: M	Race: W	D.O.B. 06-17-56	8. Home Address: 473 South Bowfield	9. Phone: 526-3365
10. Business Address: Dale Industries		11. Business Phone: 528-0696	12. Person Arrested: None at time of report	Sex / Race	D.O.B.
13. Complainant: Victim	Sex: M	Race: W	D.O.B. 06-17-56	14. Home Address: #8	15. Phone: #9
16. Additional Property: Describe: 1983 Ford LTD, 4-door, black					17. Total Value: $9,000.00
18. Reporting Officer: Tom Smith/Detective Mel Becker		Badge: 191	Unit: P-21	19. Approving Supervisor: Sgt. John Thomas	

20. NARRATIVE: Describe Any Additional Information Discovered About Or Investigative Effort Expended On The Reported Offense. Be Careful To Include The Name, Sex, Race, Date Of Birth, Address, Phone Number And Relationship To Case Of Any Additional Persons Referred To In This Supplement.

On January 27, 1984 at about 1535 hours, Mr. Mark Wilkerson's 1983 Ford LTD was located in a secluded area on Mayton's Gap Road. The vehicle was towed by McClain's Wrecker Service to the Cookeville Police Department for processing.

STATUS: Active ☐ Pending ☐ Inactive ☐ Closed ☐ Assigned To: Authority: Date:
NCIC/TIES Entries Have Been Made By: Date: All Items Have Been Cleared From NCIC/TIES By: B. Henley Date:
TDS-BLER 3-B (7/76)   RECORD COPY

FIGURE 7.7. Police department supplementary report. Reprinted with permission of the Cookeville Police Department, Cookeville, Tennessee.

News for Newspapers: Complex Stories 181

9. Write a story for your newspaper based on the facts in the police department arrest form in Figure 7.8.

1. Last Name	First	Middle	TN ORI 0710100	84 YEAR	01 MONTH	27 DAY	1141
White	Margaret	L.					

2. Aliases or Nicknames	Sex	Race	D.O.B.	3. Place of Birth (POB)	4. C.I.D. #
None known	F	W	10-25-46	Putnam County	

5. Home Address	6. Fingerprint Classification (HENRY)
43 Miller Avenue, Cookeville	NA

7. Height	8. Weight	9. Hair	10. Eyes	11. Marks, Scars, Tatoos, Physical Defects, Medical Appliances (SMT)
5'3"	113	Blk.	Grn.	None visible

12. Soc. Sec. or Military Ser. # (SOC/ASN)	13. Driver's Lic. # (OLN) Type	State	14. Occupation and/or Business Address
413-65-8483	None		Unemployed

15. Complainant	Sex	Race	D.O.B.	16. Home Address	17. Phone
Gene Holiday	M	W	Unknown	Manager, JJ's Discount Store	526-9876

18. Witnesses' Name	Sex	Race	D.O.B.	19. Home Address	20. Phone
a. Pat Burgess	F	W	Unknown	a. Clerk, JJ's Discount Store	526-9876
b.				b.	b.

21. VEHICLE — NA

22. WEAPON — None

23. PROPERTY — One lady's blouse, price $8.86

24. Location of Arrest	25. Date of Arrest	26. Number Others Arrested
JJ's Discount Store	01-27-84	none

27. Charges	28. TCA Code	29. Court	30. Date	31. Final Disposition
a. Shoplifting	a.	a. G.S.	a. 02-16-84	

32. Arresting Officer	Badge	Unit	33. Approving Supervisor
Gary Farris	184	P23	Sgt. John Thomas

34. NARRATIVE: Give All Details Of Arrest Including Probable Cause For Each Charge And Any Action Taken By The Arresting Officers. If Juvenile Arrest, Note Parent's Or Guardian's Name, Address And Phone Number As Well As School Juvenile Attends. List The Name, Sex, Race And D.O.B. Of All Others Arrested With This Subject. If Arrested On Warrant, So Indicate And Note Warrant Number.

Subject was apprehended by store personnel as she left the store with merchandise concealed in her purse. Subject was arrested in the office at JJ's Discount Store. She was transported by writer to the City Jail where a warrant for Shoplifting was signed by Pat Burgess, an employee of JJ's.

FIGURE 7.8. Police department arrest report. Reprinted with permission of the Cookeville Police Department, Cookeville, Tennessee.

10. Write a story for your newspaper based on the facts that appear on the accident report forms in Figures 7.9, 7.10 and 7.11.

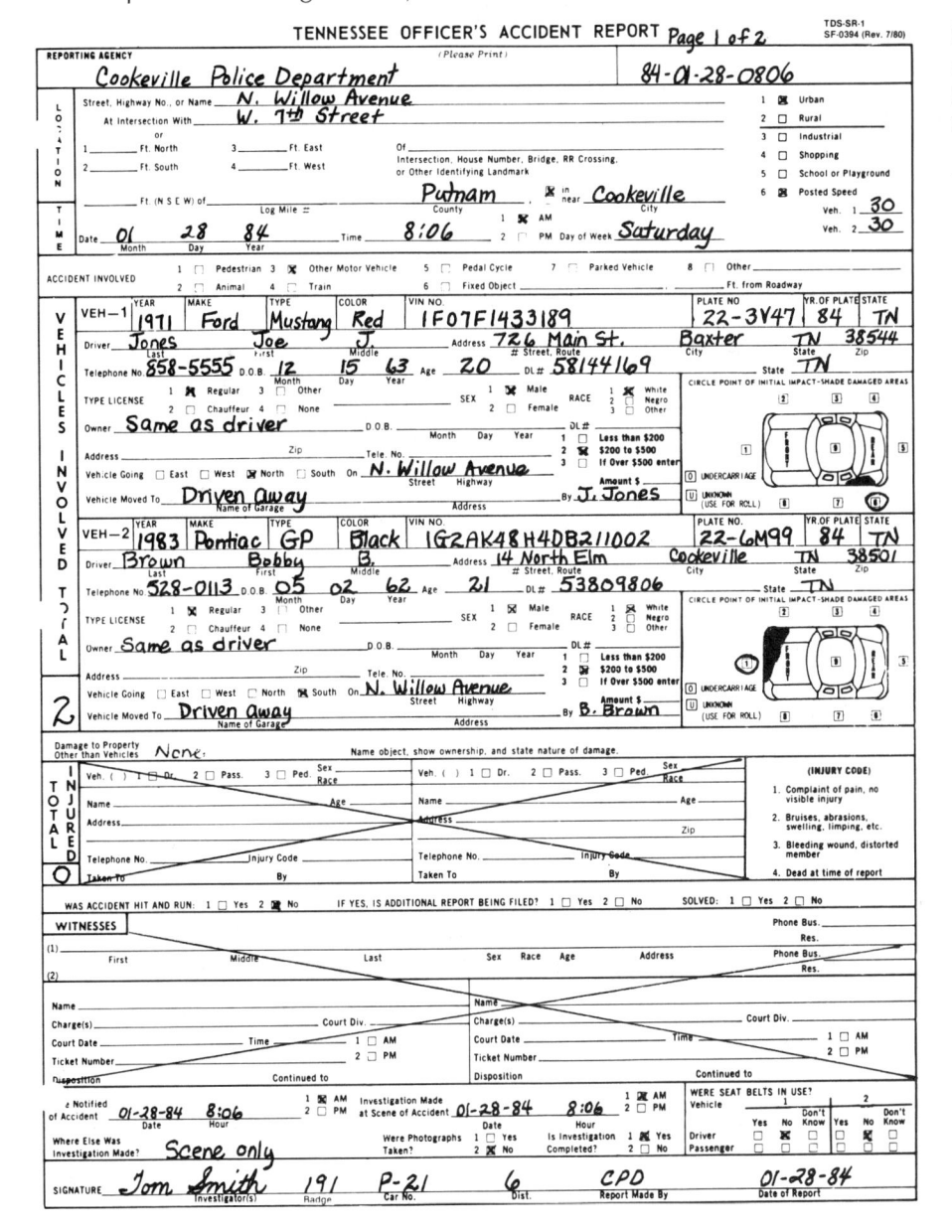

FIGURE 7.9. Police department accident report. Reprinted with permission of the Cookeville Police Department, Cookeville, Tennessee.

FIGURE 7.10. Police department accident report. Reprinted with permission of the Cookeville Police Department, Cookeville, Tennessee.

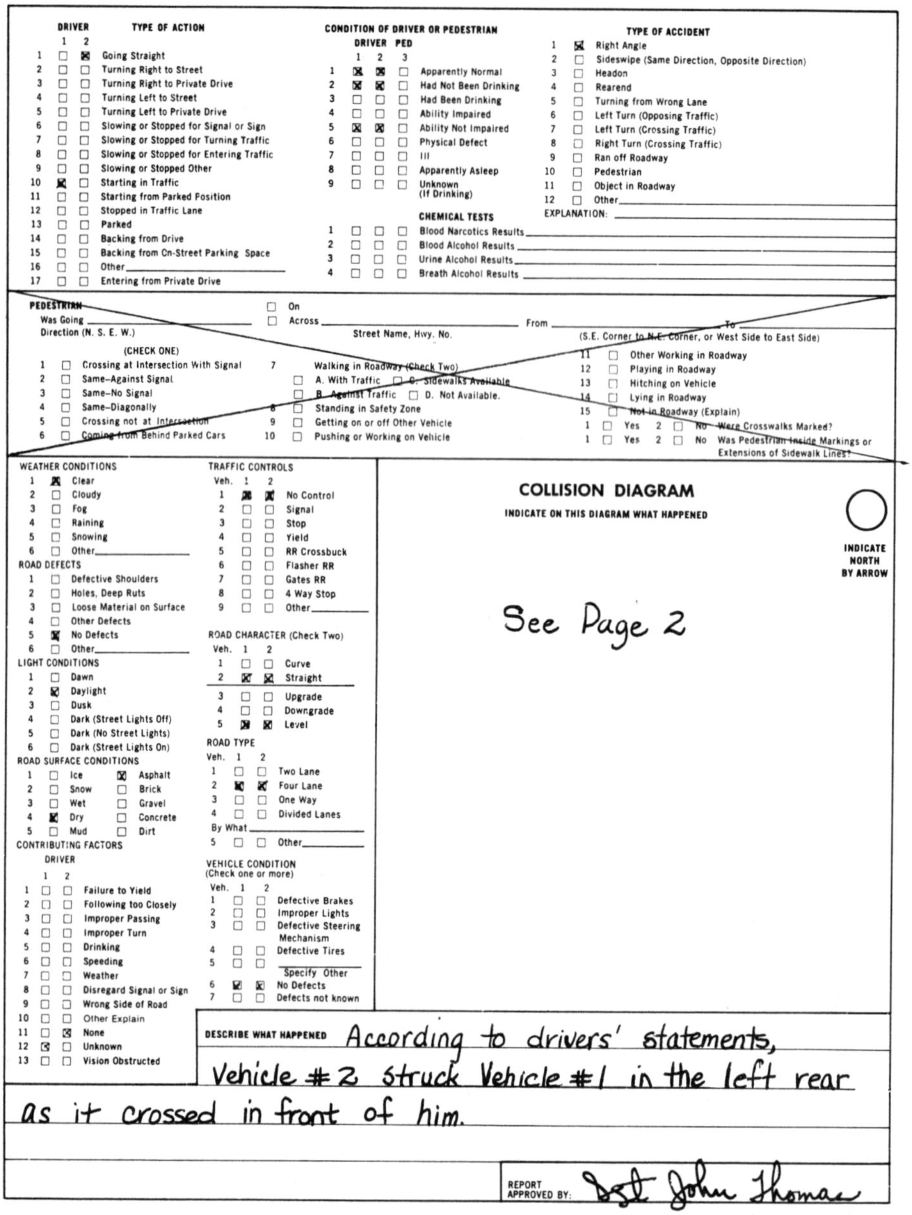

DRIVER 1 2 — TYPE OF ACTION
1 ☐ ☒ Going Straight
2 ☐ ☐ Turning Right to Street
3 ☐ ☐ Turning Right to Private Drive
4 ☐ ☐ Turning Left to Street
5 ☐ ☐ Turning Left to Private Drive
6 ☐ ☐ Slowing or Stopped for Signal or Sign
7 ☐ ☐ Slowing or Stopped for Turning Traffic
8 ☐ ☐ Slowing or Stopped for Entering Traffic
9 ☐ ☐ Slowing or Stopped Other
10 ☒ ☐ Starting in Traffic
11 ☐ ☐ Starting from Parked Position
12 ☐ ☐ Stopped in Traffic Lane
13 ☐ ☐ Parked
14 ☐ ☐ Backing from Drive
15 ☐ ☐ Backing from On-Street Parking Space
16 ☐ ☐ Other______
17 ☐ ☐ Entering from Private Drive

CONDITION OF DRIVER OR PEDESTRIAN — DRIVER 1 2, PED 3
1 ☒ ☒ ☐ Apparently Normal
2 ☒ ☒ ☐ Had Not Been Drinking
3 ☐ ☐ ☐ Had Been Drinking
4 ☐ ☐ ☐ Ability Impaired
5 ☒ ☒ ☐ Ability Not Impaired
6 ☐ ☐ ☐ Physical Defect
7 ☐ ☐ ☐ Ill
8 ☐ ☐ ☐ Apparently Asleep
9 ☐ ☐ ☐ Unknown (If Drinking)

CHEMICAL TESTS
1 ☐ ☐ ☐ Blood Narcotics Results______
2 ☐ ☐ ☐ Blood Alcohol Results______
3 ☐ ☐ ☐ Urine Alcohol Results______
4 ☐ ☐ ☐ Breath Alcohol Results______

TYPE OF ACCIDENT
1 ☒ Right Angle
2 ☐ Sideswipe (Same Direction, Opposite Direction)
3 ☐ Headon
4 ☐ Rearend
5 ☐ Turning from Wrong Lane
6 ☐ Left Turn (Opposing Traffic)
7 ☐ Left Turn (Crossing Traffic)
8 ☐ Right Turn (Crossing Traffic)
9 ☐ Ran off Roadway
10 ☐ Pedestrian
11 ☐ Object in Roadway
12 ☐ Other______
EXPLANATION: ______

~~PEDESTRIAN~~
Was Going ______ ☐ On ☐ Across ______ From ______ To ______
Direction (N. S. E. W.) — Street Name, Hwy. No. — (S.E. Corner to N.E. Corner, or West Side to East Side)
(CHECK ONE)
1 ☐ Crossing at Intersection With Signal
2 ☐ Same–Against Signal
3 ☐ Same–No Signal
4 ☐ Same–Diagonally
5 ☐ Crossing not at Intersection
6 ☐ Coming from Behind Parked Cars
7 Walking in Roadway (Check Two)
☐ A. With Traffic ☐ C. Sidewalks Available
☐ B. Against Traffic ☐ D. Not Available.
8 ☐ Standing in Safety Zone
9 ☐ Getting on or off Other Vehicle
10 ☐ Pushing or Working on Vehicle
11 ☐ Other Working in Roadway
12 ☐ Playing in Roadway
13 ☐ Hitching on Vehicle
14 ☐ Lying in Roadway
15 ☐ Not in Roadway (Explain)
1 ☐ Yes 2 ☐ No Were Crosswalks Marked?
1 ☐ Yes 2 ☐ No Was Pedestrian Inside Markings or Extensions of Sidewalk Lines?

WEATHER CONDITIONS
1 ☒ Clear
2 ☐ Cloudy
3 ☐ Fog
4 ☐ Raining
5 ☐ Snowing
6 ☐ Other______

ROAD DEFECTS
1 ☐ Defective Shoulders
2 ☐ Holes, Deep Ruts
3 ☐ Loose Material on Surface
4 ☐ Other Defects
5 ☒ No Defects
6 ☐ Other______

LIGHT CONDITIONS
1 ☐ Dawn
2 ☒ Daylight
3 ☐ Dusk
4 ☐ Dark (Street Lights Off)
5 ☐ Dark (No Street Lights)
6 ☐ Dark (Street Lights On)

ROAD SURFACE CONDITIONS
1 ☐ Ice ☒ Asphalt
2 ☐ Snow ☐ Brick
3 ☐ Wet ☐ Gravel
4 ☒ Dry ☐ Concrete
5 ☐ Mud ☐ Dirt

CONTRIBUTING FACTORS — DRIVER 1 2
1 ☐ ☐ Failure to Yield
2 ☐ ☐ Following too Closely
3 ☐ ☐ Improper Passing
4 ☐ ☐ Improper Turn
5 ☐ ☐ Drinking
6 ☐ ☐ Speeding
7 ☐ ☐ Weather
8 ☐ ☐ Disregard Signal or Sign
9 ☐ ☐ Wrong Side of Road
10 ☐ ☐ Other Explain
11 ☐ ☒ None
12 ☒ ☐ Unknown
13 ☐ ☐ Vision Obstructed

TRAFFIC CONTROLS — Veh. 1 2
1 ☒ ☒ No Control
2 ☐ ☐ Signal
3 ☐ ☐ Stop
4 ☐ ☐ Yield
5 ☐ ☐ RR Crossbuck
6 ☐ ☐ Flasher RR
7 ☐ ☐ Gates RR
8 ☐ ☐ 4 Way Stop
9 ☐ ☐ Other______

ROAD CHARACTER (Check Two) — Veh. 1 2
1 ☐ ☐ Curve
2 ☒ ☒ Straight
3 ☐ ☐ Upgrade
4 ☐ ☐ Downgrade
5 ☒ ☒ Level

ROAD TYPE — Veh. 1 2
1 ☐ ☐ Two Lane
2 ☒ ☒ Four Lane
3 ☐ ☐ One Way
4 ☐ ☐ Divided Lanes
By What ______
5 ☐ ☐ Other______

VEHICLE CONDITION (Check one or more) — Veh. 1 2
1 ☐ ☐ Defective Brakes
2 ☐ ☐ Improper Lights
3 ☐ ☐ Defective Steering Mechanism
4 ☐ ☐ Defective Tires
5 ☐ ☐ ______ Specify Other
6 ☒ ☒ No Defects
7 ☐ ☐ Defects not known

COLLISION DIAGRAM
INDICATE ON THIS DIAGRAM WHAT HAPPENED
INDICATE NORTH BY ARROW
See Page 2

DESCRIBE WHAT HAPPENED According to drivers' statements, Vehicle #2 struck Vehicle #1 in the left rear as it crossed in front of him.

REPORT APPROVED BY: Sgt John Thomas

FIGURE 7.11. Police department accident report supplement. Reprinted with permission of the Cookeville Police Department, Cookeville, Tennessee.

11. Use this legislative status report to write a news story for your paper.

NASHVILLE, Tenn. (AP) — Here is the status of major legislation at the end of the fifth week of the Tennessee Legislature's 1981 session:

Taxes

—Increase gasoline tax 1 cent per gallon, introduced.

—Increase diesel fuel tax 4 cents per gallon, introduced.

—Give cities and counties added taxing authority, introduced.

—Extend 4.5-cent sales tax another year, on Senate floor, in House Finance Committee.

Motorists

—Allow 80,000-pound, 60-foot trucks on state highways, introduced.

—Permit officers to issue citations in lieu of warrants at accident scenes, in Senate Judiciary, House Transportation committees.

—Repeal 55 mph speed limit, in Senate Transportation Committee. No House bill.

—Require passengers younger than 4 be harnessed in restraint device, passed Senate, on House floor.

Consumers and Commerce

—Transfer from Legislature to Insurance Department regulation of credit life insurance, introduced.

—Permit statewide branches by Tennessee banks, Senate and House Commerce committees.

—Forbid statewide branches by bank holding companies, in Senate and House Commerce committees.

—Establish commission to approve increases in hospital charges, in Senate and House Welfare committees.

Education

—Provide more take-home pay increase for teachers and state employees through statepaid pensions, introduced.

—Turn state-owned educational television stations over to local communities, in Senate Education, House Government Operations committees.

—Require high school seniors to pass proficiency tests to graduate beginning in 1982, in Senate and House Education committees.

—Require kindergarten as prerequisite to first grade, in Senate and House Education committees.

Courts

—Reduce base salaries of judges beginning in 1982 with 5 percent cost-of-living escalator, in Senate and House Judiciary committees.

—Transfer from governor to Legislature the job of filling judicial vacancies, in House and Senate Judiciary committees.

—Give judges, rather than juries, power to levy criminal sentences, in Senate and House Judiciary committees.

—Reorganize court system, in Senate and House judiciary committees.

—Require General Sessions judges to be lawyers, on Senate calendar, in House Judiciary Committee.

Environment

—Ban no-deposit bottles, in Senate Environment, House Conservation committees.

—Ban non-aluminum beverage cans, in Senate Environment, House Conservation committees.

—Increase tax on bottlers from 1.5 percent to 2.1 percent to help finance prisoner pickup of litter, introduced.

12. Write a news story based on the following report issued by the state department of public health. It involves a comparison study of hospitals in your university county. The hospitals are in the Class I category of medical facilities—the smallest of hospitals, providing from 50 to 200 beds. The report is the 1986 Joint Annual Report of Hospitals. The average total charge, average daily charge and average length of stay categories refer to patients, of course. University General Hospital, the hospital used by most of your newspaper's readers, is indicated by the initials UGH.

Average Total Charge

Harton Memorial, $1,134.
UGH, $1,399.
Warren County General, $1,409.
White County Community, $1,481.
Franklin County, $1,553.
DeKalb County General, $1,716.
River Park, $1,948.
Stones River, $2,048.

Average Daily Charge

Warren County General, $240.
UGH, $256.
Harton Memorial, $263.
Franklin County Community, $285.
River Park, $286.
Stones River, $291.
DeKalb County General, $359.

Average Length of Stay

Harton Memorial, 4.3 days.
DeKalb County General, 4.77 days.
White County Community, 5.19 days.
UGH, 5.5 days.
Warren County General, 5.86 days.
River Park, 6.8 days.
Stones River, 7.02 days.

13. Write a news story based on the graph in Figure 7.12.

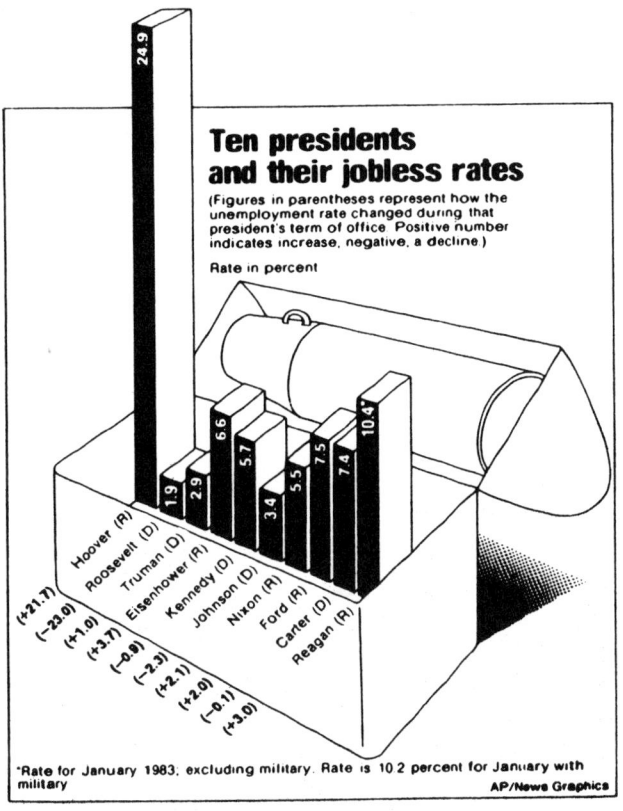

Ten presidents and their jobless rates

(Figures in parentheses represent how the unemployment rate changed during that president's term of office. Positive number indicates increase, negative, a decline.)

Rate in percent

- Hoover (R) 24.9 (+21.7)
- Roosevelt (D) 1.9 (−23.0)
- Truman (D) 2.9 (+1.0)
- Eisenhower (R) 6.6 (+3.7)
- Kennedy (D) 5.7 (−0.9)
- Johnson (D) 3.4 (−2.3)
- Nixon (R) 5.5 (+2.1)
- Ford (R) 7.5 (+2.0)
- Carter (D) 7.4 (−0.1)
- Reagan (R) 10.4* (+3.0)

*Rate for January 1983, excluding military. Rate is 10.2 percent for January with military.

AP/News Graphics

FIGURE 7.12. Unemployment rates under 10 U.S. presidents. Reprinted with permission of A.P./Wide World.

14. Write a news story from the chart in Figure 7.13.

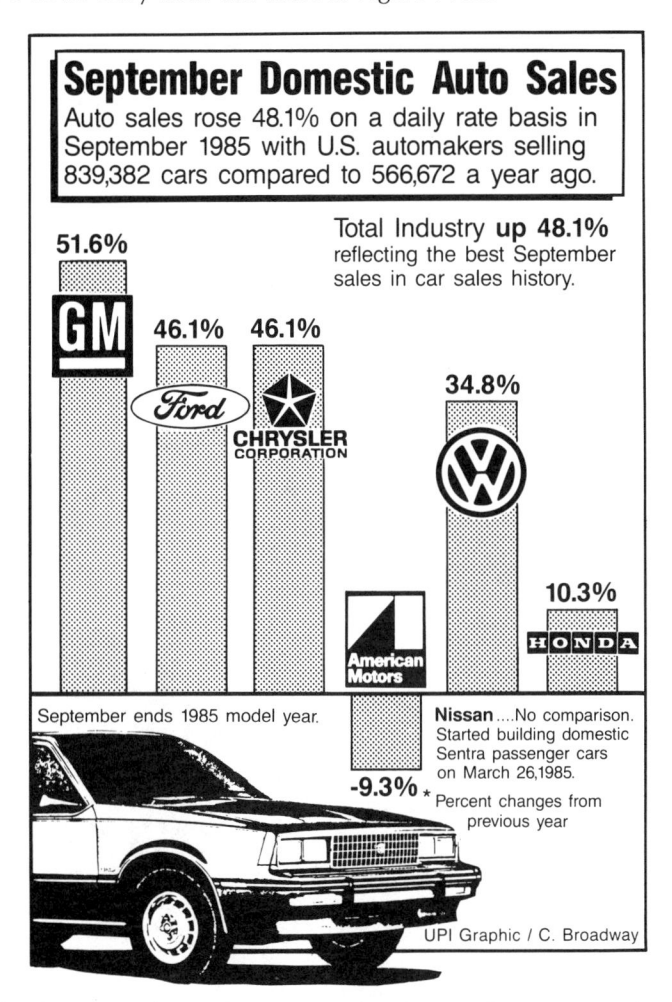

September Domestic Auto Sales

Auto sales rose 48.1% on a daily rate basis in September 1985 with U.S. automakers selling 839,382 cars compared to 566,672 a year ago.

Total Industry **up 48.1%** reflecting the best September sales in car sales history.

- GM: 51.6%
- Ford: 46.1%
- Chrysler: 46.1%
- VW: 34.8%
- American Motors: -9.3%
- Honda: 10.3%

Nissan....No comparison. Started building domestic Sentra passenger cars on March 26, 1985.

September ends 1985 model year.

*Percent changes from previous year

UPI Graphic / C. Broadway

FIGURE 7.13. Summary of car sales. Reprinted with special permission of United Press International.

15. Sometimes you have to ferret out the news from statistics handed to you. These are state statistics that you will be turning into a news story:

> From reports filed with the Department of Public Health's Division of Vital Records:
>
> Total deaths for first half of year—20,812. This equals a death rate of 8.9 per 1,000 population.
>
> Last year there were 21,574 deaths, 5 percent more than this year. A rate of 9.4 per 1,000 population.
>
> Marriage certificates filed this year = 26,640. Marriage certificates filed last year = 26,954. Five percent more filed last year for the first six months.
>
> Abortions for the first six months = 10,339. Abortions for same period last year = 11, 278.
>
> Birth rate decreased by 2 percent.
>
> Number of live births increased slightly.

Write a news story from these facts.

16. Attend a sporting event. Write an account of it using a featurized lead (you may leave out the statistics if you wish). How does it compare with your classmates' version (if any attended the same event) or with the local newspaper's version?

CHAPTER 8
NEWS FOR NEWSPAPERS: WRITING FOR IMPACT

No matter what beat a reporter covers or what a free-lancer's area of expertise is, both rely on basic rules of sentence structure in writing their stories. A lead is only as sharp and attention-getting as the language and sentence structure used to write it. The power of the articles, scripts and news releases you will compose during your career as a professional writer is directly related to your command of the English language and your understanding of various forms of sentence structure.

Recall our comparisons of good leads and poor leads. What made the difference between them? Bad grammar wasn't at fault; choice of words diminished only a few. What caused some leads to be weak was inappropriate arrangement of concepts in sentences that made the reader work too hard in trying to get to the heart of the story.

To sustain a reader's interest in an article, sentences and paragraphs have to have a rhythm, a flow, a beat. After all, there is a wide choice of reading in a newspaper—lots of stories capped by enticing headlines. To keep the reader engrossed in your story, you should vary the composition of your sentences so that the reader will anticipate with interest the disclosures of each succeeding paragraph. In short, the sentences you use to build an inverted pyramid must have maximum impact.

SENTENCE PATTERNS

When you advance beyond the beginner stage in writing, you will consciously vary your sentence patterns to avoid stringing a series of subject-verb sentences together. Nothing labels an elementary writer more clearly than this rudimentary pattern. Though the sentences may be more complex than the simple subject and verb—"She smiled"—the structure is still the same. Within the subject-verb construction you may use these variations:

Subject + linking verb + object:
She served the ball.

Subject + linking verb + indirect object + object:
He served her breakfast.

Subject + linking verb + predicate:
He was an angry fool.

Though they appear to be different in complexity, all three sentences start with subjects and are followed by verbs.

Now there's nothing wrong with using sentences with this pattern. If you know nothing about writing, this is a "safe" construction. Perhaps 90 percent of all sentences written follow this pattern. But strung haphazardly together, with little thought to the effect they create or the relationships of the ideas in them, they can be repetitious and boring. They lack rhythm or flow. They are short, choppy things. They hit like a hammer. They dull the senses. They try readers' patience.

Did you notice how wearying the last five sentences were? They all contain only four or five words—truly elementary lengths. Your audience deserves more intelligent treatment than this, and if it's not forthcoming, they will simply stop reading.

VARIATIONS

How can you vary your sentence patterns to add spice to your writing?

Reverse the order. You can vary the subject-verb pattern by reversing the order. Start out with a verb: "Strive for sentences that flow." The subject in that sentence (*you*) is understood; it need not be stated. Most questions you use in writing reverse the subject-verb order: "Are your sentences varied?" Do you now use questions in your writing? They can be effective if used judiciously.

Place the Object First. You may vary the pattern by placing the object first: "That article's been revised five times."

Use Intervening Phrases and Clauses. Although you essentially repeat the subject-verb pattern when you place a phrase or clause between the subject and the verb, the variation is so radical that you've effected a pattern change: "The sentences, lacking rhythm and flow, are short, choppy things."

Use Phrases and Clauses at the Beginning. To change the pattern completely, however, you can place the intervening phrase or clause at the beginning, like this: "Lacking rhythm and flow, the sentences are short, choppy things."

Combine the Offending Series of Sentences. One of the obvious ways of varying a series of choppy sentences is to combine them. Look, once again, at the sentences we are discussing:

1. They lack rhythm or flow.
2. They are short, choppy things.
3. They hit like a hammer.

4. They dull the senses.
5. They try readers' patience.

Some of the statements made in these sentences are more important than others. Yet in their subject-verb constructions, they all stand as equally important. All are independent clauses—they stand by themselves and make sense. But if some statements are more important than others, why not relegate them to a less important status? Why not reduce them to phrases or dependent clauses? When you do that, the more important statements will receive more emphasis.

Look at the first two sentences: "They lack rhythm or flow. They are short, choppy things." The second sentence is more important. Revise the sentences to reflect that. Reduce the first sentence to a participial phrase and use it to introduce the second statement: "Lacking rhythm or flow, the sentences are short, choppy things." That sentence now contrasts a phrase that suggests rhythm and flow—"Lacking rhythm or flow" (note the even beat and pleasant sound)—with a phrase that doesn't have any flow or pleasantness to its sound—"short, choppy things." The grammatically necessary comma after *short* emphasizes the choppiness; it makes the reader pause yet one more time.

Now let's look at the third, fourth and fifth sentences:

3. They hit like a hammer.
4. They dull the senses.
5. They try readers' patience.

All three are related to effect. Why not combine them into one sentence? How would you do that? Play around with different combinations until you find the one that's just right.

The position of greatest emphasis in a sentence is the end:

Positions of Emphasis in a Sentence

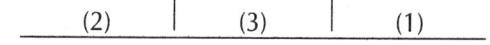

```
_____(2)____|____(3)____|____(1)_____
```

The least important position (3) is in the middle of the sentence. That means that the least important element should be placed there. Since "patience" is the least important of the three statements, it goes in the middle of the sentence. The most important element is "dulling the senses." It goes at the end. That leaves the "hammer" statement for the next most important position at the sentence beginning: "They pound like a hammer, trying readers' patience and dulling their senses."

In this revision—sentence combining—the opening of the sentence states an action, and the sentence ending emphasizes the most important result of that action. For more impact, *hit* was changed to the more concrete and colorful *pound*, a word that seems more appropriate to use with the word *hammer*.

Here's what we have done: We have converted five short, choppy, elementary sentences into two more mature 10- and 12-word sentences. In one case we varied the sentence structure from a subject-verb pattern to an introductory phrase–subject–verb pattern. In the other we moved from a subject-verb construction to a subject–verb–modifying phrases construct. Most important, we combined the sentences to reflect the importance of the statements being made.

Most writers vary sentence patterns during revisions. Students of writing tend to write sentences and then act as if they have been carved in stone. Experienced writers realize that nothing is sacrosanct about sentences written in the first draft. Indeed, most of those sentences can literally be cut up into words and phrases, shaken up and dropped on a table. They will make some sense by the way they fall. Take this truncated sentence, the first part of the opening of Charles Dickens's *Tale of Two Cities:* "It was the best of times, it was the worst of times. . . ." You could rewrite that sentence in a number of ways:

1. It was both the best and the worst of times.
2. It was the worst and the best of times.
3. The times were both the best and the worst.
4. The best and the worst of times it was.
5. Both the best and the worst of times were embraced by the era.
6. Timewise, it was both the best and the worst.

We have to credit Dickens with having considered alternatives such as these and discarded them in favor of his memorable beginning. Work hard enough at revising your sentences and you will arrive, with a small shock of recognition, at that one best way of phrasing your words for the greatest impression.

Sentences may be shaped and primed for impact by leading up to the most important idea and placing it at the end of the sentence. Look at that graphic representation of a sentence again. The same principles and graphic representation apply to paragraph patterns:

```
_____(2)_____|_____(3)_____|_____(1)_____
```

Let us recapitulate: The most important position is at the end, next most important at the beginning, least important in the middle. What this means is that you guard, zealously and jealously, the beginnings and endings of sentences and paragraphs. Bury unimportant details and transitions in the middle of sentences and paragraphs. For example, why say, "She said, 'Your sentences have no rhythm or flow,'" when you can say, "'Your sentences,' she said, 'have no rhythm or flow'"? Placing that attribution inside the direct quotation even adds a rhythm—a satisfying beat—to the sentence.

Bury unimportant phrases like "as anticipated" and "at 2 o'clock Thursday" in the middle of your sentences, after natural pauses. To determine exactly where they should be placed, read the sentences aloud. Place the unimportant phrases after a pause, where it sounds natural to do so.

ATTRIBUTION

Attribution, and its placement, can help a writer to vary the structure of sentences. For newspaper articles, attribution is best placed in the middle of a sentence or after the quote has been completed. It should not be placed at the beginning. Here is an example:

```
"It's not known how many people are still on board,"
one source said, "but the hijackers appear to be serious
about killing them if their demands are not met."
```

The first clause sets up the suspense; the attribution (the least important part of the sentence, in the middle position) provides a pause after which a conclusive statement can be made.

In the following example, attribution appears after the quote, allowing the full impact of the statement to be made first:

```
"They are all dead," he said.
```

Attribution is an important part of reporting. Readers need to know who said what, and with what degree of conviction. Occasionally, beginning writers feel that they must constantly vary the verbs they use for attribution. While it's important to demonstrate variety in the vocabulary you use in newswriting, it's best to use straightforward words for attribution. The all-around favorite is "said." If someone is asking a question, however, it's all right to use, "he asked." If someone is answering that question, it's all right to say, "she answered" or "she replied." But unless someone actually shouts, don't say, "he shouted." Unless someone actually makes a declaration, avoid the attribution "she declared." Unless someone gives an order, avoid "he commanded."

Here is a list of verbs used for attribution, in descending order of popularity:

said	commented	concluded	cried
added	explained	declared	shouted
continued	remarked	asserted	screamed
replied	suggested	averred	commanded
answered	reported	stated	
asked	repeated	exclaimed	

PARAGRAPH PATTERNS

Where you put your topic sentence in a paragraph creates different paragraph patterns. Moving from a general statement to the details or particular facts supporting that statement is the deductive reasoning approach. If you reversed this pattern, starting out with details and leading up to the climactic topic sentence at the end of the paragraphs, you would be using an inductive reasoning approach. Most paragraphs are written using one or the other, with the preponderance using the deductive approach. Sometimes, however, the topic sentence may be placed in the middle of a paragraph. Sometimes the topic sentence may not even be stated: As the paragraph develops, the idea is implied or implicit. Vary your paragraph patterns in much the same way you do your sentence patterns.

One way to provide your reader with variety and relief from long gray columns of paragraphs in newspaper articles is to use quotes (see Figure 8.1). But you don't need quotes to use short paragraphs. For emphasis, you might write a paragraph consisting of just three words or even one word.

I mean it.

Honestly.

As noted earlier, media requirements actually dictate sentence and paragraph lengths. The most finicky of audiences are those of radio and television. The result is shorter and simpler sentences and paragraphs. Newspaper and magazine readers tend to be more educated and more tolerant of longer and more complex sentences and paragraphs. The most tolerant of all, however, are book readers.

THE TRIADIC STRUCTURE

When you write and you use examples or illustrations, we suggest you consider using the triadic structure—multiples of three. To the Greek mathematician Pythagoras, the magic number was 3. William Carlos Williams's poetry is written with the triad in mind. As you survey our rituals and our society, you can see that the number 3 figures prominently: Our dramas usually have three acts. Series of books on one subject are often written in trilogies. We plan three meals a day. Our days consist of morning, afternoon and night. Our government is composed

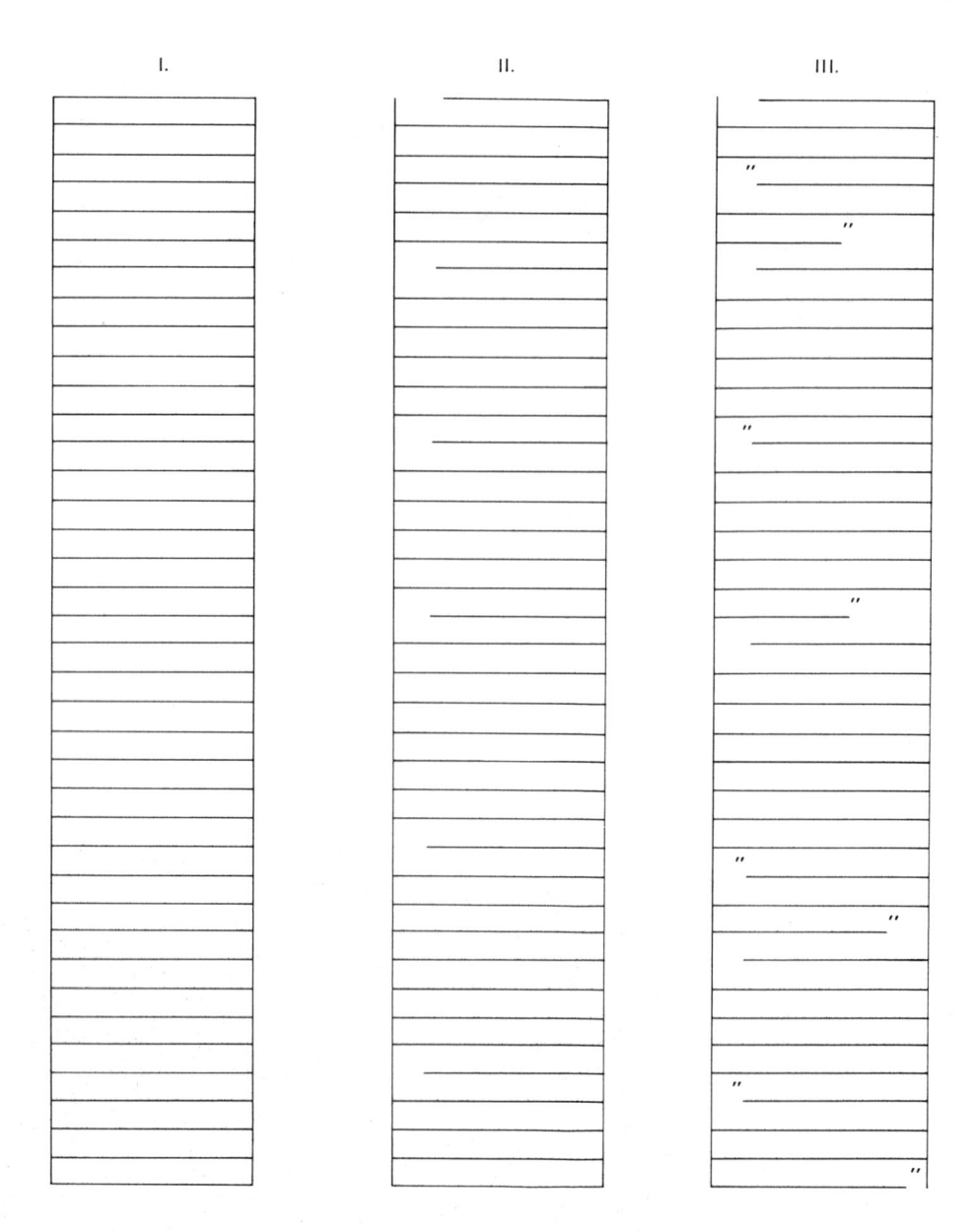

FIGURE 8.1. Importance of paragraph indentations and direct quotations. No reader will be enticed by long, gray column 1. Paragraph indentations lighten column 2. The added quotations make column 3 especially lively.

of three major branches—executive, legislative and judicial. One of our major religions speaks of a trinity—the Father, the Son, and the Holy Spirit.

Most people seem to feel an intuitive rightness about examples coming in threes. One example is insufficient evidence; two help to prove a point; but three are convincing and somehow satisfying—and four seem almost like overkill.

So write with the triadic pattern in mind, but be certain to arrange your examples or illustrations for climactic effect. Progress from the weakest argument to the strongest, from the least vivid to the most vivid language. Any other arrangement lessens the impact on your reader, as do these examples of anticlimactic order:

```
    He knocked the man to the ground with an uppercut after
 hitting him in the stomach and slapping him in the face.
```

FIGURE 8.2. Frames 1, 2 and 3 each contain three examples. In addition, frames 1, 2 and 3 themselves constitute examples leading to the conclusion in frame 4. Cathy, Copyright, 1984, Universal Press Syndicate. Reprinted with permission. All rights reserved.

```
Prior to renting the house, she painted it, replaced
three windows and fixed three dripping faucets.
```

Reversing the order of things done to the man and the house not only provides climactic and chronological order but also places the most important things done in the greatest position of emphasis—at the end of the sentence:

```
In quick succession, he slapped the man in the face,
hit him in the stomach, and knocked him to the ground
with an uppercut.
```

```
Prior to renting the house, she fixed three dripping
faucets, replaced three windows and painted the
exterior.
```

Nearly everybody uses the principle of the triad. Here are two examples (a third appears in Figure 8.2):

By GAIL McKNIGHT*

1. When Timothy Demonbreun signed his will in March 1827, he bequeathed $500 each to his three illegitimate children, and left a blank space for the name of his daughter's husband.

2. James K. Polk asked in his 1831 will that his slaves be freed.

3. Andrew Jackson's 1845 will bequeaths "my body to the dust, whence it come, and my soul to God who gave it: hoping for a happy immortality."

These are just some of the yellowed and tattered records stored haphazardly in the Metro Courthouse in a way that would make historians cry. Metro has no permanent archives and no money to establish a place to store historic records, according to officials.

By ELLEN HALE
and JUDITH HORSTMAN
Gannett News Service†

1+2. Verdi was writing operas as an octogenarian. Pablo Picasso painted until his death at the age of 91.

3. Ronald Reagan, at 73, is running the most powerful country in the world. He is, by three years, the oldest president the United States has ever had.

But after his faltering performance in the presidential debate last Sunday night, some people—politicians, physicans and public—are wondering if Reagan is showing the effects of his advanced age. They are asking if his age could affect his performance as president.

* Reprinted with permission of *The Tennessean*.
† Reprinted with permission of Gannett News Service.

LANGUAGE AND IMAGERY IN NEWSWRITING

Unless it is unnatural to do so, write in the present tense. Readers like the idea that the facts they are reading are timely. The present tense gives them that feeling.

And just as you guard jealously the beginnings and endings of sentences and paragraphs, so should you guard against the use of colorless verbs and abstract detail. "I got the mail" is dull compared to "I picked up the mail from Paul Wilmoth at the Student Center post office." "I went to the hotel for refreshments" is drab compared to "I stopped in at the Brookshire Inn for a Heineken."

Little things mean a lot. Without vivid verbs and strict attention to details, not only will your writing be uninteresting, but it will also fail to communicate effectively.

Two of the most sophisticated things you can do to improve your writing is to consider the rhythm and flow of it and to wed the sense of what you are saying to the sound of how you are saying it. Most writing should be written in a conversational style. Although you use in writing words that you do not use in speaking, writing still stems directly from speaking—we speak the words in our mind before we write them on paper. If you write the way you speak, your writing should have a rhythm or flow to it. If you are tired, for example, you reflect that in your conversation. You reflect your excitement in your conversation. The words you choose to say determine how you will say them. Would you say "I'm tired" in an animated way? Of course not. You would say it wearily. You might even sigh.

In writing, too, the sense of what you are saying should be reflected in the way you say it. Listen to the violence in these sentences:

```
Jake slapped the man's face. His sharp uppercut
knocked the man over a garbage can. Then, drawing his
.45, Jake shot him between the eyes.
```

The sense of what is happening is wedded to the sound of the sentences. The words were selected to convey the sound as well as the sense of violence: *slapped, face, sharp, uppercut, knocked, gargabe can, .45, shot,* and *eyes*. Those harsh-sounding words mimie the violence taking place. The sentences, composed into short bursts, emphasize each phase of violence. The sentences are ordered so that the violence escalates to the climactic death-dealing shot. The sense of a man slowly drawing a pistol from a holster is accomplished by softening and slowing the action by using, first of all, the soft-sounding "Then, drawing his . . ." The commas slow the reader down. Those commas and the words convey the "sound" of a man silently and purposefully drawing a .45 from a holster.

Writers who know what they're doing always wed the sense to the sound—some call it wedding the substance to the form. Listen to this sound of impending violence in these sentences from "The Open Boat," by Stephen Crane. A gull has landed on an open boat:

> *The cook and the correspondent swore darkly at the creature. The captain naturally wished to knock it away with the end of the heavy painter, but he did not dare do it, because anything resembling an emphatic gesture would have capsized this freighted boat . . .*

The words selected to convey impending violence hit the ears hard: *darkly, creature, knock, heavy, painter, did, not, dare, emphatic, gesture, capsized, freighted, boat.*

The gull, however, must now be gently shooed away from the boat. Crane conveys the gentleness of these motions by slowing down the rhythm of the sentence with commas and by using soft-sounding words:

and so, with his open hand, the captain gently and carefully waved the gull away.

Crane interposed *gently and* between *captain* and *carefully* because placed together the words sound harsh and would not convey the gentle wave of the hand. Say "captain carefully" out loud and you will see that it is impossible to convey a gentle motion with these words.

Edgar Allan Poe transports the readers over waves and washes them safe onto the shore in his poem "To Helen." He speaks of Helen's beauty and likens it to ships, "Those Nicean barks of yore / That gently o'er a perfumed sea, /

```
                              bore
                    wanderer      To
         way-worn             his
      weary                   own
    The                           na-
                                     tive      shore.
```

The words, composed as they are, force the readers to read them as if they were a wave transporting the ship, with the poet on it, "to his own native shore." The *sense* of what is happening is wedded to the *sound* of what is happening. The substance to the form.

Let's briefly recapitulate what you can do when you use sound as a handmaiden to meaning:

To convey unrest or violence, you may consider using short, emphatic words and sentences, even sentence fragments. You may want to use words with hard-sounding consonants like *k, j, p* and *d* and hard-sounding vowels like long *a, e* and *i*.

To convey the impression that all is at peace in the world, you may want to use longer words and flowing sentences, with soft-sounding consonants like *m, n, l, r* and *th* and soft-sounding vowels like *o* and *u*.

You can enrich your writing by using a dominant theme of imagery or metaphors. But if you start out using nature imagery in an article or story, you would not want to disrupt the unity of the work by switching, for no good reason, mechanical imagery. Having used such expressions as "gray mists" and "icy dew" and "cavelike opening," you would hesitate to shift abruptly to expressions such as "robotlike" or "metallic smell" unles the scene were invaded by some mechanical creatures from *Star Wars*.

Nor would you want to mix metaphors as this person did in describing the stock market:

```
In this kind of a bull market, people really begin to
believe they have invented some kind of a money tree.
Invariably this kind of froth leads to a period where
greed turns to fear, and that is exactly what has been
happening. All the while you have been building up a
ticking time bomb, you're running out of gas.
```

or this person, quoted in the *Congressional Record:*

With at least $263 billion already obligated to be spent by Congress over *the next 40 years on public housing, we have dug a deep trench by obviously biting off more than we could chew.*

An Arabic proverb says, "Four things come not back: the spoken word; the sped arrow; time past; the neglected opportunity." It's a good proverb to remember when you are revising.

SUMMARY

Writing for newspapers is a precise art. With so much information moving over the wires and being gathered by reporters each day, newspaper editors are under tremendous pressure to select the most significant fraction of news—and it is only a fraction—to include in each day's editions. Newspaper reporters must be experts on their beats, and their writing must reflect their ability to cut to the heart of the matter by leading with the facts and developing their stories with succinct, vivid phrasing.

Since newspaper readers face so many choices of stories to read in each day's paper, it's the reporter's obligation to deliver information in as compact and interesting a format as possible. To provide relief from long gray columns of type, writers should vary their sentence patterns, the placement of attribution, and the structure of their paragraphs. They should use a quote within the first three paragraphs. They should constantly test their writing by reading sentences aloud, checking to be certain that they have wedded sense to sound and that they've chosen the best possible words to describe events and personalities.

EXERCISES

1. For each sentence, list five different verbs that could be used, in order of your preference.

    a. The groom came down the aisle.

    (1)

    (2)

    (3)

    (4)

    (5)

    b. The girl went to the candy store.

    (1)

    (2)

    (3)

    (4)

    (5)

    c. The boy on the bicycle went over the cliff.

    (1)

    (2)

    (3)

    (4)

    (5)

2. Rewrite these sentences, using active verbs, concrete details, and so on. Try showing rather than telling.

    a. We left for the beach early in the car and arrived by late afternoon.

b. After the rain, everything in the yard was wet and soggy.

c. The dog at the bowl was hungry, and it looked hungry, as it ate the food.

3. Rewrite the following quotation so that it has a climactic sequence of events.

"We can't say it was a tornado, but it was definitely high winds that took the roof off the courthouse, blew down Mary Ann Cummins' barbeque, and blew trees down over in the park and in our yard and on South Main," said Eddie Johnson, a Putnam County sheriff's dispatcher.

CHAPTER 9

THE NEW NEWS TECHNOLOGIES
Helen E. Aller

An exciting part of the journalism explosion that has taken place in America since the mid-1960s involves the new electronic technologies of cabletext, teletext and videotex. Many new jobs are opening up in the electronic publishing industry as media organizations explore new ways to deliver information to the home. Electronic delivery systems bypass the newspaper carrier and newsstand to reach consumers via television and home and office computers. They offer new options to journalism students now setting career goals.

Accounts of the impact of the "information age" or "information revolution" can be read in virtually every magazine and journal published in America. Computers continue to play an ever-growing role in American life. To many people, a "bit" no longer means just a little, and a "chip" may have nothing to do with potatoes. Some 12.7 million video display terminals, personal computers, word processors and the like are now in use in the United States. The number is expected to rise to 41 million by 1987, according to International Data Corporation's market research.

Computers have found acceptance in the newspaper business, too. The familiar click-clack of typewriters is only a memory in most newsrooms. Reporters now write and edit stories on VDTs. Many can read and edit wire service stories on the same terminal. As a result, the old teletype machines that churned out rolls of yellow paper are gathering dust.

Helen E. Aller, B.S., M.A., is Assistant Dean of the College of Journalism and Communications of the University of Florida, Gainesville, and has been director of the university's Electronic Text Center since its inception in September 1981. A 1975 graduate of the University of Florida, Aller was assistant managing editor of Gulf Publishing Company, Houston, Tex., from 1976 to 1979, and a copy editor and reporter for the *Gainesville Sun* from 1979 to 1981. In addition to directing the College of Journalism and Communications' cabletext channel, Gainesville Cable Press, she developed and teaches two videotex courses at the college.

FIGURE 9.1. Helen Aller, *left*, and Kim Cordasco, *right*, edit cabletext stories for the Gainesville Cable Press, the University of Florida's 24-hour cable news channel. Reprinted with permission of the Electronic Text Center, University of Florida, Gainesville.

THE NEW TECHNOLOGIES

The computer technologies that make the changes in newspaper publishing possible also foster what many people believe is the next logical step in the information revolution, the computerized *delivery* of news to the reader at home and at work.

VIDEOTEX: THE ELECTRONIC NEWSPAPER

No longer does a person have to walk out on a lawn wet with dew to retrieve a soggy newspaper filled with news eight to 10 hours old. Instead, with the flip of a switch, up-to-the-minute news from around the world is available in full text or in news summary form through the standard television set and personal computer. Readers can choose news summaries or can read the full text of a story.

With full-text service, no longer will the reader have to depend on a news editor's judgment as to what is a significant story. The reader becomes editor, with a vast choice of news and information. The number of stories placed in the electronic newspaper's "news hole" will be determined by the database's storage capacity, not by how many advertisements are sold by the sales staff. Nearly unlimited computer memory can offer home readers more than a thousand times the amount of information available in a daily newspaper.

Videotex is usually transmitted through a telephone connection between a home or office computer terminal screen or a TV screen and a central computer located at the videotex company. The user merely chooses the most interesting and relevant article, punches in the appropriate key words or selection numbers to call it up for viewing, and sits back and reads from the screen. Articles the user wants for future reference can be printed out on a printer attached to the computer terminal.

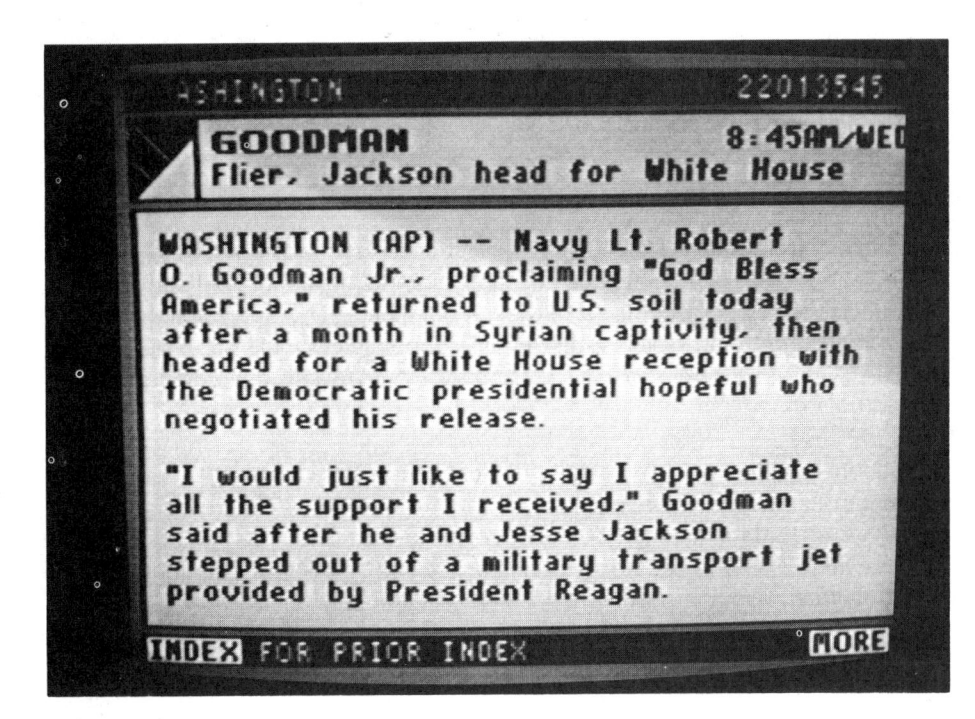

FIGURE 9.2. Sample videotex page. Note the "more" in the bottom right portion of the screen. This indicates that there are subsequent pages to the story, often as many as 10 or more. Reprinted with permission of the Electronic Text Center, University of Florida, Gainesville.

TELETEXT

Text and graphics broadcast to the home TV through the regular television signal are called teletext. The reader uses a hand-held keypad—which looks like a calculator—to select which television screen of information to read. The news on that screen will remain in view until a different screen is selected. Because teletext is usually broadcast as part of an existing television signal, rather than through additional equipment like a cable, the amount of information that can be transmitted at any given time is limited. A typical teletext system might include only 100 pages of information, whereas videotex systems can contain many thou-

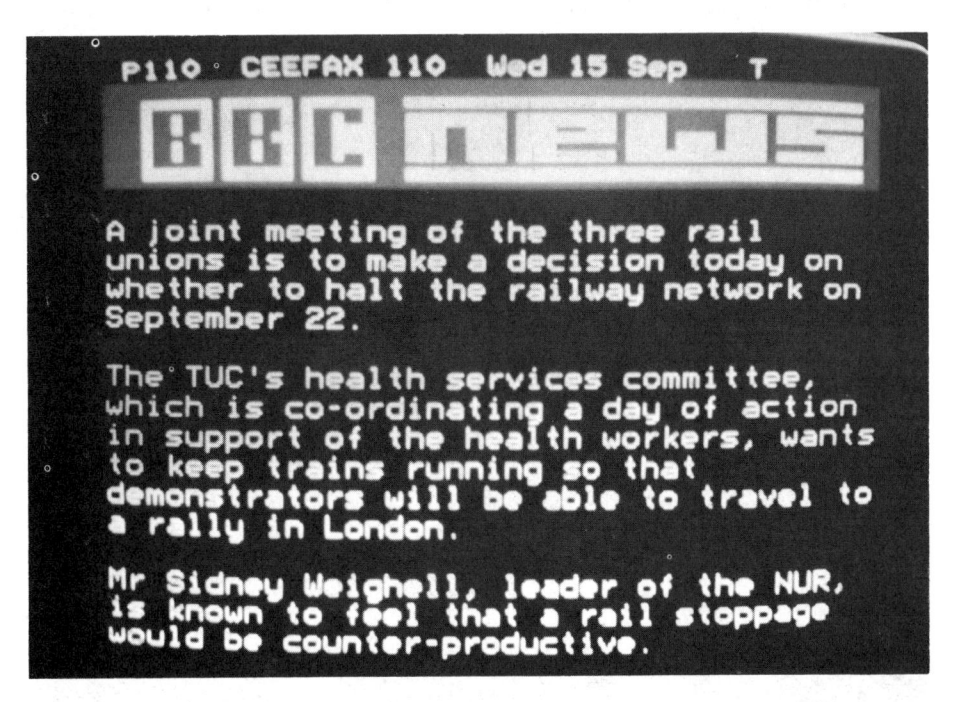

FIGURE 9.3. A news page from a British teletext service. Photo by Kurt Kent, University of Florida, Gainesville.

sands of pages. Teletext is limited because the amount of information space contained in a television signal is far less than what can be stored in a mainframe computer that would service a videotex operation.

Cabletext

A cabletext system sends text and graphics to cable television subscribers. Cabletext news is available on a separate cable channel on an automatically rotating basis. Every 15 to 20 seconds, a new screen appears. This is the simplest of the electronic information systems; the reader cannot select material to be viewed. Readers watch the screen passively, as they would watch any television news station they tune in to.

Videotex, teletext and cabletext are subscription services. Some require extra equipment besides a PC or TV; some do not. Most current teletext and cabletext systems are local or regional. Some videotex news is available nationally; some is still available only to certain service areas, such as Viewtron in southern Florida and Gateway in southern California.

Newspaper Companies Lead the Way

If you aren't employed directly by the electronic text companies, you may find your way into them through the newspaper world. Because electronic text services are seen by publishers as a way to increase revenue with the addition of new information products, newspaper companies have invested the most money in them.

A survey conducted in 1983 by the American Newspaper Publishers' Association and the National Advertising Bureau discovered that nearly half of the more than 1,000 publishers polled are "considering, planning or participating in or operating some kind of venture" in electronic news dissemination. Cabletext services dominate current projects, though most newspapers going into electronic text ventures are considering interactive videotex, which allows the user to tell the system what he or she wants to read. In other words, the system would be

Figure 9.4. A cabletext "page," or *frame*. Note how the screen is divided into different regions, each containing different information. The top and bottom *crawls* feature information moving from right to left across the screen. Reprinted with permission of the Electronic Text Center, University of Florida, Gainesville.

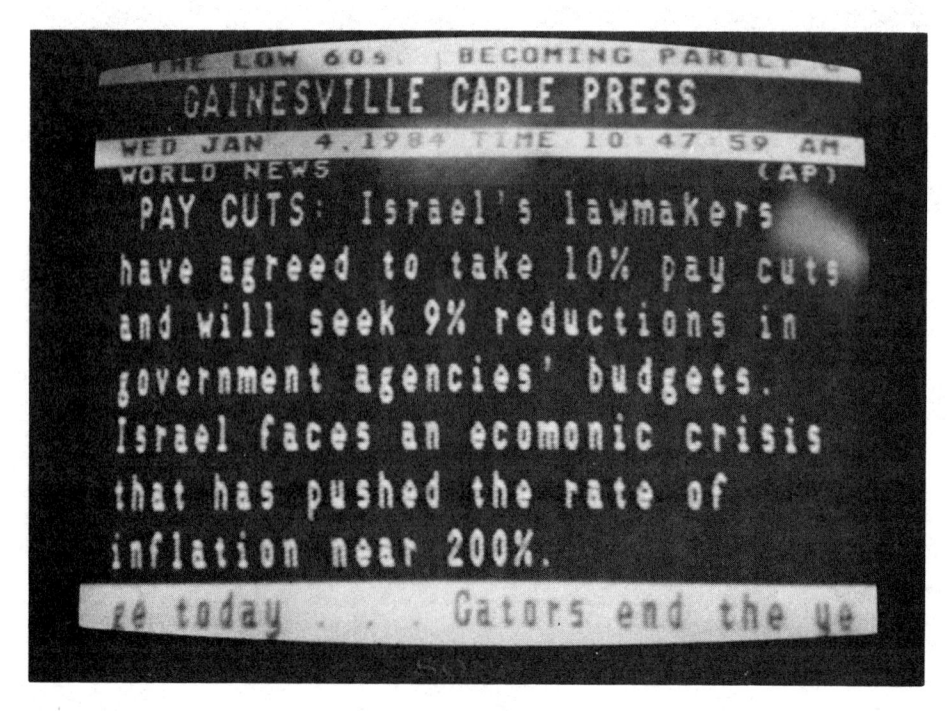

two-way, allowing the user to "talk back" to the system and get an electronic response.

Knight-Ridder Newspapers Inc. has invested more than $34 million in the first U.S. commercial videotex system, Viewtron. Concentrating on the home consumer market, commercial operations in the Miami, Fla., area began in 1983. Viewtron offers home shopping and airline flight schedules as well as news. This service is being closely imitated by Videotex America's service called Gateway, a joint venture by the *Los Angeles Times-Mirror* and Infomart, a Canadian videotex company.

Another media giant, The Tribune Co., publishers of the *Chicago Tribune* and other dailies, is investing millions in the videotex market. Unlike Viewtron or Gateway, however, The Tribune Co. is focusing on commercial videotex applications in public places, such as shopping malls and hotel lobbies. (Early tests of these electronic billboards, which include directory services and sales specials, have proved financially successful.) The Tribune Co. is also producing, in conjunction with the Associated Press, a nationally distributed cabletext service called AP News Plus. Available to any cable television system in the country, it features high-resolution color graphics, a trademark of sophisticated videotex systems.

Keycom Electronic Publishing launched a videotex service, Keyfax, in the Chicago market in 1984. Modeled on Viewtron, it features a large and varied database with eye-pleasing color graphics.

Other media giants also are involved in electronic news transmission. The Gannett Co., publisher of 85 newspapers and *USA Today*, in late 1984 launched USA Today Update, which sends news summaries to subscribers with personal computers. USA Today Update offers hourly updates of world, national, financial and weather news, plus daily industry news summaries and special news reports that interpret breaking events.

Also offering a large range of on-line general news and business news and services is Dow Jones News Retrieval, owned by the publisher of *The Wall Street Journal*.

Still in the planning stages is the videotex service being developed by corporate giants IBM, CBS and Sears. Trintex will feature videotex services marketed to the home consumer. IBM will supply the equipment and transmission expertise. CBS will provide the editorial content. Sears will provide marketing through its nationwide chain of retail stores. Two other giant corporations, J.C. Penney and RCA, also announced home videotex projects in 1984.

While perceptions vary, most media analysts predict that electronic text services will fill a highly specialized role. While news will continue to be included in videotex databases, it may become ancillary to other kinds of "value-added" features. Those include educational sections with "drill and practice" quizzes, on-line encyclopedias, transactional services such as shopping and banking, and business or commercial information such as current stock market price quotes. Videotex systems exploit the unique capabilities of an electronic database with a two-way connection to the home. The Trintex project, for example, will likely include computerized versions of the Sears Financial Network services such as its Dean Witter Investments and Coldwell Banker Real Estate divisions.

SKILLS FOR ELECTRONIC JOURNALISM

Many of the skills you'll need for the new technologies will be those you've honed working on a newspaper or a radio or television station. A videotex service, for example, combines the immediacy of radio with the thoroughness of newspapers. As such, it is a hybrid medium and will require a combination of skills.

FORMAT

Videotex, teletext and cabletext all require that the 5W+H and Significance questions be used as a guide for writing news items. "What" leads are the best for electronic news media, where there is little room to flesh out detail. The inverted pyramid really doesn't apply to these writing forms, since the stories themselves are so abbreviated. The electronic newsroom style calls for only three essentials:

1. Announcement of an event
2. Its significance
3. Its impact

EDITING IS STILL MOST IMPORTANT

Most important, you must be a good editor. Entry-level electronic text jobs almost always involve editing and rewriting. While videotex will increase the number of reporting jobs, because so much more room exists to store information than in a newspaper, jobs in today's electronic newsrooms involve recasting articles originally written for newspapers, radio or TV.

A thorough knowledge of the rules of grammar, spelling and style will be absolute prerequisites for a videotex editor. Many cabletext, teletext and videotex systems have their own particular stylebook that you will have to commit to memory. Many more abbreviations are used in writing electronic news because of the tight word limits for most stories. Even full-text stories are written with word economy in mind.

Sloppy or careless editors will not survive in electronic text projects. As soon as you hit the "store" key on your edited story in most electronic text systems, the story becomes available to thousands of readers. Some projects have several editors who read every article edited by junior staff, but others rely solely on one editor per story. There is no margin for error.

Editors and writers for electronic news services face special challenges writing stories about crimes, criminals and crime victims. To include all details and mitigating circumstances in a 30-word story is difficult. Sometimes merely fitting in the words *alleged* or *accused* is difficult. Many libel suits have been brought

FIGURE 9.5. Electronic Text Center assistant director Kim Cordasco (*left*) works with an advertising student on a space shuttle graphic. Reprinted with permission of the Electronic Text Center, University of Florida, Gainesville.

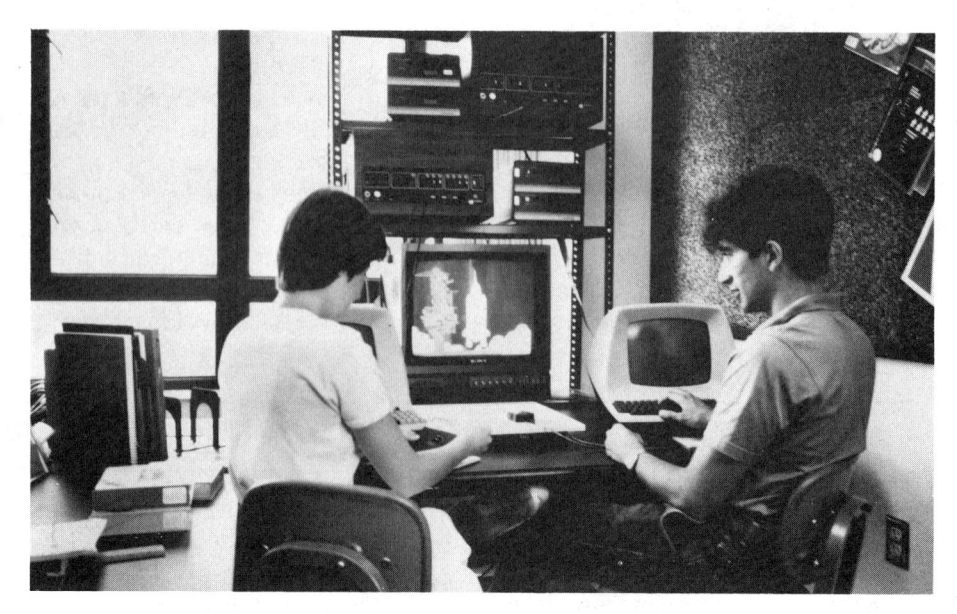

simply because the name of the accused was misspelled or the fact that someone was only *charged* with the crime, not convicted of it, was left out.

If you are an electronic text editor, every minute is your deadline. *Timeliness* and *immediacy* are the buzzwords used most by those who promote videotex. Within minutes of an event's occurrence, written accounts are available to the home subscriber. Unlike newspapers, television and magazines, there really is no end to the day's work. When you end your shift, your replacement immediately starts updating the database. There is no first, second or final edition, nor does the news day wrap up with the 10 or 11 o'clock news.

Information Management

As an electronic text editor, you'll keep track of numerous information sources all day long. A large videotex system may include every major story filed from all the major wire services in the nation. You must keep track of which stories need to be updated, which stories duplicate others, and which stories need to be filed in several different sections of the database. The videotex system for which you work may present news under different headings: foreign, national, regional, health, etc. You must decide which section a story belongs in so that interested readers will know how to locate it.

A major story about an artificial heart recipient might be filed under national news as well as medical news. News of a hurricane in Florida would be carried in the national, state and weather sections. When one section is updated, all must be updated. Some of this routing of material into the database is accomplished automatically through computer instructions coded into the system. Much of it, however, is decided by highly organized videotex editors who make decisions about story length and placement. They keep lists of information in their editing terminals and know where stories are located, when they were last updated, and when they need to be freshened.

Even on a relatively simple cabletext service, the editor keeps track of constantly changing weather forecasts; local news from internal or external sources; state, national and world news from one or more wire services; and other specialized kinds of content developed by the cabletext staff, such as local entertainment or movie listings.

Some cabletext systems will subscribe to broadcast news wires because the stories are already edited succinctly. The AP also produces a wire service, called AP Cable, specifically for cabletext. It can be automated to appear on a cabletext service if the service's office is unstaffed late at night or on holidays.

Newspapers that also program a cable channel or teletext service will provide news directly from their computers. Usually, the most information that can be included in a cabletext or teletext story will amount to only one or two paragraphs of the original newspaper story. Only the most pertinent—and interesting—information can be used. This means that editors must master economy of expression and must learn how to write succinct phrases with descriptive key words. It's a disciplined style of writing that is a challenge even for a polished writer.

Good News Sense Is a Must

Any good news reporter or editor must keep up with current events. But for the electronic text editor, it is imperative to know the ongoing and breaking stories. Most monitor the news wires, all-news radio and TV to be current. If your major goal is to "scoop" the local daily with your most current version of the news, you must know when you are updating an old story or putting in a new one. For cabletext and teletext, you will have only a limited number of articles on the air at any given time. For this reason, it is crucial that you have good news judgment. If you can write only 10 local stories, 10 state stories and 10 world stories at any given time, you need to have confidence that the ones you are including are the most important of the day.

THE IMPORTANCE OF CONCISENESS

If you learn one thing in college or on the job—to be precise and economical in the use of words in writing stories—you will never want for employment in traditional or non-traditional organizations. Electronic text editors keep a thesaurus handy to find short synonyms for long words. Sometimes three or four letters are all that stand in the way of a finished story. Editors in this field must condense news stories from several hundred words to only 30 or 40. Writers for cabletext or teletext always use two or three short sentences rather than one long one.

Like radio and TV, videotex services often use the present tense to highlight the immediate and timely nature of the news. And verbs should be active rather than passive. Unlike newspaper writing, where sentences may end with "she said," with videotex you end those sentences with "she says."

Cabletext writers never include the day of the week in a story. It is assumed that the event happened "today." You even delete "today" in "Pres [note abbreviation] Reagan told his cabinet today." Videotex writers are also acutely conscious of time references, taking care to change "today" to "yesterday" or day of the week when updating reports that remain in their database longer than 24 hours.

Let's look at several examples that show electronic news versions of wire stories.

COMPOSING FOR VIDEOTEX

Different videotex services have different length requirements for articles they offer. Read AP's story of Eastern Airlines' union negotiations; then read the way it would have been written to fit USA Today Update's news summary format:

Novel Offer to Eastern from Union
Report: Machinists Ask for Percentage of Gross

MIAMI (AP) — Eastern Airlines' largest union is proposing a labor contract that would give its members money off the top — a percentage of the airline's gross annual revenues — instead of a share of whatever is left after expenses are paid, *The Miami News* reported Monday.

Citing a source who requested anonymity, the *News* said the International Association of Machinists "is going after 10 or 11 percent of the gross revenues."

The union represents about a third of Eastern's 37,500 employees.

Another anonymous source was quoted as saying there "is a percentage tie-in of some kind, but those details all have to be worked out."

Spokesmen for the union and the airline were attending meetings Monday and could not be reached for comment on the report or on the status of lender-mandated negotiations with the Machinists.

Charles Bryan, president of Machinists District 100, said earlier that his union was seeking a "very upbeat and innovative" long-range solution to Eastern's labor-management problems, but he would not discuss specifics.

Gross revenue is the total

amount of money taken in by a corporation before deductions are made for expenses such as operations, marketing or administration. Eastern's gross grew 10.7 percent last year to $4.36 billion. According to the *News*, the contract sought by the Machinists would key directly to that figure instead of to the airline's profit.

Eastern is in technical default on $2.5 billion in loans and leasing agreements because it failed to reach new labor contracts with its pilots, flight attendants and the Machinists before a lender-imposed deadline last week.

Agreements in principle were reached with the pilots and flight attendants by Friday morning.

```
EASTERN UNION ASKS REVENUE SHARE
Eastern Airlines machinists negotiating with the carrier are said
to be asking for 10-11% of the airline's gross annual revenues,
reports the Miami News. Eastern's gross last year: $4.36 billion.
Anonymous sources say details must still be worked out on such a
proposal. The machinists are the last holdouts among union employees
negotiating new contracts with Eastern. The airline reached
agreements in principle with pilots and flight attendants Friday. (AP)
```

This format is a "news summary" article, rather than a full-text article. A reader interested in the entire story could dial up a full-text service and read AP's account on his or her screen.

USA Today Update's short headline, followed by a single-paragraph summary (32-character-wide headline, 68-character-wide body, 5 to 7 lines long) is designed to maximize the usefulness of swift electronic news transmission by boiling articles down into versions that themselves are "quick reads." Reporters write both the headline and the text. Copy editors edit both as necessary.

Again using the Eastern Airlines AP story, look at the following teletext version. Teletext calls for the writer to compose the article on an electronic grid. The grid restricts the length of the article and requires the writer to remember a number of technical requirements at the same time as he or she is doing the creative work involved in writing a condensed version of a wire story.

Here is the teletext version:

```
UNION MAKES NOVEL OFFER TO EASTERN
Eastern Airlines' largest union is
proposing a labor contract that would
give its members money off the top—a
percentage of the airline's gross annual
revenues—instead of a share of
whatever is left after expenses are
paid, the Miami News reported Monday.

The union represents about a third of
Eastern's 37,000 employees. It is
reportedly "going after 10 or 11 percent
of the gross revenues," according to an
anonymous source.
```

Teletext stories are 40 characters wide, 14 lines long, in caps and lowercase. Headlines are all caps.

Though the teletext format offers more room for details (than cabletext and some videotex), it still provides scant space for background information. Editors will be able to use about two full paragraphs from a wire story, as opposed to one paragraph for a cabletext story.

Composing for Cabletext

Cabletext has a much smaller screen than teletext. Cabletext stories are 32 characters wide and 7 lines long. Instead of headlines they have a one- to three-word all-caps slugline to lead off a story. Cabletext asks for tremendous economy of expression from those who write for it.

Writers use abbreviations whenever possible. They drop first names in identifiers if the person is well-known. They constantly look for shortcuts. The discipline of writing for this medium is that it forces writers and editors to search for the nugget of news that tells the entire story. That's not easy to do.

Here's an AP article and its cabletext companion.

New York Defends Plan to Plant Cops at Schools

NEW YORK (AP) — The New York City police commissioner Monday defended a plan to use undercover police in public schools to fight drug abuse, saying officers would not pose as teachers or others trusted by children.

Commissioner Benjamin Ward also said the flap over the undercover officers has obscured other facets of the anti-drug program, especially an education project.

Ward, at a City Hall press conference with Mayor Edward I. Koch and Board of Education officials, said officers would pose as custodial workers or cafeteria employees, not as teachers, counselors or others that "children have come to rely on."

Koch was particularly critical of the New York Civil Liberties Union, which opposes the use of undercover officers in schools.

"Frankly, I am at a loss to explain why the New York Civil Liberties Union attacks this program," Koch said. "They should support it."

The education elements of the program, involving drug awareness classes, lectures and assemblies, begins this week. The deployment of undercover officers also takes effect immediately, but authorities have not said when or where officers would be working.

The commissioner said 2,836 arrests have been made since Sept. 20 in an anti-drug crackdown near schools, and that 109 of those arrested, or 4 percent, were students. That, the commissioner said, indicated student drug peddlers were not as big a problem as adult drug peddlers.

```
COPS IN SCHOOL: The NYC police
commissioner defended a plan to
use undercover cops in public
schools to fight drug abuse.
Part of an anti-drug crackdown,
the plan has drawn fire from the
NY Civil Liberties Union.
```

This is a complex story with several interesting news elements. Here, the "when" of the story is not as important as elaborating on "who" is opposing the plan.

The use of *cops* is a judgment call. In a more liberal community it would not be offensive, but in a conservative one, *police* might be a better word.

Graphics

Many of the major electronic text projects use color graphics to illustrate sections of the database. Although there are different beliefs about the importance of graphics in electronic publishing, those that include some graphic frames are based on the belief that certain types of information—such as products that can be ordered using the system—cannot be adequately or accurately described using words alone. Some editors use graphics to highlight news and weather reports. The electronic text writer working for a service with graphics capability thinks not only in words but also in images and graphics in writing stories: How can this information be presented more clearly and concisely using a chart, table or illustration? On smaller systems, the videotex editor and graphic artist may be the same person. But even on big projects, editors work closely with an artist to achieve an overall harmony of graphic art style throughout the database.

Graphics training will likely become more available in university-level videotex programs in the near future. AT&T recently began donating more than 50 of its state-of-the-art graphics creation terminals to colleges and universities. As these terminals are distributed across the nation under the company's Grant Awards Program, videotex training will take a giant leap forward.

Computer Programming

Will you have to be a computer whiz to work on an electronic text project? No. The terminals you write stories on are quite similar to editing terminals used in traditional newspaper or broadcast newsrooms. You write and edit electronically using commands most reporters can master in less than a week. The only difference is that your story will be sent to the home or office electronically.

When you move into senior editing positions, however, a basic understanding about computers and information processing will be necessary. An understanding of the different forms of computer input, storage and transmission is important for a videotex editor. One or two basic computer courses at your university should stand you in good stead for understanding the principles underlying a videotex system.

On smaller cabletext projects, you will need to know a good deal more about your computer. A cabletext screen is typically divided into four or five regions, each of which contains different information. Across the top might be weather instrument and forecast readings. The second region might feature the name of your cabletext service, the third the day and the date, the fourth the main news story, and the fifth a headline "crawl" (moving letters crossing the screen). Cabletext editors need to know how to send information into each of these regions, as well as how to update the news and information. Different computer disks load program information into cabletext systems. Cabletext editors must know how to load these disks in the event that a power failure causes the system to "crash."

SUMMARY

Writing and editing for electronic media requires a discipline in expression that is even tighter than that called for in writing for broadcast. But practice in writing and feedback from good editors and teachers can help even the most wordy writer

FIGURE 9.6. A Gainesville Cable Press student editor at a workstation. Reprinted with permission of the Electronic Text Center, University of Florida, Gainesville.

harness his or her vocabulary to create the effective news and feature briefs that consumers will read on a television set or personal computer.

The "what" component of the 5W+H and Significance questions dominates in electronically transmitted news. It best captures the "news nugget" around which a 50-word story can be shaped. It is also the element that determines whether a story will even make it into the limited news space of teletext and cabletext and what prominence it will have among the reports available in the large databases of videotex.

Regardless of the technical differences among the three systems, the basic rules of effective print and broadcast reporting and writing apply to the new technologies as well. Electronic text editors who write clearly and briefly and show imagination and flair will never lack opportunities in traditional or non-traditional fields of journalism.

Guidelines for Writing Electronic News

☐ Put only one idea in a sentence.
☐ Some stories will need the Who, What, When and Where only; others will not be clear without a Why or How. Use your best news judgment to determine which story elements are most crucial. Generally speaking, the What element will work best for you.
☐ Do not hyphenate words at the end of a line.
☐ Use active verbs and the present tense wherever possible. Use few prepositions.
☐ Abbreviate titles: "Pres Reagan," "Sec of State Shultz." Use no periods after abbreviations, and do not include the first names of very well known people.

EXERCISES

1. Condense these paragraph groups* into a single sentence (one sentence for each set of paragraphs).

   a. Weinberger made clear that he considers a $3.2 billion expense for basic research on a space-based strategic defense system to be inviolable and said any reduction in it would "send the worst possible message" to the Kremlin at a time when U.S.-Soviet arms control talks are about to resume.

   That holds true for spending for the advanced MX intercontinental strategic missile, he said.

   b. Sen. John Stennis, D-Miss., a former Armed Services chairman and a staunch military advocate, told Weinberger: "I have a growing apprehension about the financial affairs of this government . . . I may not vote for all these items this year . . . I'm going to vote for something that I think has a chance of passing."

   "The defense budget is going to be cut," said Sen. Carl Levin, D-Mich. "Everybody around here knows it. The issue is where it's going to be cut and how much it's going to be cut."

   Sen. Mark Hatfield, R-Ore., chairman of the Senate Appropriations Committee, issued a statement saying that "a freeze on defense spending remains the absolute minimum requirement" in the face of budget deficts projected at $180 billion for fiscal 1986.

   c. The defense budget presented by Reagan calls for spending growth of 5.9 percent above the rate of inflation during fiscal 1986. With inflation aside, Weinberger said that amounts to a 10 percent growth over fiscal 1985.

* Reprinted by permission of United Press International.

2. Rewrite this story for teletext and cabletext, setting up your typewriter to conform to the character and line specifications given in this chapter (teletext on page 221, and cabletext on page 222).

By IKE FLORES
The Associated Press

ORLANDO — Gov. Bob Graham declared a state of emergency Tuesday and federal inspectors were sent to assess damage to citrus and vegetable crops from a two-day cold wave that ranks as one of Florida's worst in a century.

The governor also said he was adjusting weight restrictions on trucks carrying citrus and sugar cane, so growers could move their frozen crops to processing plants as soon as possible before they rot.

Whatever crops escaped Monday's wind and cold were ravaged by a second round of the Arctic blast Monday night and early Tuesday.

"Florida's agriculture industry is being deeply affected," Graham said in Tallahassee. "The state is closely monitoring the situation on an hour-to-hour basis and we will be providing whatever assistance we can."

Temperatures during the night ranged from the low teens to the low 30s in most of the growing regions, rising into the 40s during the afternoon.

State Agriculture Commissioner Doyle Conner compared the cold spell to the disastrous freeze of Christmas 1983, but said the damage this time is "more widespread, more crops destroyed."

Oldtimers in the citrus industry said this may have been more destructive than earlier freezes, such as those in 1977, 1962 and 1945. Wilson McGee, retired citrus executive, said it was "more democratic and systematic — it seemed to hit everywhere."

Spokesman Earl Wells of the state's largest growers' organization, Florida Citrus Mutual, said "growers are in shock . . . It has covered the entire industry. We suspect we will have severe fruit damage, and there will be tree damage in the north end" of the 760,000-acre citrus belt.

"The northern belt is in jeopardy," said Conner.

John Jackson, a citrus specialist in Central Florida, said many growers may quit because of the back-to-back freezes. "Psychologically, it's going to be a crushing blow to a lot of growers," he said.

Carl Reynolds, a DeLand-area grower, said Monday's cold persuaded him to get out of the citrus industry in which his family has worked for 52 years.

"I'm going to turn what I've got into something else," he said. "This will finish off citrus."

3. Paste a popular newspaper columnist's column below. Condense it first to 100 words, then to 60. Write a 32-character headline for it.

4. Collect five Page One news stories over a three-day period and condense each into stories of five to seven lines each. Compare your summaries with those of your classmates.

CHAPTER 10

NEWS FOR RADIO

Unlike news for the printed page, which is written for the eye, news for radio is written for the ear. You write to be heard, not to be read. You write to inform, to create images and paint pictures in the mind for a listener, not for a reader.

Media reporting and radio reporting differ primarily in the treatment and style of writing. The basic organization of the news story for radio is similar to that of the newspaper story. Radio relies on "what" leads to get the most detail across as possible in the short time allotted to radio news. Once the listener's attention has been captured, the story is usually told in chronological order to the end.

You can better understand the reason for this basic radio news story form if you think of the radio audience. More often than not, they're doing something else while listening to the radio. If that radio audience could afford to devote their undivided attention to the radio, they'd turn it off and turn on the television set. It's been that way since television invaded the radio scene in the 1950s. The primary radio audience is driving automobiles—between 6:30 and 9 in the morning and between 4 and 6:30 in the afternoon. If the radio audience isn't driving during these time periods, they're working or playing. In any event, most of the time the audience is only half-listening to the radio. Yet many of them will start twirling the dial if they don't hear the music or news that interests or pleases them. They are the most fidgety and fickle of all media audiences. For these reasons, the radio news lead must be written to catch and hold the attention of these potential non-listeners.

THE FOUR BASIC RADIO NEWS LEADS

The four basic radio news story leads are the soft news lead, the hard news lead, the throwaway news lead, and the umbrella, or comprehensive, news lead. All are "what" leads.

THE SOFT NEWS LEAD

The soft news lead "featurizes" the news to catch the ear of that half-hearted listener. Soft radio leads are the most fun to write because they call for imagination and creativity. Here are three soft lead examples:

All radio broadcast material quoted in this chapter is reprinted by permission of United Press International.

```
    MORE BAD NEWS FOR PITTSBURGH STEELER QUARTERBACK
TERRY BRADSHAW.
    A TEAM SPOKESMAN SAYS BRADSHAW'S SORE RIGHT
ELBOW— ON WHICH HE HAD OFF-SEASON SURGERY— HAS
BEEN DRAINED AND PLACED IN A SPLINT.
    BRADSHAW HAS BEEN THROWING FOR INCREASING
LENGTHS OF TIME AT THE ST. VINCENT COLLEGE
TRAINING CAMP IN PENNSYLVANIA, BUT HE SKIPPED
PRACTICE YESTERDAY BECAUSE THE ELBOW WAS TENDER.
    TODAY, HE WAS EXAMINED BY ORTHOPEDIST PAUL
STEELE IN PITTSBURGH... AND DISCOVERED THE JOINT
WAS INFLAMED.

    THE Y-12 NUCLEAR WEAPONS PLANT NEAR OAK RIDGE
WAS DESCRIBED TODAY AS A "WITCHES' CAULDRON" OF
POLLUTION PROBLEMS. DOCTOR MICHAEL BRUNER...
HEAD OF THE STATE HEALTH DEPARTMENT'S DIVISION OF
WATER MANAGEMENT... SAID CONTAMINATION AROUND
THE PLANT POSES MAJOR HAZARDS. BRUNER TESTIFIED
DURING A DAY-LONG CONGRESSIONAL HEARING ON THE
PLANT AT THE AMERICAN MUSEUM OF SCIENCE AND
ENERGY. THE HEARINGS ARE HOSTED BY REPRESENTATIVES
ALBERT GORE AND MARILYN LLOYD TO DETERMINE HEALTH
AND ENVIRONMENTAL HAZARDS AT THE OAK RIDGE PLANT.

    CHRYSLER CALLS IT A GREAT OCCASION, AND THE
REAGAN ADMINISTRATION IS HAILING IT AS ANOTHER
SIGN OF ECONOMIC RECOVERY.
    BOARD CHAIRMAN LEE IACOCCA ANNOUNCED TODAY IN
WASHINGTON THAT CHRYSLER WILL PAY OFF THE
REMAINDER OF ITS ONE-POINT-TWO-BILLION-DOLLAR
FEDERALLY GUARANTEED LOANS BY SEPTEMBER. THAT'S
SEVEN YEARS EARLY. THE AUTOMAKER OWES 800-MILLION
DOLLARS ON THE LOANS. IT REPAID 400-MILLION
DOLLARS LAST MONTH.
    IACOCCA SAYS THIS WILL RE-ESTABLISH CHRYSLER AS
A SUCCESSFUL PRIVATE CORPORATION THAT "PAYS ITS
OWN WAY." AND HE ADDS THAT THE EARLY PAY-OFF WILL
SAVE HIS COMPANY 56-MILLION DOLLARS A YEAR.
    CHRYSLER GOT THE GOVERNMENT LOANS THREE YEARS
AGO WHEN IT WAS ON THE BRINK OF BANKRUPTCY.
IACOCCA IS CLEARLY OPTIMISTIC ABOUT THE FUTURE. HE
SAYS IT LOOKS LIKE THE AUTO INDUSTRY IS IN THE
MIDST OF A BIG RECOVERY, AND HE SAYS CHRYSLER WILL
BE RECALLING SOME LAID-OFF AUTOWORKERS.
```

The Hard News Lead

The hard news lead wastes no time in alerting the audience to what's coming up. It gives the news immediately. The drawback to this type of lead is that it gives the listener little time to start paying attention. It's best to use it in the first story of the newscast, immediately following the attention-getting opening of the newscast ("Good morning and welcome to WXVZ's 10 o'clock news"):

>   VICE PRESIDENT BUSH CAST A TIE-BREAKING VOTE
>   TODAY, AS THE SENATE VOTED CONDITIONAL APPROVAL TO
>   RESUME PRODUCTION OF NERVE GAS AFTER A 14-YEAR
>   MORATORIUM. THE VOTE AUTHORIZES 112-POINT-FIVE-
>   MILLION DOLLARS FOR THE EQUIPMENT NEEDED TO
>   PRODUCE THE BIG EYE BOMB, AN AIR-DELIVERED
>   CHEMICAL WEAPON... AND ANOTHER 18-MILLION
>   DOLLARS TO INITIATE PRODUCTION OF A TWO-CHAMBER
>   155-MILLIMETER ARTILLERY SHELL.
>
>   A GROUP CALLED THE "ARMENIAN REVOLUTIONARY ARMY"
>   CALLS THE DEATHS OF SIX GUNMEN KILLED IN TODAY'S
>   ATTACK ON THE TURKISH EMBASSY IN PORTUGAL—
>   QUOTE— "OUR SACRIFICE TO THE ALTAR OF FREEDOM."
>   ONE GUNMAN WAS KILLED BY A GUARD... AND FIVE
>   OTHERS BLEW THEMSELVES UP WITH A GRENADE AS ANTI-
>   TERRORIST POLICE CAPTURED THE BUILDING. THE WIFE
>   OF A TURKISH DIPLOMAT ALSO WAS KILLED AND THERE IS
>   AN UNCONFIRMED REPORT OF AN EIGHTH PERSON KILLED.

Hard leads are usually easy to spot. Sometimes, though, as in the following example, the hard lead can be tinged with soft lead material. Most of the time, however, the hard lead takes a no-nonsense approach to the events being told:

>   THE STREETS OF SANTIAGO, CHILE, ARE QUIET TODAY
>   ... AFTER LAST NIGHT'S PROTESTS DEMANDING
>   RESTORATION OF CIVILIAN RULE.
>   A TEEN-AGE GIRL DIED AND HUNDREDS OF PEOPLE WERE
>   ARRESTED AS RIOT POLICE FIRED TEAR GAS TO BREAK UP
>   SEVERAL LARGE CROWDS.
>   POLICE SOURCES SAY 110 PEOPLE WERE ARRESTED...
>   BUT PUBLISHED REPORTS PUT THE FIGURE AT 565.
>   AT THE VATICAN, POPE JOHN PAUL TODAY CALLED ON
>   THE CHILEAN GOVERNMENT AND OPPOSITION FORCES TO
>   WORK TOGETHER TO AVERT FURTHER BLOODSHED.

THE THROWAWAY LEAD

The throwaway lead, as it says, can be thrown away, and the story can then be read starting with the second sentence or so. Like the soft lead, it alerts the listener to what's coming. The major difference is that it headlines what is to come in the same way a headline tells what's in a newspaper story.

>   THE DEPARTMENT OF HEALTH AND HUMAN SERVICES SAYS
>   THERE'S A "GLIMMER OF LIGHT" IN THE FIGHT AGAINST
>   THE DEADLY AIDS DISEASE. FEDERAL SCIENTISTS HAVE
>   FOUND THAT A VIRUS-FIGHTING BLOOD-CELL PRODUCT IS
>   USEFUL IN RESTORING SOME OF THE INFECTED WHITE
>   BLOOD CELLS DAMAGED BY AIDS. THE AGENCY'S DR.
>   EDWARD BRANDT SAYS IT'S NOT A "QUICK CURE," BUT
>   SHOULD HELP POINT THE DIRECTION TOWARD TREATMENT.
>
>   PRESIDENTIAL AIDES ADMIT THAT FOR SEVERAL DAYS,
>   THE WHITE HOUSE WAS PREOCCUPIED WITH THE CARTER

> CAMPAIGN BRIEFING BOOK INVESTIGATION. BUT OFFICIALS NOW REPORT "BUSINESS AS USUAL" AT THE WHITE HOUSE.
> SPOKESMAN LARRY SPEAKES SAYS CHIEF OF STAFF JAMES BAKER AND SEVERAL OTHER KEY OFFICIALS SPENT SEVERAL DAYS LOOKING FOR THE 1980 PAPERS USED BY THE REAGAN CAMP... BUT ADDED THAT NOW— QUOTE— "WE'RE BACK TO FULL STEAM AHEAD."
> MEANWHILE, A HOUSE SUBCOMMITTEE THREATENS TO ISSUE A SUBPOENA UNLESS IT IS GRANTED DIRECT ACCESS TO SOME OF REAGAN'S 1980 CAMPAIGN FILES. THOSE FILES ARE STORED AT A STANFORD UNIVERSITY LIBRARY.
> WASHINGTON ATTORNEY AND FORMER LAWYER FOR THE SENATE WATERGATE COMMITTEE JAMES HAMILTON IS TRYING TO NEGOTIATE WITH WHITE HOUSE COUNSEL FRED FIELDING ON ACCESS TO THOSE FILES.
>
> SENATOR EDWARD KENNEDY HAS HARSH WORDS FOR PRESIDENT REAGAN'S PROPOSAL TO TOUGHEN ENFORCEMENT OF THE FAIR HOUSING ACT.
> THE MASSACHUSETTS DEMOCRAT DESCRIBES REAGAN'S PROPOSAL AS "HALF-HEARTED" AND "PLAINLY INADEQUATE."
> BUT THE PRESIDENT ASSERTS HIS PLAN WOULD PUT "REAL TEETH" INTO THE NATION'S FAIR HOUSING LAWS.
> AND THAT'S WHAT HE'LL TELL REPUBLICAN CONGRESSIONAL LEADERS THIS MORNING WHEN HE MEETS WITH THEM IN WASHINGTON.
> THE FAIR HOUSING ACT IS A SECTION OF THE CIVIL RIGHTS ACT OF 1968. IT FORBIDS DISCRIMINATION IN THE SALE OR RENTAL OF HOUSING ON THE BASIS OF RACE, COLOR, RELIGION, SEX OR NATIONAL ORIGIN.

The Umbrella Lead

The umbrella lead—also called a round-up or comprehensive lead—is a sentence or two under which a round-up story, or several stories in a newscast, may fall. It also serves as an attention-getter for that elusive radio audience likely to turn the dial if you don't serve them properly:

> DRY BRUSH AND DRY STANDS OF TIMBER ARE GIVING WESTERN FIREFIGHTERS ALL THEY CAN HANDLE. MORE THAN THREE-THOUSAND FIREFIGHTERS ARE TRYING TO DOUSE BLAZES THAT HAVE CHARRED 15-THOUSAND ACRES IN CALIFORNIA AND SOUTHERN NEVADA. A 45-HUNDRED-ACRE BLAZE... IN A NATIONAL FOREST NORTHWEST OF LOS ANGELES... HAS BEEN PARTLY CONTAINED AT A COST OF NEARLY ONE-MILLION DOLLARS AND AT LEAST 39 INJURIES.
>
> WITH THE ALL-STAR BREAK OVER, BASEBALL RETURNS TO THE MORE IMPORTANT BUSINESS OF DECIDING ITS PENNANT RACES TONIGHT.

> THE AMERICAN LEAGUE'S TWO SURPRISING DIVISION
> LEADERS... TORONTO IN THE EAST AND TEXAS IN THE
> WEST... OPEN A THREE-GAME SERIES IN EXHIBITION
> STADIUM. THE BLUE JAYS LEAD BALTIMORE BY ONE GAME
> AND THE RANGERS HOLD A TWO-GAME EDGE OVER
> CALIFORNIA.
> THE NATIONAL LEAGUE DIVISION LEADERS...
> MONTREAL AND ATLANTA... ALSO CLASH IN OLYMPIC
> STADIUM. THE EXPOS HAVE A ONE-AND-A-HALF GAME
> ADVANTAGE OVER PHILADELPHIA IN THE EAST, AND THE
> BRAVES, SHOOTING FOR THEIR SECOND STRAIGHT TITLE
> IN THE WEST, ARE ONE GAME AHEAD OF LOS ANGELES.

In this whole business of writing radio news leads, there are gray areas. This next umbrella lead example could also be called a soft lead. Perhaps we could start a new category of leads of "soft umbrella leads":

> IT MIGHT BE SAID THE EUROPEANS ARE RATHER THIN-
> SKINNED WHEN IT COMES TO HEAT. AND WITH A HEAT WAVE
> SWEEPING THAT CONTINENT— AND THE MIDDLE EAST—
> MORE OF THAT THIN SKIN IS BEING EXPOSED.
> ACCORDING TO ONE HEADLINE IN A WEST GERMAN
> NEWSPAPER... "GERMANY IS TAKING OFF ITS CLOTHES."
> AND SO IT IS. WEST GERMAN FAMILIES HAVE BEEN SEEN
> WALKING NUDE IN THE PARKS. SOME JOGGERS HAVE EVEN
> PEELED BEFORE TAKING THEIR RUN IN RECORD
> TEMPERATURES.
> PLUNGING INTO FOUNTAINS IS BECOMING A PASTTIME
> AS THE MERCURY RUNS ABOUT 10 DEGREES HOTTER THAN
> NORMAL.
> THE WEATHER'S BEEN BLAMED FOR KILLING AT LEAST
> 10 PEOPLE IN FRANKFURT— WHERE ANOTHER 170 GERMANS
> REPORTEDLY COLLAPSED FROM TEMPERATURES HITTING 86
> DEGREES.
> TEMPERATURES ELSEWHERE IN EUROPE, INCLUDING
> SWEDEN, EXCEEDED 93 DEGREES, DRIVING THOUSANDS OF
> PEOPLE OUTDOORS.

What really matters in radio news leads is getting the attention of the radio audience in the appropriate way. That way is dictated by the story materials you have to work with.

A rewrite and updating of the weather heat wave story used this strict umbrella lead:

> AS WEATHER FORECASTERS PREDICTED NO IMMEDIATE
> RELIEF FROM TEMPERATURES INCHING ABOVE 90,
> THOUSANDS OF EUROPEANS TOOK OFF THEIR CLOTHES TO
> BEAT THE HEAT.
> SOME WEST GERMANS WALKED NUDE IN THE STREETS,
> BRITONS PUT UP THEIR OWN NUDE VOLLEYBALL TEAM, AND
> LONDON ZOOKEEPERS SOOTHED SCORCHED ANIMALS WITH
> SUNTAN LOTION.
> THE CELEBRATION OF SUMMER HAS TURNED INTO A

```
      NIGHTMARE FOR AUTHORITIES COPING WITH BLOCKED
      BRIDGES, WATER SHORTAGES AND MELTING ROADS.
        FOR OTHERS, IT'S BEEN TRAGIC. A PARISIAN INFANT
      DIED TODAY OF DEHYDRATION WHILE SLEEPING IN A CAR
      ... AND THERE HAVE BEEN WEATHER-RELATED DEATHS IN
      FRANKFURT AND BERLIN SINCE THE HEAT WAVE BEGAN.
```

What you do, and how you do it, depends on your imagination, your training, your newscast style and your news director.

RADIO NEWSWRITING: THE CONVERSATIONAL STYLE

Once you've written the lead, how does the rest of the story go? In terms of style, the story is written in much the same way as the lead. You expand on details in the order in which they were introduced, in a conversational style. That shouldn't be hard for you to do. After all, most of your writing should follow the natural flow of your speech patterns. Look at radio newswriting this way: The lead alerts the listener in the same way you would alert a friend about a story you're going to tell or a piece of information you're going to divulge; for example, "I finally know what the mass communications exam is going to be like," you say to your friend. Having got your friend to focus on what you're going to say, you then tell what's actually involved in the exam. You do it all in conversational style with a nice informal touch, just the way you would talk. You'll use some contractions and some sentence fragments. That's the way it is with radio newswriting.

Radio Writing Checklist

Be Concise. Few stories run more than 250 words; most are less than 30 or 60 seconds long. You've got a highly fidgety audience, remember? You've got to keep things moving. You've got to keep everything simple. If your audience doesn't understand you the first time, there's no going back over a paragraph. Use short declarative sentences with subject-verb-object constructions. Keep the subject and the verb close together. Long introductory phrases or clauses starting off a sentence or a paragraph or stuck in between subjects and verbs place too much strain on your listeners' minds. When that happens, your listeners will tune you out.

Be Current. Radio, always in competition with the print and television media, capitalizes on its sense of immediacy. If a train is derailed near your city and dangerous chemicals are spilled, you, like the rest of the citizens in the city, will turn on the radio to discover what's happening. (More and more, however, television is moving into this area, especially with the advent of ENG, electronic news gathering, which enables TV stations to do live reports from news sites.) To capitalize on radio's sense of immediacy, use the present tense whenever possible. Use timely phrases—"at this hour," "just moments ago," etc. The impression you want to give is that the news or event just happened. Newspapers use "yesterday" or "today"; radio tends to do away with those time tags and uses words with more recency.

Read the following news story. The woman lost in the story was found yesterday. Did the lead of the radio story say this? Of course not. It came over the

UPI wire this way:

```
A PROMINENT SURGEON'S WIFE WHO WENT FOR A WALK
OUTSIDE HER SIGNAL MOUNTAIN HOME AND GOT LOST
THREE DAYS AGO HAS BEEN FOUND PERCHED ON A CLIFF
AND CLINGING TO A TREE.
    SUSAN HAYES ALERTED RESCUERS YESTERDAY BY
YELLING AT THEM. SHE WAS LOWERED FROM A 60-FOOT
CLIFF IN GOOD CONDITION. OFFICIALS SAID THE 43-
YEAR-OLD WOMAN WENT FOR A WALK WITH THE FAMILY DOG
MONDAY AFTERNOON AND GOT LOST WHILE WANDERING
WITHIN A MILE RADIUS OF HER HOUSE. SHE BECAME
TRAPPED ON THE CLIFF ABOUT 15 HOURS BEFORE HER
RESCUE.
```

Of course, the fact that she was discovered yesterday has to be revealed eventually. It was—after the lead.

When you do use the time in radio newswriting, try to use it right after the verb.

Use Helpful Identifiers in the Lead.   In the radio news story you just read, was Susan Hayes's name used in the lead? No. Why not? Because the radio listener needs to be alerted first by a more general identifier. Otherwise, the name would be lost on the listener. So first you talk about the lost surgeon's wife; then you give her name. Names are used on radio for the same reason they're used in the newspaper—they lend a sense of intimacy and credibility to the story, whether you know the person or not.

Sometimes, however, names are omitted. This short news item omits a production secretary's name without damaging the story:

```
    LOS ANGELES COUNTY GRAND JURY TESTIMONY RELEASED
YESTERDAY SHOWS DIRECTOR JOHN LANDIS AND HIS TOP
AIDES APPARENTLY COVERED UP THEIR ILLEGAL
EMPLOYMENT OF TWO YOUNGSTERS KILLED IN THE
"TWILIGHT ZONE" MOVIE SET HELICOPTER CRASH.
    A PRODUCTION SECRETARY TOLD THE GRAND JURY THAT
FILM SCRIPTS MENTIONING USE OF THE CHILDREN WERE
CLOSELY GUARDED TO AVOID DISCOVERY.
    THE JULY 23RD, 1982, ACCIDENT ALSO KILLED ACTOR
VIC MORROW.
```

Names of places, like names of persons, are also used later in the story.

If you do use a person's name in a lead, precede it with the title that goes with the name (not Mr., Miss or Mrs., but "President," "Chrysler chairman," etc.). Once again, that alerts the radio audience to the significance of the name to follow. Titles frequently follow names in newspaper stories, but in radio news, unless the title is exceedingly long, it precedes the name. Look at this example:

```
    INTERIOR SECRETARY JAMES WATT SAYS THE UNITED
STATES IS FACED WITH A BATTLE BETWEEN THE MEDIA
AND WHAT HE CALLS THE SPIRITUAL FORCES OF TRUTH.
    IN A SPEECH TO FIVE-THOUSAND FUNDAMENTALIST
CHRISTIAN BUSINESSMEN IN DETROIT LAST NIGHT...
WATT DESCRIBED REPORTERS AS "ENEMIES OF TRUTH" OUT
```

```
TO DESTROY THE COUNTRY. BUT WATT SAID HE HAS GIVEN
UP FIGHTING NEWS MEDIA REPORTS THAT CRITICIZE HIS
CONSERVATION EFFORTS.
```

Use Pronunciation Guides. Names that are difficult to pronounce are followed by a phonetic pronunciation guide for radio news announcers. Pronunciation guides are composed by wire services as a courtesy to their subscribers. UPI begins its radio transmission each day with a pronunciation guide. This partial example of UPI's daily guide identifies the person as well as provides pronunciation aids.

```
WORD-PRONUNCIATION GUIDE
  AGCA (AH'-JAH), MEHMET ALI, TURK CONVICTED IN
1981 PAPAL SHOOTING
  ARAFAT, YASSER (YAH'-SEHR AHR-AH-FAHT'), HEAD OF
THE PALESTINE LIBERATION ORGANIZATION
  ARENS, MOSHE (MOH'-SHEH AIR'-EHNZ), ISRAELI
DEFENSE MINISTER
  ASSAD, HAFEZ (HAH'-FEHZ' AH-SAHD'), PRESIDENT OF
SYRIA
  BIEBER (BEEB'-EHR), OWEN, UNITED AUTO WORKERS
UNION PRESIDENT
  CONTADORA (KOHN-TAH-DOHR'-AH), GROUP OF FOUR
LATIN NATIONS SEEKING PEACE IN CENTRAL AMERICA.
FOUR ARE MEXICO, PANAMA, COLUMBIA AND VENEZUELA.
```

When you write a news story, if you think your announcer will have trouble pronouncing names like Gemayel or Dursun Aksoy or places like the Awali River or even more familiar words like *attaché*, place a phonetic pronunciation after them:

```
  TWO ARMENIAN NATIONALIST GROUPS SAY THEY'RE
RESPONSIBLE FOR THE POLITICAL ASSASSINATION TODAY
OF A TURKISH DIPLOMAT IN BRUSSELS, AND ONE SAYS IT
WILL KILL MORE TURKISH DIPLOMATS, POLICE SAY.
  A WELL-BUILT GUNMAN WEARING BLUE JEANS CALMLY
WALKED UP TO THE PARKED CAR OF TURKISH EMBASSY
ATTACHE (A-TUH-SHAY') DURSUN AKSOY (DUHR'-SUHN
AHK'-SOY)... AND PUMPED TWO BULLETS INTO THE
DIPLOMAT'S HEAD AT POINT BLANK RANGE.
```

As you can see, no hard and fast rules are set in this commonsensical approach to phonetic pronunciation. Anyone can play:

```
  ISRAEL'S CABINET HAS PUT OFF A DECISION ON A
PARTIAL WITHDRAWAL OF ISRAELI TROOPS FROM LEBANON.
BUT ARMY CHIEF OF STAFF LIEUTENANT GENERAL MOSHE
LEVY SAYS IF JEWISH FORCES PULL BACK THEY'LL STOP
AT THE AWALI (AH-WAH-LEE') RIVER IN SOUTHERN
LEBANON. LEVY SAYS THE MOVE WON'T LEAD TO THE
PERMANENT PARTITIONING OF LEBANON, ALTHOUGH HE
SAYS IT WOULD REDUCE TERRITORY CONTROLLED BY THE
GEMAYEL (JEH-MAYL') GOVERNMENT.
```

REWRITING RADIO WIRE COPY

You might think that Associated Press or United Press International radio news wire copy would be good enough to "rip and read." It's not. Much of the time, the copy for radio has initially been written for newspapers. In addition, a wire story may have a local angle not played up in the story. These conditions call for a rewrite to "customize" the news for your audience. For example, a fact-finding committee appointed by the Senate may have 10 senators on it. If one of those senators represents your state, that fact should lead off the story.

Here's another example of a local angle: If a person from your city is one of 55 persons killed in an air crash, that fact should probably lead off your radio story. Just remember that wire stories from AP and UPI are written for radio in the same way they are written for newspapers—for general national, state or regional interest. You must find the local angle, if there is one, and rewrite the story to reflect it.

One of the major reasons for rewriting radio news is to update it. Perhaps something new has happened, or comments on the event have been gathered and need to be added to the story. But even if nothing new has happened, most copy, whether from the wire or from a local news source, must be rewritten to keep your newscasts from sounding like an echo from an hour ago when your story was first read. A major story used on every newscast has to be rewritten so that it does not sound repetitious or boring. If you don't rewrite your news copy, your disgruntled audience will either turn you off or start twirling the dial for something less stale.

These five examples show you how UPI rewrites a story. First we'll read the full story, then highlight the different leads:

```
    AFTER TWO WEEKS OF HAGGLING OVER ACCESS TO
PRESIDENT REAGAN'S 1980 CAMPAIGN FILES, THE WHITE
HOUSE HAS AGREED TO LET A HOUSE SUBCOMMITTEE
CONDUCT A PARTIAL REVIEW OF THE DOCUMENTS.
    UNDER THE AGREEMENT, THE PANEL WILL GET FILES
FROM THE REAGAN ARCHIVES AT STANFORD UNIVERSITY
WHICH THE F-B-I DECIDES MAY BE RELEVANT TO
INVESTIGATIONS OF THE MYSTERY.
    THAT INCLUDES MATERIAL PREPARED FOR THE
PRESIDENTIAL DEBATE AND CARTER WHITE HOUSE
INTELLIGENCE DOCUMENTS THAT MAY HAVE BEEN
"IMPROPERLY" GIVEN TO THE REAGAN CAMPAIGN.
    A REAGAN ADMINISTRATION OFFICIAL, WHO DOESN'T
WANT TO BE NAMED, SAYS THE CONTROVERSY APPEARS TO
HAVE FADED AND THE ADMINISTRATION PROBABLY IS HOME
FREE.

    THE HEAD OF A HOUSE SUBCOMMITTEE INVESTIGATING
HOW CARTER CAMPAIGN DOCUMENTS MADE THEIR WAY INTO
THE REAGAN CAMP IN 1980 SAYS HIS PANEL HAS REACHED
AGREEMENT WITH THE WHITE HOUSE FOR DIRECT ACCESS
TO PART OF REAGAN'S FILES.

    THE WHITE HOUSE HAS REACHED AGREEMENT WITH A
HOUSE SUBCOMMITTEE TO GIVE CONGRESSIONAL PROBERS
"DIRECT ACCESS" TO SOME 1980 REAGAN CAMPAIGN
```

FILES, THE PANEL WANTS TO KNOW HOW CARTER WHITE
HOUSE DOCUMENTS GOT TO THE REAGAN CAMP.

A HOUSE PANEL SAYS IT'S REACHED AGREEMENT WITH
THE WHITE HOUSE ON ACCESS TO PART OF PRESIDENT
REAGAN'S 1980 CAMPAIGN FILES. UNDER THE AGREEMENT,
THE PANEL WILL GET MATERIAL THE F-B-I SAYS IS
RELEVANT. BOTH ARE CONDUCTING INQUIRIES TO FIND
OUT HOW CARTER WHITE HOUSE PAPERS WOUND UP IN
REAGAN CAMPAIGN FILES.

TWO WEEKS OF NEGOTIATIONS HAVE RESULTED IN WHITE
HOUSE AGREEMENT TO LET A HOUSE PANEL HAVE ACCESS
TO PART OF PRESIDENT REAGAN'S 1980 CAMPAIGN FILES.
THE PANEL IS PROBING HOW THE REAGAN CAMPAIGN GOT
CARTER WHITE HOUSE PAPERS.

The UPI newspaper story ran much longer, and the sentences were much more complex, as you will see:

Panel to Get Look at Reagan Files

WASHINGTON (UPI) — The White House has agreed to give congressional investigators the Reagan campaign files it needs to discover how Reagan's camp got information from the Carter White House, a congressman said yesterday.

In the compromise agreement, reached in three weeks of tense negotiation, the House post office and civil service subcommittee will have direct access to "relevant" materials but not to unrelated Reagan political data, said aides to chairman Rep. Donald Albosta, D-Mich.

"Direct access to these files is very important to our ability to complete our work" in investigating whether ethics were violated when the Reagan campaign got hold of Carter White House materials, Albosta said.

The six-page agreement only permits subcommittee investigators to review files already cleared as "relevant" by the FBI.

It lets investigators from Congress' General Accounting Office review, for the congressional panel, records of a dozen top Reagan political workers, including former campaign director William Casey and White House chief of staff James Baker. The files are stored at the Hoover Institution Library in California.

Albosta said he had confidence the FBI would not engage in a "coverup."

"The fact would still remain that we would know what was there that was relevant to our investigation," he said, and the subcommittee then could decide whether to issue subpoenas.

Albosta called the agreement signed by White House counsel Fred Fielding "both fair and equitable" and "a good compromise."

The accord apparently was approved by one or more of the trustees for the campaign files — Reagan, presidential counselor Edwin Meese and deputy White House chief of staff Michael Deaver. . . .

After reading radio news copy for a while, you may never again be satisfied with newspaper stories—they simply don't flow as naturally. And this story ran on half again as long as the segment reprinted here!

Here are UPI's updates to a presidential announcement of military maneuvers in Central America:

```
   PRESIDENT REAGAN SAID LAST NIGHT DURING HIS NEWS
CONFERENCE THAT THE PLANNED SEA AND AIR EXERCISES
IN CENTRAL AMERICA ARE ROUTINE. REAGAN ASKED WHY
THE MANEUVERS ARE BEING TREATED WITH SUSPICION
WHEN NO ONE GOT EXCITED ABOUT LAST YEAR'S
MANEUVERS IN HONDURAS AND THE CARIBBEAN. THE NEW
MANEUVERS INVOLVE MORE MEN THAN EVER BEFORE AND
WILL LAST FOR A LONGER TIME.
   PRESIDENT REAGAN SAYS THE PLANNED LAND, SEA AND
AIR EXERCISES IN CENTRAL AMERICA ARE LITTLE MORE
THAN ROUTINE. HE DISCUSSED THE MATTER DURING A
BROADCAST NEWS CONFERENCE LAST NIGHT.
   CUBAN PRESIDENT FIDEL CASTRO SAYS HE IS ARMING
ANOTHER ONE-MILLION CUBANS TO COUNTER AMERICAN
MOVES AGAINST HIS COMMUNIST NATION. IN A SPEECH
YESTERDAY... CASTRO DESCRIBED AS "AN EXTREMELY
GRAVE ERROR" THE U-S DECISION TO SEND U-S WARSHIPS
TO WATERS OFF NICARAGUA— AN ALLY OF CUBA.
```

You will note from these examples that just as in reporting for other media, in a developing story or a follow-up story, the latest development usually forms the lead. A recapitulation of the story follows in succeeding paragraphs. The same logic applies when you use the latest developments to update radio news stories.

THE RADIO NEWSCAST FORMULA

The organization of your newscast depends on your station manager or news director. You may be directed to lead off with the local news, go on to state and national news, and then move to the world news, sports and weather. Other directors will want you to write a newscast leading off with the most important news story of the day—national, local or otherwise—and then go to the world, national, state and local news, then sports and weather. As a member of the team composing the newscast, your job is to write it as you've been directed.

Generally, the smaller the radio station, the more varied the tasks you'll find yourself doing. If you are in a very small market—a city of under 50,000—you may be the person to coordinate the newscast and anchor it. A sports director may help in compiling the sports segment for you and even delivering it. Different radio stations in the same market area will have different methods of gathering and handling the news. But the format for writing radio stories and fidelity to radio newswriting style are standard in all broadcast markets.

A newscast may be 30 or 45 seconds in length and presented every half-hour during prime time, or it may be anywhere from five to 15 to 30 minutes presented at times like 6:30 a.m., noon, 6 p.m. and 11 p.m. Prime time for radio is morning and afternoon rush hours, when commuters listen in their cars.

Let's say you must put together a five-minute newscast. That actually means you have 3½ minutes of air time. The introduction, standard close and commercials will take care of the other minute and a half.

To compose the newscast, first select the major stories to be used from the world, national and state wires. Choose the local news stories developed by the station's reporters, with two or three "actualities" or "voicers" (taped or live news feeds of interviews conducted by the reporters). Select the major sports stories, and phone the local weather bureau to get the latest report. The local news story you have—perhaps a controversial high school principal in your area has been fired—is important enough to lead with. It's a fairly big story—teachers and students lined up on opposite sides over the school board's decision not to renew his contract—and interesting, so you use an actuality and let the story run for 60 seconds. That means you have 15 lines of copy, at 65 characters per line. That's the average number of lines your radio newscaster reads in one minute.

Think in terms of time rather than space when you write the newscast. Two world news stories take 20 seconds each, after you've heavily edited and rewritten them. Two national stories total another 30 seconds. That means you have one minute and 20 seconds left to fill. A story about a state prison riot takes 15 seconds. A story about the state income tax takes another 10. You have 55 seconds to fill. Another local story about an automobile accident and a fatality in the city takes up another 15 seconds. Two sports story round-ups, first on the national and then on the local level, bring you up to the five-second mark—just enough time left for the weather.

As you staple these stories to sheets of paper, one story per sheet, you compose the transitions from one story to another. They will tie the newscast together. After the world news stories, for example, you might type in, "Back home in University City . . . ," or "Meanwhile on the national scene. . . ." From the national news, you might type or write in, "Closer to home . . . ," or, "In state news tonight. . . ."

These geographical transitions may give way to subject matter transitions at times. If you've just finished talking about a state income tax story, you might move on to local news by saying, "A tax increase is also being considered here in Athens. . . ." That's the way a newscast is coupled together. Sometimes transitions are called "coupling pins."

A 15- or 30-minute newscast will be composed in much the same way. In these longer newscasts, a "kicker" or "brite" is usually used at the end of the cast. With the world as grim as it sometimes is, it's a good idea to leave the audience with a smile on its face. Any radio or television newscast of any length attempts to incorporate a brite to sign off. Here's one:

```
WHEN HOWARD AND LOIS EMDEN AND SEVEN GUESTS ATE
DINNER AT A PHOENIX RESTAURANT, THE SOUP WAS FREE
OF FLIES, BUT THE EMDENS CLAIM THEY DID FIND A
COCKROACH IN A WINE GLASS ... AND A SCORPION ON
THE HAND OF MR. EMDEN, WHO WAS STUNG. THEY'RE
SUING THE DIFFERENT POINTE OF VIEW RESTAURANT FOR
MORE THAN 400-THOUSAND DOLLARS.
```

Some Technical Aspects

The radio wire copy and the announcer copy prepared in radio station newsrooms may differ according to the guidelines of the news directors of particular radio stations. Some may want you to write copy in all caps; others may want you to use upper- and lower-case letters. Whatever the case, here are some guidelines you should follow in preparing radio copy for any announcer: Radio copy may be double- or triple-spaced. Underline words that require special emphasis. Never split words or phrases—or words that naturally flow together—from one line to another.

Although radio wire copy does not follow this last rule, and your news director may not require you to do it, there is a natural tendency when reading aloud to pause at the end of a line of copy. If you follow the rule of not splitting words and phrases from one line to another, you'll save your announcer (or yourself) some awkward reading moments. The following weathercast illustrates this.

```
The lowest temperature this morning
in the continental United States was
45 degrees Fahrenheit
at Yellowstone Park, Wyoming.
Yesterday's highest
afternoon temperature
was 108 degrees at Bullhead City, Arizona,
and Thermal and Palm Springs, California.
```

When pauses are needed after phrases or sentences, they may be indicated by ellipses, as in this example:

```
Six hours after she handcuffed herself to a chair
in Governor Lamar Alexander's outer office yesterday
. . . a Memphis babysitter was cut loose with a promise
of meeting with the governor in 30 days.
Mary Maxwell had sought a meeting with Alexander
to discuss a state licensing law that prevents her
from operating a day care center at her home. . .
a service she says is desperately needed.
```

Any misspelled words should be crossed out and the whole word rewritten above it. Numbers under 10 are spelled out. Figures are used for numbers 10 through 999. Hyphenated combinations are used for figures and words above 999: "45-thousand dollars." However, write "April 5th," etc., and "45th Avenue at 33rd Street." When you write numbers, round them off. If 989 people are involved in a demonstration, write, "nearly one thousand people." (Don't write "a thousand"; pronounced with a long *a*, it sounds too much like "*eight* thousand.")

You will want to use direct quotes in your radio news story, but you'll want to keep those quotes short and simple. Some people you are quoting will ramble or utter a long, complex sentence. To recast for radio, you will have to break the sentence up and paraphrase it or use just a part of it. Avoid saying "quote" and "unquote," but make certain your audience knows you are quoting a source when that is the case. Use such phrases as "in these words," "as she put it" or "in the mayor's words" to indicate direct quotes. If you are reading the news or know the announcer who will be reading the news, it might be all right simply to use quotation marks. The announcer, through inflection, can indicate that those words are direct quotes, as in this example:

```
   White House spokesman Larry Speakes gave
the administration's reaction today to Nicaragua's call
for region-wide peace talks on Central America. He said,
it's "a positive step". . . but that the plan
has "serious shortcomings" that should be refined
in Nicaragua's discussions with its neighbors.
Speakes said one problem is that it seems to put
the Salvadoran rebels on the same level as
the elected government.
```

SUMMARY

Capturing the audience's attention is more difficult in radio than in any other medium. Radio news competes with many activities for the listener's attention. Rarely can it capture all of it. So it's important that the radio listener be served with attention-getting leads that launch succinct, clearly worded stories that are smoothly linked in a newscast with helpful transitions.

Radio stories rely on "what" leads. Radio style usually paraphrases direct quotes or, at most, uses just a few words from a direct quote for impact. Radio style is conversational. It doesn't follow the conventions of print-media stories because the limited air time available doesn't permit full development of details. Those selected for a story must be the most significant, and they must be updated regularly, either with new information or through revision, to keep the story fresh for subsequent newscasts.

Radio's strength is its ability to reach listeners immediately. Radio newswriting must build on that strength with stories that convey a story's importance and immediacy.

EXERCISES

BASIC RADIO NEWS LEADS

1. Write a hard news lead story for broadcast from this newspaper story.

Ad Experiment Brings Public TV $3.7 Million

WASHINGTON (AP) — A report concludes that nine public TV stations raised $3.7 million by broadcasting commercials for 15 months and that the experiment resulted in few complaints from viewers.

The report was prepared by the National Association of Public Television Stations.

The special experiment was authorized by Congress in 1981 when it created the Temporary Commission on Alternative Financing for Public Telecommunications.

2. Write a soft news lead story for broadcast from this newspaper story.

SPACE CENTER, Houston (AP) — Two women astronauts let a male colleague at Mission Control know he should watch his language — and drop the sexist stereotypes.

Discovery astronaut Rhea Seddon, a physician, helped craft a flyswatter-like device that was to be used to hook a switch on the side of the Syncom satellite. Included in the work was a number of stitches with string and a sailmaker's needle.

Astronaut Dave Hilmers, acting as the Mission Control communicator with Discovery on Tuesday, complimented Ms. Seddon on her "seamstress" work.

Later, he told Ms. Seddon she would now be hearing the "dulcet" voice of astronaut Sally Ride on the microphone.

Ms. Seddon replied: "That's a sexist remark."

Ms. Ride, America's first woman in space, shot Hilmers a piercing look, and then said she wanted to correct the earlier comment about "seamstress work."

"That was the work of a surgeon," said Ms. Ride.

She said it with a smile.

3. Write a soft news lead story for broadcast from this newspaper story.*

The nationwide death toll from back-to-back heat waves approached 200 yesterday as 90-degree temperatures threatened to do more damage in the southern Plains.

The northern Plains and Western states basked in cool temperatures while thunderstorms refreshed the Ohio Valley and Great Lakes states. Humid conditions smothered the East as thunderstorms moved along the Gulf Coast.

"It's been getting cooler each day," said National Weather Service meteorolgist Nolan Duke.

"But the southern Plains could be looking at some 90-degree readings for the next few days."

The heat waves, which have been blamed for 189 deaths nationwide this summer, were producing 90-degree temperatures yesterday in the southern Plains. The 90-degree readings were expected to bring some relief, compared to Saturday's 100-degree-plus readings, Duke said.

The hot dry weather has also taken a heavy toll on crops in the Midwestern states.

* Reprinted courtesy of The Tennessean.

4. Write an umbrella lead for all three of the following items.

   GOVERNMENT OFFICIALS IN PERU SAY A "SEVERE BLOW" HAS BEEN DEALT TO A LEFTIST REBEL GROUP KNOWN AS THE SHINING PATH. THEY SAY 40 REBELS WERE KILLED IN A TUESDAY-NIGHT CLASH 230 MILES SOUTHEAST OF LIMA (LEE'-MAH), THE CAPITAL. THREE GOVERNMENT SOLDIERS ALSO DIED IN THE FIGHTING.

   IRISH NATIONALISTS IN NORTHERN IRELAND SAY THEY'VE KIDNAPPED THREE RELATIVES OF AN INFORMER AND WILL KILL THEM UNLESS THE MAN WITHDRAWS HIS EVIDENCE AGAINST 18 ACCUSED TERRORISTS. THE IRISH NATIONAL LIBERATION ARMY— AN OFFSHOOT OF THE I-R-A— SAYS IT WILL ISSUE A DEADLINE... AND IF IT IS NOT MET, THE INFORMER'S WIFE, SISTER AND STEPFATHER WILL BE EXECUTED.

   THE PRESIDENT OF ZAIRE (ZAH-EER') — BEING PRAISED BY U-S OFFICIALS FOR HIS MILITARY AID TO CHAD— HOLDS MEETINGS IN WASHINGTON TODAY WITH SECRETARY OF STATE GEORGE SHULTZ AND PRESIDENT REAGAN. PRESIDENT MOBUTU SESE SEKO (MOH-BOO'-TOO SAY'-SAY SAY'-KOH) HAS DISPATCHED 16-HUNDRED TROOPS AND SIX AIRCRAFT TO CHAD IN THE LAST MONTH. HE WANTS TO HELP THE GOVERNMENT OF PRESIDENT HISSENE HABRE (HIHS-SEH'-NEH AHB'-RUH) COUNTER LIBYAN MOVEMENTS IN CHAD.

5. Write a hard news lead story from the following facts. Use an actuality in it.

   Mary Dieringer, president of the local chapter of the Daughters of the Cumberland, announces a new membership drive.

   The chapter usually solicits members by mail and telephone.

   Next month, the drive will be made on a person-to-person basis to gain 30 new members.

   Members and volunteers will be asked to invite friends to their homes to acquaint them with the DOC.

   "The chapter hopes to increase its membership to replace those who have dropped out and moved away," she said.

   "If we cannot do so, we must discontinue the DOC chapter," she said.

6. Write a throwaway news lead story from the following facts. Use an actuality in it.

> The Buck Mountain Volunteer Fire Department is involved in controversy.
>
> Been so involved for almost a month.
>
> With Buck Mountain Police Chief.
>
> Chief Ned Sampson had ordered his men not to stop traffic at intersections to let volunteer firemen's cars through even though their lights are flashing.
>
> Fire department, made up of volunteers, believe this interferes with their all-important work of putting out fires. They're unhappy.
>
> Firemen complained to Mayor Danforth Reynolds Ross and to the Buck Mountain City Council.
>
> Last night at an executive session of the mayor and board, the chief handed in his resignation.
>
> The chief said, "No longer can I work under the constant stream of invective and hostilities being directed at me by two members of this board and members of the fire department."

7. Turn the following account into a soft lead news story. Use an actuality in it.

   Donald Skoller is a policeman in your community. Last year, because of his heroic rescue of seven persons held at gunpoint during a robbery, Police Chief Harry Holden named him the department's Police officer of the Year. Holden fired Skoller when he reported for duty at 7 a.m. today. The department adopted certain grooming standards, and Holden said Skoller's mustache was a quarter-inch too long and his sideburns a half-inch too long, and he refused to trim them. Holden added that he warned Skoller a month ago to trim his hair, then ordered him to do so at the start of last week. Holden fired Skoller for failing to obey the order of a superior officer.

Rewriting for Radio

8. Rewrite this newspaper sports story for radio.

INDIANAPOLIS (AP) — Jimmy Brown ranked 77th in the men's tennis computer ratings, upset top-seeded defending champion Jose Higueras 6-2, 6-2 in second-round play at the U.S. Open Clay Court championships yesterday.

"I'm playing well," said Brown, an 18-year-old from Brentwood, Tenn., who won the national 18-and-under clay court championship in 1981. "The more matches I play, the better I play. . . . I get my rhythm and timing, so I get a little bit stronger as I go on."

"I have not been playing very well for a few weeks," said Higueras, currently ranked sixth in the world and No. 1 on clay. "My concentration is pretty bad."

Higueras fell behind 2-0 in the opening set and Brown was in control nearly all the way. Brown, who has not won a Grand Prix event since joining the pro circuit last year, jumped to a 4-0 lead before Higueras came back with one futile charge to win the next two games.

Higueras might have won the next game had he not decided to tell the umpire a call by a linesman in his favor was incorrect.

Brown became irate, claiming a fault on a serve by Higueras, but the linesman and umpire refused to change the call. After a brief delay, which included Brown drawing a circle around the spot with his racquet, Higueras went over to check where the ball landed and notified the umpire the serve had been a fault.

"He played well," Higueras said. "I play shoddy. I had no concentration at all."

There was one other mild upset in the second round of men's play. Francesco Cancellotti of Italy eliminated ninth-seeded John Alexander of Australia, 6-4, 7-5. Fourth-seeded Henrik Sundstrom of Sweden downed Jairo Velasco of Columbia 6-3, 6-4, while No. 7 Shlomo Glickstein took care of Mark Dickson, 6-3, 6-4.

9. Rewrite this newspaper story for radio.

WASHINGTON (AP) — The House passed 282-148 last night a $165.3 billion Social Security rescue plan which raises the retirement age to 66 and later 67 in the next century.

The vote to pull the fund from the brink of bankruptcy ends two years of party warfare.

The bipartisan bill, which would make all American workers and retirees alike share the burden of bailing out the system, was approved by 185 Democrats and 97 Republicans, while 79 Democrats and 69 Republicans voted no. It now goes to the Senate, which likely will vote next week.

The plan would:

• Make affluent retirees pay income tax on half their benefits.

• Delay this July's cost-of-living increase for six months.

• Accelerate payroll tax increases.

• Boost the levy on the self-employed.

• Force new federal workers to join Social Security in 1984.

The House wrapped up work on the rescue plan after approving, 228-202, an amendment championed by Rep. J.J. Pickle, D-Texas, to make today's 40-year-olds wait until 66 to draw full Social Security benefits. Today's 23-year-olds — and those younger — would have to wait until 67.

That tally was reaffirmed later on a nearly identical 230-200 procedural vote forced by opponents of the change.

The lawmakers also soundly rejected, 296-132, a rival amendment sought by a tearful Rep. Claude Pepper, D-Fla., to leave the retirement age of 65 intact — and rely instead on a 0.53-point payroll tax hike in 2010 to solve the final third of the system's long-term, $1.9 trillion deficit.

Seventy-six Democrats joined 152 Republicans on the first critical vote to raise the age. Only 14 Republicans voted against it, along with 188 Democrats.

The rescue bill, closely following the blueprint prepared by the National Commission on Social Security Reform, would generate $165.3 billion in new revenues or savings over seven years. That would also solve two-thirds of the long-range problem, and the change in the retirement age would wipe out the rest.

Writing the Newscast

10. Select, edit and rewrite the following world and national news items* and with an opening of 20 seconds compose a world and national newscast. It will have a brief introduction, two cart (taped) advertisements, and an outro (a closing tape of 20 seconds), which will take up 1½ minutes of the newscast. After composing the newscast, list the items on the form provided after the news items. Your newscast, at 15 lines per minute, should have 75 lines of copy. Tape it or deliver it orally in class. (Don't forget transitions.)

```
F-B-I DIRECTOR WILLIAM WEBSTER SAYS THE AGENCY
IS TRAINING A SPECIAL ANTI-TERRORISM SQUAD FOR THE
1982 OLYMPIC GAMES IN LOS ANGELES. THE IDEA IS TO
PREVENT ANOTHER MUNICH, WHERE 11 ISRAELI ATHLETES
WERE KILLED BY PALESTINIAN TERRORISTS AT THE 1972
GAMES. AN F-B-I SPOKESMAN SAYS THE 42-MEMBER
"HOSTAGE RESCUE TEAM" IS TRAINING AT QUANTICO,
VIRGINIA. THE F-B-I IS PLANNING TO HAVE 700 AGENTS
PROVIDE SECURITY AT THE OLYMPICS.

    NASHVILLE— A FEDERAL COURT JURY IN NASHVILLE
ACQUITTED TOPLESS CLUB OWNER DANNY OWENS ON SEVEN
COUNTS OF FIREARMS VIOLATIONS AND STOLEN JEWELRY
CHARGES AFTER 11 HOURS OF DELIBERATIONS. THE
MEMPHIS CLUB OWNER WAS CHARGED WITH TRANSPORTING
100-THOUSAND DOLLARS WORTH OF STOLEN JEWELRY AND
WITH POSSESSION AND ILLEGAL TRANSPORTATION OF
FIREARMS, INCLUDING SILENCERS. OWENS WAS GRANTED A
CHANGE OF VENUE FROM MEMPHIS TO NASHVILLE'S U-S
DISTRICT COURT BECAUSE OF EXTENSIVE PRE-TRIAL
PUBLICITY.

    BETTE MIDLER IS REPORTED IN STABLE CONDITION AT
PONTIAC GENERAL HOSPITAL IN PONTIAC, MICHIGAN,
BEING TREATED FOR A STOMACH AILMENT AFTER
COLLAPSING DURING HER SHOWN AT THE PINE KNOB
AMPHITHEATER. MIDLER SLIPPED AND FELL DURING HER
FIRST SONG... BUT IN "SHOW MUST GO ON" SPIRIT,
GOT UP AND CONTINUED. HALFWAY THROUGH HER SET, SHE
HAD THE SPOTLIGHTS TURNED OFF, TOOK A DRINK OF
WATER AND AGAIN RESUMED. FINALLY, IN THE MIDDLE OF
"BOOGIE WOOGIE BUGLE BOY," SHE WALKED OFF STAGE,
COLLAPSED AND WAS RUSHED TO THE HOSPITAL.

    ON LONG ISLAND, NEW YORK, THE VILLAGE OF
AMITYVILLE HAS MOVED TO SILENCE ITS LATEST HORROR
... DOGS HOWLING AT THE MOON. THE VILLAGE BOARD'S
CANINE CURFEW MEANS A 250-DOLLAR FINE FOR OWNERS
WHOSE DOGS ARE OUTSIDE WITHOUT A LEASH FROM 11 P-M
TO 7 A-M. THE MAYOR SAYS THE CURFEW SHOULD PUT A
GAG ON DOGS WHO DISTURB THE TOWN'S NIGHTTIME
PEACE.

    STATE-RUN TEHRAN RADIO SAYS IRANIAN AUTHORITIES
```

---

* Reprinted by permission of United Press International.

GAVE AN OFFICIAL OF THE INTERNATIONAL COMMITTEE OF THE RED CROSS THREE DAYS TO LEAVE THE COUNTRY FOR "ABNORMAL" ACTIVITIES. THE REPORT... MONITORED IN BEIRUT... CLAIMED THE RED CROSS OFFICIAL WAS "STIRRING UP" PRISONERS CAPTURED IN THE 35-MONTH-OLD PERSIAN GULF WAR WITH IRAQ.

IN A BITTER VERBAL ATTACK ON THE U-S... THE SOVIET NEWSPAPER PRAVDA TODAY ACCUSED THE REAGAN ADMINISTRATION OF VIOLATING THE HELSINKI HUMAN RIGHTS ACCORDS WHILE "BRAZENLY USING MILITARY FORCE" TO ACHIEVE ITS AIMS. AS AN EXAMPLE, THE PAPER NOTED PLANNED U-S MANEUVERS IN CENTRAL AMERICA... INTENDED TO FORCE NICARAGUA TO CHANGE ITS POLICIES.

THE REAGAN ADMINISTRATION IS LOBBYING FOR AN EIGHT-POINT-FOUR BILLION-DOLLAR BOOST IN AID TO THE INTERNATIONAL MONETARY FUND. BUT WHETHER IT'S WON ENOUGH SUPPORT IN CONGRESS ISN'T CERTAIN. YESTERDAY HOUSE SPEAKER TIP O'NEILL SAID HE WOULD NOT BRING THE ISSUE TO THE FLOOR TODAY, UNLESS IT LOOKS LIKE IT HAS THE VOTES TO PASS.

THE SENATE YESTERDAY CONFIRMED PRESIDENTIAL NOMINEE PAUL VOLCKER AS CHAIRMAN OF THE FEDERAL RESERVE BOARD FOR ANOTHER FOUR YEARS. BUT ANOTHER REAGAN NOMINEE... NORTH CAROLINA LAWYER THOMAS ELLIS... MAY WITHDRAW HIS NAME FROM CONSIDERATION FOR A POST ON THE BOARD FOR INTERNATIONAL BROADCASTING. ELLIS HAS COME UNDER CRITICISM FOR HIS RACIAL VIEWS.

ARMY OFFICIALS ARE LOOKING FOR CLUES IN THE FAILURE OF A PERSHING-TWO MISSILE YESTERDAY. THE WEAPON— ON A TEST FLIGHT FROM CAPE CANAVERAL IN FLORIDA— WAS DESTROYED OVER THE ATLANTIC WHEN IT BEGAN TO BREAK APART. THE MALFUNCTION WAS A SETBACK TO PROPONENTS OF THE CONTROVERSIAL MISSILES, WHICH ARE SCHEDULED FOR DEPLOYMENT IN WESTERN EUROPE LATER THIS YEAR.

FIGHTING JARRED LEBANON TODAY. PRO- AND ANTI-SYRIAN GROUPS FOUGHT IN THE NORTHERN PORT OF TRIPOLI... AND WARRING P-L-O FACTIONS CONTINUED THEIR BATTLES IN THE BEKAA (BEH-KAH') VALLEY.

ISRAELI AUTHORITIES SAY THEY ORDERED THEIR CHRISTIAN PHALANGE ALLIES FROM A BASE 24 MILES SOUTH OF BEIRUT, CITING A "LACK OF COORDINATION" WITH THE ISRAELI ARMY. THE PHALANGE REPLIED WITH ROAD BLOCKS AND MOTORCADES OF PROTESTORS.

POLAND'S PARLIAMENT TODAY GATHERS FOR ITS FIRST READING OF FIVE IMPORTANT CONSTITUTIONAL AMENDMENTS. ONCE ENACTED, THOSE LAWS COULD LEAD TO THE LIFTING OF MARTIAL LAW AFTER 19 BITTER MONTHS.

DEPUTIES ATTENDING TODAY'S ONE-DAY SESSION WILL ALSO GIVE PRELIMINARY CONSIDERATION TO A MEASURE REGULATING THE OPERATION OF THE POLISH MEDIA. THAT BILL IS AMONG SEVERAL PIECES OF LEGISLATION THE WARSAW REGIME CONSIDERS NECESSARY BEFORE MILITARY RULE IS FINALLY ENDED.

GOVERNMENT SPOKESMEN SAY THE FINAL DECISION ON MARTIAL LAW IS UP TO THE 21-MEMBER MILITARY COUNCIL OF NATIONAL SALVATION— WHICH WAS NAMED TO RUN POLAND IN 1981.

THE UNITED STATES HAS REPEATEDLY INDICATED WESTERN ALLIES ARE PREPARED TO RESPOND FAVORABLY IF POLAND RESTORES HUMAN RIGHTS TO ITS CITIZENS.

U-R-G-E-N-T

M-X SUB

WASHINGTON— THE SENATE VOTED OVERWHELMINGLY TONIGHT TO APPROVE A 200-BILLION-DOLLAR MILITARY SPENDING BILL... WHICH INCLUDES FUNDING FOR THE FULL-SCALE PRODUCTION OF THE M-X MISSILE, BEGINNING NEXT YEAR. EARLIER THIS EVENING, BY A 58-41 VOTE, THE SENATE KILLED AN AMENDMENT THAT WOULD'VE STRIPPED THE BILL OF TWO-POINT-SIX BILLION DOLLARS EARMARKED FOR THE MULTI-WARHEAD WEAPON.

PRESIDENT REAGAN IS SCHEDULED FOR A ROUND OF TALKS TODAY WITH ISRAELI LEADERS IN WASHINGTON. ISRAELI FOREIGN MINISTER YITZHAK SHAMIR (YIHTS'-HAHK SHAH-MEER') TOLD ISRAEL RADIO JERUSALEM ALREADY HAD ALLAYED ONE OF WASHINGTON'S FEARS. SHAMIR SAYS HE TOLD ADMINISTRATION OFFICIALS THE RE-DEPLOYMENT OF ISRAELI TROOPS IN LEBANON WILL LEAD TO A COMPLETE WITHDRAWAL... AND NOT A PARTITIONING OF THAT COUNTRY.

THE HOUSE TAKES UP A BILL TODAY THAT WOULD END COVERT U-S AID TO ANTI-SANDINISTA REBELS IN CENTRAL AMERICA. THE MEASURE IS BACKED BY MOST OF THE MAJORITY DEMOCRATS. A REPUBLICAN COMPROMISE WOULD STOP WASHINGTON'S UNDERCOVER SUPPORT ON THE CONDITION NICARAGUA STOP EXPORTING REVOLUTION.

IN PITTSBURGH, CANDI THOMAS IS LISTED IN CRITICAL CONDITION AFTER MORE THAN 10 HOURS ON THE OPERATING TABLE FOR DELICATE LIVER TRANSPLANT SURGERY. CANDI IS THE ONE-AND-A-HALF-YEAR-OLD DAUGHTER OF A WHITE HOUSE ELECTRICIAN. HER BID FOR LIFE WAS HELPED BY PRESIDENT REAGAN, WHO ORDERED AN AIR FORCE JET TO FLY HER AND HER PARENTS TO PITTSBURGH FOR THE OPERATION

WORLD AND NATIONAL NEWSCAST
(five minutes)

Item	Length in lines	Length in seconds
1.		
2.		
3.		
4.		
5.		
6.		
7.		
8.		
9.		
10.		
11.		
12.		
13.		
14.		
15.		

11. Visit a local radio station and observe the news operation at work. In the space below, report on the staff, the reporting procedures, editing, rewriting, etc.

CHAPTER 11

NEWS FOR TELEVISION
David G. Clark

Television needs writers who understand its language.

When you write for print, you have at your disposal all the devices that three-quarters of a million English words provide: the rhythm of poets, the freshness you get when you put words into new combinations, the images words can create in the reader's mind. And you have typographical devices of print: space, headlines, different styles of type.

When you write for radio, you have words plus sounds (music, crowd noise, explosions, screams), silences, raw accents of real people and inflections announcers provide.

But when you write for television after writing for print, it's as if you are Dorothy, moving from plain, old, black-and-white Kansas to the richly colored, spectacularly peopled world of Oz. It's as if your old language had only words of one syllable, and suddenly you discover polysyllables. It's as if before you had no punctuation marks, but now you have periods to end a thought, commas to pause during, and colons to introduce. It's as if you have a new pair of magic red shoes that will do all kinds of wonders if you can just learn to dance in them.

Writing for television means shifting from describing events to showing them, from telling about them to letting them happen. Television is words plus sounds plus action plus color plus life. And every bit as much as life, television is nonverbal.

David G. Clark, who earned a Ph.D. in Mass Communications at the University of Wisconsin-Madison, has been professor and chairperson of the Department of Technical Journalism, Colorado State University, Fort Collins, since 1973. He has taught at the University of Cincinnati, Stanford University and the University of Wisconsin-Madison. Clark has worked as a reporter for the *Lincoln* (Nebr.) *Star* and the *Lubbock* (Tex.) *Evening Journal*. He has also been news editor of KCBD-AM-TV in Lubbock. His publications include *The Random House Guide to Technical Communication* (with D. E. Zimmerman, in press), *You and Media: Mass Communication and Society* (with W. B. Blankenburg, 1973), *Mass Media and the Law: Freedom and Restraint* (co-edited with E. R. Hutchison, 1970) and *The American Newspaper* (co-edited with Clifford Weigle, 1969).

TELEVISION TECHNIQUE

TV Talk

Professor Fred Shook, whose books on electronic news gathering are used in more than 200 universities and in hundreds of television newsrooms, identifies four components of television's language. Anyone wishing to "write" effectively in television must know, be at ease with, and use these four components.

Visual Image. Without visuals, television is radio. If the visual image is a TV reporter standing in front of a camera, television is dull. If the image is a still picture or an unmoving chart or graph, it may be informative, but it is not good television. If the image moves purely for the sake of movement—the speaker gets up from behind a desk and moves around it—TV has failed again. To be effective, the visual image must be a crucial part of the event being shown. The visual image should show the audience something words cannot convey.

Sound. Shook argues, and the best television proves, that sound can be as eloquent as the visual image. The crunch of a runner's feet pounding a training track in counterpoint to the noise of lungs seizing air tells much about the price Olympic runners pay for their fame. The chaos you hear when 20 reporters shout questions all at once during a news conference demonstrates the pressure national politicians undergo.

Tape Editing. As in motion pictures, editing can lift the good to greatness or can bring ruin. When you write for print, you edit to put your ideas into the proper relationship. The same is true in television. The sequence of shots, their length, their overall pacing and their juxtaposition can clarify a story or confuse the viewer.

Writing with Words. In print, words carry almost the whole burden of getting the story across, but the written word in television requires an extremely light touch. Often written words are used simply to bridge scenes, to tie similar threads together in transition, or to add facts the visual image has not revealed. Always, words are used for television in ways that they are not used for print. Words must be put to work as part of the total effort, which entails coordinating visual image and sound as well.

One chapter of a book cannot teach you to edit videotape, to photograph effectively, or to obtain the sounds that tell your story best. But this chapter can help you begin to make the transition from print writer to television writer.

First, the advice given in Chapter 10, "News for Radio," applies here, too. Be concise, be current and be conversational. Use pronunciation guides, ellipses to indicate pauses and oral devices to guide the viewer or listener ("in the mayor's words," "as she put it"). Move from the general to the specific, to alert the audience to what is coming so they can pay special attention.

Television Scripting

The news values of good journalism apply to television news, with one big qualification: *Every* story must and will have visuals. Often your job will be to figure out how to supply visuals. But you will have help from the field reporters, photographers, artists and researchers who will screen the station's files and develop new footage or slides, if needed. At times, in addition to writing, one or all of these jobs may fall to you. If newsworthiness dictates, you will occasionally use a very brief story with no visuals other than the camera trained on the anchor, but generally, a story with no visuals is no story for television. The following checklist is an important tool for television writers. Notice the assumption that you are using words, sounds, silences and visuals.

*Television News Checklist**

- ☐ Lead instantly telegraphs story to come.
- ☐ Be hard on self and script. Pare, edit, rewrite.
- ☐ Use strong, natural sound.
- ☐ A point of view.
- ☐ Moments of silence built into script.
- ☐ Strong central character(s) engaged in compelling visual action.
- ☐ Elements of the unexpected: surprises, little moments of drama.
- ☐ Short sound bites that *prove* the story you are *showing*.
- ☐ Only a few main points.
- ☐ Historical perspective, when appropriate, that defines the story's larger context.
- ☐ Strong closing that story builds toward throughout its entirety. Something you can't top. A logical place to end the story.
- ☐ VISUAL PROOF FOR EVERYTHING.

In writing news for television, you deal with essentially three types of situations. We'll discuss them one by one.

Announcer-on-Camera (AOC) Scripts. In an AOC situation, the anouncer simply reads what you have written. The news story may be rewritten from wire service accounts or written as an original report from a story you have gathered by telephone or from talking with news sources in person. Such writing is the same as writing for radio, but the script's physical format differs in that the announcer is shown on screen and you must provide directions for the cameras.

Prerecorded Scripts. Documentaries often fall into this category, which is essentially the system used by filmmakers to do feature films, commercials, instructional films and any other type of production in which the content can be determined or specified in advance. (This technique has limited value for television news.)

Taped News Events Broken into Segments. The segments combine studio announcer on camera, narration behind previously taped action, field reporter describing events or setting the scene for previously taped or live action, and backup narration either by the studio announcer or the field reporter as live events unfold. Each type of coverage presents special challenges to the writer, who may also be announcer, field reporter, camera operator, tape editor and/or overall producer and thus may have several tasks to juggle at once.

Let's examine scripts for two of these situations. Here is an announcer-on-camera script:[†]

---

* From *The Broadcast News Process*, second edition by C. F. Shook and D. L. Lattimore. Copyright © 1982 by Morton Publishing. Reprinted by permission of the publisher.

[†] Reprinted by permission of WSMV-TV, Nashville, Tenn.

```
METRO LAYOFFS 6 pm 7/23                        RUNS :20
MILLER/                           Metro councilman Kenneth
LAYOFF SLIDE                      Smith today charged that
SUPER :15 (LOWER RIGHT)           what he called "scare
(LAYOFFS WERE "SCARE              tactics" in the form of
TACTICS"?)                        worker layoffs were used to
                                  increase Metro's recent
                                  property tax hike. The
                                  layoffs, which were
                                  originally expected to
                                  reach more than 1,000, now
                                  total fewer than 200. Also
                                  today, Mayor Fulton
                                  requested that his
                                  department heads explain
                                  why layoff figures were
                                  apparently overestimated.
```

This brief story has most of the ingredients of a standard television news script. The common format is to use the left-hand column for video instructions to the control booth. Directions for what is to be seen on the screen are given in that column. The right-hand column is reserved for audio, or what is heard.

The top line contains a story slug, the newscast for which the story was written (6 p.m. on July 23) and the length of the story. The left-hand column contains instructions to the show's director. Miller is the announcer's name. Thus the director knows whom to show on camera. When the announcer starts the story, a slide reading "Layoffs were 'Scare Tactics'?" is to be shown for 15 seconds on the lower right of the projection screen behind the announcer. The right-hand column contains the news story. The story is identical to a radio news story.

A more common method of preparing television news combines on-scene taping of events, on-location narration or reporting by the field reporter, and studio narration by the anchorperson. This complex approach is frequently embellished by live conversation between the reporter on the scene and the studio anchor.

One example of such a script is the following, produced by WSMV-TV in Nashville, Tenn.* The anchor opens the story, giving the lead. A still picture of then Senator Howard Baker is shown on the screen behind the AOC. Then the anchor introduces the station's political reporter, Alan Griggs. Earlier, Griggs prepared a video and sound cartridge (cart) that shows scenes of Baker while Griggs is narrating. Then the sound comes up and we hear Baker making his announcement. When Baker finishes, Griggs comes back with more narration; then we see Ted Welch, the national finance chairman of the Baker campaign. Griggs offers more interpretation, we see Baker one more time, and Griggs signs off. The piece runs almost four minutes. At the start and end of each sound "bite," the writer has copied the exact words of the speaker, so that the tape can be properly cued at entry and left at the correct time.

```
BAKER 6 pm 3/5 sony griggs-                    RUNS 3:45
smith
A2
MILLER/                           Senator Howard Baker
```

* Reprinted by permission of WSMV-TV, Nashville, Tenn.

CK BAKER SLIDE SUPER :20 (LOWER RIGHT) (BACK TO SENATE)	quit the hectic and often grueling race for the Presidency today, saying his campaign was going nowhere. 　　Baker's action followed disappointing showings in the Vermont and Massachusetts primaries yesterday. 　　Alan Griggs has more. . . .
ROLL SONY SILENT ROLL GRIGGS CART	FROM THE BEGINNING, HOWARD BAKER'S EFFORT TO BE THE REPUBLICAN PRESIDENTIAL NOMINEE APPEARED TO BE AN UPHILL FIGHT. 　　HE CAMPAIGNED VIGOROUSLY . . . YET WAS OUTSPOKEN ABOUT THE TIME IT TOOK AND THE UNENDING PRESSURE A CANDIDATE MUST ENDURE. 　　TODAY, HIS DECISION TO QUIT MIGHT NOT HAVE BEEN AS SURPRISING AS ITS TIMING. 　　FOR THE SENATOR, HIS DECISION TO ENTER THE RACE WAS A CALCULATED RISK. WHEN HE VISITED THE SOVIET UNION LAST YEAR IT WAS TO PREPARE HIMSELF FOR A LENGTHY DEBATE ON THE STRATEGIC ARMS LIMITATION TREATY. AS SENATE MINORITY LEADER, HE SAW THAT DEBATE . . . AND A GOOD GIVE AND TAKE WITH SOVIET LEADERS . . . AS A POTENTIAL IMAGE BUILDER MUCH LIKE WHAT THE WATERGATE HEARINGS DID FOR HIM. BUT THE SALT DEBATE NEVER TOOK PLACE . . . AND BAKER FOUND HIMSELF A LATECOMER TO THE CAMPAIGN.
SONY SOUND UNDER GRIGGS CART CONTINUES SONY SOUND FULL	TODAY, HE CONCEDED IT WAS TOO LATE. . . . OPENS: I WANTED TO GAIN THE . . . RUNS :54 ENDS: REPUBLICAN MEMBER OF THE UNITED STATES SENATE.
SONY SOUND FULL CONTINUES SUPER :29	OPENS: A MAJOR PROBLEM FOR HOWARD BAKER WAS MONEY. RUNS :09

(GRIGGS)	ENDS: BUILDING HERE IN GREEN HILLS.
SONY SOUND UNDER	THAT IS WHERE TED WELCH SERVED BAKER AS NATIONAL FINANCE CHAIRMAN. WELCH, WHO MANAGED TO RAISE MUCH OF THE SIX MILLION DOLLARS THE BAKER CAMPAIGN SPENT, RECEIVED A PHONE CALL FROM THE SENATOR THIS MORNING. . . .
SONY SOUND FULL (TED WELCH) FINANCE CHAIRMAN	OPENS: WELL, HE ASKED ME HOW . . . RUNS :29 ENDS: THAN WAS TRUE THIS TIME.
SONY SOUND FULL CONTINUES	OPENS: SOMEONE ASKED ME THIS MORNING . . . RUNS :19 ENDS: TO CHANGE MY POSITION ON THAT.
SONY SILENT ROLL GRIGGS CART	SO, DESPITE HAVING MORE CONVENTION DELEGATES THAN FIVE OTHER REPUBLICAN PRESIDENTIAL CANDIDATES. HOWARD BAKER'S DREAM OF THE OVAL OFFICE ABRUPTLY ENDED TODAY. WHO WILL HE SUPPORT? HE'S NOT SAYING . . . BUT UP UNTIL THE FINAL FEW DAYS HE MADE IT CLEAR HE FELT HE WOULDN'T NEED TO MAKE THAT DECISION.
SONY SOUND FULL SUPER :21 (AGAIN) (BAKER)	OPENS: THROUGHOUT THE CAMPAIGN YOU'VE HEARD . . . RUNS :30 ENDS: TO STAY IN IT, I PROMISE YOU THAT.
SONY SOUND UNDER ROLL GRIGGS CART	ALAN GRIGGS . . . CHANNEL FOUR NEWS. ###

The Griggs story is also known as a VTR package. A "package" is a stand-alone report put onto a cartridge that can be plugged into the news program. It's fully edited and must run as assembled. Carefully timed, it is surrounded with other news stories that can be added or deleted to make the news program fit the allotted time. At the time the Griggs story actually aired, Griggs himself might have been working on a different story, out to dinner or sitting at home watching.

The package consists of an opening section, a middle and an end. Common openings include the reporter on the scene, looking into the camera; the scene itself with voice-over narration; or a combination of the two, such as the reporter's voice over the scene, followed a few seconds later by a shot of the reporter on the scene. The middle section may include interviews, changes of location or other devices that present various aspects of the story. The close contains the reporter's sign-off, which can be done in fashion similar to the opening.

The actual putting of words on paper for a package is often done at the end of the production effort and may involve mainly construction of transitions. Your job as a television news reporter is to let the story tell itself as much as possible. You may have to compose while the camera is on and recording. Therefore, the "writing" you do is truly a multimedia combination of visuals, sound and words. How well you succeed will depend on your ability to see and tell a story in its visual components. Words *are* important in television, but the other aspects are of equal, and often greater, importance.

The major challenge for television newswriters is to tell, as simply as possible, what has happened in the news of the day. Translating complicated events, particularly business and economic news, and political news into short, easy-to-understand reports takes tremendous discipline. For example, contrast the way this story on the gross national product was written for the *Washington Post* on June 21, 1985, with the way it might have appeared as an item in a 6 p.m. newscast:

GNP Growth Resumes*

2nd Quarter 'Flash' Estimate Puts Rate at 3.1 Pct.

By JANE SEABERRY
Washington Post Staff Writer

The economy appears to be expanding at a 3.1 percent annual rate in the second quarter ending this month, after showing virtually no growth from January through March, the government reported yesterday.

The apparent acceleration may not be strong enough, however, to prevent the federal budget deficit from rising beyond administration estimates, economists said.

The Commerce Department said its "flash" estimate of gross national product in the current quarter — based on data for one or two months — shows the economy growing at an annual rate of 3.1 percent, to $3.9 trillion. At the same time, the department revised downward its earlier report of first-quarter results to show GNP growth of 0.3 percent rather than 0.7 percent.

In a more positive vein, the Labor Department reported yesterday that prices remained stable in May, and analysts see little likeli-

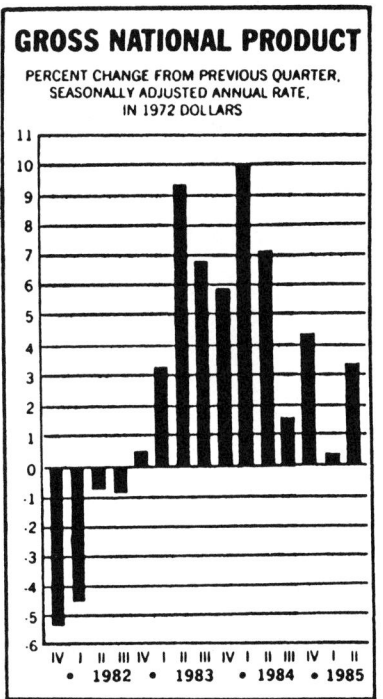

* © 1985 The Washington Post. Reprinted by permission.

hood of an inflationary surge soon. The department said the consumer price index rose 0.2 percent last month as food and transportation costs declined. Gasoline price rises were small, and the costs of new and used cars declined, the department said.

Reagan administration officials had been awaiting the flash estimate of the gross national product for a sign of how much their estimates of economic growth — and hence, federal budget deficits — may have to be revised.

Government economists said yesterday that if the flash estimate for the second quarter holds up, growth will have to accelerate to a 6 percent annual rate in the third and fourth quarters to reach the administration's 4 percent growth target for the year.

If the economy grows at about a 3 percent pace for the year, as many private forecasters have suggested, the federal budget deficit could swell by about $70 billion by 1988, according to administration calculations.

White House spokesman Larry Speakes said the GNP estimate and consumer price index "point to a renewal period of stable growth with low inflation" and that the growth figures "indicate we're headed toward a solid second-quarter performance."

"We feel that with the drop in the prime rate to 9.5 percent, along with the rise in the nation's

See ECONOMY, B2, Col. 1

```
GNP 6PM 6/21                                    RUNS :30
ANNCR                         The Commerce Department
                              announced today that the
ANNCR                         nation's economy is
GNP CHART SLIDE               growing again. The gross
                              national product was
                              practically dead in the
                              water for the first quarter
                              of 1985. . . growing only
                              zero point three percent
                              from January through
                              March. Today's figures
                              show that the economy now
                              appears to be expanding at
                              a rate that would lead to
                              annual growth of three
                              point one percent. That's
                              still a little short of the
                              Reagan administration's
                              goal of four percent growth
                              in G-N-P for 1985.
```

News features for television call for bright, punchy phrasing. Features help sustain viewer interest during a newscast because they lend themselves to interesting, attention-getting treatment. Compare this article from the *Philadelphia Inquirer* of June 21, 1985, with the TV news version that might have appeared on the nightly news:

Coty Drops Fashion-Awards Role, Leaving Their Future in Doubt*

By MARY MARTIN NIEPOLD
Inquirer Staff Writer

The fashion world was caught by surprise yesterday when Coty, sponsor of the American Fashion Critics Awards since their inception 42 years ago, announced its withdrawal as sponsor of the awards.

Coty is "stepping aside to permit others to determine the criteria of excellence by which new, young designers are encouraged and properly recognized," according to Donald D. Flannery, chairman of the American Fashion Critics Awards board of trustees and an executive of the fragrance company.

As a consequence, the most prestigious accolades for excellence in American design — popularly known as "the Cotys" — will not be presented this year. The ceremony had been scheduled to take place at the Fashion Institute of Technology on Sept. 23.

Coty's withdrawal leaves the future of the American Fashion Critics Awards in doubt. It was not known yesterday whether another organization or corporation would eventually take over their sponsorship.

"The Coty awards were established to help a fledgling, struggling American fashion industry gain recognition and prominence," Flannery said. "From the first award presentation in 1942, Coty has continued its sponsorship and commitment, until today we proudly see American fashion leadership is established throughout the world. Indeed, then, the long-sought goals of the Coty awards have been achieved."

Designers expressed regret yesterday that the Cotys would be no more. For them, the awards have meant increased business and worldwide recognition.

"As a designer, it was the highest award that I could get other than people buying my clothes," said Philadelphia's Will Smith, 1983 winner for his women's wear line, WilliWear. "Once I received it, the press and the stores always put 'Coty award winner' before my name. It added a tremendous amount of prestige to my product, and I'm really

See COTY on 6-C

FASHION 6pm 6/21
ANNCR
SLIDE/COTY AWARD TROPHY
:15

RUNS :36
Fashion took a fall
yesterday when Coty
announced it would no
longer sponsor the 42-
year-old American Fashion
Critics Awards. Designers
reacted with dismay to the
news that the cosmetics
film was bowing out of the
most prestigious awards
program in fashion design.

---

* Reprinted by permission of *The Philadelphia Inquirer*, 1985.

SLIDE/MODEL WALKING DOWN RUNWAY :31	This year's awards ceremony had been scheduled for September 23rd at the Fashion Institute of Technology. A Coty spokesman says the company is dropping out because it has reached its goal of seeing American designers rise to an established spot in the world fashion limelight. It's not known if another corporation or organization is interested in filling Coty's designer shoes.

SUMMARY

Because studies show that the majority of Americans obtain their news from TV, the role of television newswriters has become extremely important in journalism. Their words, their stand-up commentary and their instant analyses and interpretations of breaking events bring us most closely to news as it happens. Through them, we participate in news events more intimately than we do through other media.

Because television involves the viewer so closely, timing, precision, and simple, compact sentence construction are absolutely essential in television news reporting. TV is such a personal medium that the slightest goof—just a few seconds of a black screen, a slide that fails to pop up on cue, a report drowning in jargon or the parlance of politics—can cause a viewer to lose patience. Television viewers want their news delivered swiftly and completely—and they want it from reporters with flair and a gift for writing clearly. Those reporters also must know, along with film editors and photographers and artists, what type of visuals will best support the story they are reporting. Working just the right audio and video elements into a news report can make the television writer among the most disciplined and effective communicators in journalism.

EXERCISES

Try your hand at writing scripts. First do an announcer-on-camera (AOC) story in which the whole story is given by the anchorperson, and the script must contain all the details. In other words, there is no film, videotape or photography to carry the story, only an artist's drawing or a still picture illustrating the subject.

Second, write the words to accompany scenes taped by a camera operator on the scene and transmitted via an electronic relay back to your TV station to be aired in the next broadcast.

In each case, write "to the clock"—to a given time allotted by your news director. To check your success, read your scripts aloud. How they sound, as opposed to how they read, is the true test. Before beginning, make up a few TV news script sheets as illustrated in this chapter.

1. Announcer-on-camera story. The following wire service story arrives half an hour before air time. The newscast is tight today. The producer asks you for a 20-second item. A similar event occurred in your city only yesterday. No pictures from the North Carolina accident are available, though you have tapes and slides from yesterday's event in your city.

> FAYETTEVILLE, N.C. — Nearly 300 persons were evacuated from their homes and businesses today when three railroad cars carrying flammable methanol derailed in the downtown area of this south-central North Carolina city.
>
> No injuries were reported, and the Fayetteville fire department appeared to have the situation under control within two hours after the derailment occurred during the morning rush hour.
>
> A 10-block square area of the city was cordoned off and evacuated when officials began to fear a spark from a car engine or fire might set off an explosion. Luckily, a light wind dissipated the cloud of methanol. Railroad and civil authorities were still uncertain late today as to the cause of the accident.

2. VTR package. It's a day when all hell seems to be breaking loose. This afternoon at a local air show, the aircraft being flown by a famous test pilot simply disintegrated in midair. The pilot parachuted safely, but pieces of the plane fell into the crowd, killing three people and injuring a dozen, some seriously. A camera operator, a sound recorder and a reporter for your station were on the scene and got good footage. But when they returned to the station to put together the VTR package, they were immediately called out on another story, this time at the other end of the county, where a grain elevator had exploded. Off they go, leaving you the job of assembling the VTR package on the air crash. You have the reporter's notes, descriptions of the scenes, timing, sound "bites" and everything else you need to assemble a great story. Go to it. Put the shots together in any order you wish, to give the story full impact. Ordinarily, this story would occupy two-thirds of your newscast. Today, though, there is a lot of other news. Still, give it what it's worth. However, tell the viewers that the station has scheduled a special on the disaster for 9 p.m. tonight.

Scenes	Time
Long shot, crowd on hill, waiting for start of air show.	:05
Governor addressing crowd Opens: "This wonderful event . . ." Closes: ". . . let's enjoy it."	1:45
Medium shot of pilot climbing into plane's cockpit.	:04
Long shot of plane taking off.	:05
Long shot to close-up of plane zooming low over field, into camera that rotates following plane as it hurtles past and disappears into distance.	:03
Close-up of young child in father's arms, smiling delightedly.	:02
Medium shot of members of the crowd, marveling at the skilled flying.	:03
Baby sleeping through it all calmly. Sound of plane roaring past.	:02
Long shot of plane doing loop; then it begins to come apart. One wing comes off, then another, then the tail section breaks loose. Camera follows as parts fall, hitting runway. A wing section lands nearby, shaking the ground and jarring the camera, which keeps running. Throughout is sound first of plane engine roaring, then explosion, then crowd screams, then explosions as wing hits and people continue screaming.	:18
Blurred camera pan back up to sky and glimpse of parachutist landing.	:04
People being put on stretchers, injured being bandaged, wreckage in background.	:05
Close-up interview of injured pilot, head bandaged, telling what he thought happened. Opens: "Everything was going fine . . ." Closes: ". . . it's awful."	:15
Close-up of woman sobbing on man's shoulder.	:05
Scene from helicopter above field, showing wreckage scattered, stretchers laid out, some white sheets covering bodies.	:05
Interview with woman eyewitness, Cecile Neff. Opens: "I'd just taken my little boy to the restroom . . ." Closes: ". . . when it hit."	:20

Those are the shots you have to work with. You have natural sound for all, meaning you can let the sound carry the story or turn it down when you wish to have the studio announcer narrate. Do the complete story, from lead-in to wrap-up.

Here are the story facts the reporter, Sarah Clark, handed you in notes:

```
Air show at Strang Field (named for Leroy Strang,
city's only World War II flying ace) sponsored by city's
service clubs (Rotary, Lions, Jaycees, Optimists) to
raise funds for local charities. This was the 13th
annual show. John Strang, son of the ace, is director.
Admissions paid amounted to $18,576. Raised a total of
$35,000 after expenses. Money to be used mainly to aid
handicapped and to provide medical expenses for those
```

needing operations. Tony Richards, test pilot and
former astronaut, scheduled as last event. He was flying
the FX-10, a flex-wing experimental jet that had set
several speed records during several exhibitions around
the country. Richards was to try to set a new speed
record this p.m. He took off shortly after 2 p.m. Though
plane had radio, he was out of touch with ground in last
few seconds before accident. Investigators have no idea
as yet what caused his plane to come apart. Identities of
victims have not yet been released, pending
notification of next of kin. The governor had been in the
crowd and had spoken briefly before show began. He had
left scene a few moments before Richards took off. The
engine of the ill-fated plane fell into the speakers'
stand. If Gov. Thurston had been there, he almost
certainly would have been killed. In addition to the
three persons killed, 12 were injured. All are at
Memorial Hospital at this hour, being treated.

PART IV
WRITING TO INFORM: FEATURES

Writing feature stories can be among your most enjoyable experiences as a media writer. Developing and then composing them blends the best of journalistic writing with whatever literary artistry you can summon from your imagination and your creative powers.

Newswriting brings color to life; feature writing infuses it with texture and hue. Features offer newspaper, magazine, radio and television audiences an opportunity to go more deeply into subjects to learn more about the human drama underlying an action or event. The feature writer is an interpreter, a storyteller who, with enterprise and imagination, moves beyond the simple and the obvious to examine events from a different angle.

Feature writing is an umbrella term that includes many kinds of articles. They can address the lighter side or the very serious drama of life. They come in all shapes and sizes, depending on their importance and depth of investigation.

News events may suggest *sidebars* (stories of secondary importance about the same events) and *color stories* (stories that ride on the coattails of the main event and may also be called features). A news story on a hotel fire may call for a sidebar on a woman who re-enters the hotel to rescue her dog, a Pekingese named Sparky. An income tax deadline provides an opportunity to focus on one last-minute income tax filer. A homecoming football game may provide a color story on reminiscenses by alumni cheerleaders invited to cheer one more time for the home team.

Features are here, there, everywhere. They fall somewhere between the news story and fiction and consequently incorporate the writing of both. Whatever captures your fancy, imagination, curiosity, emotions, memories or awe will no doubt catch and hold the interest of your readers. What you have to do, however, is investigate, recapture and put on paper the things that moved your emotions and imagination in the first place. If you do this well, your readers will also be captivated by your features.

In broad terms, features can also be said to include humor and advice columns, specialty writing on topics such as food and fashion, society columns and entertainment reviews.

Feature writing for the print or broadcast media isn't nearly as stylized as newswriting. You can try any technique of expression. With features, you write for impact. You pull away from strict formats of organization and use your creativity to show the shades of gray behind something that, in a news story, may have appeared to be black and white.

The three chapters in this part discuss writing features for newspapers, magazines, and radio and television. While the technical aspects of writing for radio and TV differ from composing features for print media, the basic principles and instruction of feature writing apply to all.

CHAPTER 12

NEWSPAPER FEATURES

The subject matter of the newspaper feature story is as varied as life. The feature may be about a prince or a pauper, a mayor or a janitor, a cat or a dog. It may be a light feature or a "brite." The following light feature came across the wires some years ago and proved irresistible to wire editors across the country.

"I'll Be Happy to Do That"

His car stalled on the New Jersey Turnpike, Dan Sullivan settled back in his seat and waited for the State Highway Patrol. A white handkerchief on the car's aerial signaled his distress.

Before the patrol could reach him, however, a middle-aged woman pulled up behind him in a 1981 Olds Cutlass.

"Anything I can do to help you?" she asked Sullivan.

"Well, actually I was waiting for a tow truck. But if you could give me a push, I think the car will start. I have a dead battery."

"I'll be happy to do that," the woman smiled.

"OK," Sullivan said, "but you'll have to get up to 30 miles per hour before it'll catch."

"No problem there," the woman replied.

Sullivan walked back to his car and put the gear in neutral and waited for the bumpers to connect. He waited. And waited.

Then he glanced through his rear-view mirror. There the woman was—bearing down upon him, he realized at the last moment, at what appeared to be 30 miles per hour.

Feature stories may just as often be serious—and unforgettable. Other feature stories blend the serious and humorous, like this UPI story.

A Maturano Rage

Suppose you were going to be married in one month, and your future father-in-law feted you with a dinner at his house where the main course was supposed to be lamb. Just what would you do, after a dessert of rice pudding, if your future father-in-law told you that the main course [had been] grilled dog?

What Amaro Maturano, 26, did was this:

Threatened to kill everyone in the house. They believed him and fled.

Strangled 40 chickens. Broke 1,200 eggs ready for market.

Cut the throats of three mules.

Shot six more mules dead.

Cut the throats of three cows. Set the truck on fire. And then set the farmhouse on fire.

In Mendoza, an agricultural center 650 miles west of Buenos Aires, the police are still trying to find Maturano.

SOURCES FOR FEATURES

Ideas for features come from news events, obviously. Some come from calendars, from the holidays noted on them, and from anniversaries of events. Other feature ideas come from unusual hobbies or occupations and national or local trends and fads. Community change, conflict and activism usually generate good leads for features too.

You may also get an idea from a casual encounter or a lucky find. For example, going through the attic of your grandmother's house, you discover an old art magazine in a dusty corner full of old newspapers. You thumb through it. You read a story entitled "Little Red Riding Hood." In part, it reads like this:

> Little Red Riding Hood, with "cheeks like an apple and a cloak as red as a poppy," is told to take a cake and pot of honey to her grandmother and not to "chatter with folks or pick flowers on the way." She promises to do as she is told. But she did loiter and she did stop to pick flowers.
> And a grim gray wolf crept near and said:
> "If I might be a flower, I'd grace that bosom."
> "Oh, what a sweet-spoken beast it is," said Red Riding Hood.
> "Grant me one little kiss before you go," exclaimed the wolf.
> She told all to the wolf's questions. And the wolf then left.
> Riding Hood sets her honey and cake down to chase a butterfly and a mouse steals the cake. A dragon fly darts by and Riding Hood is off again. The ants devour the honey. What can she do, she wonders.
> Sobbing as she enters Grandma's house, where she has been preceded by the wolf who gobbles up the grandmother and dons her garments, she answers the wolf's queries in this way:
> "Where is the cake your mother promised to bake? And where is my honey?"
> "Please, Grandmother, Ma is not able to bake to-day, and as for the honey, what makes you expect any?"
> The wolf asks Riding Hood to warm the bed for him and Riding Hood strips and "into bed goes." Then come the questions and answers, slightly different from today's:
> "Oh, Granny, I view your long ears with surprise?"
> "They're to hear all you say to the letter."
> "Oh, Granny, how fiery and big are your eyes!"
> "They're to see you all the better."
> "Oh, Granny, your teeth are tremendous in size!"
> "They're to eat you!" And he ate her.
> And so the curtain rings down on Grandma's cottage small.

You look at the cover of the magazine again: *The Aldine*. You check the year. December 1873—more than a hundred years ago. Times have changed, you say to yourself. In today's version of Little Red Riding Hood, she is saved by the woodsman. Even Grandmother manages to scramble to the closet and hide from the big bad wolf. You think about that for a while. Is the change in the story for the good or the bad?

You ask a local pediatrician and a child psychologist. You ask the local librarian who reads children's stories to children every Saturday morning at the library. They all believe that the original version of Little Red Riding Hood would not harm the children reading it. Indeed, they believe the story would instruct them in the hard ways of the world and in the value of heeding parental advice. You go on with your investigation. You check with a folklorist and some parents and a kindergarten teacher. They see value in the original version. You discover that the original version of the "Three Little Pigs" has also been dramatically altered, as have many other familiar tales.

Is there feature material here? Of course. For newspapers, radio and television. Under the title "These Modern Children's Tales," just such an article was first published in a weekly newspaper, then a daily newspaper, and then in *Elementary English* magazine. A condensed news feature of the subsequent controversy it stirred up in *Elementary English* was published in *Parents Magazine.*

As has been said, feature stories are everywhere—in stocking designs, in new products, in power blackouts, in bumper stickers, in snowstorms, in joy and tragedy. And whether you are on a news assignment or a feature assignment, your job as a media writer is to be alert for them.

What you need in this search for feature material is a trained eye and imagination. Often the feature angle or treatment isn't obvious. The writer's intuition will alert him or her to the "extra something" the subject can offer.

The newspaper writer working under the beat system is likely to have a feel for features in his or her territory. These reporters can suggest good feature possibilities to their editors and, with a go-ahead from an editor, can begin the research and interviewing needed to shape the piece. Or an editor may assign a feature to a reporter.

STRUCTURE OF A FEATURE

Short feature stories are usually written using the suspended-interest story organization. The suspended-interest news story, you will recall, starts with a lead paragraph that captures the audience's interest and holds it through the explanatory paragraphs of the story. Those paragraphs build on the interest generated by the lead. A graphic representation of a suspended-interest story looks like this:

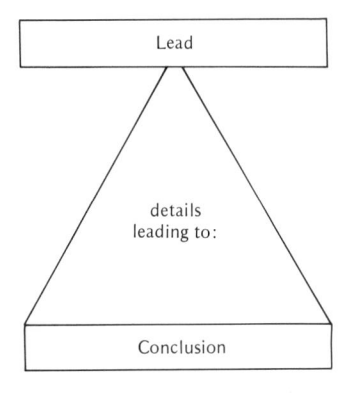

```
        Lead
         /\
        /  \
       / details \
      / leading to: \
     /_____\
       Conclusion
```

Longer feature stories may be more easily organized and written if you think in terms of the lead, then valleys and peaks of information, leading to the concluding paragraph. That graphic representation would look like this:

```
[Lead]  ～～～～～～  [End]
```

The valleys represent the expository material that carries the story forward. The peaks represent the examples, anecdotes and illustrations used to amplify the expository material. They are usually more interesting paragraphs than the valley paragraphs.

MAKE EACH LEAD A SURE-FIRE HIT

If you are going to ask an audience to read (or listen to or view) a lengthy feature story, you must write a lead that will entice them into the story. The feature lead follows the HIT pattern: a narrative *hook* for readers to bite on, an *idea* of what the feature is about and a *transition* into the body of the story. (The straight news story lead, you will recall, usually starts off emphasizing what happened—a "what" lead—or, on occasion, who was involved in the happening—a "who" lead.) The next three feature story leads include these three elements. As you read each lead, pick out the hook, the idea and the transition before reading the commentary that follows.

The Poor Shall Inherit Crime

It's common knowledge—the crime rate is worse in those parts of the city where buildings are run down and people are poorer. But why is that so?

Social psychologists and police officers have noted that if a window in a building is broken and is left unrepaired, all the rest of the windows will soon be broken. This will happen in good as well as bad neighborhoods.

The hook in this lead is the first sentence: "the crime rate is worse in those parts of the city where buildings are run down and people are poorer." The sentence attracts the interest of the audience. The idea of what the feature will be about is also implied in this sentence. The question "But why is that so?" not only serves as the transition into the body of the feature story but also lets the audience know, more explicitly, the idea to be explored in the feature.

Against the Bubbly Tide . . .

EVANSTON, Ill. (AP) — Against the bubbling tide of liquor, wine and beer, the ladies of the WCTU bow their heads in prayer but never in despair.

They have been fighting the flood for 84 years. They haven't stopped it. But it hasn't stopped them either.

The hook in this lead is the first sentence: "Against the bubbling tide of liquor, wine and beer . . ." The second paragraph makes more explicit the idea to be explored in the feature: A brief history of the Women's Christian Temperance Union and its fight against alcohol. The whole second paragraph also serves as a transition into the body of the feature by starting with the idea that the ladies of the WCTU "have been fighting the flood for 84 years. They haven't stopped it. But it hasn't stopped them either."

Feature leads can be deceptively simple. The "bubbling tide" phrase probably did not come easily to the writer.

A first-person, "in their own words" feature lead can be interesting, especially when it is as graphic as this lead:

Under the Thumb: Battered Women

"I don't remember what the argument was about, but as usual, my husband was drunk. First he threw me on the hardwood floor and then against the wall. He ripped off my brand new sweater and the rest of my clothes.

"As he made threats against my life, I decided to run out the door. He grabbed me and dragged me to the shower, sticking my head under the cold water. I cried hysterically. Finally, I broke away and ran out of the room and the apartment, screaming, naked and dripping wet."

This is the story of Anne, as reported to psychologist Lenore Walker. It's a typical story of a battered woman . . .

The first two paragraphs are the attention-getters—the hook of the feature. The third paragraph serves as the idea element in the lead as well as the transition into the body of the feature story.

SETTING THE TONE

In the leads you've read so far, you've probably noted that the feature will be a serious feature story about crime or battered women or a light feature about the WCTU. The subject matter of the feature and how you intend to deal with it in the story should be indicated in the lead. The next two feature lead examples illustrate that the features will be humorous in tone.

It's That Pesky Blue Clay*

It's that pesky blue clay over there in Ogdensburg that's causing all the trouble. As the *Courier* goes to press, that 300-foot tourist ship enters into its seventh day on a St. Lawrence River sandbar 150 yards off the Rutland Railway dock at Ogdensburg.

A herd of wild horses wouldn't budge her. You can believe that, for at last count, six tugboats with a combined horsepower in the neighborhood of 9,000 moved her only a degree or so.

The tone for this feature is set in the lead. Readers are prepared for a Mark Twain–style account of the efforts to dislodge the tourist ship.

Heaven Is . . . †

By RANDY MOORE

Heaven is many things to many people.

To Orson Welles, it might be stumbling into a wrecked food truck. To Howard Cosell, it might be a world without sportswriters. To sportswriters, it might be a world without Howard Cosell.

---

* From the Potsdam *Courier-Freeman*.

† Reprinted courtesy of *The Tennessean*.

To a hard-core basketball junkie, it might be 11 days of non-stop, championship-level hoop action.

If you happen to fall into that last category, get ready to overdose. Heaven is on the way.

A similar tone is set in this feature. The third paragraph, of course, eases the audience into the body of the story.

The following lead has flaws in it:

An Unhappy Christmas

Christmas, the time of love and joy and peace, just won't be this year for Theresa (Terry) De Francesco. It will be the unhappiest Christmas of her young (23) life.

For Terry, a petite auburn-haired Rochester girl, will spend Christmas Eve and Christmas Day in the Canton County Jail — waiting for Jan. 16.

Then, Supreme Court Judge Felix Aulisi will sentence her for the July 17 slaying of a Canton golf pro on the St. Lawrence University campus. Terry testified that she shot Richard Smith, 27, because he spurned her love.

All of these feature leads are acceptable, but some are better than others. The last writer is obviously attempting to move readers to tears. This first paragraph of "An Unhappy Christmas" is also confusing for readers. The parenthetical words stop the flow of the lead. And you also tend to read "just won't be this year" without placing the emphasis on *be* and without pausing momentarily after it.

In Potter's Field*

By JIM SQUIRES

A man was buried in a muddy grave at Nashville's Potter's Field yesterday, without eulogy and without a name.

It was a $100 funeral. Nobody cries at a $100 funeral.

BODY PARAGRAPHS

Your feature stories must flow from the lead idea, by way of the transition, into the body of the feature. Your feature story then must flow from sentence to sentence and paragraph to paragraph. That flow comes primarily from a logical organization of ideas connected by transitions.

As you read or write stories, you may find that some paragraphs or sentences do not flow naturally from one to the next. They seem to be disjointed parts of the story. The connecting tissue is missing—the thigh bones are not connected to hip bones.

Transitions transport the reader from sentence to sentence and from paragraph to paragraph, from different facts and actions to still other facts and actions. Most transitions—and, for the most part, the best transitions—are subject transitions. A repetition of a mayor's name or a pronoun are examples of subject matter sentence or paragraph transitions. They flow naturally from the subject matter of the story itself.

On the other hand, mechanical transitions may also be pressed into service

---

* Reprinted courtesy of *The Tennessean*.

for flow, continuity and clarity of expression. And although they may be more unnatural than subject matter transitions, they still bring to the story a flow and continuity that every story should have. What are examples of mechanical transitions? The start of the first two sentences of this paragraph may be considered examples of mechanical transitions: "On the other hand," "and although." Sometimes it is necessary to use mechanical transitions; most of the time, however, subject matter transitions will serve just as well.

FEATURE ANALYSIS

Let's analyze an entire feature. This particular feature grew out of an interview. The paragraphs are numbered for easy reference.

"A Father's Tale"

PEORIA, Ill. (AP) — Donald Shreeves buried the last of his four daughters a week ago. [1]

"It's one of those things you figure, God, it can't be," Shreeves, a retired Army Corps of Engineers worker, said yesterday. "But it is." [2]

All four of his daughters died violently at different times in different ways in less than a decade. [3]

"Don't do nothing now, not a thing. Don't want to," he said. "I haven't been to bed all night. You just wake up in the middle of the night and walk the floor." [4]

His last surviving daughter, Candace Lang, 33, was buried last Thursday in a family plot in Iowa. Her husband has been charged with shooting her to death. [5]

Shreeves found out about her death Feb. 22 when he was listening to the car radio. He was driving from his new home in Princeton, Mo., to Peoria to do some work on the old family house he had put on the market. [6]

A few months ago, Shreeves and his wife, Bea, had given up their house here. It held too many bad memories, he said. [7]

The radio newscaster was saying something about a woman being shot to death in Schaeferville. [8]

"I knew that's where my last living daughter, Candy, lived," he said. "But I quickly dismissed it as impossible. It couldn't be Candy. A man simply does not lose all four of his daughters." [9]

Shreeves lost his first daughter, Debbie, "the saint of the family," in a fiery car wreck in 1972. She was 19. [10]

Beverly died in Chicago, where she had moved in the summer of 1977. A man in an apartment next to hers was killed in what people believe was an underground war. Beverly, then 27, opened the door of her apartment to see what the shooting was about. The killers saw Beverly, pushed her back into the room and forced her onto a bed. They put a pillow against her head and fired two shots into her skull. [11]

Denise was two years younger than Beverly and followed her older sister everywhere. She moved to Chicago and tried to find out who killed Beverly. [12]

Soon after she wrote her father that she believed she had found Beverly's killer, Denise was discovered dead in an elevator in Chicago. She had been injected with enough drugs to kill a horse, the medical examiner said. [13]

But the father's tragedy did not end there. When Shreeves went to Chicago to try and find out what happened, he learned that his girls were not secretaries. They were prostitutes, he said. [14]

"I raised them since they were babies," he said, "I held down two jobs, washed their diapers and ironed their dresses. I thought I knew them." [15]

So he and his wife moved to Missouri last October, to put it all behind them. [16]

A week after burying his last daughter, Shreeves stares at an old portrait and says he can't believe all his girls are gone. [17]

"It's like looking at a blank piece of paper," he said. "What the hell was wrong with us? That's what I'd like to know. Did we drink out of the wrong side of the cup or what?" [18]

The copy editor who wrote the headline for this feature (and it will probably be copy editors who will write the headline-titles for your features) did a masterful job. It is a father's lament. The copy editor has selected the focal point of the feature and placed it, succinctly, in the headline, or title. The headline also prepares the reader for the tone of the feature.

The hook of the lead is in the first three paragraphs. Few persons have undergone this dreadful experience. The audience will read on to discover what happened. The idea of the feature is implicit in the first paragraph—"Donald Shreeves buried the last of his four daughters a week ago—and the third paragraph—"All four of his daughters died violently at different times in different ways in less than a decade."

The feature lead transition is also the third paragraph. After reading it, the audience knows the feature will explore the deaths of those daughters. The word *daughters,* incidentally, and their names, serve as transitions throughout the feature, sometimes carrying readers from sentence to sentence, at other times from paragraph to paragraph.

You should note how including the name of the father, Donald Shreeves, lends credibility and authenticity to the story. The impact of this feature is also increased by using the exact words of the father in the second paragraph. Just as they are used in news stories, quotes should be used profusely in feature stories.

Audiences want to hear the exact words of the person telling the story in a feature. Every feature should have a quote, beginning a paragraph, within the first three paragraphs, and at least every two or three paragraphs thereafter. Quotes also add authenticity and break up long gray columns of type.

VALLEYS AND PEAKS

The fourth paragraph in the lead might be classified as a valley. You'll remember from our wavy-line characterization of features that valleys consist of expository prose that moves the story line along to the conclusion. Most of them are not as interest-provoking as this one: "His last surviving daughter . . . was buried last Thursday . . . Her husband has been charged . . ." Usually the interest comes in the peak paragraphs following the valleys. In the peak paragraphs, examples, illustrations and details amplify the expository statement made in the valley paragraphs. In these particular peak paragraphs, the audience gets the specific details of how "Shreeves lost his first daughter, Debbie, 'The saint of the family,' in a fiery car wreck in 1972. She was 19." The audience knows the next few paragraphs will be peak paragraphs describing how the other daughters died.

This feature story, like most good feature stories, follows the valley-and-peak organizational structure to the end. The next valley that moves the feature along is paragraph 14: "But the father's tragedy did not end there.—" His reaction in the next paragraph is a peak: "'I raised them since they were babies. . . . I held down two jobs, washed their diapers and ironed their dresses. I thought I knew them.'"

The next paragraphs are valley paragraphs—more in the way of uninteresting expository prose:

"So he and his wife moved to Missouri last October, to put it all behind them."

"A week after burying his last daughter, Shreeves stares at an old portrait and says he can't believe all his girls are gone."

The peak paragraph following the valley paragraph is also the concluding paragraph. The audience is given the specific details of his disbelief:

" 'It's like looking at a blank piece of paper,' he said. 'What the hell was wrong with us? That's what I'd like to know. Did we drink out of the wrong side of the cup or what?' "

STYLE OF THE FEATURE

The unity of this feature is assured by the author's focus on one man's grief over the death of his four daughters and the logical organization of the story. This unity of impression wavers, however, when the reader is momentarily confused by paragraph 7's being allowed to stand alone. That is an organizational flaw. If it were wedded to the sixth paragraph by simply tacking it onto the end, readers would be spared this brief moment of bewilderment. And to lead the reader from paragraph to paragraph and daughter to daughter, the 11th paragraph should start out with a clear transition: "Beverly, his second daughter, . . ."

Feature story unity would also be strengthened if the next paragraph, 12, were revised to include stronger transitions in this manner: "Denise, two years younger than Beverly, had always followed her older sister everywhere. After Beverly's death, she moved to Chicago to try to find out who killed her."

THE IMPORTANCE OF DETAILS

We have been pointing out how lack of stronger transitions can affect the all-important unity of a feature, but that is not to denigrate a story such as this. Readers forgive certain flaws as they follow the story. Note that Shreeves is quoted profusely throughout. The writer allows him to tell the story in his own words. The verbs are active, and the prose indicates that the writer is very conscious of word economy. The selection of words and details by the writer makes this a good feature.

What does it mean to "raise daughters since they were babies?" Washing diapers and ironing dresses. What does it mean to lose four daughters? How would you describe that tragedy and the hurt that it caused? The concluding paragraph has a master's touch about it. Hemingway or Faulkner would have been hard-pressed to convey the father's feelings of loss and bitterness better than "It's like looking at a blank piece of paper. What the hell was wrong with us? That's what I'd like to know. Did we drink out of the wrong side of the cup or what?" What these words from a simple man describe, what these figures of speech tell us, is so moving that we are led to the brink of tears.

CONCLUDING PARAGRAPHS FOR THE FEATURE

The conclusions of features should strongly suggest that this is the last to be said on the subject. Like a gift in a box, the feature story should be tied with a ribbon before being delivered to the audience. The ribbon is the final touch to the feature—the concluding paragraph.

There are as many ways to conclude a feature as there are features. However, most endings can be placed into four major categories:

1. Sometimes the ending may be suggested by the lead of the feature. The unity of the feature may be assured by this circular organization. The ending may

then flow naturally from the subject matter and the tone of the feature and may be ready to use in the subject matter you've gathered in your research. An example would be the ending of the feature just analyzed. The audience is left in awe by ending the feature with the words of the grief-stricken father of four dead daughters. The ending brings the reader back to the lead.

2. A note of finality may be added to the feature by telling what action is now being taken on the subject matter of the feature, as it does with the feature on the rage of Amaro Maturano:

"In Mendoza, an agricultural center 650 miles west of Buenos Aires, the police are still trying to find Maturano." (This conclusion also suggests, with its flowing words, that things are relatively calm now.)

3. Conclusions can refer to what may be done in the future as far as the subject matter of the feature is concerned. That ending, too, will keep the audience thinking about the feature.

4. Another major conclusion category involves reader action. If you have been writing about the hazards of waste disposal, for example, and the cavalier attitude exhibited by private industry and the government toward that problem, you might end by asking the audience what they propose to do about it. Or, you could be more of a journalistic advocate and exhort them to action.

The conclusion of your feature, of course, depends on your subject matter and your audience. Those elements generally dictate the ending.

WRITING A FEATURE

ASSIGNMENT

Assignments for features may be dictated by your beat and the news events that occur on it. Or you may be assigned by an editor to write a feature. Let's say that the editor of the New York City newspaper you work for calls you in Wednesday morning: "Drive on up to Hyslip, Connecticut, and find out what's going on there," Warren Titus says. "In the past three months Hyslip's been racked by a series of automobile accidents that killed three high school students. And there's been heavy drinking and drug use and all that kind of stuff. That's not quite the picture of suburban living that most people have in mind when they move to the suburbs. Most of the Hyslip citizens moved there to get away from those evils, which are only supposed to exist in big cities like New York."

"When do you want the story?" you ask.

"We'd like to play it big in the Sunday edition," Titus replies.

GETTING THE FACTS

After going to the newspaper morgue and noting the contents of four major stories on Hyslip's problems, you know you have a feature on your agenda. You go to your apartment, pack an overnight bag, pick up your portable computer and drive to Hyslip.

OBSERVATION

You arrive there at twilight. The New England autumn is breathtaking. You drive around the community of about 25,000, trying to get a "feel" for it. Some residents are burning leaves; several of them wave to you with their rakes. A sports car full of young people zips past you.

At the Anchor Inn motel, you wait to check in behind two extremely young-looking couples. As you register, you make small talk with the desk clerk: "Is most of your clientele as young as those kids who just registered?"

The clerk smiles courteously and answers, "Yes."

Research

The next morning you stop by the town's newspaper, *The Hyslip Courier*, the first stop of many in your efforts to research thoroughly the problems of Hyslip's youth. The path you follow is the path followed by all feature writers of stories such as this. The staff is receptive. The two reporters, Steve Williams and Julie Simpson, tell you about some of the goings-on about Hyslip. You spend the rest of the day looking through the morgue's clippings and last year's editions of the newspaper. Late in the afternoon, the *Courier's* editor, Joe Farris, gives you that day's edition featuring an editorial on the current trouble in Hyslip. You read it, then ask him more questions that occurred to you as you were going through the morgue's clippings during the day. How do the current problems differ from those in the past? What does he think is causing the problems? What may be solutions to them? You list the people you're planning on talking to the next day and ask him if there are others you should see. After dinner, you spend the night in the motel, going over your notes and writing down on 3-by-5 cards the questions you're going to ask the next day. How does this high school population differ from those of the past? How do these sons and daughters differ from those of a few years ago? How are their relationships with the schools, churches and parents different? What is the absentee rate? The dropout rate? The number of pregnancies? How do the students regard the laws of the community and the state? You arrange the question cards in the order in which you plan to ask the questions of principals, parents and church figures.

Interviewing

You go to bed knowing that the initial interviews will provide you with facts you can use in interviewing still other people. You will have to listen carefully to the answers. You know that a feature story assignment such as this calls for extensive interviewing and investigation. After breakfast the next morning, you drive to the police station and introduce yourself to the police chief. As you shake his hand, you say, "Joe Farris told me to come down here to check out some accident reports and talk about the kind of trouble the young people here in Hyslip get into."

"Police blotter's right there. You might want to talk to these two officers who are on duty at night."

He introduces you to Sergeants Jeff Salansky and Juan Rodriguez. You talk to them about the auto accidents and about drinking and drugs among teen-agers. You check the police blotter; later in the morning you ask the police chief and other police officers more questions about the arrests and accidents and drug usage and the attitude of the parents and community toward those incidents.

You drive to the parish house of St. Thomas' Roman Catholic Church. Like the newspaper office building, the church architecture is elegant and stately. You talk with the priest, the Rev. Robert J. McCabe. You ask him about the role of the church in all this and the attitude of his parishioners. He is a little defensive and remarks that many of the answers are treated in the sermon he will be delivering this Sunday. You persuade him to give you a copy of the sermon. You then stop by the high school and talk with the principal, Dr. Mildred S. Ross, about the discipline problems she's having and the parents' attitudes toward them.

Although she is reluctant to talk at great length about the problems in the high school, you discover, among other things, that the parking lots have to be patrolled before classes, during lunch breaks and after classes because of the heavy necking and other things that go on during those times. In the hallways of the high school, between periods and at a lunch break, you talk to high school teachers and students about sex and drugs. You corroborate all that's been said to you about the lifestyle of high school students at Hyslip. You call the head of the Parent-Teacher Association, Jennifer Rowland. She puts you in touch with two concerned parents, Michelle Gaps and Heidi L. Hewitt, and a minister of the Richard Street Methodist Church, Donna Watson.

On the way out of Hyslip, late in the afternoon, you cross the railroad tracks leading to New York City. The rusty-looking railway station is in a sad state of repair. Pigeon droppings plaster everything.

OUTLINING

As you drive to New York City, you mentally compose the outline of your feature story. (Remember the details on outlining from Chapter 5.) Some facts and statements fall naturally together into blocks of information: the car accidents, the arrests, the attitude of the community. Some remain stubbornly by themselves at this time: the roles of the newspaper, the church and the parents. You think about what should go into the feature lead to get the readers' attention. What should follow the lead? What goes after those paragraphs? You think about a good conclusion. Can it stem from the lead? While doing this, you review the interviews to determine if you have left anything out of your notes. You retrace your drives through the suburban town. You are struck by the mixture of modern and old houses and by the incongruities of the various architectural settings and the community's jet-set lifestyle. Those architectural incongruities, you decide, will be the underlying and unifying motif of the feature story. They help tie in the roles of the newspaper and the church. By the time you arrive at your apartment at 10 o'clock, you have the feature outline in mind. You can hardly wait to type it out in detail, making changes in your mind's outline as your intellect directs you. The outline looks good:

"Trouble in Suburbia"
I. Introduction
    A. Autumn glory
    B. Eagle on *Courier*
    C. Leaf fires and turbulence
II. "Little Kinsey Report"
III. Auto accident deaths
IV. Citizens' reactions
    A. Father McCabe sermon
    B. Church architecture
    C. Hyslip setting, houses, etc.
V. *Courier* editorial "On Name-Calling"
    A. Luxurious living
    B. Pampered children
    C. Good conscience not "bad press"
VI. Weeks' record of arrests
VII. Conclusion
    A. Dull-red train station
    B. Tracks lead back to New York City (connect Hyslip to City)

First Draft

The next morning at 8, you sit down at your portable computer with a cup of coffee in easy reach. Reviewing the outline, you make minor changes here and there. When you are through, you still don't like what you see. The outline looks good to you, but you actually thought it would be more detailed than it is. You're uneasy because you know that the more detailed your outline is, the better your first draft will be. You know it's difficult enough just to put "proper words in proper places" without having to worry about where you are going and where you have been. You study the outline once more. Opening and closing with a setting description makes good sense to you. It helps unify the feature. Although your headline (or slugline or title), "Trouble in Suburbia," isn't likely to appear over your story when it is published (the copy editor will supply one), it keeps you focused on the subject of the feature.

You can't put it off any longer. You start writing the first draft of your story—a dreary task for you. As you write, you recall the beauty of the autumn scene in Hyslip. Your flair for the picturesque and your love of nature carry you away when you write the hook.

```
HYSLIP, Conn., September 21 – Streaks of rose lie across
the western horizon at twilight here in the evening, and
the russet hills are pure New England glory. The
weather-vane eagle that poises, wings spread, on the
roof of the newspaper office of the Courier seems made of
freshly poured gold.                                    [1]
```

You know the hook is more "literary" than most newspaper features. But this is for your Sunday edition and, consequently, for readers who expect more from a feature and have more time to read it. You decide to keep the lead.

You then indirectly suggest the agitation underlying Hyslip—the main idea of the feature—by using leaf fires and sports cars zipping through the streets.

```
In autumn, this prosperous town is a beautiful haven
from the noisy city. The tang of leaf fires rides the
air. At night, long, low imported sports cars with loud
engines, filled with young people, zip through tree-
lined lanes.                                            [2]
```

You like the idea of smoldering fires and loud engines in young people's cars to symbolize the underlying conflict in Hyslip. And it makes good, vivid reading.

Like a good feature writer, in the third paragraph you spell out the idea of the feature story and provide the transition for the reader to follow into the main body of the story.

```
The face of Hyslip appears serene. Underneath,
however, lies agitation and turbulence.         [3]
    The turbulence surfaced in May, when the Council of
Hyslip School Parents published what one adult labeled
"a little Kinsey report" on drinking, vandalism,
shoplifting, gang activity and sex play among teen-
agers. Some citizens called it unfair.          [4]
    But three weeks ago, after two house parties, 16-year-
old Shirley Atchison was killed at 3:55 a.m. in a
station-wagon crash. As a result of this death, 13
```

> adults, including business and professional men and
> their wives, were arrested and charged with serving
> liquor to minors. Four days later, Harvey Haddox, 17,
> died in another early-morning car wreck in what
> authorities called apparently similar circumstances. [5]
>
> Hyslip is self-conscious now, and a little angry. Some
> citizens feel it is being made to serve as a symbol of
> modern suburban moral decay. [6]

The fourth paragraph really pleases you. Its expository prose is supposed to be a valley in the feature because it moves the story line along. But with the "little Kinsey Report" and other examples in it, it represents a peak as much as a valley. The fifth paragraph, with its auto deaths, is definitely a peak.

You also like the opening of the sixth paragraph: "Hyslip is self-conscious now . . ." The feature is marching right along. The detailed outline is doing its job.

> "It could have happened in any one of hundreds of
> communities in America," The Rev. Robert J. McCabe said.
> He is pastor of St. Thomas' Roman Catholic Church – a
> small stone building with a peaked roof and tower. At all
> masses last Sunday, he echoed an anguished truism: [7]
>
> "Editorial writers across the country have had a field
> day at our expense. They have made us the victims of
> their editorial guillotines." [8]
>
> But Father McCabe admitted that "in recent years
> there has been an ever-increasing disregard for law. In
> the eyes of some, all obligations are becoming a
> nuisance." [9]

These paragraphs about the sermon are peak paragraphs, representing reader peaks of interest. As you write McCabe's comments, you review the interview you had with him. You're never too concerned about the peak paragraphs. Because they elaborate on the exposition in the valley paragraphs—through illustrations, examples or anecdotes—peak paragraphs tend naturally to make interesting reading. And McCabe's remarks make good reading, especially the "editorial guillotines" comment.

> Surburban living and all its happy values seem to be
> summed up in the neatness and simplicity of the weekly
> *Courier*'s office. Published in a handsome, semicolonial
> office, four wooden columns stand at the portico
> entrance. Those values also seem to be symbolized by the
> saltbox cottages with weathered shingles, lovely old
> wooden manors with tall pines towering over them,
> rambling suburban homes, and the long rock walls so
> familiar to New England. [10]

As you write this paragraph—a valley paragraph—you fear it will be the valley of death—reader interest death. The exposition and the lengthy architecture description of Hyslip countryside may turn readers away and onto another story. You make a note in the margin to check it out closely when you revise. But if you've carried readers this far, you reason, you have their interest. That interest will probably sustain some of that long description. But you don't want the reader to suffer needlessly—to wallow through uninteresting detail.

> But in a blistering editorial titled, "On Name-
> Calling," the current issue of the *Courier* scalds some
> parents for pampering children.   [11]
>
> "This sordid, tawdry spectacle, where children are
> allowed all sorts of excesses," the editorial says,
> "includes too many material comforts and luxuries and
> too much license to do as they please."   [12]
>
> (Typical of the resident comforts is the listing of
> family after family on Buttonwood Lane with separate
> numbers marked "children's telephone.")   [13]
>
> "The standards and values this sad series of events
> exposed is false and superficial," the editorial said.
> "We should be more concerned with real accomplishment
> than social status, with more worry about a good
> conscience than about a 'bad press.'"   [14]

A rush flows through you as you write these paragraphs. They're another peak.

So far, you've been doing what you should be doing as a feature writer. After the opening narrative hook, idea and transition, the lead elements, you've been alternating valleys and peaks, and you're now nearing the end of the feature. Joe Farris's editorial remarks makes good copy in the feature—colorful and to the point. What's nice about them is that they also carry your story line along while entertaining the readers.

You move with confidence into the concluding paragraphs.

> Meanwhile, this week's record of arrests on the police
> blotter discloses that Juan Rodriguez, a policeman
> patrolling Weed Beach at night, came upon two 15-year-
> old girls with liquor. And a 21-year-old unmarried
> woman, of Middlesex Road, was arrested and charged with
> secret delivery and concealment of birth.   [15]
>
> Not too far from Weed Beach, at Hyslip's old, dull-red
> train station, not much more, really, than a bird roost
> needing several coats of paint, two tired, rummage-sale
> Victorian cast-iron benches face the New York-bound
> tracks – 27 miles and 45 minutes from Grand Central
> Station.   [16]

The week's arrests seem made for the feature. But the last paragraph sounds a little too literary to you. You make another note in the margin to revise it so that the meaning will be clear to the reader.

REVISION

You fix another cup of coffee and then go back to the first paragraph and start revising. Back in college, one of your writing professors said that all good writers go through a revision process—that there's no such thing as good writing; it's all good rewriting. You know that you should have more time before looking over your first draft to revise effectively, but you like what you've written and you want to revise it now. Sometimes the flow and rhythm of the feature can be improved by revision immediately after the first draft. But you'll still let it sit overnight and revise it once more.

As you revise, you recall the scenes and the persons you interviewed as you come to them in the feature so that you can picture them more accurately if necessary and use still other quotes you may not have used in the draft. You keep in mind that, above all, you want unity, clarity and economy.

You check the lead—it has the three elements of HIT: hook, idea, transition. Your first paragraph serves as a good contrast to the concluding paragraph. You especially like the "freshly poured gold" phrase in the beginning. It contrasts beautifully with the "dull-red bird roost" in the concluding paragraph.

Your use of direct quotes in the first three paragraphs leaves something to be desired. You decide to pull "a little Kinsey report" to the front of the fourth paragraph. After that, the quotes appear liberally sprinkled throughout the rest of the feature. Quotes at the beginning of paragraphs provide the reader with a variety of typographical display. They make the long gray column of type less foreboding. And readers like to think they're reading the exact words of persons, not some paraphrase of them.

You check your verbs to eliminate the passive ones and insert action verbs. Vivid words, along with specific details and figures of speech, make or break a good feature. You check for clichés; there are none. You read the feature aloud and listen to the flow and rhythm of it. You mark the sixth paragraph. The second sentence sounds stilted: "Some citizens feel it is being made to serve as a symbol of modern suburban moral decay." The phrase "it is being made to serve" must be changed. You draw a mental block on how to do it now, but you know that during tomorrow's revision session the change will come to you.

The valley paragraphs don't flatten out too much, and the following peak paragraphs nicely amplify, with examples, the exposition in the valley paragraphs. You're beginning to think you've written a good feature. But beware of overconfidence. When you revise, you can't afford to let rose-colored glasses slip over your eyes. Nevertheless, you're pleased.

You read the next-to-last paragraph. You compliment yourself on using details so well: If a woman has to be charged with concealment of birth, what better street for her to live on than Middlesex Road? And since part of Hyslip's problem is a problem facing most American communities—the gap between youth and law enforcement officers who no longer know every person on their beat—what better name for a policeman than Juan Rodriguez? After all, Hyslip is a WASP community, and for the reader between the lines—the sophisticated reader—the name Rodriguez does not fit in. The paragraph's perfect.

"Better watch that attitude!" you caution yourself again.

You look once more at the last paragraph. You started the feature with the eagle on the *Courier* building, the first stage of the architectural motif. The description of the Catholic church—the "small stone building with a peaked roof and tower" (paragraph 7)—suggests that the church is lagging behind the times: The church is not counseling its flock in the wise conduct of modern living. In the same fashion, in the 10th paragraph, the *Courier* building's architecture—the "semicolonial office, four wooden columns . . . at the portico"—suggests that the newspaper isn't doing its job of keeping a surveillance on the community and letting the citizens know what's going on. Instead, it has merely mirrored and reacted to events, not forewarned the citizens of them. The mixture of saltbox cottages with rambling suburban homes suggests the mixture of old values with the new in Hyslip (paragraph 10). You have even mentioned the values in the paragraph.

You read the last paragraph and decide that the "Victorian cast-iron benches" evoke the Victorian age in England, when, on the surface, respectability was mightily striven for, while below the surface, morals were more than a little loose. The connection of the Victorian age with Hyslip may or may not be noted by the average reader, but it doesn't hurt the ending at all. The New York–bound railroad tracks, meanwhile, suggest to the reader that suburbia is still connected to the temptations of the big city. But the ending is still not as smooth as it could be. The next day's revision will have to take care of that.

Overall, you are pleased with most of the paragraphs. But you know that as you revise, still more changes in imagery and details will occur to you. You take the last sip of coffee and place the feature aside until tomorrow.

INTERVIEW FEATURES AND SIDEBARS

In Chapter 7 we gave some examples of news stories written from interviews. However, unless an interview is conducted to glean information while an event is happening, the material gathered is usually more suitable for more feature-oriented handling. The two most common formats are the question-and-answer interview and the pure-feature interview story. Both "A Father's Tale" and "Trouble in Suburbia" in this chapter were pure features that were based on interviews. The question-and-answer interview is quite a different beast.

THE QUESTION-AND-ANSWER INTERVIEW FEATURE

The question-and-answer technique provides a deceptively simple approach to writing an interview story. Some question-and-answer interviews begin with a brief introductory paragraph to ensure a smooth transition into the body of the story; others do not need one. Likewise, a concluding paragraph may or may not be used to end the story.

A greatly abbreviated story on how married couples argue is presented here in question-and-answer form. The original article by Anthony Brandt appeared in the October 1982 issue of *Psychology Today*.

Avoiding "Couple Karate"

If you are happily married, chances are you possess good arguing skills. Anyway, that's what investigations of marital conflict by University of Illinois psychologist John M. Gottman indicate.

Q: How exhaustive was your investigation into marital conflict?

A: Throughout a nine-year period we studied some 487 couples, using aids such as videotapes and devices for measuring physiological reactions.

Q: What are some of your findings?

A: We discovered that skills in relating to one another were more important than wealth or education.

Q: What kind of marital discord were you studying?

A: Actually we found that most fights have three stages: agenda-building, then arguing and, finally, negotiating.

Q: You obviously have been able to help couples in conflict. What other relationship skills do you find important?

A: Helping couples to solve conflicts is obviously important. But no one yet has been able to instruct them in how to become friends. I intend to do that.

If you ask the right kind of questions in the right order and if you get the proper responses, you don't have to engage in much creativity in writing the story. The creativity comes in shaping the answers so that they are succinct and still keep the spirit of the response. And creativity must take place in the background research that was necessary and in formulating the questions.

Sometimes you may have just the right answer to end the story. If not, you may have to use a concluding paragraph such as this:

> Having helped couples resolve their conflicts, Gottman now intends to teach them how to become friends.
>
> "No one," according to Gottman, "has done that yet. That's my goal now."

THE SIDEBAR

The sidebar is a valuable tool for both editors and readers. It helps the editor keep a story's length and precision under control by separating out an important detail for treatment in a second story. It helps the reader obtain a better understanding of the events because of the double treatment of related information.

Sidebars can be small boxes that add hard information—such as statistics and comments from analysts—or full articles that amplify an aspect of a story that appears next to it or near it in the newspaper—an interview with a newsmaker is one outstanding example. If a story is so complex that all elements of it can't be explained in the main piece, a sidebar is an excellent way to capture an important element and explain it fully outside the main piece.

One good example of a sidebar is on page 446. And here is an example of the way in which the *Washington Post* developed a sidebar on polygraphs to run with a larger story on how Congress is instituting new penalties and deterrents for U.S. citizens who deal with classified information:

[Page One news story—
continues on Page A11]

House Votes Execution for Spies*
Peacetime Penalty Could Be Levied by Military Courts

By SHARON LaFRANIERE
Washington Post Staff Writer

The House of Representatives passed without debate yesterday a measure that would permit military courts to impose the death penalty on those convicted of espionage in peacetime.

The approval of the measure by voice vote was the House's second action in less than 24 hours to strengthen anti-espionage efforts following the recent arrests of four alleged Navy spies.

Yesterday's vote represented a dramatic turnaround for the House, which last year refused to take up a Senate-passed measure that would have allowed the imposition of the death penalty in cases of espionage, treason and attempts on a president's life.

The vote followed overwhelming House approval Wednesday night of a measure that would allow the Defense Department, for the first time, to test the loyalty of more than 4 million military and civilian employes with access to classified information through the use of polygraph tests. It would require polygraphs before employes are allowed to see the most sensitive information.

[This precedent-setting action by the House is fleshed out in a sidebar.]

Proponents and opponents of the two measures agreed yesterday that neither would have passed so

---

* ©, *The Washington Post*. Reprinted by permission.

easily had it not been for mounting concern over the alleged spy ring said to be headed by retired Navy Chief Warrant Officer John A. Walker Jr. Federal officials have described the spy case as one of the most damaging in decades.

Voicing a sentiment widely shared by civil liberties advocates, Rep. Don Edwards (D-Calif.) said the House was acting out of "hysteria. That's the only reason these worthless amendments are being

See PENALTY A11, Col. 1

☐ *Polygraphs: 'Witchcraft' or 'effective tool' to detect spies?* Page A12
[Prompts reader to look at sidebar]

[*Sidebar* appears on Page A12]

Polygraphs: 'Witchcraft' or 'Effective Tool'?*

Spy Case Refuels Debate Over Tests' Validity

By RUTH MARCUS
Washington Post Staff Writer

To its detractors, such as the late Sen. Sam Ervin, the lie detector test smacks of "20th century witchcraft." To its supporters, such as William Kotapish, director of security for the CIA, the polygraph is "the single most effective tool available" to ferret out spies.

The polygraph's ability to determine an individual's veracity by measuring changes in pulse, blood pressure and perspiration has been a matter of controversy almost since the forerunner of the modern device was invented about 60 years ago.

But with the arrest of four Navy men on espionage charges, the issue of using lie detectors to uncover spies and potential spies has come to the forefront of debate about what should be done to stem the loss of defense secrets.

The House of Representatives voted overwhelmingly Wednesday to grant the Pentagon broad power to subject to lie detector tests more than 4 million military and civilian employes cleared to see classified information. Under the measure, passed 333 to 71 as an amendment to the Defense Department authorization bill, polygraphs would be required of those seeking clearance to see the most sensitive information.

A similar measure, backed by Majority Leader Robert J. Dole (R-Kan.), is pending in the Senate.

Polygraph proponents applauded the House vote. "If a person is a spy, and if he's being asked on the polygraph, 'Have you ever spied?' he's going to react to it on the polygraph, and the chances of his being detected are very good," said Gordon Barland, a Utah polygraph expert.

According to the American Polygraph Association, the test is accurate more than 90 percent of the time in cases where trained examiners are able to reach a conclusion about a person's truthfulness.

Backers of polygraphs also maintain that the threat of being subjected to a test would deter workers who might otherwise be tempted to spy. The author of the House amendment, Rep. C.W. Bill Young (R-Fla.), cited testimony last month by convicted Soviet spy Christopher Boyce, who told a Senate committee that if he had thought he might be required to take a polygraph test, "I would never have considered an act of espionage."

But critics of lie detector tests

* ©, The Washington Post. Reprinted by permission.

describe the devices as unreliable in general and particularly unsuitable in screening rather than in investigating specific crimes or incidents. Increased use of the tests for determining clearances, they warn, would finger innocent people as security risks while failing to unmask real spies trained to outwit the tests.

"The polygraph can detect lies just as well as Laetrile can cure cancer," said Dr. John F. Beary III, associate dean at the Georgetown University School of Medicine and former principal deputy assistant secretary of defense for health affairs. "The soldier or sailor now has his career determined by a device with the accuracy of a roulette wheel."

Beary cited a 1983 study by the congressional Office of Technology Assessment that concluded, "While there is some evidence for the validity of polygraph testing as an adjunct to criminal investigations, there is very little research or scientific evidence to establish polygraph tests validity in screening situations. The scientific evidence is clear—that a polygraph test cannot reliably and in any valid way determine whether somebody is lying."

"I'm as concerned as any other citizen about spies and preventing people in the armed forces from selling information to foreign governments, but the polygraph is not a device that is going to enable us to determine who's doing these things," said the author of the report, Boston University psychology professor Leonard Saxe.

A principal concern among critics of lie detector tests is the threat of "false positive" readings — finding deception by a person who actually is telling the truth — that would brand honest employes as security risks.

"Truthful people are going to be victimized," said David Lykken, a polygraph expert at the University of Minnesota. He said studies show that innocent people have a 40 to 50 percent chance of being classified as deceptive. "A lot of innocent people and especially conscientious people who are not accustomed to having their word questioned are going to fail a polygraph test," he said.

"Certainly false positives can occur," said Frank Horvath, director of the American Polygraph Association Research Center at Michigan State University. However, he said, such results "do not present a serious problem [because] most employers do not make a decision solely on the basis of a polygraph test outcome. They use that to correlate with other information about an applicant."

Critics also warn that actual spies trained to outsmart polygraphs might evade detection. Subjects can throw examiners off the track of their lies by biting their tongues or stepping on a tack hidden in their shoes when answering "control" questions, critics said.

"It can be beaten and the KGB knows how to beat the polygraph," Lykken said. "When the examiners say you can easily detect [evasive measures] from the charts they are thinking about uninformed criminal suspects who don't know how to do it and try to beat the test on the spur of the moment by coughing or squirming."

But Lynn P. Marcy, chairman of the American Polygraph Association and a former Air Force security investigator, said that examiners were able to discern even more sophisticated attempts to fool them. "To a skilled polygraph examiner, the type of reaction that occurs from pain is entirely different than the typical type of reaction caused by fear of detection or the stress of telling a lie," he said. "We have developed anti-countermeasure techniques to help us sort out those kinds of attempts."

BLUEPRINT FOR IMPACT

A balanced blending of journalism and art characterizes the best efforts of feature writing. Notice how Jules Loh's great feature story, like all features, starts out with a narrative hook, the idea of what the feature is going to be about and a transition or bridge leading into the body of the feature story.

Starting with the lead, you are pulled into the story and hurtled along at great speed—leaping over the valleys and skimming the peaks of the feature. Notice how Loh works a quotation into the story early—at paragraph 3. He didn't bury the quotation marks, either—he started the paragraph with them. Note also how he depicts the small town of Skidmore in six newspaper lines in paragraph 7. As you read, notice particularly the details, the transitions and the concluding paragraphs.

The Saga of Ken McElroy

By JULES LOH
AP Special Correspondent

SKIDMORE, Mo. (AP) — No sooner had Ken McElroy walked out of the courtroom where they found him guilty of shotgunning the village grocer than, sure enough, there he was back at the D&G tavern. [1]

He showed no remorse. He was sullen. When Ken McElroy was sullen, prudent people gave him room. Even when he was not sullen, tough guys in saloons all across Nodaway County called him mister. It was recognized as unhealthy to cross Ken McElroy. [2]

"He never knelt down to nobody," his young, blonde wife of five years, Trina, reflected the other day. "He didn't care who they were or how many there were. He didn't need nobody beside him." [3]

Just so. He was a big, thickset man of 47 ill-spent years, 5 foot 10 and 265 pounds, massive arms, low forehead, bushy eyebrows and sideburns. [4]

He wasn't a street brawler. He was specific. He struck fear in your soul by staring you down, flashing a gun, occasionally using it. If you were his prey for today, he stalked you. He glared at you in silence, and when he spoke it was in a slow whisper. Chilling. [5]

He was born on a farm just outside of town. When he was a boy, he fell off a hay wagon, requiring a steel plate to be implanted in his head. Some wondered if that was what made him so mean. [6]

This is a small town: 440 people, filling station, bank, post office, tavern, blacktop street, grain elevator. Beyond are rolling meadows, ripening corn, redwing blackbirds, fat cattle, windmills and silos, a scent off a Sweet Lassy feed calendar. Ken McElroy jarred that pastoral serenity. So it is with outspoken relief that the citizens of Nodaway County now speak of him in the past tense. He is dead. The fear he brought them, though, still lingers in a new, unexpected form. [7]

At the D&G tavern the day of his conviction, last June 26, he was very much alive, and he was decidedly sullen. [8]

"I been fighting prosecutors since I was 13 years old and I'm damn near 50," he muttered in his beer. "This is the first time I've lost." [9]

For the next two weeks the townspeople muttered, too. They wondered why Ken McElroy was in the D&G tavern in the first place, or anywhere else than where they had wanted him to be approximately since he was 13, which was in a well-barred jail. [10]

Here he was again, scot free on a $40,000 appeal bond, terrorizing the countryside. Bond or no bond, he had swaggered into the D&G tavern toting an M-1 rifle with a bayonet on it. [11]

"Same old story," Lois Bowenkamp said. "Police arrest him, courts let him go." Lois is the wife of Ernest Bowenkamp, known affectionately as Bo, the 72-year-old grocer who McElroy shot in the neck. Bo survived and is back to work. [12]

On the day of a hearing to revoke McElroy's bond for carrying the rifle, July 10, about 60 men gathered downtown. They figured a big crowd at the hearing would impress the judge, and they figured to go to the courthouse together. [13]

When the men got to town, though, they learned the hearing had been postponed. Another maddening delay. In their frustration they gathered at the Legion hall, and invited the sheriff, to discuss how to protect themselves from the county menace. [14]

The meeting broke up when someone burst in with a message that more than once had cleared the streets of Skidmore. [15]

"McElroy's in town." [16]

This time they didn't clear the streets. This time they strode over to the D&G, and when McElroy finished his beer, they walked out with him. They stared wordlessly as he got into his pickup. Suddenly, someone put at least three bullets in McElroy's head. [17]

Now a new terror grips the people of Skidmore. Having survived their fear of the lawless, they now fear the law. Not one person in that crowd has been willing to say who it was who shot and killed Ken Rex McElroy. [18]

Trina McElroy, who was with him, told a coroner's jury she saw who it was and named his name. Nonetheless, the jury concluded McElroy was killed by a "person or persons unknown." Now a Nodaway County grand jury will investigate. [19]

Trina was not McElroy's first wife. She was his fourth, the mother of three of the 15 children he fathered over the years. [20]

They were married when their first child was a year old and Trina was 17 — married under circumstances the prosecutor termed "suspicious." The townspeople had other words for it. [21]

The prosecutor had charged McElroy with raping Trina. Trina says it was a lie, that they wanted to get married all along. Fair enough, except that Ken already had a wife and, besides, Trina would need her parents' consent, which they refused to give. [22]

A few days before the rape trial, four things happened. [23]

One, Ken got a divorce. Two, a house burned down. Three, Trina's parents gave their consent. Four, Ken and Trina found a magistrate in another county who married them. The house that burned down belonged to Trina's parents. [24]

Thus ended the possibility of Trina's testifying against Ken. The rape charges were dropped. [25]

Charges being dropped for lack of people willing to testify against Ken McElroy was the theme of his long criminal record. His lawyer said he had been run in and turned loose "for lack of a case" so many times he couldn't remember them all. [26]

Rustling livestock, threatening people, molesting a minor, arson, you name it, McElroy had been charged with it, but witnesses had a way of backing off. [27]

So it went, until he shot Bo Bowenkamp. Guilty. Finally. [28]

"Oh, he was intimidating," Lois Bowenkamp said. "You can't know how awful it was. My neighbor and I took turns sleeping at night. [29]

"Before the trial, he would drive up in his pickup at night and sit there. Occasionally he would fire a gun. We knew him, knew his reputation. It was frightening." [30]

You could never know what small thing might set McElroy off. His falling out with Bo Bowenkamp resulted from Bo's clerk asking McElroy's daughter to put away a candy bar she hadn't paid for, or from McElroy's view, "accusing her of raiding the store." [31]

When McElroy roared into town in his pickup with the big mud flaps and the gun rack, his wife in a second pickup ("backup," she explained), everybody fled, not so much for their immediate safety but for fear they might see McElroy do something they would have to testify to later. [32]

In fairness to the late Ken McElroy, it is also true that, like another who once prowled these parts and met his Maker just south of here, Jesse James, he was suspected of every crime in the county. [33]

Especially rustling. Last year, Nodaway County led the state in stolen livestock — six times the thefts in any other county — and the ranchers who were aware of that were also aware that Ken McElroy always had a pocket full of money. [34]

He lived on a small farm not likely to win any agricultural awards, so where did he get it all? He claimed also to trade in antiques, to which everybody said, but not to his face, whose antiques? [35]

We're talking money. He paid for his pickups in cash. He paid his lawyer in cash. He tossed $8,000 on the bar at D&G and told the bartender, "If that ain't enough I've got a suitcase full at home." He peeled a hundred-dollar bill off his wad and told Lois Bowenkamp it was hers if she would try to whip Trina on the Skidmore street. [36]

People here are looking to see what happens to the rustling problem now that Ken McElroy is laid in his grave. [37]

It will be more interesting to see what happens to Skidmore. [38]

The McElroy shooting has thoroughly shaken this rural community. The townsfolk don't want to talk about who might have shot him, they don't want to talk about "the incident," as they refer to it, at all, not even among themselves. [39]

"All we want to do," Lois Bowenkamp said, "is to go back to doing what we do best, which is minding our own business." [40]

This feature blends the best of journalism and literary art.

The first paragraph provides a narrative hook that a reader will find hard to resist; the idea of what the feature will be about—Ken McElroy and the trouble he creates; and the transition to the body of the story: "there he was back at the D&G tavern."

The third paragraph starts with a direct quote from McElroy's wife that functions as an expository or valley paragraph. But the quote also characterizes the wife and her feelings about her husband. It is entirely appropriate to leave in her grammatical lapses. Loh renders the speech of the townspeople so faithfully that you seem to hear them talk. In the peak paragraphs that follow we discover why McElroy "didn't need nobody beside him."

For impact, Loh uses fragmentary sentences. He ends paragraph 5 this way: "He glared at you in silence, and when he spoke it was in a slow whisper. Chilling."

The peak valleys end with paragraph 6, and in paragraph 7, a valley paragraph, Loh paints a picture of the setting in which all this action takes place (a beautiful portrait in one small paragraph), lets the reader know that McElroy is now dead, and then uses this transition into the next paragraphs: "He is dead. The fear he brought them, though, still lingers in a new, unexpected form." The reader is now ready for examples, in peak paragraphs, of how that fear lingers on.

Loh flashes back to the day of McElroy's conviction and tells all that happened in the next few days in the present tense, for more impact. The feelings of the townspeople are explored. More quotes are used.

Paragraph 13 prepares us for the events that are to follow the hearing to revoke McElroy's bond for carrying the rifle. It functions primarily as a valley paragraph, moving the feature along to the climactic scene, when "Suddenly, someone put at least three bullets in McElroy's head." That sentence comes at the end of paragraph 17, the most emphatic position in a paragraph, and the reader is ill-prepared for the suddenness of McElroy's death. But that coincides with the way it happened.

Paragraph 18 is a valley paragraph that talks about the new terror that now grips the people of Skidmore—the fear of the law. Loh states it ironically: "Having survived their fear of the lawless, they now fear the law."

The following peak paragraphs explore that fear and, in the process, flash back to McElroy's wife's experiences with him and how charges of rape against him were dropped.

Paragraph 27, a valley paragraph, points out that charges against McElroy were always being "dropped," and the next peak paragraphs describe how McElroy operates to get them dropped. The occasion leading to McElroy's shotgunning of the grocer is included.

Valley paragraph 33 states that McElroy was, like Jesse James, suspected of every crime in the county. The next paragraphs touch on rustling, trading in antiques and the money he flashed around. They end with paragraph 37: "People here are looking to see what happens to the rustling problem now that Ken McElroy is laid in his grave."

The next two paragraphs function as valley paragraphs, touching on the fear that permeates Skidmore and the townsfolk's reluctance to talk about "the incident."

The concluding direct-quote paragraph illustrates the feeling of the townsfolk in this regard and ties up the feature in a neat bow: "'All we want to do,' Lois Bowenkamp said, 'is to go back to doing what we do best, which is minding our own business,'" To make the quote and the conclusion more emphatic, Loh buries the attribution, "Lois Bowenkamp said," in the least important place in the sentence and paragraph, the middle.

These are only highlights of the artistry evident in the writing of this feature, major factors Loh blended into a great feature story.

SUMMARY

What's in a feature lead? A narrative *hook*, the *idea* of what the story's about and a *transition* to move the audience into the main body of the story. Put the first letter of these words together and they spell HIT, an acronym to remind you of what should go into every lead.

What's in the feature itself? Nuggets of information that will inspire readers to read on for fulfillment. To satisfy them, avoid overly long expository paragraphs ("valleys of death") and make sure that the high peaks of interest are composed of examples, illustrations and anecdotes. All of this should parallel a reader interest plane of constantly mounting interest.

Include details and vivid words, especially verbs. Direct quotations should open a substantial number of paragraphs to break up the long gray columns of type. Each sentence and each paragraph should have a transition that keeps the feature flowing along, like Ol' Man River. The concluding paragraph ties the whole feature up for the audience in a neat bow.

To ensure that you've infused your feature writing with polish and power, review these pointers before you begin writing and before you revise.

EXERCISES

1. Critique the effectiveness of each feature lead in the space provided.

    a.   Absolutely and forevermore, the people in the refrigerator had found the end of animation.
    Indeed, the bearded man rolled out in cold drawer No. 68 had collapsed into death while he was dancing at a discotheque.

    b.   The ABC Monday night football telecast team has been catching no end of flak lately. Critics claim Howard Cosell, Frank Gifford and Don Meredith talk too much, get plays and players confused, don't know the rules and in general distract from the action on the field.
    Ah, that's a bit harsh. Who in the world would have trouble following this typical telecast: . . .
    [The three commentators comment on an imaginary game. This is a satirical feature.]

c. "I don't know the name of the detergent," a shopper said to the clerk, "but I can hum the tune for you."

That highly resilient gag has been making its way up and down Madison Avenue for years, generating a few light moments in the intensely competitive business of providing music that sells soap—or anything else.

d. Emily Freeman, [the first woman] USFL football broadcaster, didn't accept the job because she wanted to break down the barriers of a male domain.

She says Bo Null, owner of the Tucson Gunslingers, offered her the job because he wants to get women interested in football so they will become paying customers.

2. Select five mediocre leads from five feature stories in the local newspaper. Paste them on the left. State what is wrong with the leads. Then write a better lead for each.

3. Write a feature lead that would be appropriate for each story.

   a. LAWRENCE, Mass. (UPI) — Steven A. Grabowski, a balding pro wrestler who fights under the name Steve Thunder, filed a $200,000 suit against the firm that attached his hairpiece.

   Grabowski, 28, of Lawrence, paid $750 for a hair replacement that he says he was assured would be fixed tightly to his real hair. Four days later an opponent yanked off Grabowski's wig in the ring. "Everybody was laughing at me," Grabowski said. "I was very embarrassed and quite humiliated, to say the least." He said he can't get bookings because "I was a laughing stock."

   b. CHICAGO (AP) — Most Americans think doctors are less compassionate these days, their dedication to patients being displaced by their desire for dollars, according to a study sponsored by the nation's largest physicians' group.

   V. Lance Tarrance and Associates, an independent Houston research company, did the telephone survey of 1,000 adults last November on behalf of the Chicago-based American Medical Association to determine public perceptions of physicians.

   Fifty-four percent of respondents agreed that "doctors don't care as much about people as they used to," the company said.

   The largest group of respondents — 44 percent — believes that people become doctors today for "the money and prestige." Only 28 percent believe the motivation is to "help people."

   Still, the survey found that the public doesn't begrudge doctors their high incomes, which now average more than $100,000 per year.

   Sixty-two percent of the respondents thought doctors' incomes "are fair because of the importance of what they do and the many years of training they have to undergo." But patients wish doctors would spend more than a few minutes with them during an office visit.

   Sixty-one percent of respondents said doctors don't devote enough time to their patients.

4. These paragraphs can be rearranged to produce a feature story* replete with narrative hook, ideas, transition, peaks and valleys, and conclusion. Cut out the paragraphs and then rearrange them by pasting them in the proper order. Underline paragraph transitions. Come up with a title for the story.

—Catherine II, empress of Russia, complained that she couldn't go to sleep unless her hair was being brushed. People who knew her said, "Yeh, sure, but who's brushing it?" They didn't say it too loud.

—Gandhi found he could pass out passively if he hauled his bed outdoors, contemplated the constellations and soaked himself in fresh air.

—Nero used to go to bed buried in baubles. The only way to sleep, he said, clutching his book matches, was in his special bed encrusted with rubies, amethysts and garnets, which were said to promote pleasant dreams.

Can't get to sleep at night because you're worried about what the world's coming to?

—Alexander Dumas got sleepy by walking downtown and eating an apple under the Arc de Triomphe. This was good for apples and it didn't hurt the tourist trade any, either.

—Charles Dickens never went anywhere without his compass. He kept it, he said, because he knew the only way to sleep was with his head to the north and his feet to the south.

Over the centuries, all sorts of people have had peculiar ideas about how to woo 40 winks.

—Van Gogh didn't care about being any too popular — and it's a good thing. His cure for insomnia was stuffing his pillow and mattress "with a very strong dose of camphor.

Benjamin Franklin's cure for insomnia, he said, was "I get up and sit naked in the middle of the room for an hour or two, according to the time of year, reading and writing."

Nervous and upset?

—The Countess de Soissons couldn't drop off unless she was propped up. She not only had pillows for her head and her back, but she also kept seamstresses, mumbling revolutionary nothings, hard at work doing petit point on teeny pillows to prop up her thumbs.

If you're interested in falling asleep, you might try and stay awake long enough to leaf through a new book, *101 Recipes for Sound Sleep*, by Mariane Kohler and Jean Chapelle. It has several good suggestions and a fair share of foolishness.

—Madame de Sevigne, who always had trouble conking out at the court of Louis XIV, finally discovered that if she played cards endlessly, admiring her infinite finesse, sooner or later she'd faint.

You can take satisfaction in the fact that you're not the first person to toss and turn over the turmoil of the time.

But if you still want to get sleepy celebrity style, here's a last but by no means least way:

—Brillat-Savarin, the great gourmet, used to eat a lot of good food, drink a lot of good liquor, talk a lot about love, think about madrigals and jump into bed concentrating on what a pleasant fellow he was.

Maybe you can get some sleep-producing satisfaction from the past. The world has always been upset, people have always lost sleep over it — and here is what some of the famous ones did about it.

In Islam today it is generally believed that kings sleep on their right side, wise men on their left, saints on their backs and the devil on his stomach. Which way [Khomeini] nestles down has never been made public, but the indication would be he tosses a lot.

* Reprinted with permission of *The Denver Post*.

PASTE EXERCISE 4 HERE.

5. Select a feature story from a newspaper and paste it on the left. To the right, criticize it, paragraph by paragraph, listing the good and bad points of the feature.

6. Rewrite the following stories in feature form.

a. A Social Insect

By HARRY E. WILLIAMS
University of Tennessee

Honeybees are social insects, with 50,000 to 100,000 living in a typical colony.

The worker bees may make 80,000 trips from the hive to flowering plants to produce one pound of honey. They fly a distance equal to three times around the world to produce one pound.

The bees use one ounce of honey to fly a distance equal to one trip around the world. This means about seven million miles of flight per gallon of honey.

The honey bees begin flying from the hive early in the morning before dawn. The last bees return to the hive just after dark. A few bees may remain out all night. On each of these trips the bees may visit several hundred flowers. However, on each trip the bee confines her visits to one plant species, collecting one kind of nectar and distributing one kind of pollen.

The honey bee's visit to the blossoms results in complete fertilization of the blossom. The fruit set is increased, the quality improved and the yield increased when the plant is adequately pollinated.

A flower garden appearance is a sign of inadequate pollination. Flowers adequately pollinated will wilt a short time after pollination.

b. Man Grips Dog, Bites Man

NORWALK, Calif. (UPI) — A young man wanted for assaulting his mother-in-law was arrested early yesterday on charges he bit two sherriff's deputies as they tried to pry a police dog from his grip.

Charles Lamping, 22, was booked on two counts of assaulting a peace officer and a count of assault on his mother-in-law.

Deputy Robert Stoneman said officers responding to the assault report tracked Lamping down to a vacant home. Lamping, who was hiding, grabbed the dog, Captain, after the canine was sent in to find him. Captain's handler, Deputy John Falkner, and a second deputy, Thomas Rosas, were bitten by Lamping during a scuffle, Stoneman said. The dog was freed just as he blacked out, Stoneman said, and was unhurt.

Falkner and Rosas were both treated at Whittier Presbyterian Hospital for bites on their right index fingers and were released. Lamping was hospitalized in the jail ward of County-USC Medical Center for treatment of multiple lacerations to his scalp. Stoneman said the circumstances of Lamping's fight with his mother-in-law were under investigation.

7. List five ideas for feature stories below, in order of preference. Swap with a classmate. Do you agree on which feature ideas are best? The instructor may ask that the best feature ideas be placed on the board for critique purposes.

8. Take your best feature idea from Exercise 7 and:

   a. List sources of information that you will check before writing the feature.

   b. Prepare the questions you will ask each source.

9. After you have completed at least part of the research for the feature idea listed in Exercise 8, outline the feature in the space below. Write the lead for the article.

10. You have been given the assignment of interviewing the mother of the four daughters who have been killed. In the space provided below, write in detail the approach and the words you will use in asking Bea Shreeves to talk to you about their daughters' deaths so that you may write a story for your newspaper.

11. Write a brief one-paragraph description of each of the following:

   a. Your room.

   b. Your mother, father or guardian.

   c. A sibling or best friend.

CHAPTER 13

MAGAZINE ARTICLES

Magazine writing offers an opportunity to explore in-depth subjects that are often given only fleeting coverage by media driven by daily or hourly deadlines. Magazines publish many of the thought-provoking, informative articles that help shape people's opinions.

Magazines have led all other media in rapid specialization by subject. Magazine publishing has exploded since the mid-1960s, with new titles being created to serve the needs of people who prefer to subscribe to several magazines with different specialties than to one or two very general magazines. Such reader preferences helped put *Life* and *Look* magazines out of business and radically changed the nature of *The Saturday Evening Post* and the eventually reincarnated *Life*.

This trend toward specialization can be seen especially clearly in the women's market, where giants such as *McCall's* and *Ladies' Home Journal* have seen their advertising and circulation nibbled by newcomers such as *Working Woman, Ms.* and *Self* and by not-so-new magazines, such as *Cosmopolitan* and *Vogue*, whose editorial content has shifted to reflect the expanding interests and lifestyles of their audiences.

Specialization can be seen in other markets as well: in business, where *Inc.*, a magazine targeted to growing businesses, joined the ranks of heavyweights such as *Fortune, Forbes* and *Business Week*; in health, where titles such as *American Health, FIT, The Runner* and *Weight Watchers Magazine* blazed a new trail for magazine readers; and in regional markets, where city magazines have established a strong niche.

A compendium of magazine research in the May 1985 *Social Science Monitor*, a newsletter for communications executives, indicates that local magazines are among the fastest-growing media in the United States. Their content varies from lifestyle and entertainment subjects to hard-hitting, investigative features on local problems. And specialization occurs even on the local levels: In Dallas, you can buy the city magazine, *D*, and a shelter magazine, *Dallas/Fort Worth Home & Garden*. In other locales, a city magazine may share the market with a city *business* magazine.

The trend indicates that magazines continue to be a popular medium for American consumers. Writers who can carve out a specialty for themselves that fits the profiles of the magazines for which they want to write can enjoy considerable success in selling features to them.

MAGAZINE ARTICLE LEADS

Like the leads written for newspaper feature stories, magazine article leads include a narrative hook, an idea of what the article is about and a transition into the body of the article. But unlike newspaper features, which are usually connected with a news event or an issue or individual personality of community interest, magazine articles often introduce brand-new ideas to their audiences. So the magazine lead has to offer a more compelling hook and the promise of value to readers who are unfamiliar with the subject.

A wide range of approaches is available in writing magazine article leads. These sample leads emphasize the fact that a little more strategy is called for in writing for magazines.

THE DRAMATIC LEAD

Suicide in the Children's Ranks*

His classmates called him "the leper," because measles had left his 12-year-old body scarred.

His mother said children tended to blame him when things went wrong.

One day, distraught, the boy in Tromsoe, Norway, took a rope and hanged himself.

In Manchester, Mo., a "nice boy" who had won a good citizenship award was taunted about his family by his junior high classmates before he pulled out a pistol and killed one student, wounded another, and took his own life, officials said.

The boy left a suicide note in his gym bag, police said.

These are just two of a growing number of cases of suicides by children, a phenomenon in our society.

The dramatic lead sets the stage for readers and draws them into the article immediately. The two examples of child suicides used in this lead might be called "minidramas." Where are the hook, idea and transition in this lead? The first five paragraphs form the hook. The sixth paragraph contains the idea and the transition.

The dramatic lead is an excellent way to lead readers into an article. The following example by John Gerstner is from an internal publication of John Deere & Co. It describes how employees brave unpredictable weather to service equipment in remote Alaskan villages.

Beating the Bush

It was nearly closing time when Hans Jensen reached his office at the large Craig Taylor dealership on the north side of Anchorage. Jensen, manager of a new power system division, was greeted by Bob Combs, service manager, who handed him a telex. It began: "Hot, hot, hot," and went on to say that the single Deere engine providing all the electricity for the village of Kotlik (across the bay from Nome) was down. Hans would have to fly up to fix the engine, cancelling the travel plans he and I had made. "Welcome to Alaska," he said with a grin, "where your plans change from minute to minute."

---

* Reprinted with permission of the Associated Press.

The Novelty or Curiosity Lead

Reagan's Problems with Women*

By ZICK RUBIN

My interest in President Reagan's sex appeal began a few months ago, when I noticed that the President was getting much lower approval ratings in the national polls from women than from men. In a CBS poll taken in late June, for example, 49 percent of the men and only 36 percent of the women approved of the way the President was handling his job. Other polls showed the same pattern. Such a wide difference between the ratings of the two sexes was unprecedented in American politics.

At first glance, the sex difference was puzzling. After all, Ronald Reagan is a good-looking, charming, fatherly man whom one would expect women to like. As his wife Nancy writes in her autobiography, "How can you resist someone who sends flowers to your mother on your birthday thanking her for making him the happiest man in the world?" Yet American women seemed to have resisted.

The writer of this lead piques the curiosity of *Psychology Today* readers in this tongue-in-cheek look at the president's impact on women. The last sentence in the second paragraph of the lead is a transition into the main body of the article.

The Question Lead

Acid Rain

Acid rain — how much is falling and where? Where does it come from? Is the problem getting worse? Are its effects cumulative?

These are some of the questions two WVU researchers are attempting to answer in separate research projects on this problem that is causing worldwide concern.

Although question leads appear easy enough to write, the question should provoke the readers into reading the article. Does this lead, by William A. Aston in *The West Virginia University Alumni Magazine*, interest you? If so, it's a good lead.

The No-Nonsense Lead

Hard Times and Presidential Luck†

Three survey findings signal the emergence of a political issue so powerful that it is likely to dominate our politics in the years ahead. The first is that most Americans (83 percent) realize that in the 1980s we will be forced to make downward changes in the way we live. The second is that a majority of Americans (60 percent) expect the recession to continue at

---

* Reprinted from *Psychology Today Magazine*. Copyright © 1982 American Psychological Association.

† Reprinted from *Psychology Today Magazine*. Copyright © 1984 American Psychological Association.

least through 1983. But the most surprising finding is that only a minority of the public (33 percent) blames President Reagan for our economic troubles.

Daniel Yankelovich began this article without any fanfare—the narrative hook rests on the paragraph's appeal to the reader of *Psychology Today*. The lead has straight summary news lead characteristics. The article then takes up the three findings of the survey in much the way a news story about the survey would.

THE SETTING LEAD

Terror in the Icy Potomac*

Thick, wet snow was falling on the nation's capital, and the freezing temperatures of one of the coldest afternoons of the century forced even well-wrapped pedestrians off the wind-swept streets. Commuters dashed through underground garages to their cars for an early escape across the 14th Street Bridge and the ice-clogged Potomac River to warm suburban houses in Virginia.

Priscilla Tirado, with her husband and two-month-old son, was riding to the airport in her grandmother's comfortably heated car. She was dressed in the in-between, layered style of Northerners flying south in wintertime: a long-sleeved red cotton top, black corduroy designer jeans and a patchwork leather jacket. As the Ford LTD cautiously maneuvered through the D.C. traffic on its way to National Airport, windshield wipers brushing away the swirling snow, she thought about what lay ahead in Florida: a new home; a new job for Jose, her husband . . .

They pulled up outside the Air Florida terminal about 1 p.m., in plenty of time for the 2:15 flight to Tampa.

The setting lead is difficult to write simply because you have to know something about the craft of fiction to carry it off. This article for *Family Circle* by Tracie Rozhon resulted from extensive interviews with one of the survivors of a plane crash, and it employs fiction techniques throughout its chronological story line.

The lead sets the stage for the reader. In this respect it is similar to the dramatic lead. Rozhon is able to unfold her drama slowly, building suspense all the while.

THE COMBINATION LEAD

Any number of combinations of openings can also be used in writing the magazine article lead. It depends on your material, the market you write for and your imagination. Scott Witte decided to start off this article in *Popular Science* with a combination lead:

Getting into Ski Mountaineering: The Ultimate Winter Adventure

"You're going camping in the mountains, in the middle of winter? Wouldn't it be simpler just to hire someone to club you over the head?"

My friend's reaction was a typical one when I told him I would be

* Copyright Tracie Rozhon. Originally printed in *Family Circle Magazine*.

spending my winter vacation ski mountaineering somewhere in the Rocky Mountains. It's a sport best described as the marriage between backpacking and cross-country skiing. Many enthusiasts consider it the ultimate expression of both.

TITLES

Magazine article titles are fun to create. A good title can provide you with the impetus you need to sit down and write the article. Titles open the wellsprings of creativity. Good titles promote good writing.

The primary function of the title is to attract the attention of the reader, to describe or hint at what the subject matter of the article is about, and to set the tone for the article. Look at the titles you have read so far in this text. Do they do that?

How were they created? The lead should provide you with an idea for the article. If there is trouble in Hyslip, Conn., a natural title is "Trouble in Suburbia." If an essay is on going back to an old haunt, say, a lake, what is more natural than "Once More to the Lake"? Sometimes a celebrity's name is enough to provoke interest and indicate what the article is about: "Woman in the News: Maureen Reagan." Most of the time, however, you must use creativity to come up with the best titles: "The House of the Dead," "The Dream of the Red Chamber," "Streams That Nobody Fords." But it may not be easy. Ernest Hemingway sometimes wrote a hundred titles for a novel or short story before selecting one. But then, easy titles are rarely the best titles.

THE READER-INTEREST PLANE

As you have seen, magazine article titles and leads can be fun to write. They require imagination and artistry. Having written them, however, you have little time to bask in glory—the rest of the article looms high and threatening on the horizon. Just how should you go about writing the body of the article?

One method is to follow the peaks-and-valleys approach stressed in the chapter on newspaper features, but organized along the "reader-interest plane" (Figure 13.1). The reader-interest plane functions this way: Reader (or editor) interest

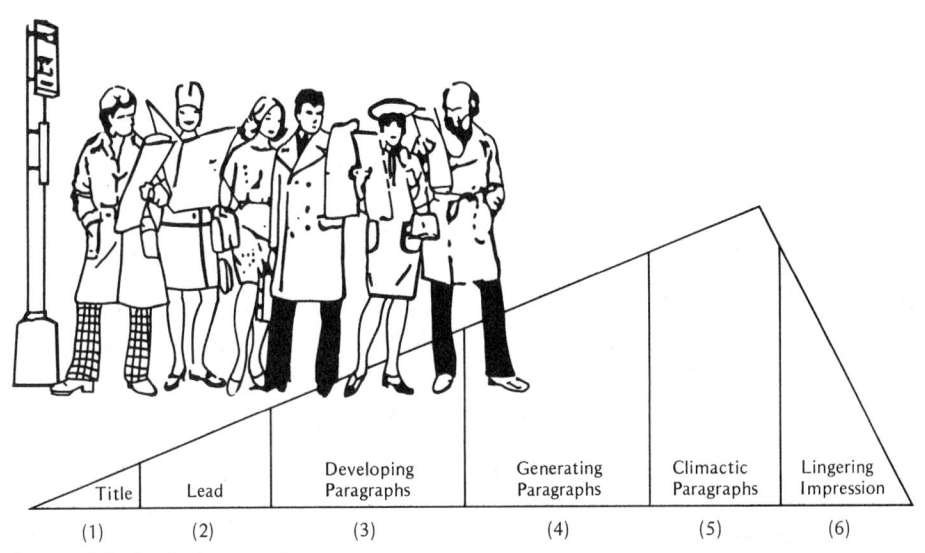

Figure 13.1. Reader-interest plane.

starts with the *title* (1). If you compose a title good enough to lure readers into the first paragraph and a *narrative hook* (2) that leads them into the *developing paragraphs* (3), you've almost surely earned an audience for the rest of your article. The developing paragraphs give readers a fuller glimpse of the main idea mentioned in the narrative hook. The *generating paragraphs* (4) embrace the major points you want to make in the article and lead up to the *climactic paragraphs* (5). Climactic paragraphs transport the readers to the article's high point of interest. Sometimes that high point of interest might be carried over and embodied in the concluding paragraph or what can be called the *lingering-impression paragraph* (6). The last paragraph should leave them with the impression you want to make.

Examine how the reader-interest plane works with several article excerpts from national magazines.

THE BUSINESS FEATURE

The one-two punch of this sentence lead from an article by Craig Stoltz in *Regardie's,* a magazine about business in the nation's capital, launches a four-paragraph narrative hook that can't fail to take readers straight to the article's idea:

Zapped!*

Richard Andreski pushes back his chair, reaches into a drawer behind his desk, and pulls out a barbecued chicken. **[1]**

"This chicken has been sitting in my credenza for over two years," he says, handling the vacuum-sealed bird as if it were a small, gravy-colored football. "You could eat this chicken today and it would taste as if you'd just taken it out of the oven. Or you could keep it in the drawer for five years and it would still be fresh. Go ahead, feel it." **[2]**

The chicken does, in fact, feel fresh. It has suffered minor bruises all over its breasts and thighs, where, at Andreski's request, dozens of thumbs have poked and prodded it over the months. But that's minor damage if you consider the black-and-green meatblob that it would be today if, on April 20, 1983, it had not been slathered in barbecue sauce, baked, and subjected to a 4,500-kilorad dose of gamma rays. **[3]**

"Here's the problem," says Andreski, taking the chicken back and standing it upright, as if to hold it for a placekicker. "If you see this chicken in the grocery store on a shelf next to the cornflakes, there's no way you're going to buy it. People simply have it in their heads that chicken needs to be refrigerated." **[4]**

Andreski is the president and founder of Miramar Industries, Incorporated, and he is betting everything he owns on the hope that people will soon be able and willing to buy all kinds of food preserved by some form of radiation—"irradiated" or "ionized" food is the language preferred by folks in the industry, "zapped" or "nuked" food by critics and media types. **[5]**

Irradiation can replace some toxic chemical preservatives and extend a product's shelf life, enthusiasts argue, thereby cutting down on spoilage and waste. After more than 40 years of experimentation and limited approvals, the federal government is on the verge of relaxing its regulations regarding food irradiation, and bills to explore and promote the technology currently

---

* "Zapped," by Craig Stoltz, from *Regardie's,* May 1985. Reprinted by permission.

sit in Senate and House subcommittees. [6]

Yet Andreski isn't the only local entrepreneur who's poised to enter the food irradiation business in a big way. As a matter of fact, he isn't the only one in his *suite*. [7]

Right down the hall from Miramar Industries is Gamma Technology, Incorporated, which Andreski launched three years ago but which is now run by his ex-friend and ex-partner, Victor L. Clavelli. Thanks to a series of personal disputes and legal actions that neither man discusses very happily, Andreski and Clavelli currently operate competing companies from offices in the same Tysons Corner penthouse suite. Andreski's Miramar and Clavelli's Gamma Tech share elevators, coffeepots, rest rooms, a Telex number, and even telephone service. Dial 556-0607 and a secretary answers, "Miramar Industries"; dial 556-9844 and the same woman answers, "Gamma Tech." Ask her if the companies are related and she says, "No, they're totally separate companies. *Totally* separate." [8]

The community of professionals involved with food irradiation is small. Currently the nation supports fewer than a dozen "service irradiators"—companies that will, for a price, sterilize pharmaceutical supplies, strengthen building materials, or preserve spices with blasts of ionized energy. [9]

Craig Stoltz's hook fairly sparkles with bright language, much of it supplied by his fast-talking interview subject. His choice of active verbs—"slathered," "poked and prodded," "reaches," "pulls"—brings a high sense of energy to the article. People can ride Stoltz's language right down to his idea, in the fifth paragraph, that this very upbeat, amusing story is really about a high-tech industry that preserves food.

Stoltz creates a smooth transition from an explanation of the industry to its competitive nature with the two-sentence seventh paragraph. The seventh paragraph rises out of the two preceding valley paragraphs necessary to explain the basic focus of the article. Stoltz follows paragraph 7 with a peak paragraph that discloses the gossip about the companies being described and the amusing anomalies that resulted from a company split. The last paragraph excerpted here is a valley, offering more information about the irradiation business. The balance of the story was a mixture of quotes, low-key explanations and upbeat paragraphs that continued the imaginative phrasing of Stoltz's opening hook.

Travel and Leisure Features

The writer of the following piece, Randy Rieland of *The Washingtonian* magazine, chose a setting lead full of immediacy for his article. He put the reader right in the environment. Such leads are effective because they get the reader involved in solving a riddle. The lead paragraph gives the clues; the second, single-sentence paragraph, the answer:

Bright Lights in Annapolis*

Overhead the neon glows, an Art Deco rainbow. The music is so loud and lively that it stirs your drink. And on the dance floor, people move with an abandon usually reserved for fraternity parties and witches' covens. [1]

Welcome to Annapolis. [2]

That's right, Annapolis, the place once described as "the gen-

---

* "Bright Lights in Annapolis," by Randy Rieland, *The Washingtonian*. Reprinted by permission.

teelest town in North America," a city where dress and demeanor are usually thought to be as low-key as Mr. Rogers on Valium. [3]

That Annapolis still exists, but the scene in Margarita Maggie's, a glitzy new disco near the Annapolis Mall, reflects a new side of the city's nightlife, one that is not only decidedly up-scale, but also flashier than anything the town has seen. [4]

The fact that John Carroll Associates, a Beltsville-based firm, spent more than $3 million on Maggie's and the adjoining restaurant, Plata Grande—including $150,000 for the disco's lighting and sound system—also suggests that the Annapolis market is becoming more and more attractive as an entertainment center. You may still see it as a quaint little sailing community, but the big money thinks there is more there than boats and history. [5]

Another case in point is Jason's, a stylish bar and restaurant that opened last month across the harbor in Eastport. Area developer Jim Foote spent $1.2 million to turn an old watering hole named Spiro's into a slick night spot where any self-respecting upwardly mobile person can find peace, or at least a seat at the long mahogany bar. Another new tavern, Griffin's, is expected to open this summer at the site of the old Dockside restaurant in the City Dock area. [6]

Does all of this mean that the city on the Severn is becoming too polished? Will people actually go out dancing when they could be sailing? Will Topsiders be banned? [7]

Not to worry. Annapolis will remain a town where a person is marked more by how he tacks into the wind than by the number of glasses of Dom Perignon he can consume. The important thing to remember is that it's no longer a quiet little burg on the bay, particularly on weekend evenings when Main Street and the City Dock can seem more crowded than a Metro escalator at rush hour. Traffic can be a headache; parking, an Excedrin headache. There are even lines outside the bars. [8]

But if you're used to all that, or if you can visit during the week, consider a night on the town in Annapolis. It has more variety in its nightlife than it's ever had, from a fancy disco to a first-rate jazz club—the King of France Tavern—to plenty of places where you can just sit on the dock of the bay. [9]

It also still has Chick and Ruth's Delly on Main Street, where you can order a corned-beef sandwich at three in the morning. [10]

Try that in Washington. [11]

Rieland establishes a strong contrast between the latest entertainment and the type traditionally associated with Annapolis, Maryland's picturesque state capital. Rieland's article is really about a trend—slick nightlife is growing in Annapolis. That idea comes in the fourth paragraph, after which he ticks off, one by one, the best places to go. Rieland uses an effective technique in the seventh paragraph, asking questions that at once stop readers and command their attention, yet make them want to move on to find out the answers. Rieland's peaks-and-valleys organization is akin to comparison and contrast. He moves back and forth between descriptions of traditional and trendy Annapolis to keep his article flowing.

THE PERSONALITY PROFILE

Articles about celebrities don't need attention-getting leads. A photo of the person, or just his or her name in the headline, will usually do it. The challenge for the writer doing an article about someone who's been written about many times is to find an *original* lead, something that tells us or shows readers something new.

For her profile of Maureen Reagan in *Working Woman* magazine, Susan Page led with a focus on Reagan's body language and personal traits, such as "her patented laughter . . . her most distinctive feature." Page echoes her lead sentence in the second paragraph to effect a transition into the main theme of the article, Reagan's professional and political interests:

Woman in the News: Maureen Reagan*

Maureen Reagan doesn't sit still for long. During an interview in her cramped office at Republican headquarters in Washington, she fiddles with a pen, swivels in her chair, leans back to ponder a question and lets loose a peal of her patented laughter. It is her most distinctive feature, starting with a whoop, cascading into unabashed giggles. [1]

She doesn't sit still for long, either, on the causes that make her the most public, most political, most influential, most controversial Presidential daughter ever. [2]

This month, she is to leave for Nairobi, Kenya, where she will head the United States delegation to the United Nations Conference on Women. When the UN Ambassador Jeane Kirkpatrick declined to lead the delegation, "Maureen was the obvious person," says Nancy Reynolds, a US delegate to the conference and a powerful Washington lobbyist. [3]

The Nairobi conference is just one of the activities that have preoccupied Reagan since her father's reelection. As a consultant to the Republican National Committee (RNC), she is encouraging the national GOP to sponsor a pilot project this fall to help elect more women to a state's legislature—the particular state has not yet been chosen—and provide a model for other states. She recently helped form the GOP Women's Political Action League, a political action committee (PAC), with Reynolds and former Housing and Urban Affairs Secretary Carla Hills, to aid in electing more Republican women at state and federal levels. She has served as a sort of role model for Republican women who are conservative on economic and foreign policy issues but are concerned about the rightward tilt of the GOP on social issues. [4]

This is relative calm after last year's seven-days-a-week travel schedule that took her to all 50 states, campaigning for dozens of Republican women candidates for congressional and state offices and for the reelection of her father, Ronald Reagan. [5]

How much did these efforts help? A lot, at least one candidate contends. "There is no question in my mind that she deserves much of the credit for our victory," President Reagan said in a written interview with *Working Woman*. Others concur. Reagan's pollster, Richard Wirthlin, credits her with "the effective way the campaign dealt with the gender gap," ultimately winning the votes of a majority of women. Ann Lewis, then the political director of the Democratic National Committee, calls her "a very, very good salesperson for a very, very bad product." [6]

The fourth paragraph reads like a résumé, but it works because it supports the quote in paragraph 3 and sets up the contrast between Reagan's present interests and her past activities, discussed in paragraphs 5 and 6. By this time, readers have a thorough knowledge of Maureen Reagan's agenda and are interested in

---

* Excerpted from "Woman in the News: Maureen Reagan," by Susan Page. *Working Woman*, July 1985. Reprinted by permission.

getting to know more about her. The intimacy of Page's lead paragraph is picked up again in the rest of the story (which does not appear here).

The next article, a *Washington Star* feature on Billy Carter, actually could have been published as is in *Time* or *Playboy*. Why? Because it would work beautifully in a magazine as well as in a newspaper. In this magazine-style newspaper article, excellent characterization, setting description and, above all, details are blended together to paint a colorful portrait of a colorful man.

By MICHAEL SATCHELL
The Washington Star*

PLAINS—Last Sunday, says Billy Carter, was just too much. [1]

"Used to be at 10 o'clock on a Sunday morning, you could walk out onto Main Street and [urinate] and nobody would see you," he grumbled. [2]

"LAST Sunday there must have been 2,000 damned tourists here. I couldn't stand it. I went off to the bootlegger, bought me a fifth, drove around the rest of the day and got good and drunk," [3]

If Jimmy Carter represents the clean-cut, God-featuring, modest-mannered New South, Brother Billy epitomizes the old. He's an absolute original, a good ol' boy as Southern as sawmill gravy and fried white meat, with a passion — but not necessarily the capacity — for strong drink and good conversation. Lots of it. [4]

"Billy," sighs Miss Lillian, "drinks too much. He's a wonderful boy and he's really my favorite son, but he drinks too much. Jimmy never tells him off for it and neither does his mother. But he does." [5]

"YES, SIR: I'm a real Southern boy," Billy chortles. "I got a red neck, white socks and Blue Ribbon Beer." And to the guffaws of his gas station cronies, Billy shows off his sun-drenched neck, his white socks, and snaps the tab off his can of the beer. It is 6:30 p.m., 90 minutes since work ceased and relaxation began for Billy and the boys. [6]

Ordinarily, Billy Carter would be just another slice of local color in a rather drab little town. But as the brother of the world's most powerful leader-elect, questions arise. [7]

What influence does he have over the next president? Will he try to exercise it? What are his concerns about national or international problems? Will he try to profit from his brother's exalted position? And by examining Billy, can one detect any clues as to what makes Jimmy tick? [8]

THERE IS only one way to examine Billy Carter close at hand and that is to drink with him after work, a risky venture at best. [9]

He runs the family peanut farm and warehouse and regards his stewardship of the Carter family business interests as his contribution to his brother, for it has freed Jimmy to concentrate fulltime on politics. [10]

Billy works from 5 a.m. or so until 5 p.m., works hard, works seriously, and will entertain no non-essential visitors. From dawn to dusk six days a week, Billy is tough, shrewd, no nonsense, very successful businessman. [11]

BUT COME 5 p.m., Billy locks up the peanut warehouse, hurries across the street to his gas station and relaxes. With a vengeance. [12]

In the back part of the station, half a dozen, sometimes more, of Billy's pals gather each evening after work to drink beer and jaw about nothing in particular. They are all working men, wearing coveralls and red caps that say "Funk's Hybrid" or "Standard Oil." One wears an ABC television cap he conned from a cameraman. [13]

No special deference is shown to

* Reprinted from *The Washington Star*, 11/14/76, p. A3. © 1976 *The Washington Star*. Reprinted by permission of the publisher.

Billy and he doesn't expect it. He plays the role, not of the President-elect's brother, but more the saloon keeper. Because there is no tavern for whites in Plains (there is a black club), Billy's gas station is essentially the town bar. Until 7 p.m. at least, when the gas station closes and everyone goes home to eat supper. [14]

THE STATION is impossibly cluttered with tools, tires, cans of Campbell Soup and 10W40 oil all mixed up. On the wall is a saucy pinup calendar from the Keena Auto Parts Co. Atop an 8-track tape deck, dusty and unused, are tapes by Lynn Anderson and Tammy Wynette. [15]

At 5:02 p.m. precisely Billy bounces in, dives into a huge cooler, pulls out a handful of cans of beer, pops a couple, lights up a Pall Mall, sucks hard on it, gives a tubercular wheeze, and downs the can in a single guzzle. [16]

"Boy, I needed that," he said, "Here, have another." [17]

Billy, 39, is the youngest of Lilliam Carter's four children. He was raised, like his brother, on the family farm at Archery, Ga., and was 14 when the family moved into Plains. [18]

AFTER HIGH school he joined the Marine Corps and married his childhood sweetheart, Sybil Spires, 16, the day after graduating from boot camp. They have six children, ranging in age from 20 to one month, and Billy is said to be the consummate family man, caring deeply for little else but his wife and his children. [19]

Physically, Billy resembles his brother closely, although he is shorter, wears glasses and is a lot thicker around the middle than Jimmy. Unlike the president-elect, Billy disdains the church. "Bunch of damned hypocrites down there at that Baptist church," is Billy's view. "The only time I ever go is when one of the kids is baptized." [20]

MISS LILLIAN's recollection of Billy's childhood is naturally glossed with a mother's concern for projecting only the best of images. But Billy, being Billy, tells it like it was. [21]

"Jimmy, Ruth, and Gloria all graduated first or second in their high school class. I was 25th out of 26. It didn't bother me none though. [22]

"I joined the Marines because I wanted to be a bad---. First time on leave I tried to whip five or six sailors and found out, I wasn't as tough as I thought." [23]

Did he ever get into trouble? [24]

"WELL, I once did 30 days in jail in South Carolina for speeding. And I went to jail in Daytona Beach for drinking in public. Nothing serious though. You ready for another?" [25]

Billy made several campaign appearances on behalf of his brother, clad often in his yellow leisure suit, yellow shoes, and pink shirt, but he says he "hated it." [26]

"I don't like to go anywhere where I can't get back to Plains the same night," he said. "I was the token redneck on the campaign. But I think my main contribution to Jimmy was staying home." Er, yes. [27]

"TO KEEP the business running smoothly so Jimmy could be free." Oh, of course. [28]

Billy said he has been to Washington only once. [29]

"I was at National Airport for 10 minutes on my way to somewhere during the campaign," he recalled. "The other time was when I drove up to Montreal with my wife and three kids. I got lost in DeeCee and spent four hours driving around. I finally hired a taxidriver to guide me out to that ring road (the Capital Beltway). [30]

"Well, I ended up going the wrong way on it. Finally found us a motel and when I hit the bar I had to have a triple to calm me down. Here, want some of this?" [31]

AFTER A tug on a Seagram's Crown Royal bottle, Billy continued: "My only regret about Jimmy being elected is that I wished he had lived in Atlanta. Plains has gone straight to hell. I went to a meeting the other night of landowners and property owners. I was the only one voting against commercialization. I'm the only person in this whole town who isn't selling peanuts to tourists. I really regret what's happening to Plains." [32]

Just then another friend strode into the gas station. From the crook of his right arm hung a 270-Ruger with a scope site. He had returned from an unsuccessful day of deer hunting. [33]

"You loaded?" asked Billy. [34]

The friend pointed the rifle into the ground and clicked the trigger. [35]

"Nope." [36]

"Well, I am," Billy giggled, opening another can. [37]

Despite the ready laughter, the constant stream of four-letter words, the role-playing and the booze, Billy Carter is no buffoon. [38]

FOR THE last eight years, with his brother campaigning or serving in public office virtually full time, Billy has built the family's peanut business into a very profitable venture. He reads four or five books a week from the Americus Public Library and subscribes to eight newspapers and news magazines. [39]

IN a quiet moment, he will discuss serious matters — the economy, world affairs — with a sound depth of knowledge, but he's happiest when talking about crops and farm problems. [40]

"I have absolutely no ambition beyond Plains," he said in answer to a question about his future role. "I'm just an unambitious person. Jimmy and I are very good friends and we talk for hours, just shooting the bull, but I don't try to influence him and I don't think I could. The only thing I'd like to see him do when he gets to the White House is appoint a working farmer as secretary of agriculture, that's all." [41]

ACCORDING to Miss Lillian, Billy and his brother are as close as two peanuts in the shell. "Billy is always the first person Jimmy wants to see when he returns to Plains," she said. They spend hours together walking in the woods and fields. They need each other." [42]

If brother Billy has any role to play in the Carter administration it will be to keep on doing exactly what he has in the past. Jimmy Carter is a good example of the old axiom that you can take the boy out of the country but not vice versa. As long as Billy is around, the next president of the United States will be able to sit in the White House and still keep a few peanut husks under his boots and a little bit of red Georgia earth beneath his fingernails. [43]

The narrative hook of this personality profile runs some seven paragraphs—not unusual for a magazine article lead. The eighth paragraph leads into the idea of the article: What influence does Billy "have over the next president? Will he try to exercise it?" And can you determine what makes Jimmy tick by examining Billy? The transition, leading readers into the body of the feature article, is the ninth paragraph: "There is only one way to examine Billy Carter close at hand and that is to drink with him after work, a risky venture at best." The writer evidently did what he had to do, drinking and all. The feature is developed further in the next few paragraphs, describing what *that's* like.

After luring you this far, the writer figures you're in for the duration. Now it's safe to discuss the background of the character, usually not very interesting stuff. Those two expository paragraphs (18, 19) are quickly disposed of. The succeeding paragraphs continue generating interest in Billy and bring the reader up to the climactic part of the feature.

The last three or four paragraphs—the climactic paragraphs—answer the questions raised in the idea part of the lead.

Remember, until you've mastered the art of magazine article writing—and even after that time—the path that promises the most success is the reader-interest plane. If you organize your materials on this plane and acquire a good grasp of writing principles outlined in this book, you should be on your way to a successful magazine-writing career.

CHARTING THE READER-INTEREST PLANE

To illustrate how to outline along the reader-interest plane, here is an outline of E.B. White's great "Once More to the Lake."

"Once More to the Lake"
(paragraphs)

I. Narrative Hook: Reminiscence about childhood and lake in Maine   [1]
II. Developing Paragraphs
   A. More reminiscence about lake   [2]
   B. Setting description of lake   [3]
   C. Illusion of dual existence—he being his son   [4]
      1. Same illusion—no passage of time motif   [5]
      2. Enchanted sea—no passage of time motif   [6]
   D. Dinner at the farmhouse   [7]
III. Generating Paragraphs
   A. Summertime! Life indelible!   [8]
   B. More remembrances   [9]
   C. Motorboat noise   [10]
      1. Sets years moving
      2. Dying revolution of flywheel—reversing years
IV. Climactic Paragraphs
   A. Description of week at camp—illusion persists   [11]
   B. Thunderstorm on lake presages his fate?   [12]
V. Lingering Impression and Concluding Paragraph: As son pulls wet swimsuit on, chill of death in his groin   [13]

Now read "Once More to the Lake," written by one of the greatest essayists of this century. The article describes how a man (symbolic of *all* people) tries to stop time—the aging process—to attain some sort of immortality through a son (or a daughter) and fails. E.B. White also examines the cycle of life. Note how the article is unified through repetition of details and the insistence, repeatedly made, that there had been no passage of years since he had last been to the lake.

White's reminiscences about childhood—replete with concrete details—form an excellent narrative hook. All readers will recall similar childhood experiences.

Once More to the Lake*

One summer, along about 1904, my father rented a camp on a lake in Maine and took us all there for the month of August. We all got ringworm from some kittens and had to rub Pond's Extract on our arms and legs night

---

* "Once More to the Lake—'Aug. 1941,'" from *Essays of E.B. White*. Copyright © 1969 by E.B. White. Reprinted by permission of Harper & Row Publishers, Inc.

and morning, and my father rolled over in a canoe with all his clothes on; but outside of that the vacation was a success and from then on none of us ever thought there was any place in the world like that lake in Maine. We returned summer after summer—always on August 1st for one month. I have since become a salt-water man, but sometimes in summer there are days when the restlessness of the tides and the fearful cold of the sea water and the incessant wind which blows across the afternoon and into the evening make me wish for the placidity of a lake in the woods. A few weeks ago this feeling got so strong I bought myself a couple of bass hooks and a spinner and returned to the lake where we used to go, for a week's fishing and to revisit old haunts. [1]

The developing paragraphs continue the recollection. Later in the article details such as "the tarred road" will be mentioned again and help tie the article together.

I took along my son, who had never had any fresh water up his nose and who had seen lily pads only from train windows. On the journey over to the lake I began to wonder what it would be like. I wondered how time would have marred this unique, this holy spot—the coves and streams, the hills that the sun set behind, the camps and the paths behind the camps. I was sure that the tarred road would have found it out and I wondered in what other ways it would be desolated. It is strange how much you can remember about places like that once you allow your mind to return into the grooves which lead back. You remember one thing, and that suddenly reminds you of another thing. I guess I remembered clearest of all the early mornings, when the lake was cool and motionless, remembered how the bedroom smelled of the lumber it was made of and of the wet woods whose scent entered through the screen. The partitions in the camp were thin and did not extend clear to the top of the rooms, and as I was always the first up I would dress softly so as not to wake the others, and sneak out into the sweet outdoors and start out in the canoe, keeping close along the shore in the long shadows of the pines. I remembered being very careful never to rub my paddle against the gunwale for fear of disturbing the stillness of the cathedral. [2]

The lake had never been what you would call a wild lake. There were cottages sprinkled around the shores, and it was in farming country although the shores of the lake were quite heavily wooded. Some of the cottages were owned by nearby farmers, and you would live at the shore and eat your meals at the farmhouse. That's what our family did. But although it wasn't wild, it was a fairly large and undisturbed lake and there were places in it which, to a child at least, seemed infinitely remote and primeval. [3]

Repeated details unify the article. So does the illusion that White is his son, first mentioned in paragraph 4, and "There had been no years," introduced in paragraph 5 and repeated thereafter. Be especially aware of these recurrent threads.

I was right about the tar: it led to within half a mile of the shore. But when I got back there, with my boy, and we settled into a camp near a farmhouse and into the kind of summertime I had known, I could tell that it was going to be pretty much the same as it had been before—I knew it, lying in bed the first morning, smelling the bedroom, and hearing the boy sneak quietly out and go off along the shore in a boat. I began to sustain the illusion that he was I, and therefore, by simple transposition, that I was my father. This sensation persisted, kept cropping up all the time we were there. It was not an entirely new feeling, but in this setting it grew much stronger. I seemed to be living a dual existence. I would be in the middle of some simple act, I would be picking up a bait box or laying down a table fork, or I would be saying something, and suddenly it would be not I but my father who was saying the words or making the gesture. It gave me a creepy sensation. [4]

We went fishing the first morning. I felt the same damp moss covering the worms in the bait can, and saw the dragonfly alight on the tip of my rod as it hovered a few inches from the surface of the water. It was the arrival of this fly that convinced me beyond any doubt that everything was as it always had been, that the years were a mirage and there had been no years. The small waves were the same, chucking the rowboat under the chin as we fished at anchor, and the boat was the same boat, the same color green and the ribs broken in the same places, and under the floor-boards the same fresh-water leavings and débris—the dead helgramite, the wisps of moss, the rusty discarded fishhook, the dried blood from yesterday's catch. We stared silently at the tips of our rods, at the dragonflies that came and went. I lowered the tip of mine into the water, tentatively, pensively dislodging the fly, which darted two feet away, poised, darted two feet back, and came to rest again a little farther up the rod. There had been no years between the ducking of this dragonfly and the other one—the one that was part of memory. I looked at the boy, who was silently watching his fly, and it was my hands that held his rod, my eyes watching. I felt dizzy and didn't know which rod I was at the end of. [5]

We caught two bass, hauling them in briskly as though they were mackerel, pulling them over the side of the boat in a businesslike manner without any landing net, and stunning them with a blow on the back of the head. When we got back for a swim before lunch, the lake was exactly where we had left it, the same number of inches from the dock, and there was only the merest suggestion of a breeze. This seemed an utterly enchanted sea, this lake you could leave to its own devices for a few hours and come back to, and find that it had not stirred, this constant and trustworthy body of water. In the shallows, the dark, water-soaked sticks and twigs, smooth and old, were undulating in clusters on the bottom against the clean ribbed sand, and the track of the mussel was plain. A school of minnows swam by, each minnow with its small individual shadow, doubling the attendance, so clear and sharp in the sunlight. Some of the other campers were in swimming, along the shore, one of them with a cake of soap, and the water felt thin and clear and unsubstantial. Over the years there had been this person with the cake of soap, this cultist, and here he was. There had been no years. [6]

Up to the farmhouse to dinner through the teeming, dusty field, the road under our sneakers was only a two-track road. The middle track was missing, the one with the marks of the hooves and the splotches of dried, flaky manure. There had always been three tracks to choose from in choosing which track to walk in; now the choice was narrowed down to two. For a moment I missed terribly the middle alternative. But the way led past the tennis court, and something about the way it lay there in the sun reassured me; the tape had loosened along the backline, the alleys were green with plantains and other weeds, and the net (installed in June and removed in September) sagged in the dry noon, and the whole place steamed with midday heat and hunger and emptiness. There was a choice of pie for dessert, and one was blueberry and one was apple, and the waitresses were the same country girls, there having been no passage of time, only the illusion of it as in a dropped curtain—the waitresses were still fifteen; their hair had been washed, that was the only difference—they had been to the movies and seen the pretty girls with the clean hair. [7]

The generating paragraphs, leading to the climactic paragraphs, start with paragraph 8. When White speaks of "fade-proof lakes, the woods unshatterable," he is repeating, in different words, that there had been no passage of years.

Summertime, oh summertime, pattern of life indelible, the fade-proof lake, the woods unshatterable, the pasture with the sweetfern and the juniper forever and ever, summer without end; this was the background, and the life along the shore was the design, the cottagers with their innocent and tranquil design, their tiny docks with the flagpole and the American flag floating against the white clouds in the blue sky, the little paths over the roots of the trees leading from camp to camp and the paths leading back to the outhouses and the can of lime for sprinkling, and at the souvenir counters at the store the miniature birch-bark canoes and the post cards that showed things looking a little better than they looked. This was the American family at play, escaping the city heat, wondering whether the newcomers in the camp at the head of the cove were "common" or "nice," wondering whether it was true that the people who drove up for Sunday dinner at the farmhouse were turned away because there wasn't enough chicken. [8]

It seemed to me, as I kept remembering all this, that those times and those summers had been infinitely precious and worth saving. There had been jollity and peace and goodness. The arriving (at the beginning of August) had been so big a business in itself, at the railway station the farm wagon drawn up, the first smell of the pine-laden air, the first glimpse of the smiling farmer, and the great importance of the trunks and your father's enormous authority in such matters, and the feel of the wagon under you for the long ten-mile haul, and at the top of the last long hill catching the first view of the lake after eleven months of not seeing this cherished body of water. The shouts and cries of the other campers when they saw you, and the trunks to be unpacked, to give up their rich burden. (Arriving was less exciting nowadays, when you sneaked up in your car and parked it under a tree near the camp and took out the bags and in five minutes it was all over, no fuss, no loud wonderful fuss about trunks.) [9]

White's sensibilities and better judgment start making inroads on his euphoria. The illusion he is trying to sustain—the dual existence with his son—is shattered from time to time by the "nervous sound of the outboard motors" that "set the years moving." Describing the old one-cylinder motorboat of his day, White says that "you could have it eating out of your hand if you got really close to it spiritually." Paragraph 10 comes close to being the climactic paragraph of the essay.

Peace and goodness and jollity. The only thing that was wrong now, really, was the sound of the place, an unfamiliar nervous sound of the outboard motors. This was the note that jarred, the one thing that would sometimes break the illusion and set the years moving. In those other summertimes all motors were inboard; and when they were at a little distance, the noise they made was a sedative, an ingredient of summer sleep. They were one-cylinder and two-cylinder engines, and some were make-and-break and some were jump-spark, but they all made a sleepy sound across the lake. The one-lungers throbbed and fluttered, and the twin-

cylinder ones purred and purred, and that was a quiet sound too. But now the campers all had outboards. In the daytime, in the hot mornings, these motors made a petulant, irritable sound; at night, in the still evening when the afterglow lit the water, they whined about one's ears like mosquitoes. My boy loved our rented outboard, and his great desire was to achieve single-handed mastery over it, and authority, and he soon learned the trick of choking it a little (but not too much), and the adjustment of the needle valve. Watching him I would remember the things you could do with the old one-cylinder engine with the heavy flywheel, how you could have it eating out of your hand if you got really close to it spiritually. Motor boats in those days didn't have clutches, and you would make a landing by shutting off the motor at the proper time and coasting in with a dead rudder. But there was a way of reversing them, if you learned the trick, by cutting the switch and putting it on again exactly on the final dying revolution of the flywheel, so that it would kick back against compression and begin reversing. Approaching a dock in a strong following breeze, it was difficult to slow up sufficiently by the ordinary coasting method, and if a boy felt he had complete mastery over his motor, he was tempted to keep it running beyond its time and then reverse it a few feet from the dock. It took a cool nerve, because if you threw the switch a twentieth of a second too soon you would catch the flywheel when it still had speed enough to go up past center, and the boat would leap ahead, charging bull-fashion at the dock. **[10]**

All that White is attempting to do, living on through his son, is described symbolically in how he used to dock the old motorboat. White wants us to associate this reversal of the "dying revolution of the flywheel" with his own dying and his attempt to reverse the aging process in himself.

The next paragraph reiterates, for the last time, the illusion he is trying to sustain: "Everywhere we went I had trouble making out which was I, the one walking at my side, the one walking in my pants."

We had a good week at the camp. The bass were biting well and the sun shone endlessly, day after day. We would be tired at night and lie down in the accumulated heat of the little bedrooms after the long hot day and the breeze would stir almost imperceptibly outside and the smell of the swamp drift in through the rusty screens. Sleep would come easily and in the morning the red squirrel would be on the roof, tapping out his gay routine. I kept remembering everything, lying in bed in the mornings—the small steamboat that had a long rounded stern like the lip of a Ubangi, and how quietly she ran on the moonlight sails, when the older boys played their mandolins and the girls sang and we ate doughnuts dipped in sugar, and how sweet the music was on the water in the shining night, and what it had felt like to think about girls then. After breakfast we would go up to the store and the things were in the same place—the minnows in a bottle, the plugs and spinners disarranged and pawed over by the youngsters from the boys' camp, the fig newtons and the Beeman's gum. Outside, the road was tarred and cars stood in front of the store. Inside, all was just as it had always been, except there was more Coca-Cola and not so much Moxie and root beer and birch beer and sarsaparilla. We would walk out with a bottle of pop apiece and sometimes the pop would backfire up our noses and hurt. We explored the streams, quietly, where the turtles slid off the sunny logs and dug their way into the soft bottom; and we lay on the town wharf and fed worms to the tame bass. Everywhere we went I had trouble making out which was I, the one walking at my side, the one walking in my pants. **[11]**

In the climactic paragraphs, following and leading into the storm on the lake, White realizes that his fate is inescapable: He will die.

One afternoon while we were there at that lake a thunderstorm came up. It was like the revival of an old melodrama that I had seen long ago with childish awe. The second-act climax of the drama of the electrical disturbance over a lake in America had not changed in any important respect. This was the big scene, still the big scene. The whole thing was so familiar, the first feeling of oppression and heat and a general air around camp of not wanting to go very far away. In midafternoon (it was all the same) a curious darkening of the sky, and a lull in everything that had made life tick; and then the way the boats suddenly swung the other way at their moorings with the coming of a breeze out of the new quarter, and the premonitory rumble. Then the kettle drum, then the snare, then the bass drum and cymbals, then crackling light against the dark, and the gods grinning and licking their chops in the hills. Afterward the calm, the rain steadily rustling in the calm lake, the return of light and hope and spirits, and the campers running out in joy and relief to go swimming in the rain, their bright cries perpetuating the deathless joke about how they were getting simply drenched, and the children screaming with delight at the new sensation of bathing in the rain, and the joke about getting drenched linking the generations in a strong indestructible chain. And the comedian who waded in carrying an umbrella. **[12]**

When the others went swimming my son said he was going in too. He pulled his dripping trunks from the line where they had hung all through the shower, and wrung them out. Languidly, and with no thought of going in, I watched him, his hard little body, skinny and bare, saw him wince slightly as he pulled up around his vitals the small, soggy, icy garment. As he buckled the swollen belt, suddenly my groin felt the chill of death. **[13]**

The rhythm, flow and unity of this article come not only from the majestic pacing and flow of the words but also from the repetition of details and the motif—no passage of time: "There had been no years"—and the artistic weaving in of nature imagery throughout. The craft of fiction in the essay is so evident that "Once More to the Lake" could easily be classified as a short story. When you search for a non-fiction effort that blends the best of journalistic writing with literary effort, no better example exists than E.B. White's article.

STEPS FOR DEVELOPING MAGAZINE ARTICLES

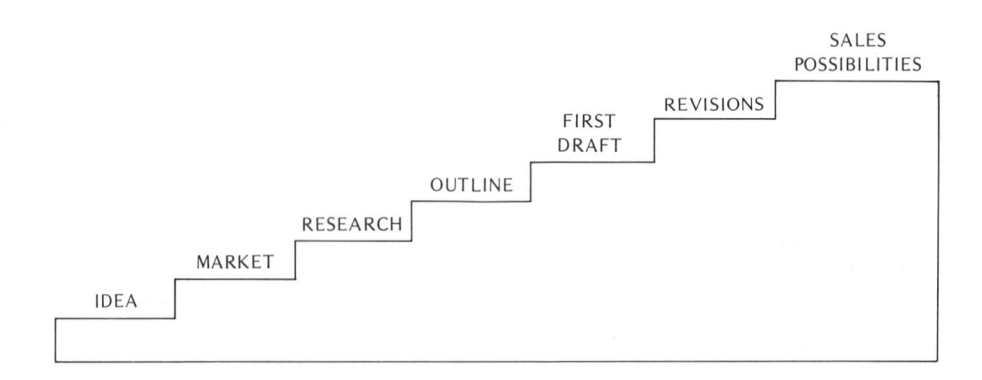

The *idea* for an article leads to a consideration of the *market* for it. Once that market's been determined, article *research* is conducted. After surveying the materials you've gathered in your research, you *outline* the article (along the reader-interest plane) and then write a *first draft*. You then make as many *revisions* as it takes to finish the article to your satisfaction. We've already examined the middle steps of researching, outlining, writing and revising; let's move back to explore the steps that precede those processes.

MAGAZINE ARTICLE IDEAS

Where do ideas for articles come from: A better question might be, Where are there no ideas for magazine articles? We live in a sea of ideas. To escape from them, we'd have to lose all five of our senses. Ideas live and thrive everywhere.

Personal experience or narrative ideas may be the easiest to discover, develop and write. Take an inventory of your life and the interesting experiences or thoughts you have had. Look around on your way to class. Note things that occur to you; tuck them away in your mind or in a notebook for further exploration. Look at the latest fashions. Listen to the latest sayings. Who knows? When you get through with this observation and inventory, you may end up writing an article about awkward behavioral patterns in elevators or about how fathers *do* know best.

You might develop how-to-do-it article ideas while helping your mother plan her garden or your father paint the house. Sort through the day's mail. If you've had the foresight to place yourself on the government's mailing list of periodicals, which include everything from building a solar energy unit to eliminating broom sage from pastures, you'll be able to mine ideas from those mailings.

Science and health article ideas may stem from recently published articles or books, phenomena reported by the press, or experiments being conducted in the science departments of major universities located near you.

Travel article ideas crop up along the highways in the form of historical road signs, tourist information booths and chambers of commerce.

Just reading through the listings in *Writer's Market* and the descriptions of the kind of articles wanted by the various magazine editors will stimulate article ideas in you.

© 1984 Newspaper Enterprise Association, Inc.

MAGAZINE MARKETS

Among the things *Writer's Market* will tell you is whether you should query the magazine before writing an article for it. A query is simply a compact letter that sells your article idea to the editor. Your query should comment on the significance and timeliness of the article and its particular suitability for the magazine. A query may include the proposed length of the article, the title and opening paragraphs, and a rough outline or summary. It also lists your qualifications and sources you will use in writing the article. A self-addressed, stamped envelope (SASE) should be included. If you want to submit an article to a magazine, address your query to the appropriate editor by name.

Just as there exist numerous ideas for the magazine writer, so too are there numerous markets for those ideas. *Writer's Market* lists more than 4,000 of them. Just about anything you write, if it's written well, can be marketed in one or more magazines. Because of this fact, you may write an article first and then locate a market for it. However, professional writers determine the market for the idea and then write the article with that market in mind. They know that wherever the article eventually goes, it will have to fit the particular magazine's editorial needs. Why go through an unnecessary editorial revision? Revisions take time, and time means lost money.

The categories of magazine markets for article ideas range all the way from the broad categories of consumer, professional and company trade journals to narrower categories such as women, men, children, farm, sports and health.

Every serious writer keeps on his or her personal library shelf (in addition to the usual writer's tools such as a dictionary, a thesaurus, an atlas and a book of quotations) a copy of *Writer's Market*. That's because once an idea for an article occurs, the *Market* can be used to select the most prestigious, best-paying markets for it. Write the names of the editors and the magazine addresses of about five of those markets on 3-by-5 cards; then study the editorial styles of the magazines in the library. Note the kind of article leads used—dramatic, no-nonsense, etc. What kind of style is preferred—breezy, formal, first-person? Are authorities cited in the articles? What is the usual length of the articles? While you are doing this market search, write down a title or two from some of the articles you read so that they can be mentioned in your query letters to the editors. That will help communicate to the editor that you are familiar enough with the magazine to be able to write to suit its needs.

Let's look at two *Writer's Market* listings:

FORD TIMES, *Ford Motor Co., Box 1899, The American Rd., Rm. 765, Dearborn MI 48121-1899. Editor: Arnold S. Hirsch, 75% freelance written. "General-interest magazine designed to attract all ages." Monthly magazine. Circ. 1,200,000. Buys first rights only. Pays kill fee. Byline given. Buys about 100 mss/year. Pays on acceptance. Submit seasonal material 6 months in advance. Computer printout submissions acceptable. Reports in 1 month. Publishes ms an average of 1 year after acceptance. Free sample copy and writer's guidelines. SASE.*
Nonfiction: *"Almost anything relating to contemporary American life that is upbeat and positive. Topics include lifestyle trends, vacation ideas, profiles, insights into big cities and small towns, the arts, the outdoors, and sports. We are especially interested in subjects that appeal to readers in the 18-35 age group. We also are beginning to use stories with international settings. We strive to be colorful, lively and, above all, interesting. We try to avoid subjects that have appeared in other publications or in our own." Length: 1,500 words maximum. Query required unless previous contributor. Pays $450 minimum for full-length articles.*
Photos: *"Speculative submission of high-quality color transparencies and b&w photos with mss is welcomed. We need bright, graphically strong photos showing people. We need releases for people whose identity is readily apparent in photos."**

McCALL'S, *230 Park Ave., New York NY 10169. Editor: Robert Stein, Managing Editor: Don McKinney. 90% freelance written. "Study recent issues." Our publication "carefully and conscientiously services the needs of the woman reader—concentrating on matters that directly affect her life and offering information and understanding on subjects of personal importance to her." Monthly. Circ. 6,200,000. Pays on acceptance. Pays 20% kill fee. Buys first rights only. Byline given. Computer printout submissions acceptable; no dot-matrix. Reports in 2 months. SASE.*
Nonfiction: *Don McKinney, managing editor. No subject of wide public or personal interest is out of bounds for McCall's so long as it is appropriately*

---

* Reprinted courtesy of the Ford Motor Company.

treated. The editors are seeking meaningful stories of personal experience. They are on the lookout for new research that will provide the basis for penetrating articles on the ethical, physical, material and social problems concerning readers. They are most receptive to humor. McCall's buys 200–300 articles/year, many in the 1,000- to 1,500-word length. Pays variable rates for nonfiction. Mrs. Helen DelMonte and Andrea Thompson are editors of nonfiction books, from which McCall's frequently publishes excerpts. These are on subjects of interest to women: biography, memoirs, reportage, etc. Almost all features on food, household equipment and management, fashion, beauty, building and decorating are staff-written. Query. "All manuscripts must be submitted on speculation, and McCall's accepts no responsibility for unsolicited manuscripts."

Columns/Departments: *"The Mother's Page (edited by Maryann Brinley); short items that may be humorous, helpful, inspiring and reassuring. Pays $100 and up. Vital Signs (edited by Judith Stone); short items on health and medical news. Pay varies. Back Talk (edited by Barbara Blakemore); 1,000-word essay in which the writer makes a firm statement of opinion, often taking an unexpected or unpopular point of view. Whether humorous or serious in tone, the piece must reflect the writer's strong feelings on the subject. Pays $1,000. VIP-ZIP (edited by Annette Canby & Anne Cassidy); high-demography regional section. Largely service-oriented, it covers travel, decorating and home entertainment. The editors are also interested in short essays (humorous or serious) and in profiles for the Singular Woman feature. The woman spotlighted here has accomplished something not expected of her and is someone our readers can admire." Pay varies.*

Fiction: *Department Editor: Helen DelMonte. "Again the editors would remind writers of the contemporary woman's taste and intelligence. Most of all, fiction can awaken a reader's sense of identity, deepen her understanding of herself and others, refresh her with a laugh at herself, etc. McCall's looks for stories which will have meaning for an adult reader of some literary sensitivity. No stories that are grim, depressing, fragmentary, or concerned with themes of abnormality or violence. McCall's principal interest is in short stories; but fiction of all lengths is considered." Length: about 3,000 words average. Length for short-shorts: about 2,000 words. Payment begins at $1,500; $2,000 for full length stories.*

Tips: *"Except for humor, query first. Material is running shorter than few years ago. We are much more open to very short pieces, 750 words up."*

After reading through thousands of market listings like these, you'll see that there's a whole wide world of publications out there just waiting for you to make your debut.

MAGAZINE MANUSCRIPT FORMAT

After you have completed the research for your article, outlined it along the reader-interest plane, written the first draft and revised it, you are ready to type it in final magazine-article manuscript form.

On the first page, in the upper left-hand corner, on four single-spaced lines, type your name, your address, and your telephone number. In the upper right-hand corner, also on four lines, write the name of your article, the number of words rounded off to the nearest hundred (e.g., 1,400 words), and then your copyright notice: the word *Copyright*, the year, your name. Start the text halfway down the page. Double-space and leave margins of at least 15 spaces. Your first page should be free from errors. Very neat erasures or Liquid Paper corrections are permitted on the following pages. At the end of each page and in the center, write (*more*). At the end of the article, in the middle of the page, two spaces after the last line, write *The End*.

Make a copy of the original article you are sending to the editor in case it is not mailed back. Manuscripts under eight pages may be folded once and mailed in a 6-by-9 envelope. Larger manuscripts should be mailed in 9-by-12 envelopes, with a cardboard insert to keep the pages wrinkle-free. Never staple pages together; use a paper clip. Use the correct postage for the envelope addressed to the editor. Include a self-addressed, stamped envelope to return the manuscript to you if that is necessary. Editors are not likely to return manuscripts unless you provide an envelope and pay the postage.

The letter accompanying the article should be to the point and short. If you queried the editor earlier, remind the editor of his or her positive response to your query, but point out again how well-suited the article is for the magazine. Ask the editor to write you if the article needs modification.

REJECTIONS

If you do not hear from the editor within the period of time in which *Writer's Market* says the magazine usually responds, wait a week or two, then write a brief note to the editor:

```
Six weeks ago I sent you an article titled ''They Drew
a Circle,'' and I have yet to hear from you. Does this
mean the article is still being considered? I hope this
is the case. I have great hopes for it. In any event,
thank you for considering the article.
```

Chances are your article will be promptly returned. You may as well resign yourself to the fact that rejections will play a large role in your writing career, especially in the beginning. When you do receive a rejection, however, don't despair. Go to the manila folder where the photocopy of your article is. On the inside of the folder, create a log for your article with these headings:

```
TITLE OF        MAGAZINE                    DATE
ARTICLE         MARKET       DATE SENT      RETURNED      COMMENTS
1. ''They Drew
    a Circle''  McCall's     1/14/86
2.
3.
4.
5.
```

Fill in the columns for the rejected manuscript. Then select the next magazine you think would be a good prospect for your article.

If the pages of your article have been damaged or wrinkled in some way, retype them. (No editor likes to receive obvious rejects from another magazine.) Then mail it with a cover letter to your next choice.

Don't let the shock of being rejected keep you from pursuing your goals as a writer. Rejections are a large part of a writer's life.

No matter how many rejections you receive, though there may be enough to set you up in the wall-papering business, do whatever is necessary to keep writing. If you've been getting rejections from national magazines, lower your sights a bit and try local and regional publications and magazines with smaller circulations. Whatever it takes to keep on writing, do it.

Remember what happened to William Faulkner. He kept a log of his rejected short stories, and when he finally wrote his first best seller, editors and publishers started calling his agent and begging for something to publish. He sent them the identical stories they had rejected, with inflated price tags on them. They paid the price. Gladly.

SUMMARY

Every magazine writer should master the various lead forms analyzed in this chapter. Creative use of these lead styles can inspire the extra-special "narrative hook" a writer must craft in order to bring readers into the body of the story.

A critical review of your article, with an eye toward balance between valley and peak paragraphs, will help even experienced writers during the revision process. A good outline, using the reader-interest plane, will assist in organizing your notes and article research and keying it to those valleys and peaks.

Most important, be aware of the trend toward specialization among magazines and write to each market's specifications. Close attention to a magazine market's requirements will help you produce an article that will build your reputation with that magazine.

EXERCISES

1. List five magazine article idea possibilities derived from your personal experiences. Under each, list the articles in the *Readers' Guide to Periodical Literature* that have explored a similar or related idea in the last two years. Include full bibliographic data for the articles.

    a.

    b.

    c.

    d.

    e.

2. List five ideas that stem from your observations of life around you that are suitable magazine-article material. Check the *Readers' Guide* for the last two years to determine if other articles have been written about the subject matter. Include the bibliographic data of the articles.

    a.

    b.

    c.

    d.

    e.

3. List 10 ideas that stem from a calendar that notes holidays, anniversaries, etc. Include the angle from which you will write the article.

    a.

    b.

    c.

    d.

    e.

    f.

    g.

    h.

    i.

    j.

4. Using *Writer's Market*, select three magazines for each of three article ideas you listed in Exercise 1. Repeat the article idea here, listing three prime markets for each. Note the pay you'd expect to receive from each.

   a.

   b.

   c.

5. Select one article idea that you want to develop. Choose and analyze the market for that article. Examine all issues published in the last year or so.

   Record here some brief comments about what you have discovered. Is the *Writer's Market* description accurate? Where does it apparently differ? What kind of leads are favored in the magazine? What point of view is used? What is the tone of the articles?

6. In the magazine you chose in Exercise 5, find an article similar to your article idea. Analyze it according to the reader-interest plane. Comment on the article's title, purpose, sources, tone, flow and descriptions. Analyze it paragraph by paragraph in the space below. Note down what you will have to do in writing your article so that it will have the best chance of being accepted by the magazine editor.

7. Write a query letter to the editor of the magazine you selected in Exercise 5. Be sure to cite one or two articles that you read in the magazine.

8. Write a detailed outline of your article, indicating at one side where parts of the outline fall on the reader-interest plane. Then write the article, following the outline—unless you have good reason to depart from it (note any such instance).

9. Reread the gas station description in paragraph 15 of the article on Billy Carter. Write a similar description of some place of business in your hometown in 50 words or less. Compare with your classmates' descriptions.

PART V
WRITING TO PERSUADE

The information explosion has made it possible for more and more voices to be heard through the American media. Hunger for up-to-the-moment information, particularly information that is valued by persons with specialized rather than mainstream interests, has encouraged more discussion and examination of events and issues. The opportunity for different points of view to find expression in the American mass media has never been greater, and audiences for different points of view have never been larger.

The professionals who meet these information needs are today's persuasive communicators. Among journalists, they are the columnists, editorial writers and essayists whose views add depth and interpretation to events on the national, international and even personal levels. Their commentary, expressed in editorials, bylined columns and guest appearances on television and radio interview programs, provides the stimulating insights that assist media consumers to come to terms with a complex world.

Among other information professionals are public relations practitioners who produce information for governments, companies and individual clients with the goal of getting them publicity for their beliefs, their programs, their products—whatever important goal is on their agenda. The PR professional is a vital link in the information loop that connects governments, businesses and organizations with consumers through the mass media.

Also counted among non-journalist persuasive communicators are advertising copywriters and creative directors, who concoct the clever campaigns that inform and entice the buying public. Advertising is among the most creative—and most competitive—work in the mass media.

All these different forms of persuasive communication require well-honed skills in analyzing, interpreting and presenting information. Opinion is powerful, and it must be clearly distinguished from fact.

CHAPTER 14

OPINION

Editorials, columns, essays, reviews—a formidable array of journalistic forms, isn't it? How do you prepare yourself to write in these various forms?

The training and experience you receive in writing news and feature articles provide you with a good foundation to write in these areas. A more fully developed curiosity and sensitivity to life's experiences may also be necessary, however. Your feeling for words and how they flow to express your views will need to be enriched. This is easily said but not easily done. The next few pages, however, should place you on the right writing track.

PREPARATION FOR WRITING COMMENTARY

"You cannot be in my business long without being asked the question: Where do you get your ideas?" columnist Ellen Goodman recently wrote. "The answer, alas, is a secret known only to me and an oracle that lurks in Boston Harbor."

The answer also lies in writers' imaginations, in their resourcefulness and in their having a keen eye on the day's events.

Editorial writers, columnists and essayists have research habits similar to those of news and feature writers. Nothing is lost on them. A government press release, a news story, a magazine article, a television documentary, a book, a conversation with a senator—all are filed away or noted in case they'll be needed for reference a day, a month or a year later.

For example, out of a conference of a newspaper's editorial staff may come a decision to publish an editorial or column on Jordan and its changing relations with neighboring Arab countries. The slaying of 10 civilians in El Salvador might prompt a decision for comment on that country's troubles. A meeting of OPEC ministers might be the catalyst for an editorial on perils to the Western economy should the price of oil drop to the 1976 price per barrel. When that time comes, the writers go back to their files and their folders of clippings saved for these assignments. The collections provide valuable background and leads.

Editorials, columns and essays fall into four broad categories: informative, interpretive, persuasive and humorous. Some may inform and interpret at the same time. Others may persuade through humor. But for purposes of discussion, let's assume that editorials, columns and essays are primarily informative, interpretive, persuasive and humorous.

The *informative* editorial, column or essay dissects events. If a complicated Medicare bill has been passed by Congress, an editorial may explain the implications of the bill to the public in a more logical manner than an inverted-pyramid-style news story. If the president presents his budget to Congress, various terms of that budget will call for interpretation and discussion. For example, what does "supply-side economics" really mean? An *interpretive* editorial, column or essay may explain that the concept is based on what is called "trickle-down" theory and what that means to the rich and the poor in this country. A *persuasive* editorial, column or essay may try to persuade readers that supply-side economics is doomed to failure through various arguments and emotional or intellectual appeals. A *humorous* article on the administration budget decision by columnist Art Buchwald may bring a smile to your lips while at the same time exposing a contradiction in political promises and the realities of the budget.

There is nothing very complicated in all these definitions, is there? The complications come only when you attempt to write them all.

Before you sit down at a typewriter or a video display terminal to write an editorial, column or essay, research is necessary. That may mean going to the filing cabinet, reviewing folders and updating that material by going to the library or by calling experts in the field to get additional information. A period of reflection on the information you have marshaled should follow.

Pick up a pen and pad and find a clean, well-lighted place or a quiet, secluded nook. Develop related ideas and thoughts and expand them with more incidents, illustrations, anecdotes and examples. As you think about these ideas and incidents, jot them down on that pad so you won't forget them. Then sit back and look at everything you have on that pad.

Ask yourself, *What does it all mean? Does it signify something more than what I initially had in mind? Does it signify less? What biases or prejudices have I allowed to intrude?* This self-examination will help you determine the precise point of view you will take and the tone and rhythm of the writing. Once you have done this, outline your article. (See Chapter 5 on outlining.)

The outline organizes still further all the facts and ideas you jotted down on the pad for more formal presentation. The outline aids you in these ways:

© 1984 Newspaper Enterprise Association, Inc.

1. It forces you to think about your subject matter and then to know it more thoroughly and to organize it for presentation.
2. It forces you to survey your materials more exhaustively. If the material and facts are lacking, the outline exposes the thin spots and prevents you from being stranded in the middle of a column, editorial or essay for lack of research.
3. It brings a sense of proportion to your ideas. Is one idea more important than another? Do more facts support this idea than other ideas? If so, that should be reflected by the idea's position in the article and the amount of space devoted to it.
4. An outline clarifies the relationship of one idea to another. Coherence and good transitions are the result.

While you are writing, outlining has these effects:

1. It creates confidence in you. You know what you're going to say and how you are going to say it.
2. It forces you to focus on the task at hand and provides a wider highway for your mind to follow.
3. It frees you to think. A good deal of creativity goes on while you write. Not having to think about what idea will be taken up next (it's on the outline), you are free to develop new and related ideas, incidents or illustrations to amplify the idea at hand.
4. It frees you to write. You can ponder the best word, the best phrase, the best figure of speech, the best image, without worrying about organization.

After saying all this, however, once you've composed your detailed outline and are writing, remember that you, and not the outline, are the master. If a deviation from it appears to be the best path, consider it fully. If it is the best path, take it.

IMPORTANCE OF THE OPENING PARAGRAPHS

No matter what you're writing, the beginning should entice readers into the article by identifying what the article is about and then providing the transition into the body of the article. The tone of the article—serious, humorous, satirical—as well as the scope of the article, should be signaled by the opening paragraphs.

When you start writing, write without stopping until the article is completed. If a word or phrase refuses to come to you immediately, leave a blank space and take care of the problem during revision—by that time the mental block will probably have disappeared. If you are discouraged by what's pouring from your typewriter, keep on writing to the end. In this first writing, however, and especially later, the words, phrases, clauses, sentences and paragraphs should be as rich with meaning as the subject matter and the audience require.

An opinion piece should conclude with dignity and finality. If you've examined problems in your article, you may want to propose solutions in the conclusion, or you may want to relinquish the solution to your readers by leaving them with a simple "What would you do?" Or you may want to compose a neat little concluding bow for your article by referring to comments made in the opening paragraphs. That will help unify the article. But this kind of concluding summary should be stated in entirely different words from those of the opening paragraph. Otherwise, you'll be engaging in amateurish verbatim repetition of what was stated in the beginning—a dreadful way to end your article when you consider all the other ways of leaving your reader: wondering, laughing, crying, cursing.

WRITING TO PERSUADE

No one formula exists for writing most editorials, columns and essays. The subject matter usually dictates the literary form. That's why the reader-interest plane is such a valuable guide to writing. It provides guidance without dictating structure.

When writing persuasively, however, it's best to stick to this form:

1. The opening paragraphs should state the problem or situation and outline the position you are taking.
2. The next few paragraphs present arguments, illustration, examples, evidence and other support for your position.
3. The succeeding paragraphs present the major arguments or evidence counter to your stand. Try not to dwell too long on opposing arguments and evidence—after all, why give aid and comfort to the enemy? Include your refutations of those opposing arguments in the same section of the article.
4. The concluding paragraph reemphasizes, in different phraseology, the stance you took in the beginning.

The following Tom Wicker column from *The New York Times* follows the form exactly. The first three paragraphs present the stand he is taking on what he believes to be President Reagan's lack of understanding of the function of the American press. The next 10 paragraphs present evidence to support Wicker's major thesis: The president thinks the press is hostile and fails to understand its adversary role. (Although in these paragraphs Wicker refutes the president's views, he is establishing the validity of the stand he took in the first paragraphs of the column.) In the third section of the column, Wicker states the major contention of the president—that reportage has endangered American forces—and refutes it. The concluding paragraph refers to the opening paragraphs and restates in different words the major stand taken there.

Read the column. Wicker is one of the most respected columnists in American journalism. And until you feel more comfortable writing in the persuasive mode, follow the formula presented here.

The Press Is on Whose Side?*

By TOM WICKER
The New York Times News Service

NEW YORK — When Secretary of State George Shultz recently observed that American reporters were not "on our side" but seemed "always against us," the White House press secretary, Larry Speakes, told reporters: "I do not think that reflects the attitude of the President."

Larry, you should have known better.

Ronald Reagan, at his latest news conference, not only agreed with Shultz; he displayed in his usual amiable manner his animosity toward the American press as well as a profound lack of understanding of its function.

It's commonplace, nowadays, to say that that only reflects the attitude of the American public. Reagan, however, is President of the United States. He doesn't have to like reporters any more than the public does; but if he doesn't understand a free press operating in a free society under a Constitution he's sworn to uphold, his high office demands that he learn.

Not Reagan. He even told editors of the Gannett papers recently that there was "no conscious decision by anyone" at the White House or State Department to bar reporters from the Grenada invasion — thus confirming earlier administration statements that this decision had been left to the military.

But who's supposed to be in charge of the armed forces in this country? Generals and admirals or the civilian government?

Then, when asked about Shultz's remarks. Reagan said of the press that "beginning with the Korean conflict and certainly in the Vietnam conflict, there was more criticizing of our forces and what we were trying to do, to the point that it didn't seem that there was much criticism being leveled on the enemy."

Now, historically, the sharpest criticism of the Truman Administration's conduct of the Korean "conflict" was "leveled" by the Republican Party; you could look it up. And throughout the Vietnam "conflict" a large segment of the American press remained determinedly hawkish; you could look that up, too.

Aside from muddled history, however, does Reagan believe that criticism "leveled" by the U.S. press at Ho Chi Minh and Hanoi would have had the slightest effect on the Vietnam "conflict"? And does he believe that a free press should *not* have reported on the military difficulties of what was the third largest war in U.S. history?

Such reporting — particularly graphic and unstaged television im-

---

* "On Reagan and the Press," by Tom Wicker, December 1983. Reprinted with permission of the The New York Times Company.

ages from Vietnam itself — probably did influence public opinion against the war. Reagan apparently assumes that that was its purpose.

This assumption not only impugns the patriotism of the capitalists who own the major newspaper and broadcasting companies; it is ignorant of the obligation of a free press.

But "I just wish," Reagan went on in his aw-shucks manner, "that we could get together on what is of importance to our national security . . . what is endangering our forces and what is helping them in their mission."

Well, Americans have learned that "what is of importance to our national security" is not always what either Democratic or Republican presidents say it is; and there's little evidence that either Reagan or any recent president has tried very hard to "get together" with those of honestly differing views.

The implication that press reporting has been "endangering" American forces is untrue and unworthy; and "helping them in their mission" is certainly not to be equated with unquestioning press support of whatever a president decides. Is it being on the Syrian or Soviet "side" to report that Marines are in an untenable military position and have been given a probably impossible assignment in Lebanon? No, it's being against Ronald Reagan's policy.

Reagan can't make that distinction, simple as it is. When asked who was the "us" reporters are always against, he said Shultz had been talking about "our side, militarily — in other words, all of America."

That's a major trouble with presidents. They assume that having been elected to temporary power by the American people, they come to embody that people — that a president's policy becomes *ipso facto* the people's policy, or "our side." In fact, it's just the President's side, often wrong, and often representing nothing more than his political interest.

The free American press, with all its human faults, nevertheless has the obligation, owing to its constitutional protection, to make that kind of distinction. Doing so doesn't please presidents and sometimes angers the public; but it's still the duty of the press to provide, if it can, "that glimpse of truth for which you have forgotten to ask." Only when doing so is it really "on our side."

To recapitulate, the persuasive mode of writing calls for four distinct sections:

1. An introduction and your stance
2. Arguments in support of your position
3. Arguments in opposition to your position and your refutation of them
4. A reaffirmation of the stance taken in the opening paragraphs

But let's look at how other writers treat various topics. All too frequently editorials appear in newspapers that need never appear at all. The following editorial is actually a news story in the guise of an editorial. What is worse, it had already appeared in the newspapers in news-story form. The editorial is printed in its entirety but without attribution. The reason? To keep from embarrassing an otherwise excellent newspaper serving some one million readers. The only editorial comment comes in the weak concluding paragraph:

AIM Shoots Itself in Foot

Gen. William Westmoreland has taken to task Accuracy in Media (AIM), a conservative group which portrays itself as a watchdog of American journalism.

In a newspaper advertisement, the group used a picture of the retired Army general, suggesting that he endorsed the organization. The ad was intended to encourage public support for the group and raise money for its activities.

There is one problem with the ad: General Westmoreland does not share the group's attitude of wholesale dislike for the news media.

The general has written the group a letter, in which he dissociated himself from the advertisement.

"I believe in the First Amendment," the general wrote.

He also noted that his much publicized fight with CBS News is a case of a single disagreement, not wholesale condemnation of the media. The general is suing CBS for libel because of its portrayal of him as a participant in a conspiracy to misrepresent North Vietnamese forces.

It appears that AIM could do a little policing of its own accuracy.

In contrast, note how the following editorial starts out editorializing and continues to the end.

Sen. Cutrer Owes Apologies*

Sen. T. Tommy Cutrer, D-Cottontown, made a serious error yesterday when he officiously removed a Knoxville *News-Sentinel* reporter from a committee hearing because he was displeased with a story the reporter had written.

Senator Cutrer interrupted a session of the Transportation Committee, of which he is chairman, to point out Mr. David Lyons, Capitol correspondent for the Knoxville newspaper, and tell the sergeant-at-arms "I want him removed from the chamber." The reporter had created no disruption, was there to cover the hearing and was entitled to do his job.

When Mr. Lyons asked why he was being removed, Senator Cutrer said: "None of your business, boy. Just get out. Do what you're told, Move! . . . I have just thrown you out. You offend me."

The article in question dealt with legislation to allow twin-trailers on Tennessee interstates and the efforts of lobbyists, especially the Teamsters Union, to win passage. The article said Mr. Cutrer "reportedly remarked to a number of people on the Capitol elevator that he would be working for the Teamsters soon. . ." Two members of the committee, Sen. Carl Moore, D-Bristol, and Sen. James Elkins, R-Clinton, objected, but not before the journalist was evicted.

Senator Cutrer said after the eviction of Mr. Lyons that he had talked with Teamsters about employment but that that had nothing to do with his vote on the twin-trailer issue.

Regardless of what Mr. Cutrer thought of the article, he had no right to evict a newsman from a public meeting. The senator does not own the Capitol Building. The people do. He does not decide the

* Reprinted with permission of *The Tennessean*.

rights of reporters covering the sessions. The law does. The state Sunshine Law and the Constitution guarantee the public and the press access to legislative meetings. The fight to open up the legislature to the press was won in 1965 when a federal court rescinded a ban the senate invoked against Mr. Bill Kovach, then a *Tennessean* reporter, now an executive of *The New York Times*.

It is Senator Cutrer's conduct that was offensive. It should be embarrassing to other senators. Senator Cutrer owes an apology not only to Mr. Lyons but also to the Senate, the press and to the people.

COMPOSING THE COLUMN

The line of demarcation between editorials and columns is wavy at best. Perhaps the major distinction between editorials and columns is that columnists speak for themselves, and as a result, although not necessarily, their comments tend to be more personal. The editorial writer writes most often anonymously for a newspaper, radio or television station. As a consequence, while the comments are more personal, the tone and the writing of the editorial are more impersonal than those of a column.

To illustrate what we mean, simply recall the two editorials you have just read and then read this greatly abbreviated column about New Year by Tom Wicker. Without any fanfare, he begins:

> Here, in no particular order, are a few things I would do without in the New Year:
> Horror movies.
> People who tell me that the press should print more good news. . . .
> Congressmen and bureaucrats who "prioritize" things. . . .
> Horror novels. . . .
> Baseball players and managers who have the knack of spitting or drooling tobacco juice just when the camera is on them. . . .
> TV horror shows. . . .
> Cheerful TV weathermen.
> The designated hitter. . . .
> The Bomb.

Wicker ends the column with the last thing he could do without: "People who will now write me letters saying that they could do without any more newspaper articles by me. But you can't have everything."

Wicker's writing is carefully revised to achieve the effect he strives for. Even in this column, which listed some 60 things he could do without and seemed haphazardly put together (reread what he says in the first paragraph), the column is unified by using, at carefully placed intervals throughout, "Horror movies," "Horror novels," "TV horror shows," etc. The final big "horror" before the last paragraph is "The Bomb."

Columnist Ellen Goodman writes about her personal life with the same unflinching honesty with which she writes about politics. It may be about herself and her relationship with her daughter. It may be about her friends and their problems. In this example, she writes about her woman friends, who find it difficult to find men who are as willing to commit themselves to a relationship as women are.

On Men and Commitments

By ELLEN GOODMAN

BOSTON — The announcement comes over the phone, from West Coast to East, a long-distance obituary to a long-time relationship.

My friend mourns her loss, eulogizes her broken connection. Her words are so familiar they might have been uttered at a hundred other such wakes: "In the end, he couldn't make a commitment."

This is the third time this month that I have been called upon as pallbearer to a love affair.

In each case, the man came up to the threshold of promise and experienced it less as a doorway than as a line drawn in the sand. A line he couldn't cross.

By the time I hang up, I share my friends' pain and frustration. I want to say something about men and their troubles with "commitment."

I know that three life stories do not make a class action or even a generalization about men. I am surrounded by exceptions, in my home, my family, my friends, my reading.

Yet when I look back, I see more men who were skittish about permanent connections than women, more who were frightened about commitment, and more who were anxious about marriage.

I am not talking about men who subscribe to *Playboy*'s magazine and philosophy. I am not talking about musical-comedy "guys" who fear being housebroken by marriage-minded "dolls."

These are men who have relationships on which they work — who may regard their reluctance to make a commitment as a problem. When pressed they may tell themselves the problem will disappear with "the right woman."

Nor do the women in their lives lay traps anymore. They do not fill hope chests or talk about men as good catches. They, too, have relationships on which they work.

Still, I wonder how much things have changed between men and women. The dimensions of the commitment problem, the description of it may be different than in the days of the tender trap, but what about the origins, the feelings?

We still grow up differently. It's not just a matter of dolls and building blocks, though there is some of that. We are taught people have to break away to become mature. People have to become independent, a condition we confuse with being alone. In real life, these people are men.

We teach men relationships are encumberances that hold them back, trap them, catch them. Men, almost always, become our lone rangers.

Women learn another double message. We are both urged toward independence and encouraged toward caretaking. We try to grow up without growing away, thinking of our selves and our lives as connected. And fearing isolation.

What happens when we come together expecting love? Men who equate maturity with independence meet women who equate it with connections. Our fears collide.

Most of us break through, but not all or always or without pain. Often, there are casualties.

I spoke with one of the three men who had caught this spring fever. It was hard, he said, but he would get

---

* © 1983 (1984), The Boston Globe Newspaper Service/Washington Post Writers Group, reprinted with permission.

through it, tough it out. I had the sense he regarded this breakup as a challenge.

Re-enacting some primal scene, he was again a real man, alone. In some odd way the new bad feelings felt right.

In the next few weeks or months, this man will use his considerable strength. He will use it to prevent himself from crossing the threshold. He will use it to deal with his loneliness. It will be easier for him that way, making no commitments.

Time and time again, what is read or seen in the media generates ideas for columns, both humorous and serious. A perfect example of how this muse is stirred by revelations in the media is this column by Erma Bombeck. Bombeck starts out by remarking that she read that the average marriage nowadays lasts about six years. Bombeck asks why that should be and then answers her own question: There's nothing mystical about it at all. By that time, the husband will have eaten some 5,000 meals and has an inkling of what's in the offing. The wife, meanwhile, will have met the sponging relatives and the father-in-law, who is a Cro-Magnon at the dinner table. Everything, by the end of six years, is out in the open—his smelly feet, her toothpaste in the basin, etc. Children add their toll to the burden of marriage until love simply becomes a note on the calendar of "things to do today." If you can put up with all this, if this is what you thought you married, then the marriage should last for another 30 years or so.

The opening of this column is similar to openings of innumerable columns and editorials. News events and revelations make excellent launching pads for flights into fantasy for columnists like Bombeck, Buchwald and Russell Baker.

Baker uses a news story about possible Russian involvement in the shooting of Pope John Paul II to launch a column in this way:

NEW YORK — Like most Americans, I suppose, I tend to think that all the dumbness is on our side. This is why it's so hard for me to believe it was the KGB that engineered the shooting of the pope.

I've tried to imagine what might have gone on at Moscow Central to produce such a botch, and none of it fits the portrait of diabolically cunning intelligence which two generations of spy literature and Senate oratory have ascribed to the place.

For example:
"Okay, Dmitri, where are we on the pope plot?"
"I've got the Bulgarians working on it right now, chief."
"You crazy or something?"

But news events serve as inspirations for non-humorous comments, as we noted earlier. In this abbreviated column example,* Carl T. Rowan starts out this way:

WASHINGTON — Last week, Ronald Reagan revealed to an Oklahoma newspaper publisher the secret about what's wrong with the economy: "erroneous" news stories have painted him as a "Scrooge," and "irresponsible" TV networks have hurt his recovery program by interviewing people who have lost jobs:

"Is it news that some fellow out in South Succotash . . . has just been laid off, that he should be interviewed nationwide?"

Does Reagan think unemployment for 11 million is not news, and the media should fail to broadcast examples of the human suffering, or

---

* By Carl T. Rowan. Copyright by and permission of News America Syndicate.

show the impact of the recession? Apparently he does, since he told the publisher of the *Daily Oklahoman*: "You can't turn on the evening news without seeing that they're going to interview someone else who's lost a job, or they're outside the factory that has laid off workers."

Reagan ought to get on his knees and thank God for his almost unlimited access to the media. He has commandeered the networks in prime time at will; editors and publishers flock to his briefings or lower red carpets and their guards when he shows up in their towns.

After pointing out that supply-side Reaganomics in the past was the rage and that administration official after administration official has appeared on television extolling the president's program, Rowan remarks how unfair the president is in his assault on the media:

> But let the networks interview mothers who tell how miserable things really are, and the president accuses them of creating a "downbeat" psychology that slows economic recovery.
>
> But the truth emerges. Reaganomics was "voodoo" in concept. It has been "no do" in application. And it can never be a success, even if we give the president what he apparently wants: a monopoly on news and talk shows, and a veto on newspaper editorials that make him look like Scrooge.

If you get the impression from Rowan that columnists can be tough on an administration, you are right. Anthony Lewis, of *The New York Times*, began a column this way:

> Two years into Ronald Reagan's presidency, Americans are beginning to suspect the awful truth: They have a government incompetent to govern, a president frozen in ideological fantasyland, an administration spotted with fools and rogues.
>
> The unmistakable symptom of incompetence is the economic disarray in Washington.

THE ESSAY

What distinguishes the essay from the editorial or the column is not the length, form or even the subject matter, although more esoteric subjects may be treated in an essay. Better writing tends to distinguish the essay from the two other forms. The major distinction between articles such as editorials, columns and magazine articles and essays may be much like that between prose and poetry. Essays tend to be more "musical." They tend to be more eloquent and moving than articles. John Stuart Mill, in making the distinction between prose and poetry, remarked that there is more inner soliloquy involved in writing poetry. Fresher channels of thought are explored. Poetry, he wrote, is more the fruit of solitude and meditation. The same may be said about essays. The essayist may sometimes simply a better writer. At other times better essay writing may stem from the fact the essayist has the luxury of time not available to the editorial writer or columnist, who is chained to a daily grist mill. That doesn't mean that some columns or editorials are not better written than some essays. But overall, the quality of writing of the essay tends to be better.

This essay follows the reader-interest plane: The title is arresting, and the opening paragraph is interesting—it tends to "hook" the reader. The idea of the essay and the transition into the main body of the essay occur in the first paragraph. The second paragraph elaborates on the idea and launches the reader into the body.

The Rewards of Living a Solitary Life*

By MAY SARTON

YORK, Me. — The other day an acquaintance of mine, a gregarious and charming man, told me he had found himself unexpectedly alone in New York for an hour or two between appointments. He went to the Whitney [Museum] and spent the "empty" time looking at things in solitary bliss. For him it proved to be a shock nearly as great as falling in love to discover that he could enjoy himself so much alone.

What had he been afraid of, I asked myself? That, suddenly alone, he would discover that he bored himself, or that there was, quite simply, no self there to meet? But having taken the plunge, he is now on the brink of adventure; he is about to be launched into his own inner space, space as immense, unexplored and sometimes frightening as outer space to the astronaut.

His every perception will come to him with a new freshness and, for a time, seem startlingly original. For anyone who can see things for himself with a naked eye becomes, for a moment or two, something of a genius.

With another human being present vision becomes double vision, inevitably. We are busy wondering, what does my companion see or think of this, and what do I think of it? The original impact gets lost, or diffused.

"Music I heard with you was more than music." Exactly. And therefore music *itself* can only be heard alone. Solitude is the salt of personhood. It brings out the authentic flavor of every experience.

"Alone one is never lonely: the spirit adventures, walking / In a quiet garden, a cool house, abiding single there."

Loneliness is most acutely felt with other people, for with others, even with a lover sometimes, we suffer from our differences of taste, temperament, mood. Human intercourse often demands that we soften the edge of perception, or withdraw at the very instant of personal truth for fear of hurting, or of being inappropriately present, which is to say naked, in a social situation. Alone we can afford to be wholly whatever we are, and to feel whatever we feel absolutely. That is a great luxury!

For me the most interesting thing about a solitary life, and mine has been that for the last twenty years, is that it becomes increasingly rewarding. When I can wake up and watch the sun rise over the ocean, as I do most days, and know that I have an entire day ahead, uninterrupted, in which to write a few pages, take a walk with my dog, lie down in the afternoon for a long think (why does one think better in a horizontal position?), read and listen to music, I am flooded with happiness.

I am lonely only when I am overtired, when I have worked too long without a break, when for the time being I feel empty and need filling up. And I am lonely sometimes when I come back home after a lecture trip, when I have seen a

---

* "The Rewards of Living Alone," by May Sarton, April 6, 1984, Op-Ed. Reprinted with permission of The New York Times Company.

lot of people and talked a lot, and am full to the brim with experience that needs to be sorted out.

Then for a little while the house feels huge and empty, and I wonder where my self is hiding. It has to be recaptured slowly by watering the plants, perhaps, and looking again at each one is though it were a person, by feeding the two cats, by cooking a meal.

It takes a while, as I watch the surf blowing up in fountains at the end of the field, but the moment comes when the world falls away, and the self emerges again from the deep unconscious, bringing back all I have recently experienced to be explored and slowly understood, when I can converse again with my hidden powers, and so grow, and so be renewed, till death do us part.

The adventure in solitary bliss awaiting the man is explored in terms of what will be revealed to him, as it has been revealed to the author. Those are the developing and generating paragraphs. The climactic paragraphs come with the last paragraphs dealing with loneliness, when the house feels huge and empty. The concluding paragraph is the climax: She describes her rejuvenation, "when I can converse again with my hidden powers, and so grow, and so be renewed, till death do us part." The last five words, "till death do us part," create the lingering impression; the reader is left to meditate and discern the full meaning of them. In doing so, the meaning of the essay is absorbed, and the reader is not likely to forget the essay.

This essay is unlikely to find its way into any newspaper, except in a Sunday magazine supplement—which is where this appeared. Another essay unlikely to be published in anything other than a magazine or book is James Thurber's "The Dog That Bit People." When you read it, try to distinguish where the developing paragraphs end and the generating paragraphs begin. Determine if the essay can be plotted along the reader-interest plane.

The Dog That Bit People*

Probably no one man should have as many dogs in his life as I have had, but there was more pleasure than distress in them for me except in the case of an Airedale named Muggs. He gave me more trouble than all the other fifty-four or -five put together, although my moment of keenest embarrassment was the time a Scotch terrior named Jeannie, who had just had six puppies in the clothes closet of a fourth floor apartment in New York, had the unexpected seventh and last at the corner of Eleventh Street and Fifth Avenue during a walk she had insisted on taking. Then, too, there was the prize winning French poodle, a great big black poodle—none of your little, untroublesome white miniatures—who got sick riding in the rumble seat of a car with me on her way to the Greenwich Dog Show. She had a red rubber bib tucked around her throat and, since a rain storm came up when we were halfway through the Bronx, I had to hold over her a small green umbrella, really more of a parasol. The rain beat down fearfully and suddenly the driver of the car drove into a big garage, filled with mechanics. It happened so quickly that I forgot to put the umbrella down and I will always remember, with sickening distress, the look of incredulity mixed with hatred that came over the face of the particular hardened garage man that came over to see what we wanted, when he took a look at me and the poodle. All garage men, and people of that intolerant stripe, hate poodles with their

---

* "The Dog That Bit People," by James Thurber, originally in *The New Yorker*. Reprinted by permission of the estate of James Thurber.

curious haircut, especially the pom-poms that you've got to leave on their hips if you expect the dogs to win a prize.

But the Airedale, as I have said, was the worst of all my dogs. He really wasn't my dog, as a matter of fact: I came home from a vacation one summer to find that my brother Roy had bought him while I was away. A big, burly, choleric dog, he always acted as if he thought I wasn't one of the family. There was a slight advantage in being one of the family, for he didn't bite the family as often as he bit strangers. Still, in the years that we had him he bit everybody but mother, and he made a pass at her once but missed. That was during the month when we suddenly had mice, and Muggs refused to do anything about them. Nobody ever had mice exactly like the mice we had that month. They acted like pet mice, almost like mice somebody had trained. They were so friendly that one night when mother entertained at dinner the Friraliras, a club she and my father had belonged to for twenty years, she put down a lot of little dishes with food in them on the pantry floor so that the mice would be satisfied with that and wouldn't come into the dining room. Muggs stayed out in the pantry with the mice, lying on the floor, growling to himself—not at the mice, but about all the people in the next room that he would have liked to get at. Mother slipped out into the pantry once to see how everything was going. Everything was going fine. It made her so mad to see Muggs lying there, oblivious of the mice—they came running up to her—that she slapped him and he slashed at her, but didn't make it. He was sorry immediately, mother said. He was always sorry, she said, after he bit someone, but we could not understand how she figured this out. He didn't act sorry.

Mother used to send a box of candy every Christmas to the people the Airedale bit. The list finally contained forty or more names. Nobody could understand why we didn't get rid of the dog. I didn't understand it very well myself, but we didn't get rid of him. I think that one or two people tried to poison Muggs—he acted poisoned once in a while—and old Major Moberly fired at him once with his service revolver near the Seneca Hotel in East Broad Street—but Muggs lived to be almost eleven years old and even when he could hardly get around he bit a Congressman who had called to see my father on business. My mother had never liked the Congressman—she said the signs of his horoscope showed he couldn't be trusted (he was Saturn with the moon in Virgo)—but she sent him a box of candy that Christmas. He sent it right back, probably because he suspected it was trick candy. Mother persuaded herself it was all for the best that the dog had bitten him, even though father lost an important business association because of it. "I wouldn't be associated with such a man," mother said. "Muggs could read him like a book."

We used to take turns feeding Muggs to be on his good side, but that didn't always work. He was never in a very good humor, even after a meal. Nobody knew exactly what was the matter with him, but whatever it was it made him irascible, especially in the mornings. Roy never felt very well in the morning, either, especially before breakfast, and once when he came downstairs and found that Muggs had moodily chewed up the morning paper he hit him in the face with a grapefruit and then jumped upon the dining room table, scattering dishes and silverware and spilling the coffee. Muggs' first free leap carried him all the way across the table and into a brass fire screen in front of the gas grate but he was back on his feet in a moment and in the end he got Roy and gave him a pretty vicious bite in the leg. Then he was all over it; he never bit anyone more than once at a time. Mother always mentioned that as an argument in his favor; she said he had

Nobody Knew Exactly What Was the Matter with Him.

a quick temper but that he didn't hold a grudge. She was forever defending him. I think she liked him because he wasn't well. "He's not strong," she would say, pityingly, but that was inaccurate; he may not have been well but he was terribly strong.

One time my mother went to the Chittenden Hotel to call on a woman mental healer who was lecturing in Columbus on the subject of "Harmonious Vibrations." She wanted to find out if it was possible to get harmonious vibrations into a dog. "He's a large tan-colored Airedale," mother explained. The woman said that she had never treated a dog but she advised my mother to hold the thought that he did not bite and would not bite. Mother was holding the thought the very next morning when Muggs got the iceman but she blamed that slip-up on the iceman. "If you didn't think he would bite you, he wouldn't," mother told him. He stomped out of the house in a terrible jangle of vibrations.

One morning when Muggs bit me slightly, more or less in passing, I reached down and grabbed his short stumpy tail and hoisted him into the air. It was a foolhardly thing to do and the last time I saw my mother, about six months ago, she said she didn't know what possessed me. I don't either, except that I was pretty mad. As long as I held the dog off the floor by his tail he couldn't get at me, but he twisted and jerked so, snarling all the time, that I realized I couldn't hold him that way very long. I carried him to the kitchen and flung him onto the floor and shut the door on him just as he crashed against it. But I forgot about the backstairs. Muggs went up the backstairs and down the frontstairs and had me cornered in the living room. I managed to get up onto the mantelpiece above the fireplace, but it gave way and came down with a tremendous crash throwing a large marble clock, several vases, and myself heavily to the floor. Muggs was so alarmed by the racket that when I picked myself up he had disappeared. We couldn't find him anywhere, although we whistled and shouted, until old Mrs. Detweiler called after dinner that night. Muggs had bitten her once, in the leg, and she came into the living room only after we assured her that Muggs had run away. She had just seated herself when, with a great growling and scratching of claws, Muggs emerged from under a davenport where he had been quietly hiding all the time, and bit her again. Mother examined the bite and put arnica on it and told Mrs. Detweiler that it was only a bruise. "He just bumped you," she said. But Mrs. Detweiler left the house in a nasty state of mind.

Lots of People Reported our Dog to the Police.

Lots of people reported our Airedale to the police but my father held a municipal office at the time and was on friendly terms with the police. Even so, the cops had been out a couple times—once when Muggs bit Mrs. Rufus Sturtevant and again when he bit Lieutenant-Governor Malloy—but mother told them that it hadn't been Muggs' fault but the fault of the people who were bitten. "When he starts for them, they scream," she explained, "and that excites him." The cops suggested that it might be a good idea to tie the dog up, but mother said that it mortified him to be tied up and that he wouldn't eat when he was tied up.

Muggs at his meals was an unusual sight. Because of the fact that if you reached toward the floor he would bite you, we usually put his food plate on top of an old kitchen table with a bench alongside the table. Muggs would stand on the bench and eat. I remember that my mother's Uncle Horatio, who boasted that he was the third man up Missionary Ridge, was

Mugs at His Meals Was an Unusual Sight.

splutteringly indignant when he found out that we fed the dog on a table because we were afraid to put his plate on the floor. He said he wasn't afraid of any dog that ever lived and that he would put the dog's plate on the floor if we would give it to him. Roy said that if Uncle Horatio had fed Muggs on the ground just before the battle he would have been the first man up Missionary Ridge. Uncle Horatio was furious. "Bring him in! Bring him in now!" he shouted. "I'll feed the _____ on the floor!" Roy was all for giving him a chance, but my father wouldn't hear of it. He said that Muggs had already been fed. "I'll feed him again!" bawled Uncle Horatio. We had quite a time quieting him.

In his last year Muggs used to spend practically all of his time outdoors. He didn't like to stay in the house for some reason or other—perhaps it held too many unpleasant memories for him. Anyway, it was hard to get him to come in and as a result the garbage man, the iceman, and the laundryman wouldn't come near the house. We had to haul the garbage down to the corner, take the laundry out and bring it back, and meet the iceman a block from home. After this had gone on for some time we hit on an ingenious arrangement for getting the dog in the house so that we could lock him up while the gas meter was read, and so on. Muggs was afraid of only one thing, an electrical storm. Thunder and lightning frightened him out of his senses (I think he thought a storm had broken the day the mantelpiece fell). He would rush into the house and hide under a bed or in a clothes closet. So we fixed up a thunder machine out of a long narrow piece of sheet iron with a wooden handle on one end. Mother would shake this vigorously when she wanted to get Muggs into the house. It made an excellent imitation of thunder, but I suppose it was the most roundabout system for running a household that was ever devised. It took a lot out of mother.

A few months before Muggs died, he got to "seeing things." He would rise slowly from the floor, growling low, and stalk stiff-legged and menacing toward nothing at all. Sometimes the Thing would be just a little to the right or left of a visitor. Once a Fuller Brush salesman got hysterics. Muggs came wandering into the room like Hamlet following his father's ghost. His eyes were fixed on a spot just to the left of the Fuller Brush man, who stood it until Muggs was about three slow, creeping paces from him. Then he shouted. Muggs wavered on past him into the hallway grumbling to himself but the Fuller man went on shouting. I think mother had to throw a pan of cold water on him before he stopped. That was the way she used to stop us boys when we got into fights.

Muggs died quite suddenly one night. Mother wanted to bury him in the family lot under a marble stone with some such inscription as "Flights of angels sing thee to thy rest" but we persuaded her it was against the law. In the end we just put up a smooth board above his grave along a lonely road. On the board I wrote with an indelible pencil "Cave Canem." Mother was quite pleased with the simple classic dignity of the old Latin epitaph.

An essay may be a personal reminiscence, a reflection on a worldly event, a political comment, a eulogy, an exhortation, a declamation, a pronunciamento. As indicated earlier, what distinguishes it, generally, from editorials or columns might be the flow, dignity and artistry of the language when it treats a serious subject and the sparkle, polish and wit displayed when the essayist engages in humor or satire. For a more complete grasp of what an essay is, and what it can be, you might pick up a modern anthology of essays or a collection of essays by George Orwell, E.B. White or E.M. Forster.

REVIEWS

Major newspapers, magazines and television stations have critics who review the arts for their readers and viewers. On a smaller newspaper or television station, a beginning reporter might be called upon to "write a couple of paragraphs" about, say, the country music festival that night at the municipal auditorium.

"But I don't know anything about country music!" the reporter might protest.

"Just go there and act like a reporter. Tell what happened and how the crowd reacted to it," the editor replies.

And so the beginning reporter will cover the performance, writing, in effect, a reportorial review of it.

THE REPORTORIAL REVIEW

Audience reaction usually forms the lead element in a reportorial review. As you read this review, you will discover that that is an effective way to conceal a reviewer's unfamiliarity with the work being reviewed.

Saturday Night at the Opry

A gala cast of country music superstars wowed a crowd of 4,000 at the Municipal Auditorium last night. A packed house of all ages stopped the show all night long to show its appreciation. As the opening bars of songs cued listeners to old and new melodies, number after number was interrupted by applause.

Favorites among the performers were Conway Twitty and his love songs and pretty Barbara Mandrell and her equally sentimental ballads.

With the exception of Willie Nelson, the country music performers bypassed plaid shirts, jeans and polka-dot dresses in favor of sharp suits and designer gowns. The Lee Greenwood and Sylvia segment of the program was notable for its sleek, colorful dress. The audience, consisting of the very young, the very old and the in-between, responded by hurrying down the aisles to take photos of their favorite singers.

The review goes on to describe the songs and the receptions of them by the audience. The final paragraph summed up the concert:

> Most of the performers were well-received, from Charlie McClain to Ricky Skaggs. And most of the fans left, as Steve Wariner noted in his last song, "Walking Down Happy Street."

This review can serve as a prototype of the reportorial review: Open with a paragraph describing the crowd's reaction to the performance. Describe the program and the crowd's reaction to various portions of it. End with a concluding paragraph highlighting the general feeling generated by the performance.

THE STANDARD REVIEW FORMAT

Until you know more about reviewing, you'll feel more secure writing reviews if you have a format to follow. The review format in Figure 14.1 provides you with your review "security blanket." If you were to plot it on the reader-interest plane, the appraisal would form the introductory paragraphs. The intent of the artist and the synopsis of the work form the developing paragraphs. The generating paragraphs are composed of the evidence supporting the appraisal. The climax comes with the restatement of whether or not the artist accomplished the intent. That may be accompanied with a concluding paragraph suggesting whether readers will benefit or not from attending the event—a lingering impression.

But reviews do not readily lend themselves to formats or patterns. Let's look at how critics review works when they *know* their subject matter, when they have prepared themselves to be critics through eduction, reading, and viewing and mastering books, music, cinema and theater. Look at these various types of reviews.

In this review from the *New Yorker*, titled "Supple Song,"* Andrew Porter writes with the assurance of a man who knows his music. His lead:

| Appraisal of the work |
| Intent of the artist |
| Synopsis of the work, performance, exhibit |
| Evidence supporting your appraisal |
| Artist's intent accomplished, not accomplished. Suggestions to the readers |

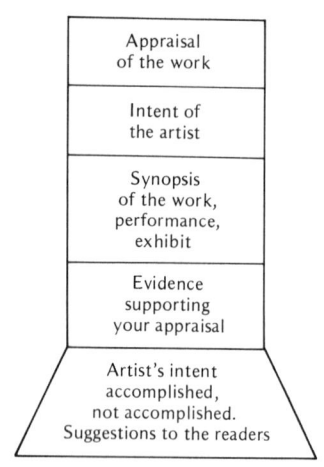

Figure 14.1. Review format.

When I last wrote about "The Pirates of Penzance," after its City Opera revival three years ago, I suggested that a good cast for the piece would be Joan Sutherland, Marilyn Horne, Placido Domingo, and Sherrill Milnes. Or, if the work were to be done in Italian translation, with sung recitatives, Montserrat Caballé, Fiorenza Cossotto, José Carreras, and Piero Cappuccilli. The New York Shakespeare Festival production of "The Pirates," which played this summer in the Delacorte Theatre, in Central Park, used vocal resources more modest and—inevitably in the large open-air, open-sided theatre—relied on amplification to get the voices across. Moreover, Sullivan's music had been rescored—resourcefully—for a stringless combo (dominated by two noisy trumpets), and that, too, was amplified. The music reached its listeners from loudspeakers high above the stage. Nevertheless, admirers of Gilbert and Sullivan, once their ears had adjusted themselves to the sound, could enjoy an attractive, animated, and even in its way stylish account of the opera. Its romance, its charm, and its high spirits were all done justice to.

The paragraphs after the introduction describe Linda Ronstadt, the leading lady, as having an accurate and pretty coloratura for Mabel's waltz song. "Lower down," however, Porter remarks, "she sounded short-breathed. . . ." Rex Smith was a "better actor than one usually sees in the role. Though he did not have the voice for the music—there was little between a husky, sexy murmur and a raw blare when he sang out. . . ."

Porter then praises the "clarity and music alertness" of the performance conducted by William Elliott. All the major figures are dealt with in a phrase or two:

> Patricia Routledge's Ruth was no trombone-voiced virago but a spry, entertaining veteran. Kevin Kline played the pirate king as Douglas Fairbanks might have done. The chorus was dapper.

Porter ends his review with:

> In an age that is serious about "Lucia di Lammermoor" and "Il Trovatore," "The Pirates of Penzance" acquires renewed freshness. The music is good enough to reward vocal prowess of the highest level—and good enough, too, to prove intoxicating even with moderate voices when it is as skillfully and spiritedly performed as it was here. The production reopens on Broadway late this year; I look forward to enjoying it again.

* Reprinted by permission; © 1980 by Andrew Porter. Originally in the *New Yorker*.

Experienced reviewers determine what the artist's purpose is and then make a judgment as to whether the artist has fulfilled that purpose. In so doing, the reviewer assists the audience in understanding the artist's work, whether it is a painting, a musical score, a novel or a drama. How harshly the reviewer criticizes the work depends on whether the artists are amateurs or professionals. A circle theater group in University City would not be expected to attain a level of performance comparable to that of a professional troupe from New York or London.

The best way to learn to write reviews is to study reviewers who are generally considered to be the best in their fields. One of the best cinema critics is the *New Yorker*'s Pauline Kael. Here she's reviewing *48 HRS.* under the title "The Cool and the Dead."

> Walter Hill's action comedy "48 HRS." socks it to the audience. The picture is a roller coaster that hurtles along—"The French Connection," "Dirty Harry," "The Defiant Ones," "In the Heat of the Night," "Butch Cassidy and the Sundance Kid" all put in a compactor, smashed, and pressed into cartoon form. It's "dynamite" entertainment—punches, exploding guns, and two men snarling obscenities at each other.

Kael briefly sketches the plot, which she says has been shaped around Eddie Murphy. Murphy, she says,

> starts his movie career as the beneficiary of [Richard] Pryor's wild flail-about. Fastidious, and with timing so precise that it seems almost surgical, he uses blackness as a pose. It's Pryor's comedy made cool.

The black and white relationship of co-star Nick Nolte and Murphy is dissected, and then Kael says that *48 HRS.* "is excitingly paced; it hooks you at the start and never lets up. But I didn't enjoy it." Most of the time, the director "isn't doing anything special—even the car chases aren't much fun. He does what other action directors have done, but he does it faster, and with tumescent instrumental music blending with city noise and whipping up the audience's emotions."

She ends the review like this:

> Murphy is a whiz of a performer; he has concentration and intensity, and he's so young that there's an engaging spirit in what he's doing. But this picture is plastic paranoia all the way through, and it has handed him a dubious victory. Pryor made white people understand his resentments, and it felt good to have that stuff out in the open. "48 HRS." brings out invented, distorted hostilities, and is being cheered for it, as if it were doing us a service.

Critics will differ with one another. Bill Hagen of Copley News Service opens his review* of the movie *Silkwood* as follows:

> HOLLYWOOD — I don't know with any certainty, no more than do the makers of a movie about her, what really happened to Karen Silkwood, but if there was foul play involved in her death what this movie does is narrow a list of suspects to about, oh, a couple of thousand.

After a synopsis of the movie, he writes:

---

* Reprinted with permission of Copley News Service.

However appealing those attributes, something still goes terribly wrong with *Silkwood*, one of its minor shortcomings being that it's mercilessly dull. And one of the reasons for that, another minor flaw, is that the characters are mercilessly dull, even, or maybe especially, the title character. That the title character is played by Meryl Streep, probably the finest screen actress working, and is still dull perhaps suggests that the fault lies not in the stars but in the writers and the director.

But *The New York Times* reviewer Vincent Canby* writes quite differently about the film:

> . . . Mike Nichols has directed a precisely visualized, highly emotional melodrama that's going to raise a lot of hackles.
>
> Though far from perfect, *Silkwood* may be the most serious work Nichols has yet done in films, and that would include *Who's Afraid of Virginia Woolf?*, *The Graduate* and *Catch-22*. Perhaps for the first time in a popular movie has America's petrochemical-nuclear landscape been dramatized, and with such anger and compassion.
>
> *Silkwood* also offers another stunning performance by Meryl Streep, . . .

Even trained observers see the same things in different ways.

Brendan Gill, under the title of "A Carol to Carroll,"† ties in this theatrical review for the *New Yorker* with Christmas:

> Not all the most welcome presents are to be found under the tree on Christmas morning. An especially delightful one was unwrapped at the Virginia Theatre a couple of days before the twenty-fifth, in the form of an exquisite production of "Alice in Wonderland"—a production that kept the attention of its audience of adults and children joyously engaged from start to finish. Eva Le Gallienne, working in collaboration with Florida Friebus, staged her first version of "Alice" just fifty years ago; successful as it was, I find it hard to believe that it could have been as tenderly heartfelt and as continuously humorous as her latest version of a work that is, at bottom, every bit as odd a manifestation of self-assertive genius as "Finnegans Wake." (Carroll and Joyce, who would have been quick to detest each other, had much in common; their minds were obsessed with puns and parodies, but whereas Joyce was a conscious voluptuary, Carroll appears to have been an unconscious one.)

Gill's lead is longer than most review leads—so long that we cut it off halfway through. But because the *New Yorker* reader is a devoted and peculiar breed and this is a magazine, Gill can get away with it. Gill is also one of the leading theater critics, and that gives him liberties beginners don't have.

Gill lauds this production, noting how Le Gallienne has faithfully followed Carroll in text and tone, and pays similar tribute to set designer John Lee Beatty and costume designer Patricia Zipprodt for adhering faithfully to the drawings of John Tenniel: "How touching they are in their familiarity, and yet how much more beautiful in their new-found colors than in black-and-white." After com-

---

* Review of the film "Silkwood" by Vincent Canby, December, 14, 1983. Copyright 1983 by the New York Times Company. Reprinted by permission.

† Reprinted by permission; © 1982 by Brendan Gill. Originally in the *New Yorker*.

menting on the actors and actresses in one sentence, Gill compliments the musical accompaniment and the lighting. The review ends:

> For all his donnish diffidence, Carroll was a hard man to please; in the case of this "Alice" I imagine his grateful ghost uttering, with a characteristic stammer, frabjous benignities of praise.

As we have seen, most reviewers present in the lead an overall appraisal or assessment of the work being reviewed. If the reviewer has some idea of what the artist intended, that aim or purpose is stated early in the review. Before the review ends, an indication of whether that purpose has been accomplished is given. The initial appraisal of the work is followed by comments, illustrations and examples that serve as evidence for that appraisal, along with a synopsis or description of the scope of the work. In the process, more critical comment and appraisals of various parts of the work are presented, along with the background of the artist and perhaps a comparison of the work with others in the same genre. All reviews end with unmistakable finality. Most have a suggestion for the audience as to the merits of the work and whether it is worth attending or viewing.

SUMMARY

Definitive guidelines for writing commentary are difficult to formulate. Although they are nice to have around when you first start out, once you have some experience, they tend to inhibit creativity. The best advice for writing commentary is this: Collect facts, ideas and thoughts you want to include in your work. Devote time to reviewing them and establishing their importance. Compose an outline with the reader-interest plane in mind. Write the first draft and revise according to the suggestions in this text and in the appendixes. Remember always that there is no such thing as good writing—it's all good rewriting.

EXERCISES

1. Comment on the effectiveness of the following editorial. Rewrite it so that it reflects what a true editorial ought to do.

Awards Program Help to State*

Several state employees and one former employee have received $27,248 in awards for making suggestions that save the state money.

It is estimated the state will save $428,000 as a result of the suggestions rewarded last week. The largest single awards — $5,000 each — went to Mr. William R. Goan, a former employee of the Department of Human Services, and Mr. Wilbert Hogan of the Department of Tourist Development.

Mr. Goan's suggestion that reports going to county offices be mailed together rather than separately is expected to save the state $142,000 annually. Mr. Hogan suggested that certain publications from his department be mailed at bulk rate rather than first class, and that is expected to save $82,000 annually.

The awards ranged down to $25. All represent thoughtful consideration of their jobs by state employees and of how the work can be accomplished more efficiently and at lower cost to the taxpayers.

The savings to be realized from these suggestions are well worth the money paid out in awards. The state should continue the awards program and improve on it whenever possible.

* Reprinted courtesy of *The Tennessean*.

2. Write a letter to the editor of your university newspaper focusing on some aspect of university life that disturbs you or gives you some pause. Use the persuasive format.

3. Write a letter to the editor of your hometown newspaper on some topic of your own choosing. Use the persuasive format.

4. Select one good and one bad example of an editorial, a column, an essay and a review. Paste or clip them to these pages and write a brief paragraph telling why each is good or bad.

5. Read two or three Erma Bombeck and Art Buchwald columns. Then write, in their style, a column based on one of these brief news items:

> The Federal Trade Commission said today that it will crack down this year and require wholesale retractions by businesses who distort or actually lie about their products or services in newspaper, magazine and television commercials.

> Television viewers will be in for some unpleasant surprises in the coming year. TV producers are being pressured by advertisers to insert commercials in much the same way it is now being done in England.
> What this means is that in the middle of a discussion on what to do about Ruth Ann's impending crisis, the doctor may ask her if that aroma of Tastee Freeze Coffee isn't the best thing that's happened to her this morning and then invite her to have a cup. Filled to the brim.

6. Write a review of a movie. Compare it with a critic's review. How does it differ? Why? Are some things about your review superior to the critic's?

7. Select an experience from your life that can be used in a reflective essay. Outline and write the essay.

CHAPTER 15

ADVERTISING
Robert L. Bishop

Advertising is a powerful form of communication that accounts for a good part of the information explosion that has characterized the second half of the 20th century. When the demand for consumer goods and services soared after World War II, the need for persuasive messages targeted to consumers also burgeoned. And new forms of communication, such as television and specialized magazines, provided more outlets for those persuasive messages. Today, advertising fills every mass medium, from newspaper and magazine pages to the radio and television airwaves. In fact, revenue derived from the sale of media space to advertisers is the main source of income for many media. The economic clout of the advertising industry is formidable.

Because advertising penetrates all mass media, advertising copywriters must possess versatile, sophisticated writing skills. A campaign designed to launch a product or to keep the public aware of the qualities of an older product may include newspaper ads, magazine ads, and radio and television commercials. The campaign must work well for all four media, and advertising copywriters must know how to take a product theme and develop it in the style of each medium.

For example, the radio commercial may grab listeners with sound effects that suggest attractive visuals. Background sounds of waves lapping a dock and seagulls flying overhead may lead into a dialogue about fishing. During the course of the dialogue, one of the actors in the commercial may say how much he's enjoying the coffee he's drinking while he's fishing. We can see nothing, but the audio effects are a pleasant frame to his verbal product pitch.

The TV commercial may actually depict the scene and the two men on the dock with their fishing poles. The dialogue will be similiar, but they may not need to say as much about the product. TV allows it to advertise itself. We can *see* the product, the steam from the thermos, the enjoyment on the fishermen's faces.

The newspaper ad may show a still photo of the same two men, with their poles in one hand and a mug in the other. The copy accompanying the photo may contain just a few words, such as "The perfect pick-me-up . . . Advertiser's Coffee."

And in the magazine, the ad may be even more simple and basic: A gleaming

---

Robert Lee Bishop, a professor at the University of Georgia since 1982, has served as reporter for the Shawnee, Okla., *News-Star* and as copy editor for the *Detroit Free Press*. After five years as public relations director for Oklahoma Baptist University, he attended the University of Wisconsin-Madison and earned a Ph.D. in Mass Communications in 1966. From 1965 to 1982 he was a professor at the University of Michigan. Among his publications are *Qilai! The Chinese Communication System* (in press), *Economics, Politics and Information* (1983) and *Public Relations: A Comprehensive Bibliography* (three volumes, 1974–1977).

color photo of a steaming mug of dark, rich coffee. The copy? Just the name of the brand.

In all four, the message is the same: Buy our coffee. But the presentation is adapted to suit different media and their audiences. The writing techniques discussed in the chapters on writing for print and broadcast media are good tools with which to design communication for the creative world of advertising.

The advertising writer has to remember two things: (1) The goal of advertising is to sell goods, and (2) selling occurs as a result of well-written, well-presented persuasive communication, targeted to a receptive audience.

SETTING ADVERTISING OBJECTIVES

The architects of advertising campaigns look closely at the information they have on potential consumers in order to target their message to the group most likely to pay attention to it. They examine the preferences of people in different age groups and different regions of the country to determine the similarities and differences among them. They study consumers' reactions to competitors' products and companies to see what they can learn about the success and failure of their advertising campaigns. Only then do they design the message that will be used to promote their product.

Advertisers must first decide what the purpose of their ad campaign is. Ads can perform many functions, including these listed by Russell Colley in *Defining Advertising Goals for Measuring Advertising Results* (commonly known as DAGMAR):

1. Making people aware of a product's existence.
2. Creating a favorable emotional disposition toward a brand.
3. Planting information about benefits and features.
4. Combatting or offsetting competitive claims.
5. Correcting false impressions or misinformation.
6. Building recognition of a package or trademark.
7. Building a corporate image and favorable attitudes.
8. Building a "reputation platform" for new brands or product lines.
9. Planting a unique selling proposition in the minds of consumers.
10. Developing leads for sales personnel.

As you can see, any of these goals might apply to international diplomacy, political campaigns, or fund raising. In fact, Colley is saying that advertising is one of the most useful tools available to a communicator.

Advertisers, then, must decide what they wish to accomplish. Then they must find out where their potential customers are and what those customers want. Finally, they have to work through ad agencies to see how these two overlapping interests can be profitably enlarged.

COPYWRITER'S QUIZ

Here are some questions that a copywriter might ask clients before starting to work on their advertising messages.

What Do You Want? Is your aim to make an immediate sale, to build a prospect file, or to protest governmental regulation? What good is your product or idea? Is it a convenience food that will make it easier for the working family? Is it a campaign to limit imports on the theory that unfair foreign competition is putting Americans out of work and therefore increasing the national deficit?

The copywriter needs to do some research—to look for anything about the company, industry or economy that might help. He or she should pay particular attention to comparative price and value. Some products sell on price alone, but it is better to emphasize comparative value per dollar spent than price by itself.

What Are Your Customers' Wants? All people have certain needs and desires. A.H. Maslow and others have arranged these into hierarchies, arguing that fundamental needs must be satisfied first, or they become dominant. After basic needs have been met, motives on the next higher level become dominant, and so forth. Finally, when all other motives have been satisfied, humans will continue exploration and activity for their own sake. We try to comprehend our world and to use that understanding to create something of value to ourselves. Figure 15.1 is an approximation of Maslow's hierarchy.

Some products operate at the lowest level—appeals to self-preservation through seat belts, for instance. But the same ad may appeal to affiliation motives by asking the driver to demonstrate love for the family through seeing that everyone buckles up for safety. Generally, advanced societies have conquered basic needs. Most of their citizens do not carry guns or starve to death. Therefore, most advertising works on the higher levels of the pyramid.

Affiliation motives make up the bulk of advertising appeals. Love and sex are very powerful motivators, though they may be mingled with other motives, such as care for the family.

(How would you classify appeals to convenience? To altruism? To novelty and curiosity? If you were advertising a residential development, how many different levels could you appeal to?)

Is Your Product Positioned Correctly? For example, have you been trying to sell a hand cleanser for mechanics in media that appeal to people in retirement homes?

In addition to the usual demographic information, more specific information is needed about potential customers. Where do they buy? Do they patronize

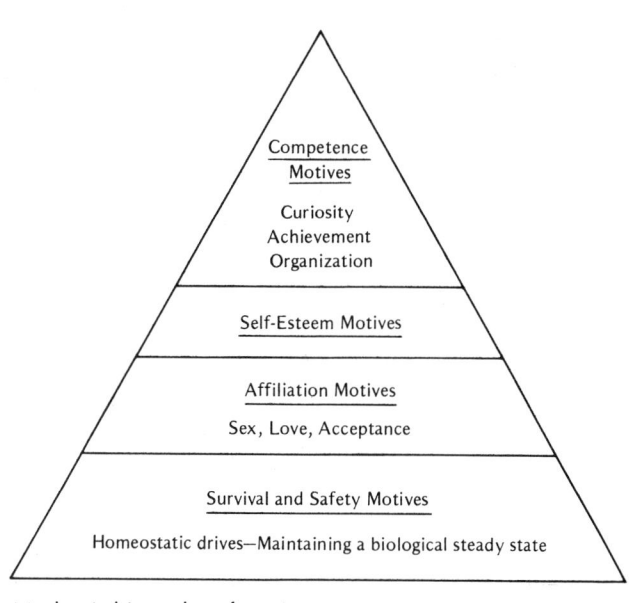

FIGURE 15.1. Maslow's hierarchy of motives.

exclusive shops or convenience stores? When do they shop? Is the product an item that must be replaced every week, such as breakfast cereal? Is it a seasonal item or a once-in-a-lifetime buy?

Who Makes the Purchase Decision?   Many manufacturers overlook the importance of women in purchases considered to be in the male domain, such as automobiles. Even children can exert a strong influence on new car purchases.

How Can the Overlap between Client and Customer Interests Be Increased?   Make a list of reasons why consumers would buy the product. Perhaps the client is marketing winter vacations in Florida; the copywriter could use a line like, "I need it bad!" The grammar is questionable, but the motivation is pretty strong to a public knee-deep in snow.

Perhaps the most important factor is the main advantage of the product—the unique selling point (USP). One USP for Mercedes-Benz is that older Mercedes automobiles have maintained their sales value. Burger King advertises hamburgers made your way, while Wendy's promotes more beef, less bun. Maytag admits that its washing machines are more expensive but maintains that their outstanding repair record is worth the higher initial investment. Some houses are sold because of low-interest financing deals that downplay the increase in interest rates after the first few years of payments. Almost every idea or product has some unique selling point, plus secondary selling points that set the product apart. These may include pride of workmanship, economy of operation, convenient repair service, or outstanding personal attention.

What Creative Strategy Is Best?   Should we use hard sell, soft persuasion, strong identification, some combination? What media should we use? Or should we rely entirely on word of mouth and direct salesmanship?

From this copywriter's quiz must evolve a *written strategy*. This will include the basic psychology of the ad, including the pairing of art and text, plus media placement, scheduling, and so forth.

For example, a Maytag ad's basic theme is reliability. The copy approach for *print* is a testimonial from satisfied users—homemakers with whom Maytag's customers can identify. Graphically, the ads show the product in use in an attractive home setting.

Maytag *television* ads use the same basic theme, though the copy approach is humorous, playing off the predicament of the lonely Maytag repairman. Visually, the approach depicts the repairman far from where the product is being used, waiting in vain in his shop for a call to arms (or wrenches)!

With a written strategy in hand and approval from the client, we are ready to compose the ad. In some cases, visual elements come first, and copy must be subordinated to fit the visuals. In other ads, the situation is reversed. But in every successful ad, all elements must work together. Let's take up copy first.

ELEMENTS OF ADVERTISING COPYWRITING

Headline

There's an old recipe for rabbit stew that begins "First, catch a rabbit." Advertising must first catch a reader, and either the headline or the art will carry most of this burden.

Some headlines are aimed at the general public: "Sail a Tall Ship to a Small Island" attracts romantics to Windjammer Barefoot Cruises. "How to Live Extravagantly for $6.95" appeals to a broad segment who would like to dine at Magic Pan restaurants, "The Extravagance You Can Afford." "Neptune Would Have Dined Here" entices people to the Fish Market Restaurant in Atlanta.

Other headlines act as "screens"—they try to draw only readers who would be in the market for a product; for example, "An Open Letter to Everyone Whose Letters Aren't Getting Opened" was intended to attract direct mailers to an ad for Western Union Electronic Mail.

Subheads

Typographically, subheads lead the reader through the text of the ad. They should emphasize main selling points. A full-page, all-text ad for Dale Carnegie training uses subheads to point out the five different courses.

Chemlawn uses a series of reinforcing subheads for its pest-control service: "No Bugs in Our Guarantee," "Inside, Outside, All Around the House," "48-Hour Bug Alert," and "Free Survey."

Text

The text follows up on the headline and illustration and presents the ad's main message. The American Humane Education Society ran an ad headlined "If you can't decide between a Shepherd, a Setter or a Poodle, get them all." The text read:

> Adopt a mutt at your local humane society and get everything you're looking for, all in one dog. The intelligence of a Poodle and the loyalty of a Lassie. The bark of a Shepherd and the heart of a Saint Bernard. The spots of a Dalmatian, the size of a Schnauzer, and the speed of a Greyhound. A genuine, All-American Mutt has it all.
>
> And your animal shelter has lots of All-American Mutts waiting for you. There are genuine, All-American Alley Kittens, too. Just come to: The Atlanta Humane Society.

There's no rule for how long copy should be. The trend is toward very short copy blocks and strict economy of words. But some clients will prefer long, even technical copy. The previously mentioned Dale Carnegie training courses ad is more than 500 words long and is designed to fill a full magazine page. Maytag runs a regular ad in *Reader's Digest* that is more than half text. And Mercedes-Benz runs ads full of engineering jargon.

Slogans, Logotypes, Signatures

If you come up with a good slogan, use it constantly. "Have you driven a Ford lately?" is the successor to "Quality is Job 1!" and "Ford Has a Better Idea."

Harley Hotels uses a slogan as a headline: "I don't hire people who have to be told to be nice . . . I hire nice people." And who could forget Karl Malden's pitch for American Express traveler's checks: "American Express. Don't leave home without them."

Logotypes are the corporate symbols that must appear in every ad. Sometimes they are called "logos" or "sigs." Something would be missing if an ad for Coca-Cola didn't include the curvy Coca-Cola typeface or the sharp, clean serifs of the Coke typeface. And a Mercedes-Benz ad would look naked without the company logo, which also distinguishes the hood ornament and trunk of the cars.

ANATOMY OF AN AD

The basic physical elements of the ad are the headline, subheads and text (or script), and logo or signature. All work together to present a product with maximum impact. They support the basic *message* elements of an advertisement:

1. Pointing out a need or desire to the consumer
2. Introducing the product as being singularly capable of fulfilling that need or desire
3. Calling for action on the part of the consumer. The call for action can be subtle or direct, but it must be there.

Television commercials have many more visual elements than print media ads. Radio commercials depend entirely on sound—music, special effects, voices—to sell a product. But all address a need or desire, a product's ability to satisfy, and the consumer's need to act to obtain that product. The following ads contain all three of these elements, but they are handled differently, depending on the purpose of the ad and the medium for which each was designed.

Figure 15.2. Reprinted courtesy of the Fairfax Hospital Association CATS Program.

Purity — Milk in the New Yellow Jug — 30-SECOND TV COMMERCIAL

Headline (Frame 1)

[1] Hey, Vernon! Purity has really done it now, buddy!

[2] Purity milk now comes in a new solid yeller jug! So light can't get to the milk...

[3] And you know what light does to the flavor of milk!

Message/solution/logo (Frames 2-4)

[4] See 'ere, Vernon, this solid yeller jug protects 'at fresh Purity taste...know what I mean?

[5] Get Purity's new solid yeller jug!

Call to action (Frame 5)

[6] Then it won't matter how long your frig light stays on...

[7] It does stay on, don't it?

[8] Yeah, it does!

YELLER...IS BETTER!

Purity Dairies, Inc.
360 Murfreesboro Road
Nashville, Tenn. 37210

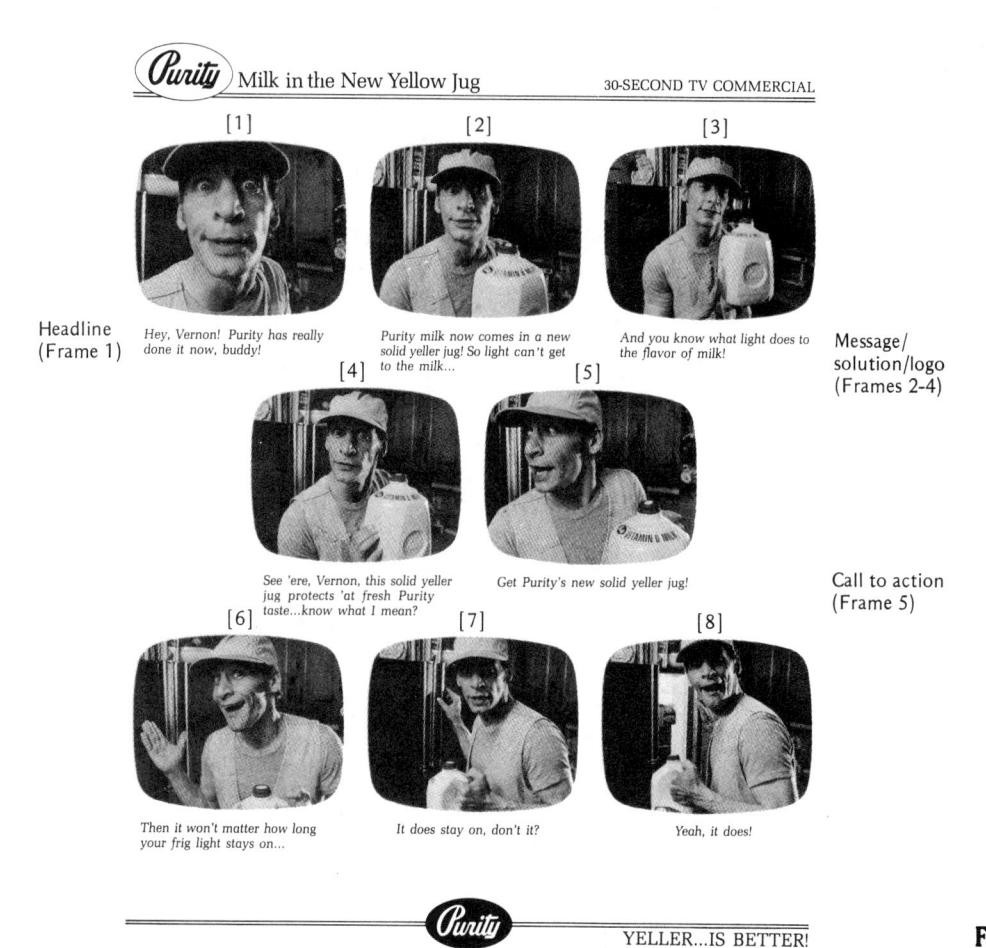

Figure 15.3. Reprinted by permission of Purity Dairies, Inc., Nashville, Tenn.

ADS THAT SOLVE PROBLEMS

Not all problem-solving ads confront issues as serious as alcoholism. Problem-solving ads have been written for power tools, air conditioning and automotive repairs. But the ad produced for the Fairfax (Va.) Hospital Association (Figure 15.2) is a good example of an ad that appeals to affiliation motives and bases its call to action on them.

Purity Dairies uses a character famous in markets even outside Purity's Nashville headquarters to sell milk in a colored container. The character, Ernest P. Worrell (played by actor Jim Varney), always speaks to "Vern," an off-camera character the audience never sees. He makes his pitch directly to Vern, who could be sitting beside you on the couch as you're watching the commercial. This device enables the actor to make a call to action directly to the viewer while appearing to be making it to his buddy, Vern.

The device is effective because it allows the character to grab the viewer's attention directly ("Hey, Vernon! Purity has really done it now, buddy!"), state the solution Purity has found to the problem of milk spoilage, and make a call to action ("Get Purity's new solid yeller jug!"). The commercial is shown in Figure 15.3 in the form of a storyboard, a sequential breakdown of film or tape into segments.

A storyboard is a series of still photos or roughed-in drawings that reflect how the ad should actually be filmed. Commercials are broken into scenes, which

FIGURE 15.4. Reprinted courtesy of Continental Savings Bank, Fairfax, Va.

are sometimes shot as separate miniproductions. A storyboard helps organize the production economically, helps avoid gaps that might otherwise require a return visit to the shooting site, and generally gives all the advantages that preplanning usually brings.

From a storyboard, a shooting script is prepared, complete with descriptions of close-ups, medium and long shots, and type of sound required for each scene, as well as the words the actors will use.

ADS THAT APPEAL TO COMPETENCE

Many ads appeal to the competence of the reader or viewer. They are results-oriented: pragmatic, direct, aggressive. The language (and typeface, in print media) reflects their strong sense of direction.

The ad for Continental Federal Savings Bank (Figure 15.4) contains no less than five calls to action. The art depicts a person taking action. He is seated in front of a chart that shows the beneficial results of action he has taken previously. Each sentence below the photo explains why the bank can help the reader to "get ahead."

ADS THAT APPEAL TO STANDARDS OF EXCELLENCE

Words that connote style, tradition and quality characterize advertisements and commercials that appeal to standards of excellence. Calls to action are implied rather than direct; the assumption is that the reader understands quality and, when presented with the details, will respond to the message without being told to.

Consider the language in the newspaper ad for Woodward & Lothrop (Figure 15.5), an upscale department store in metropolitan Washington, D.C. The words and phrases target a successful consumer with an appreciation for quality and value.

Look at the language:

"Investment Strategy"—This headline suggests an intelligent, thoughtful attitude toward purchases. Contrast that with the message "Don't miss out on our great sale! Bargains galore for the budget-conscious shopper!" What differences in appeal does each suggest?

FIGURE 15.5.   Reprinted courtesy of Woodward & Lothrop, Washington, D.C.

"Wool . . . remains trim and beautiful"—The subtle message here is that the consumer can remain trim and beautiful, too.

"Better Dresses"—The name of the store department in which the suit can be found reinforces the idea of quality.

"Your natural choice"—Soft-sell phrasing rather than an aggressive command to "buy now"; a very subtle call to action.

Likewise, notice how American Telephone & Telegraph (Figure 15.6) conveyed a strong sense of tradition and quality in ads introducing a new product line, computers. The reminder of the Bell tradition is anchored in the "Watson" theme, a thread that runs through a number of advertisements. The Watson ads were created for the purpose of showing that the AT&T technology after divestiture would maintain the level of excellence for which it had been known and to stress that the company would continue to be an innovator. (Watson, of course, was the first person to hear a voice on a telephone: Alexander Graham Bell's.)

The language of excellence appears in the opening sentence (the equivalent

Figure 15.6. Reprinted courtesy of AT&T.

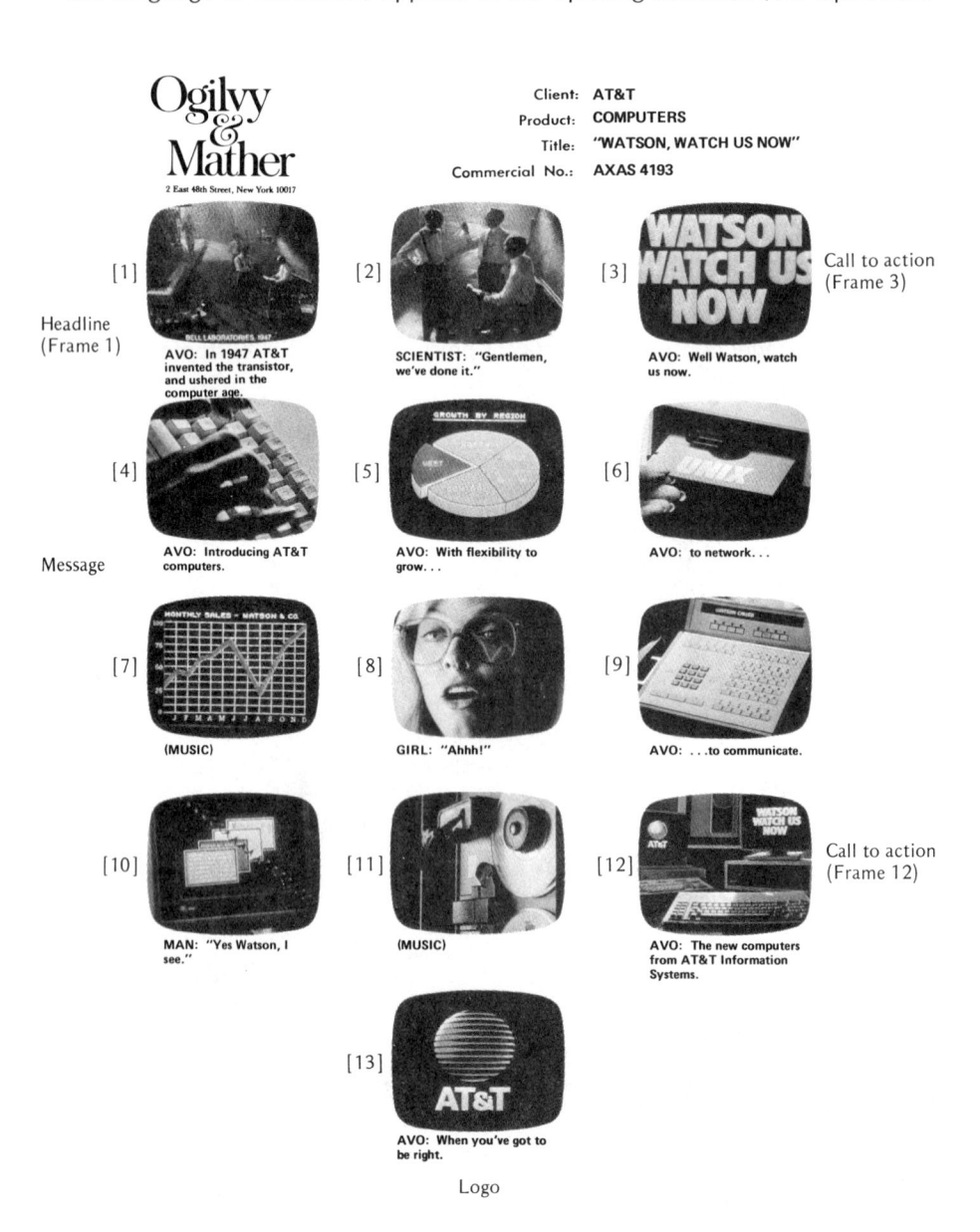

Ogilvy & Mather
2 East 48th Street, New York 10017

Client: AT&T
Product: COMPUTERS
Title: "WATSON, WATCH US NOW"
Commercial No.: AXAS 4193

[1] Headline (Frame 1)
AVO: In 1947 AT&T invented the transistor, and ushered in the computer age.

[2]
SCIENTIST: "Gentlemen, we've done it."

[3] Call to action (Frame 3)
AVO: Well Watson, watch us now.

[4] Message
AVO: Introducing AT&T computers.

[5]
AVO: With flexibility to grow. . .

[6]
AVO: to network. . .

[7]
(MUSIC)

[8]
GIRL: "Ahhh!"

[9]
AVO: . . .to communicate.

[10]
MAN: "Yes Watson, I see."

[11]
(MUSIC)

[12] Call to action (Frame 12)
AVO: The new computers from AT&T Information Systems.

[13]
AVO: When you've got to be right.

Logo

of a headline), with the invention of the transistor, which "ushered in the computer age." This historic communication breakthrough in 1947 is followed in the storyboard by the introduction of AT&T computers. The implication is that this is an event of comparable importance. The statement that these computers have "flexibility to grow" reminds viewers that AT&T, too, has demonstrated a "flexibility to grow." The words chosen, the use of logos and symbols and the thread of tradition that runs through the ad work together to establish an environment of excellence in which the product is presented.

Like the Woodward & Lothrop ad, the AT&T commercial doesn't beat the consumer over the head. Appeals based on standards of performance and excellence—usually to sell to an upscale audience—are more sophisticated, less insistent.

TESTING

Some brilliant and highly successful ads are the intuitive work of one writer. But with millions of dollars at stake, most agencies demand careful evaluation before committing to production and publication costs.

Many agencies have a checklist similar to that of Benton & Bowles, shown in Figure 15.7. Once an ad or series of ads has passed such a review, and after innumerable conferences within the agency and with the client, it may pass on to the testing stage.

CONSUMER RESPONSE

A *consumer panel* consists of a group of present or potential customers, brought together to rate various ad approaches. The panel must be interested in the product and representative of the expected customer profile.

A variation, usually used before the ad campaign is built, is the *focus group*. This is a group of informed consumers who are united for a freewheeling discussion of the product, the company, the circumstances—whatever topic is of importance. Skillfully guided, their ideas can be very useful.

Consumer panels generally work; that is, there is a correlation between their purchase decisions and the client's actual product sales. They do not cost a lot of money or require much time. Carefully chosen panels do represent the marketplace. But there can be difficulties.

For example, the panel may turn out not to be representative. And unless there are about 200 members of the panel, it will be very dangerous to generalize from their responses, especially when you look at subgroups from the panel—women with household incomes of less than $15,000 as compared to women with household incomes of more than $45,000, for instance.

It may be difficult to get the panel to look at elements of the ad separately. Weak copy might be offset by strong graphics, for instance, so you would not be able to determine the effectiveness of the copy itself.

The panel may have very favorable responses to a new refrigerator but no great need to purchase it. So their positive responses will not necessarily translate into purchase decisions.

Sometimes they can be swayed, especially if there is any group pressure or if they feel a subconscious obligation to please the tester. This makes their responses less valid.

Finally, the cumulative effect of ad campaigns will not show up when you test single ads or elements in an ad.

Six questions to ask before you approve an advertisement.

1. Is there a big idea?
Nothing else is so important to the success of an advertisement. A genuine selling idea transcends execution. Before you approve any advertisement, ask yourself if it really has a big idea and if that idea emerges clearly, emphatically, and single-mindedly. Ask yourself: Is it an *important* idea—such as Scope's "medicine breath," the positioning of Pledge furniture polish as a dusting aid, or AMF's "We make weekends."

2. Is there a theme line?
A theme line that presents your selling idea in a memorable set of words can be worth millions of dollars of extra mileage to your advertising. Provocative lines like "When E.F. Hutton talks, people listen," "Please don't squeeze the Charmin," "We really move our tail for you" (Continental Airlines) make it easy for the customer to remember your selling message. Incidentally, when you get a great one, treasure it and use it prominently in every print ad and television commercial you run.

3. Is it relevant?
If your advertising is remembered but your product forgotten, you might as well run "compliments of a friend." Jokes that steal attention from the selling idea, inappropriate entertainment devices, celebrities who have no logical connection with your product, and other irrelevancies can be devastating. Look for relevance in every advertising execution.

4. Is it hackneyed?
Is the advertisement fresh, innovative, and original or is it merely a pale carbon copy of somebody *else's* advertising? Too much advertising is look-alike, sound-alike advertising. These advertisements are often costly failures. Don't run the risk of being mistaken for your competitor. Demand an execution that is all your own.

5. Does it demonstrate?
Nothing works harder or sells better than a demonstration of your product's superiority, especially in television. Look for every opportunity to demonstrate. If you can't demonstrate, at least show the product in use. Demonstrations—such as the simple exposition of how the Trac II razor works or the coating action of Pepto-Bismol—are convincing ways to sell.

6. Is it believable?
Does the advertising overpromise? Does the selling idea sound a false note? An advertisement can be totally truthful, yet sound unbelievable. Better to underpromise and be believable than to overpromise and lose credibility.

We know that great advertising is not made by rules nor created by guidelines. It comes from creative people. However, we also know from experience that most successful advertising has certain readily identifiable and wholly predictable qualities. We have listed six. There are others. We would like nothing better than to show you some of the advertising that illustrates these points.

Benton & Bowles
New York, Chicago, Los Angeles, and other major cities worldwide.
It's not creative unless it sells.

Figure 15.7. © Benton & Bowles, Inc., 1980. Reprinted, by permission, from Benton & Bowles, Inc.

Theater Testing. For television commercials, respondents are brought into a theater, given a pretest attitude scale on which to rate the product, shown the commercial and given a posttest. The audience may be given buttons to push to register reactions to various parts of the commercial or film. Sometimes their bodies are wired to test their galvanic reponses, which presumably are more accurate than verbal answers.

Readership Studies. For print ads, readership studies are conducted by outside companies. Readers of a publication are asked about each element of the ad or campaign under study.

Motivational Research. Motivational research attempts to explore the subconscious reasons for purchase. It is sometimes spectacularly successful, but the results seem to depend more on the insight of the interviewer than on his or her method.

SUMMARY

Advertising copywriting presents great challenges (and sometimes great frustrations) to people in the profession. It takes real genius to attract the attention of consumers, describe the range of benefits offered by a product and motivate consumers to action with a minimum of words. And if the ad message is rejected by either the client or a testing panel, it's back to the drawing board for the copywriter. It's not entirely different from being a reporter whose editor asks for a rewrite, but because the preferences of clients and consumers are far more fickle and less connected to factual matter than those of journalists, the advertising copywriter may have to take a number of stabs at the project before satisfying self, client and customer.

The key principle the copywriter must remember is that he or she is using persuasive communication to sell a product. The message crafted must be both brief and descriptive. The language employed must be appropriate for the product, the medium in which the ad is presented and the audience to which it is presented. Most important, it must accomplish three things:

1. Point out a need or desire to the consumer.
2. State that the product is singularly capable of fulfilling that need or desire.
3. Call for action on the part of the consumer.

The language used for each of these three elements should be appropriate to the type of appeal made by the ad. This will help ads survive testing by potential consumers, who will quickly reject an ad if the appeal doesn't fit with their attitudes toward or beliefs about the product.

EXERCISES

1. Outline an advertising campaign for selling each of the three types of houses listed. Be sure to state your objectives, your appeals and the type of call to action you would use (mild or aggressive). Then write a prototype ad for each for a newspaper real estate section.

   a. Single-family, ranch-style suburban homes, selling for $85,000 and available on easy credit terms

b. Condominiums, specializing in single adults

c. A retirement village with heavy security, restricted to people above the age of 55

2. Compare real newspaper ads for each type of housing in Exercise 1 with the ones you've written. Be sure to compare the headlines, messages or solutions, calls to action and length of text. Which are better? Why?

   a.

   b.

   c.

3. Write an ad for the Ford Motor Co., stressing the reliability of the Ford Escort. The company gives you the following information:

Over five years or 50,000 miles, the Escort requires only 20 different maintenance operations. The Toyota Tercel requires 37, the Nissan Sentra 54 and the Honda Accord 58.

The Escort gets an estimated 37 mpg in town, 56 mpg on the highway.

A consumer survey indicates that Ford makes the best-built American cars. The survey measured reported problems during the first three months of ownership of 1983 cars designed and built in the United States.

Participating Ford dealers stand behind their repair and maintenance work with a written free Lifetime Service Guarantee.

The company's slogan is "Have you driven a Ford . . . lately?"

4. Write a paragraph comparing a current advertisement with one written for the same type of product 10 years ago. Be sure to evaluate all the basic elements for each ad. According to the BBDO advertising agency, today's ads should be better. Is the one you chose better than its earlier counterpart?

5. Clip an advertisement from a magazine or newspaper and paste or clip it at the left below. To the right of it, analyze the appeals of the advertisement. Determine what needs and wants in Maslow's hierarchy (Figure 15.1) are targeted by the advertisement.

CHAPTER 16

PUBLIC RELATIONS AND PROMOTION WRITING

Robert L. Bishop

Public relations is an occupation that has become increasingly attractive to journalism and communication majors. Public relations encompasses all professions and organizations. The business of making news about products and ideas and seeing that it is communicated to the public has become a major American industry.

Public relations is persuasive communication. Its objective is to serve the best interests of an organization by informing the public of that organization's products, activities and ideals in such a way that they are newsworthy. Public relations targets may be the general public, special segments of that public or what are known as "internal" publics: groups within the organization or the organization's industry or interest area.

Public relations practitioners may communicate directly with the audience through oral, written, audio or audiovisual messages they prepare themselves, or they may work with representatives of the media to communicate their message.

Public relations professionals help to supply much of the news that is aired on radio and television newscasts and printed in newspapers and magazines. Their major role is to help reporters and editors learn about specialized information. It would be impossible for most reporters and editors to keep up with the developments in all the political, medical, scientific, entertainment and industrial sectors of today's world. By supplying information about those sectors and answering journalists' questions about activities in those sectors, public relations practitioners make a major contribution to the media consumer's understanding of the world in which he or she lives.

Writing for public relations has much in common with writing directly for the mass media. The differences stem from the degree to which persuasive communication is the goal of public relations. A public relations message may make a simple statement—such as disclosing a company's quarterly earnings or a new movie's performance at the box office—but it may also communicate a point of view.

One of the more famous examples of a persuasive public relations campaign was mounted during the Tylenol crisis of 1982. Although Johnson & Johnson, the manufacturer of Tylenol, was in no way responsible for the deaths of people who had used its product, until the company's innocence had been clearly established it had to conduct an aggressive, expensive public relations campaign that demonstrated that Johnson & Johnson was a professional, completely responsible manufacturer of over-the-counter drugs. The company made every attempt to assure the American public that its products were made with quality, were safe and were produced by a firm with years of professional experience behind it. Theirs was *persuasive* communication that was based on facts.

EXTERNAL PUBLIC RELATIONS

Public relations professionals have many tools with which to communicate messages to the public. But before they choose which ones would be most effective, they must determine precisely who their audience is, says Carole Howard, vice president–public relations and communications policy, Reader's Digest Association Inc. Only then can decisions be made about how best to reach that audience.

It's critically important, too, that public relations practitioners understand what constitutes *news*. They must share the same news values as members of the press in order to be able to interest the press in covering news about their organization. A PR department with a poor conception of news value will have very little credibility with the press, whose attention it wants to attract.

Consequently, public relations professionals have to present their information in such a way that the press will perceive it as newsworthy. They must avoid "hard-sell" techniques, opting instead for being a reliable source of information that will help a writer do a better job on an assignment. A spirit of cooperation, rather than one of pressure, will advance a public relations department's cause more rapidly.

TOOLS

Whether Johnson & Johnson is trying to handle a crisis or to introduce a new product, its public relations staff relies on the same tools and techniques as other corporations, large and small. Certainly, a corporate giant will employ more expensive technology (such as simultaneous, multicity press conferences that hundreds of journalists will attend) than a small company that is interested mainly in attracting the attention of the local newspaper's business writer. But public relations has a set of tried-and-true communication tools that are used in every organization, regardless of size:

- ☐ News releases
- ☐ Speeches and public statements
- ☐ Media kits
- ☐ Annual reports
- ☐ Brochures
- ☐ Feature articles
- ☐ Public service announcements

☐ Novelty items, such as T-shirts, pens and other accessories carrying the organization's logo

All these public relations tools, used in groups or individually, have the potential to generate publicity, to inform and to persuade—the goals of public relations. Let's look at these tools more closely.

News Releases. The most-used instrument of public relations communication is the news (or press) release. Usually written on a company's letterhead, it is used for a variety of purposes: to announce new products, describe personnel changes, disclose company earnings, preview upcoming events sponsored by the group—whatever information an organization wants to get out into the media. News releases are often the stimuli for reporters' stories. They use them to get started, to find interview prospects and to get leads for ferreting out additional information.

News releases are written in the inverted-pyramid style, with a news lead, fleshed out by detailed paragraphs. Releases should also contain certain key features:

☐ A headline
☐ A release date or other indication of when the information is to be released (for example, "For release Aug. 24, 1986" or "For Immediate Release")
☐ A contact and that person's phone number
☐ An address

Many public relations professionals strive to keep releases to one page to make them easily scannable for reporters and editors who have many other releases to scan and evaluate each day. But that's not always possible. Some complex announcements require more space to inform the journalists who will be receiving the information.

The Warner Bros. release announcing a record-setting box-office gross for actor-director Clint Eastwood (Figure 16.1) is typical.

The Gannett Co. news release disclosing its 1985 second-quarter earnings (Figure 16.2) is a good tool for business writers. Like most such business releases, it offers journalists comparative statistics and recent corporate events as background for the news of the day. Although this release lacks a headline, it contains an attention-getter of equal value, a dateline—Washington, D.C.

Note that a home phone number is given for the contact person named at the bottom of this release. This is intended to make follow-up easy for reporters, whose workday is often quite different from that of people involved in public relations.

News releases are distributed by the thousands every day in the United States. There is even a wire service, PR Newswire, that moves nothing but copies of news releases. PR Newswire takes releases it receives, keys them into its system and moves them electronically to printers that print them out for subscribers. Figure 16.3 is one such example, announcing the appointment of a new executive by a New England company.

Because news releases are churned out so regularly, public relations writers must go to special lengths to make theirs stand out. Here is a checklist for writers who prepare them:

☐ Have I written a clear headline and a compelling lead?
☐ Has my choice of words been interesting without being overly dramatic? Have I been careful not to overreach?

NEWS from WARNER BROS.

FOR IMMEDIATE RELEASE

TEN DAY GROSS OF $21.5-MILLION ON "PALE RIDER"
SETS NEW RECORD FOR ITS DIRECTOR/STAR CLINT EASTWOOD

"Pale Rider," Clint Eastwood's first western in nine years, has struck a mother lode of box-office gold in its initial ten days, and set a new ten-day box-office record for its star and director, according to D. Barry Reardon, President of Warner Bros. Distribution.

The 10-day U.S. and Canadian gross, according to Reardon, now stands at a sensational $21,553,618 for 1,710 theatres, a figure which eclipses the previous 10-day figure for an Eastwood picture held by his Summer 1984 police-action drama "Tightrope," which brought in $20,909,060. The new Eastwood western also broke the first full week record established by his Christmas 1983 film "Sudden Impact," which grossed $13.7-million in its initial week of release, while "Pale Rider" took in $14.5 in its first seven days.

Eastwood stars in the Malpaso Production for Warner Bros. Michael Moriarty, Carrie Snodgress, Sydney Penny and Chris Penn also star in the picture; with Richard Kiel, Richard Dysart, John Russell, Doug McGrath, Charles Hallahan, Marvin McIntyre and Allen Keller co-starring. Written by Michael Butler and Dennis Shryak, it was produced and directed by Eastwood, with Fritz Manes serving as executive producer and David Valdez as associate producer. The music was by Lennie Niehaus.

070885ECdb   -wb-

Motion Picture News Dept., Warner Bros. Inc. / 4000 Warner Blvd., Burbank, CA 91522 (818) 954-6290 • 954-6217 / Cable: Warbros
A Warner Communications Company

FIGURE 16.1. Reprinted courtesy of Warner Bros.

- ☐ Have I got all the mileage out of the information that I could have? For example, have I done enough homework to interpret the information in every interesting way it deserves? Have I provided background and comparative information as well?
- ☐ Is the release authoritative? Does it need a quote or a statement from an expert?
- ☐ Have I made it easy for recipients of the release to contact me for more information? What kinds of calls from them can I anticipate? Could I add any information to the release now that would make it unnecessary for them to make that call?
- ☐ Have I double-checked facts and figures to make certain there are no errors in what I've said?
- ☐ Is the release tightly written? Can I trim it down?
- ☐ Is it timely? Have I presented today's news in a way that will make reporters think about the future and perhaps come back to me for more information?

> **News For Release**
>
> GANNETT
> USA TODAY
>
> FOR IMMEDIATE RELEASE   Wednesday, July 17, 1985
>
> WASHINGTON, D.C. -- Gannett Co. Inc., today reported a 20 percent increase in net earnings for the second quarter of 1985, marking the 71st consecutive quarter of earnings gains since the company went public in 1967.
>
> Chairman Allen H. Neuharth said, "Gannett's record earnings reflect sustained strength in the company, particularly in the newspaper division. USA TODAY continued its strong revenue gains."
>
> For the second quarter, Gannett's net income increased by 20 percent to $71,803,000, up from $59,685,000. Earnings per share were 90 cents, up from 75 cents a year ago. Operating revenue increased to $556,928,000, up 13 percent from $491,682,000.
>
> For the first half of 1985, Gannett's income increased 20 percent to $113,131,000, up from $94,522,000. Earnings per share were $1.41, up from $1.18 a year ago. Operating revenue increased to $1,039,616,000, up 13 percent from $916,886,000.
>
> For the second quarter, newspaper lineage increased by 6 percent, broadcast revenues improved over last year by 17 percent and outdoor advertising revenues increased 4 percent.
>
> Advertising revenues at USA TODAY increased 106 percent in the first half of 1985 compared to the first half of 1984. The three year old national newspaper averaged 12.5 pages of paid advertising daily, compared to 6.8 pages during the same period in 1984.
>
> "The trends at USA TODAY are very encouraging," Neuharth said in a letter to shareholders.
>
> On July 1, Gannett completed its purchase of the Des Moines Register, The Jackson (Tenn.) Sun, and four Iowa weekly newspapers. Gannett also purchased a minority interest in the Minneapolis-based Cowles Media Co.
>
> In the second quarter, Gannett announced plans to renovate Family Weekly, the weekend magazine for newspapers with 13 million circulation. The plans include expanded use of color, increased news and features and a redesign, and changing the name to USA WEEKEND.
>
> Gannett is a nationwide information company that publishes 86 daily newspapers, including USA TODAY, 38 non-daily newspapers and Family Weekly magazine; operates six television and 14 radio stations and the largest outdoor advertising company in North America; as well as marketing, news, television, production, research, satellite information systems and a national group of commercial printing facilities. Gannett has operations in 36 states, Guam, the Virgin Islands and Canada.
>
>   #   #   #
>
> **For More Information:**   Charles L. Overby, Vice President/Communications
> Gannett Co., Inc., P.O. Box 7858, Washington, DC 20044
> Office:(703) 276-5960 Home:(703) 276-5959, (703) 425-7658

FIGURE 16.2. Reprinted with permission of Gannett Company Inc.

Going over this checklist until you know it by heart will help you to produce public relations messages that will establish you and your organization as reliable sources of information.

Speeches and Statements. Important events in the life of a corporation, non-profit organization or neighborhood civic association often call for speeches and public statements to be made by an official of the company or group. These persons also are often asked to speak at dinners, luncheons and conventions. Because they represent something larger than themselves—the organization to which they belong—their speech or public statement must strengthen and enrich the relationship of their organization and the audience.

Some executives are very thoughtful about the craft of speech writing. They will spend time with the writer, outlining the occasion, the problem and their own philosophy or feelings. Others simply order up a 20-minute speech for Friday. If you are unfortunate enough to hook up with someone like that, you must do

FIGURE 16.3. Reprinted courtesy of P.R. Newswire.

```
• NE NY NJ BU BL PP WA CC CE
  NE2     /FROM PR NEWSWIRE BOSTON 617-482-5355 OR NYC 212-832-9400/
  TO BUSINESS DESK %

       SIGNAL CAPITAL NAMES SEYMOUR SMITH SENIOR VICE PRESIDENT AND CFO

       HAMPTON, N.H., JULY 15 /PRNEWSWIRE/ -- SIGNAL CAPITAL CORP., THE
  FINANCIAL SERVICES SUBSIDIARY OF THE SIGNAL COS. INC. (NYSE: SGN),
  HAS APPOINTED SEYMOUR K. SMITH TO THE NEW POSITION OF SENIOR VICE
  PRESIDENT AND CHIEF FINANCIAL OFFICER, THE COMPANY ANNOUNCED TODAY.
       SMITH JOINS SIGNAL CAPITAL FOLLOWING 15 YEARS WITH CONNECTICUT
  BANK AND TRUST CO. OF HARTFORD, CONN., WHERE HE MOST RECENTLY SERVED
  AS EXECUTIVE VICE PRESIDENT AND TREASURER.  HE HELD THAT POSITION FOR
  FIVE YEARS.
       A NATIVE OF CONNECTICUT, SMITH ATTENDED LOOMIS SCHOOL IN WINDSOR,
  CONN., AND HAMILTON COLLEGE.  HE WAS IN THE U.S. NAVY FROM 1963 TO
  1968, SERVING AS A FLIGHT OFFICER AND RISING TO THE RANK OF
  LIEUTENANT.
       SMITH AND HIS WIFE, TIA, HAVE RELOCATED TO BOSTON.
       SIGNAL CAPITAL, WITH A LOAN PORTFOLIO THAT EXCEEDS $2 BILLION,
  PROVIDES PROJECT FINANCING, SECURED LENDING AND OPERATING LEASES.  IT
  FINANCES SIGNAL ENVIRONMENTAL SYSTEMS REFUSE-TO-ENERGY FACILITIES,
  OTHER SIGNAL PLANTS AND A WIDE RANGE OF EQUIPMENT, INCLUDING
  COMPUTERS, WORD PROCESSORS AND AIRCRAFT.
       THE SIGNAL COS. INC., WITH HEADQUARTERS IN LA JOLLA, CALIF., IS A
  HIGH TECHNOLOGY AND ENGINEERING COMPANY OPERATING WORLDWIDE.  IT
  SERVES THE AEROSPACE, ELECTRONICS, ENERGY AND AUTOMOTIVE INDUSTRIES,
  AMONG OTHERS, WITH SOPHISTICATED TECHNOLOGY AND HIGH QUALITY
  PRODUCTS.  SIGNAL HAD 1984 SALES OF $6 BILLION, AND THE COMPANY
  EMPLOYS APPROXIMATELY 54,000 PEOPLE.
       -0-              7/15/85
       /CONTACT:  NORMAN R. RITTER OF SIGNAL COS., 603-926-5911/
       -NE2-
```

a lot of research on your own. Ask, What is the occasion? Why has the executive been asked to speak? What does the audience really expect from him or her?

Find out as much as you can about your speaker. Is he or she a dry reader? Does he or she ad-lib brilliantly or awkwardly? Does the speaker freeze in front of an audience or warm to the occasion?

Most important, you need to determine what company or organizational purposes may be served by the speech. A garden club does not want to hear about the company's efforts to dispose of nuclear waste unless you can tie it to local environmental concerns, in which case you'll have an interested audience and, more than likely, media coverage.

Should you spell out the conclusions you want the audience to draw? Research indicates that it is wise to be explicit. However, if the issue is clear and the audience is *not* sympathetic, make your arguments first and then present your conclusions—stating the conclusion too early may make the audience tune out.

On the other hand, if the message or the issue is likely to be confusing, it's best to state your conclusion at the beginning of the message, then interpret it as you move through your speech.

By all means, find out who has spoken to the group recently and on what topics. This is crucial if you are to prepare a speech as part of a panel or continuing seminar. All speech writers have horror stories of opening with the same story that the last speaker told—and both speakers claimed it happened to their grandmother!

After you have researched the topic of the speech, choose *one* main point that you want to get across, plus two subordinate points. (George McGovern, the 1972 Democratic presidential candidate, said he had always thought it was possible to educate the public on three issues during one campaign. After 1972, he lowered his estimate to one issue!) Then relate your ideas to the audience's interests. For example, higher productivity isn't of much interest to a labor union unless productivity means job security or a higher income.

Now you can begin to build an outline. Build up layers, with each fact or each proposition immediately followed by illustrations and anecdotes.

Decide what action, attitude or impression you want the audience to carry away, and work that into your conclusion.

Remember to state every key point two or three times, but always in a different way with a fresh slant. Audiences hear very little of what most speakers have to say. One psychology professor tested that proposition by firing off a gun at random points throughout the semester. Students then wrote down what they had been thinking about when the gun went off. It turned out that they were thinking about the lecture only 20 percent of the time!

So don't be afraid to simplify issues and hammer them home over and over. Just be sure to be entertaining while you are being informative.

When the speech is completely outlined, work on the opening. It is the most crucial part of the speech. If the speaker's opening remarks fail to establish a rapport with the audience and to convince listeners that he or she has something important to say, the audience is likely to go blank for the rest of the hour.

We reprint here in its entirety a statement by Robert J. Casale, executive vice president of AT&T Information Systems.* Casale gave this brief talk to the press immediately after AT&T's chairman announced that the company was getting into the personal computer business. Casale opened with a short reference to the information he knew the audience had already heard, then launched into a discussion of AT&T's "proud heritage" in voice communications, which included, according to Casale, far-seeing marketing strategies that moved the company toward this new expansion.

Casale's main objective was to present the innovation in the context of the company's past technological strengths. He also made a point to use the company's slogan developed specifically for the product launch: "Watson, watch us now!" The slogan would soon appear in ads and other promotional materials.

You've heard us describe our newest product introductions. We feel we're going to have strong success in this market. Let me tell you why—present our credentials, so to speak.	Opening is upbeat, builds on established rapport.
AT&T Information Systems springs from a proud heritage in voice communications systems. It's our traditional strength. Today, we offer an outstanding voice communications product line. Our systems are highly interactive, open-ended, "growable" and, of course, communications-based.	Picks up historical thread of quality right away.
We're leading the way in providing a true integration of voice and data communications. And we will continue to offer systems with strong price-performance capabilities.	
In entering the office automation market—the computer business—we're building on that traditional	Forward-looking innovations build on strong innovations of past.

---

* Reprinted courtesy of AT&T.

strength. Our market strategy emphasizes compatibility, system integration and an open architecture—all characteristics of a communications-based approach.

> *After building case for quality, speaker underlines unique business position.*

That puts us in a unique position. We're the only information management company offering both voice-based and data-based solutions under the same logo.

> *Returns to historical precedents.*

This is not a new market strategy for us. It's one we began to develop nearly 10 years ago, based on what we saw as emerging market opportunities. We were limited by regulation then, but we were planning for the future. We knew where we wanted to be today—and tomorrow.

The potential now widely recognized in this market supports our assessment. Price-performance improvements in silicon-based processing and storage have created opportunities for productivity gains that were only dreamed of 10 years ago. Information movement and management is now a $65-billion market—and will reach $185 billion by 1988.

> *"Hit 'em with the numbers to prove point!"*

The largest part of that market—75 percent—is in data products. And it's growing at between 30 and 35 percent per year, compounded. The voice portion, on the other hand, is growing at only 9 percent per year.

Since it makes good business sense to follow the opportunity, we've selected those markets offering the highest growth potential for us. And with our new market entries, we're doubling the size of that target market.

> *Spells out bold sales initiatives.*

We expect that our new computer offerings will quickly attract a broad base of customers. And we're going to make it as easy as we can for them to do business with us.

> *Backs up sales initiatives with numbers as proof.*

The people in our 150 branch sales offices have helped us establish a deep market presence over the last 18 months. And all 6,000 sales and technical support people—and 27,000 service technicians—are ready and willing to help our customers put these new products to work in their businesses.

And . . . we're also entering new distribution channels—Sears, Microage, Compushop, Amerisource, Genra. By 1985, we'll have some 900 retail outlets.

We're setting new standards in bringing products to the marketplace. This announcement is arguably the largest and broadest in our industry's history. But we had to go a long way to beat the second largest announcement—our own, only three months ago. In fact, in less than three months, we have introduced an entirely new, robust product set, with offerings in every area of our information systems architecture.

> *Again picks up historical precedents, proven track record.*

We've shown our ability to compete successfully in business automation. We've demonstrated our expertise at integrating voice-based systems. We offer high system functionality at competitive prices. Our pricing options are numerous and flexible. And in service support, we've set the standards which others must now try to follow.

But the strongest evidence of our competitive strength is our people. We have an enthusiastic and professional sales force, which has been rated among the top three in the world.

Again uses numbers to quantify quality.

And it's no accident. As we developed our market strategy in the mid-1970s, we began to seek the sales and technical skills to match our requirements. Those requirements included data processing and data communications expertise right from the start.

As a result, we recruited some 20 percent of our present force from outside our company—and we went after the best the industry had to offer. The 80 percent who came from within the company were hand-picked for their new roles, and they, like their ''outside'' colleagues, have been through rigorous certification and training programs.

Our sales force has attended internally offered courses ranging from introductory BASIC to advanced systems programming. In addition, we send many of our people to Cambridge training courses.

Our technical consultants all complete 12 to 18 months of coursework before they meet our high qualification standards. A high percentage of these people came to us with technical degrees and data processing experience, which we enhanced with both training and field experience.

And we continue to add new courses to our internal training curriculum. For example, we've already trained more than 75 percent of our sales force on the products we announced today.

Expands on growth theme . . .

We've provided several layers of product support for our sales force. For example, specialized expertise is available in our Systems Marketing Centers. There are experts there on local area networking, applications processors, the 3B line, and other complex products—and I don't use the term *experts* lightly. And there is a highly skilled special sales support team, a SWAT team, so to speak, at every area headquarters in the country. These people are not just trained in data processing; they're from the industry—software specialists, computer specialists, UNIX specialists.

and discusses means to support it.

In addition, we've developed strong customer-support programs. We have classes tailored for senior executives, for technical managers, for administrative managers and for programmers. We'll be able to help our customers with everything from a review of industry trends and system integration strategies to advanced C-language programming.

So that's a capsule review of our credentials for entering this market. But what do our customers—the people with all the votes—say about our chances for success? Well, so far they've expressed their opinions by helping our salespeople to exceed our expectations across the board.

Refers to rapport established with other publics.

More references to good track record.	Allow me to share the results of some of our most recent announcements. We've already sold more Dimension System 85s than we had anticipated, even despite limited availability. And we've sold three times our initial projections for the Dimension System 75 through May. And the demand for all models of 3B processors has been phenomenal, even though they were initially offered primarily through OEMs and value-added resellers. We anticipate even stronger performance for the 3B line with the announcement of general availability. Finally, our trends on productivity are significant enough to point out. We have doubled the dollars generated per AE over this time last year — we expect to do that again next year — while at the same time we have reduced support costs as much as 30 percent. We are committed to further success.
Begins conclusion with eye toward the future—again picks up theme of unique qualifications.	Where does this put us? I firmly believe we have an AT&T exclusive.
	We're the only company to offer such a complete product line under one logo. We're the only company to announce such depth so quickly. We offer the richest integration of voice-based applications. And we have linked the power of UNIX to an open architecture, which promises an almost unlimited vista for business automation advances.
Rest of speech is testimonial, display of confidence, invitation for continued interest.	We have outstanding strength and leadership in microelectronics, photonics and systems software. We offer unparalleled service-support capability. *Forbes* magazine rates our manufacturing organization among the top 10 in the world.
	We have an unquestioned financial stability and a corporate commitment that has transcended the legal and regulatory issues we faced for so long.
	We have the sales force, the technology, the service support and the commitment.
	WE HAVE IT ALL!
	We have linked the power of UNIX to an open architecture. Today's announcement is only one point on a continuum. We're committed to being the leading provider and the leading integrator of business automation systems. You'll be hearing from us again soon. You can bet on it.
	The first words ever transmitted by telephone were from Alexander Graham Bell to his associate, Mr. Watson. They were "Mr. Watson, come here, I want you." This afternoon we communicate with words equally prophetic: "Watson, watch us now!"

Casale's statement is a good model for speeches for four reasons:

1. It contains simple sentences and paragraphs. They are short without being terse. The speech is easy for the listener to follow because it is well-integrated and faithful to several key themes.
2. He uses facts to impress.

3. He builds a list of past accomplishments and future plans with authoritative language. Notice his words: "The potential now wisely recognized in this market supports our assessment." "With our new market entries, we're doubling the size of that target market." "We're setting new standards in bringing products to the marketplace." "In less than three months, we have introduced an entirely new, robust product set, with offerings in every area of our information systems architecture." "We have an enthusiastic and professional sales force, which has been rated among the top three in the world."
4. He closes with an invitation to keep an eye on his company: "You'll be hearing from us again soon. You can bet on it." A good speech leaves an audience thinking about what the speaker said and raises their level of interest in the speaker and the organization he or she represents. Casale's fits the bill.

Media Kits. Public relations writers keep very busy producing media kits, comprehensive packages of information made available to the press upon request. Many organizations have on hand "generic" media kits that contain standard, unchanging information about the organization, its goals, its history and accomplishments, its staff and headquarters, etc. Reporters use these for background when they're working on a story.

The generic media kit will be added to when a special event is planned. For example, when AT&T announced its new line of computers, reporters attending the press conference were able to pick up a media kit packed with news releases, detailed descriptions of the products, a schedule of events for the announcement period, copies of biographies of senior executives involved in the product launch and copies of their speeches. A media kit can also be sent to a reporter who was unable to get to the press conference, assuring that the company doesn't lose an opportunity to get coverage just because the reporter couldn't be present.

An agenda, such as the one shown in Figure 16.4, helps reporters plan which parts of a large-scale event they wish to cover. Not every reporter attending AT&T's press conference was interested in every single aspect of the announcement agenda. For example, reporters who cover technology probably weren't as interested in the marketing aspects of the new computers as were financial writers. A published agenda enables them to pick and choose. Some events were repeated for the convenience of the press.

Annual Reports. A company or organization's annual report is a very important document. It usually contains three main pieces of information:

1. A statement from the chief operating officer
2. The earnings statement of the company
3. One or more articles about the organization's activities during the past year and plans for the following year. Sometimes, this includes profiles of employees who work in different areas of the organization.

Producing the annual report is one of a public relations department's biggest responsibilities. The annual report is like a yearly biography of an organization; it's the first thing stockholders and people outside the company look at to try to get an understanding of the organization's goals and operating style.

Writing copy for an annual report is a big challenge. Usually, the content has to be cleared by a tier of executives before it goes off to the typesetter. Annual reports of large companies look like glossy, slick magazines. They are designed with sophistication and are very expensive to produce.

ANNOUNCEMENT AGENDA
Essex House, New York City

Monday, June 25
  8:00-10:00 am   *Market Operations Staff Meeting*
                       Blue Room, 2nd Floor

  8:30-9:00   Announcement Overview
                       S. Mencher

  9:00-10:00   Product Demonstrations
                       South Casino, Main Floor

  10:00-Noon   *Final Demo Rehearsals*
                       North Terrace

  Noon-1:00 pm   *News Conference Dress Rehearsal*
                       South Casino, Main Floor

  3:00-6:00 pm   *Industry Analysts Briefing*
                       South Casino, Main Floor

  2:30-3:00   Nondisclosure Registration
  3:00-3:10   Opening Remarks (C. Marshall)
  3:10-3:25   Information Systems Architecture (F. Vigilante)
  3:25-3:55   Processor Overview (S. Bauman)
  3:55-4:10   Information Systems Network (L. Dooling)
  4:10-4:25   Service Support (B. Pigott)
  4:25-4:40   Marketing Thrust (B. Casale)
  4:40-5:00   Q&A Panel (Marshall/Casale/Vigilante)
  5:00-6:00   Product Demonstrations
  6:00-7:30   Reception

Tuesday, June 26
  9:00-11:00 am   *Security Analysts Briefing*
                       South Casino, Main Floor

  9:00-9:10   Opening Remarks (C. Marshall)
  9:10-9:20   Information Systems Architecture/New Products (F. Vigilante)
  9:20-9:30   Marketing Thrust (B. Casale)
  9:30-9:45   Q&A Panel (Marshall/Casale/Vigilante)
  9:45-11:00   Product Demonstrations

  Noon-2:00 pm   *News Conference*
                       South Casino, Main Floor

  Noon-12:10   Opening Remarks (C. Marshall)
  12:10-12:20   Information Systems Architecture/New Products (F. Vigilante)
  12:20-12:30   Marketing Thrust (B. Casale)
  12:30-1:00   Q&A Panel (Marshall/Casale/Vigilante)

  1:00-1:30   Technical Briefing
                       Blue Room, 2nd Floor

  1:00-2:00   Product Demonstrations
                       South Casino, Main Floor

Tuesday, June 26
  (EDT)
  1:00-3:30 pm   *Customer Area Announcements*
                       (17 Cities)

Figure 16.4. AT&T press conference agenda. Reprinted courtesy of AT&T.

```
1:00-1:15       Product Announcement (AVP)
1:15-2:00       Product Overview (ASSG Manager)
2:00-2:15       Q&As
2:15-2:30       Support Program (AVP)

2:30-3:30       Product Demonstrations

4:00-6:30 pm    New York Customer Announcement
                Essex House, South Casino

Tuesday, June 26/27
   Advertising    • 30-second TV spot-full line (6/26)
                  • WSJ & dailies, 30 top markets-full line day after announcement
                    ad (6/27)

July 9-12
   Exhibit        • National Computer Conference (Las Vegas)
                    (primary emphasis-full computer line)
```

Figure 16.4. (continued)

Brochures. Brochures are brief presentations of programs or products. They usually consist of a single sheet of paper, folded once or twice, and printed on all sides. The basic function of a brochure is to be an attention-getter. It invites the reader to follow up for more information, much as an advertisement does.

Feature Articles. Many public relations agencies representing companies, or a company's own public relations department, will offer to write articles for magazines and newspapers. They will tailor the content to suit the audience of the publication that has agreed to publish the article. The article usually contains information about the products produced or ideas advocated by the organization writing the article. The organization may or may not be mentioned in the article, and the products may or may not be mentioned by brand name, depending on how the editor feels. Some editors who feel that the mention of the product name amounts to an endorsement of the product avoid doing so.

Other articles are sent out by mail and by wire in the expectation that they'll be picked up. The article "Tips for Summer Vegetable Gardening" (Figure 16.5), from the PR Newswire, mentions the product right in the lead: Peters Professional Plant Food. It's a standard "how-to" feature article. It's very likely that medium-sized and small newspapers who subscribe to the PR Newswire used it in a garden or home section. Magazine editors who received it in the mail but who work six months or more in advance may have filed it as filler for an issue to be produced the following spring.

Public Service Announcements. Public service announcements (PSAs) are aired by radio and television stations as a service to their listeners. They are "mini-ads," but there is no charge for them. Generally speaking, PSAs are produced by non-profit organizations that cannot afford paid advertising and are involved in community affairs. Most are notices of upcoming events or invitations to call a group for helpful information on a specific topic, such as health. An example is shown in Figure 16.6.

TV stations will expect to receive a typed script or a videotape; radio stations, a typed script or a cassette. A press release about the topic or event should also be included. The announcements will be aired as air time becomes available.

Here are some guidelines on writing PSAs from Lindy Keane Carter, now on the staff of the Council for Advancement and Support of Education in Washington,

```
US CH CH AP AB
     CH
FNS1     /FROM PR NEWSWIRE BOSTON 617-482-5355 OR NYC 212-832-9400/
TO LIFESTYLE EDITORS %

            TIPS FOR SUMMER VEGETABLE GARDENING

    BOSTON, JULY 15 /PRNEWSWIRE/ -- A SUMMER VEGETABLE GARDEN CAN BE A
SOURCE OF GREAT SATISFACTION, RELAXATION, AND -- OF COURSE -- FRESH
PRODUCE. A FEW KEY TIPS CAN MAKE A BIG DIFFERENCE IN THE SUCCESS OF
ALL GARDENS, ACCORDING TO DR. RAY SHELDRAKE, CONSULTANT FOR W.R.
GRACE & CO./PETERS PROFESSIONAL PLANT FOOD AND PROFESSOR EMERITUS IN
THE FIELD OF HORTICULTURE.
    TIP NUMBER 1:  STAKING TOMATOES.
    ALMOST ANY VARIETY OF TOMATO CAN BE TRAINED-UP VERTICALLY WITH
GREAT SUCCESS. STAKING THE PLANTS CORRECTLY IS ALL-IMPORTANT IN
PRODUCING HIGH QUALITY FRUIT.
    FIRMLY PLACE A 6-FT. HIGH STAKE ABOUT 12 INCHES INTO THE GROUND.
USE ONE FOR EACH PLANT AND SET THEM 18 INCHES APART. WHEN PLANTS ARE
ABOUT 12 INCHES TALL, BREAK OFF THE SIDE SHOOTS WHICH WILL APPEAR ON
THE STEM AT THE POINT WHERE EACH LEAF IS GROWING. REMOVE THESE SIDE
SHOOTS 16-18 INCHES UP THE PLANT; LET THE PLANT BUSH OUT AND TIE THE
BRANCHES TO THE STAKE. TO GROW PLANTS 6-8 FEET HIGH, REMOVE THE SIDE
SHOOTS ALL THE WAY UP AND TIE THE CENTRAL STEM TO THE STAKE.
FERTILIZE THESE PLANTS ONCE A WEEK. DISSOLVE A TABLESPOON OF A
BALANCED 20-20-20 WATER SOLUABLE FERTILIZER, LIKE PETERS ALL PURPOSE,
PER GALLON OF WATER. WATER THE PLANTS WITH THIS SOLUTION TO PROVIDE
THE NECESSARY NUTRIENTS FOR STRONG, HEALTHY DEVELOPMENT. GROWING
TOMATOES VERTICALLY IS AN EXCELLENT WAY TO SAVE SPACE AND PRODUCE
HIGH-QUALITY FRUIT.
    TIP NUMBER TWO:  WATERING/FERTILIZING THE GARDEN.
    A SUCCESSFUL VEGETABLE GARDEN REQUIRES ABOUT 1 INCH OF WATER A
WEEK. PLACE A STRAIGHT-SIDED CAN IN THE GARDEN NEAR A PLANT, TURN
ON THE SPRINKLER AND NOTE THE TIME. IN THIS WAY, IT WILL BE POSSIBLE
TO DETERMINE THE AMOUNT OF TIME TO LEAVE THE SPRINKLER ON FOR AN
APPROPRIATE WATERING. ALSO, LEAVE A CAN IN THE GARDEN DURING THE
WEEK TO SERVE AS A RAIN GAUGE.
```

FIGURE 16.5. Reprinted courtesy of P.R. Newswire.

D.C., and a former public service director of WCIV-TV in Charleston, S.C.:

- ☐ Write PSA copy conversationally. Open with an attention-getting sentence or phrase. Give the who, what, when, where and why, and then end the message neatly. Keep the message simple. Give a start and stop date for the PSA.
- ☐ If there are tricky words, include phonetic respellings.
- ☐ Check the length of the PSA by a clock with a second hand. Assume that about 2½ words can be said in one second. Most stations use PSAs in lengths of 10, 15, 20 and 30 seconds.

Novelty Items. Items such as T-shirts, bumper stickers, balloons and pens are often given away in connection with a promotion of an organizational event. These types of tools are extensions of major events and serve to remind those who receive them of the group whose event they attended or whose viewpoint they were recently exposed to. They also help publicize the organization's name to others.

```
    SOIL TYPE WILL ALSO AFFECT THE AMOUNT OF WATER REQUIRED FOR GOOD
GROWTH.  SANDY SOILS WILL DRAIN MORE QUICKLY THAN HEAVIER SOILS.
CHECK THE SOIL ABOUT 3 TO 6 INCHES BELOW THE SURFACE TO MAKE SURE
PLANTS ARE RECEIVING ADEQUATE MOISTURE.
    TIP NUMBER THREE:  HARVESTING SWEET CORN.
    IT TAKES ABOUT 21 DAYS FROM SILKING UNTIL THE EARS ARE EDIBLE.
THE SILK WILL START LIGHT GREEN AND TURN TO A DARK BROWN OR BLACK
WHEN THE CORN APPROACHES MATURITY.  THE KERNELS ON THE EAR FILL OUT
FIRST AT THE BASE PROGRESS TOWARD THE TIP.  DELICATELY PEEL BACK SOME
OF THE HUSKS AND CHECK THE DEVELOPMENT OF THE KERNELS.  THE KERNELS
NEAR THE TIP SHOULD BE LIGHT YELLOW AND IF PIERCED, THE JUICE SHOULD
BE CLEARED TO SLIGHTLY CLOUDY.  THIS IS THE BEST TIME TO HARVEST THE
CORN.  DON'T PICK CORN TOO YOUNG OR WAIT TOO LONG BECAUSE IT GETS OLD
AND TOUGH IN A FEW DAYS.
    TIP NUMBER FOUR:  THINNING YOUR VEGETABLES.
    A COMMON PROBLEM IN MANY VEGETABLE GARDENS IS OVERCROWDING.
PLANTS GROWN TOO CLOSELY WILL NOT GROW WELL DUE TO THE COMPETITION
CREATED FOR THE WATER AND NUTRIENTS IN THE SOIL.
    FREQUENTLY SMALL SEEDS ARE SOWN TOO CLOSELY BECAUSE THEY ARE
DIFFICULT TO HANDLE.  AND, ALTHOUGH WE ALL LIKE TO SEE THE GARDEN
FLOURISH, IT IS NECESSARY TO THIN OUT OVERCROWDED PLANTS -- OTHERWISE
THEY ACT LIKE WEEDS, HINDERING THE GROWTH AND DEVELOPMENT OF ALL THE
PLANTS IN THE GARDEN.
    THE FOLLOWING CHART OUTLINES SOME SIMPLE PLANTING GUIDELINES:
    VEGETABLE                       SEED DISTANCE
LETTUCE (ICEBERG, BIBB)         10-12 INCHES APART
CARROTS                         1-3 INCHES APART
CORN                            8-12 INCHES APART
PUMPKINS                        8-10 FEET APART
MUSKMELONS (A)                  2-3 FEET APART
    (A) OFTEN REFERRED TO AS CANTELOUPES.
    -0-           7/15/85
    /CONTACT:  KATHE BIENEMANN OR CYNTHIA LOWE OF INGALLS PUBLIC
RELATIONS, 617-437-7000, FOR W.R. GRACE & CO./PETERS PROFESSIONAL
PLANT FOOD/
    -FNS1-
```

(continued)

CAMPAIGNS

Choosing Your Tools.   Different events call for different types of messages. Budgets, too, dictate the extent to which certain tools can be used. So does the ability to plan. The Johnson & Johnson public relations department was caught completely by surprise when seven Tylenol users died and was forced to *react* to the event. But most public relations information campaigns are planned. Their aim is to inform a public about a new project and to gain the public's support. A good public relations plan also includes a strategy for keeping that support once it has been obtained.

Consider these examples of how groups use different tools to accomplish their goals of informing the public and gaining its support.

Fund Raising.   A group of university students organizes to stage a 48-hour "dance-a-thon" to raise funds for cancer research. Their aim is to raise $75,000 through admissions to the event, fees for sponsoring the dancers, solicitors at the door and in the parking lot, and call-in pledges. They also want to cut expenses by having a site, food and other supplies donated. Here is their selection of PR tools:

```
            :20     PSA FOR INTERNATIONAL CRAFT FESTIVAL

      START:        Nov. 7
      STOP:         Nov. 20

      ANNOUNCER:    The Greater Buffalo Junior League and
                    University of Buffalo faculty invite you to
                    sample handmade crafts from around the world
                    at their international craft festival on
                    Saturday, November 21, at Norton Union on the
                    U-B campus. Proceeds will benefit African
                    famine relief. The festival is free! That's
                    Saturday, November 21, from 9 till 5.
```

Figure 16.6. Sample radio-TV public service announcement copy.

1. A news release to the local newspapers and radio and television stations announcing the event and explaining how money and goods can be donated. Accompanying the release is a complete schedule of activities during the dance-a-thon.
2. Follow-up calls to the stations asking for on-site coverage.
3. Close work with the local chapter of the American Cancer Society, which offers to do the publicity mailing to the media and supply brochures and bumper stickers to be handed out to attendees and mailed to people who call in pledges.
4. Personal visits to local merchants to ask for their support by donating materials and displaying posters in their stores.
5. Radio public service announcement prepared and mailed to area stations.

Here's what happened:

1. Local newspapers covered the event on the front page of the city section; one paper also ran a sidebar on cancers common among college-age persons. The campus newspaper wrote an editorial in advance of the dance-a-thon, encouraging students to attend, and did a major photo spread in the edition published the morning after the dance-a-thon began.
2. One of the two TV stations in the area sent a reporter to do a live feed from the dance-a-thon for the 11 p.m. news on opening night. Her report on the event's second night included interviews with students who had lost friends and relatives to cancer and with one dancer who was herself in remission from leukemia. The public service announcement prepared by the organizers was aired six times daily during the week preceding the telethon and 10 times daily during the event itself.
3. A total of 4,000 brochures and 1,000 bumper stickers were distributed.
4. Local grocery stores and beverage outlets supplied food and drinks for the dancers. Campus officials waived the fee for the dance hall. The T-shirt shop gave free shirts to the dancers. A sporting goods store gave shoes as prizes in dance contests held during the event.
5. Most media interviewed the dance-a-thon chairman, including his hometown paper 200 miles away. The paper had been included on the mailing

list for news releases, which had noted his participation as the group's chairman.
6. A total of $90,000 was raised, including one anonymous donation of $10,000.

Announcements. Announcements of research findings, survey results, scientific breakthroughs, and business successes and failures also call for adroit use of public relations tools. The people responsible for releasing such information will use a different assortment of PR tools than the students did to help get the word out. Why? Because they are trying to reach a different audience. Consider this scenario:

A media watchdog group releases its analysis by gender of authorship of Page One stories published by major American newspapers, according to bylines, and ranks the papers in order of most female bylines. The group's goal is to monitor equal opportunity in journalism by assessing whether the gender of a reporter or of a story's subject affects the prominence given to the story. To announce their findings, the group plans this public relations campaign:

1. A news release announcing a press conference at the National Press Building in Washington, D.C., at which the researchers and the group's director will be present is mailed to all the newspapers surveyed, to writers interested in women's issues and professional development in journalism, and to professional journalism organizations, unions and publications.
2. An effort is made to place the researchers and the director on radio and television programs to discuss the study's findings. The organization's staff begins contacting the networks and talk-show producers in large broadcast markets. The staff also attempts to interest journalism groups in having the researchers and the director on the program at their conventions.
3. A statement is prepared for the director to read at the news conference. It summarizes the study, calls for action by newspapers to expand opportunities for female reporters, and is made available to the press at the news conference and to callers to the organization's office who request it.
4. Statements from media observers and scholars who've had a sneak preview of the study are made available to the press. These third-party comments help to give the findings some perspective and verify and support the researchers' conclusions.

Here are the results:

1. Several papers that did well and several that did poorly in the rankings asked columnists to write on the subject of sexism in journalism. These columns were published on the papers' op-ed pages.
2. Numerous television and radio interview programs responded with invitations for the researchers and the director to appear on news interview programs with journalists and media scholars to discuss the findings.
3. Two magazines for journalists assigned writers to explore the topic of the "gender gap" in front-page bylines. Two very different types of stories resulted. In one, the author interviewed observers who attacked the study, insisting that it proved very little. In the other, comments were mixed.
4. Journalism organizations planned programs around the findings and began to organize panels to discuss the event.
5. The study was used in upper-level journalism courses that cover newsroom management and journalism ethics.

6. A textbook publisher invited the researchers to contribute to a book on the journalism profession.

There *are* similarities between the two PR campaigns discussed here. Both groups wanted to persuade the public about an issue: the students, that their cause was worthy of support; the media watchdog group, that their study drew attention to a situation that bears watching and improving. Their choice of public relations tools was different, because their needs were different. But both followed the single most important principle of public relations: They chose the PR instruments that were most likely to bring their message to their target audience.

The results of both campaigns were very positive. But public relations efforts can fizzle. Why? The media simply cannot and will not respond to every group's pitch for coverage—there are only so many reporters, so many camera operators, so many minutes before deadlines, and, as the saying goes, "There are a million stories in the naked city." The ones that will get covered have a solid, fresh news angle, and the public relations professionals handling the information will have made it as easy as possible for members of the press to get the information and whatever else they need to write the stories.

Other Kinds of Campaigns. A public relations (or public affairs) effort can be mounted to raise awareness of many other kinds of causes. Community activists, for example, use these public relations tools to draw attention to problems in their neighborhoods and to move people to action to solve them. A trade association representing an industry that will suffer if the government passes regulations forcing it to invest heavily in equipment to protect the environment will use some of the same tools to launch an information campaign showing why such heavy investment might not achieve the goals the government wants. In sum, almost any organization can rely on public relations techniques to place its goals and points of view on the public agenda.

INTERNAL PUBLIC RELATIONS

Tools

House Organs. Many organizations have newsletters, magazines and newspapers for their employees or for other people involved with the organization. Communicating with people "in-house" is known as *internal* public relations.

The "house organ" is published in the interest of employees. It contains news about the organization's activities and short features about the individuals who work or volunteer for it. House organs help keep employees informed about organizational activities and foster good will and a feeling of teamwork by highlighting their special contributions.

AT&T Information Systems' *Challenge:* is published for its employees. The content of the issue shown in Figure 16.7 reflects the big events involving the company at that time: AT&T's entry into the personal computer industry. *Challenge:* devoted most of that edition to the new product announcement and the different ways employees were involved in the production and promotion of the new products.

This issue of *Challenge:* also demonstrates how AT&T Information Systems got its employees involved in a bit of *external* public relations: the bumper sticker campaign (Figure 16.8). The "Watson, Watch Us Now!" theme was carried through in designing the bumper sticker, which employees put on their cars. The

inside

Great opportunity
Bartz on "networking": potential multi-billion dollar revenue source. — page 2

A real performer
AT&T introduces competitively priced personal computer. — page 3

Stick it to 'em!
Bumper sticker inside for your car. — page 5

Marvelous motif
New packaging adds pizazz to computer line. — page 6

AT&T Information Systems

Challenge:

The newspaper of AT&T Information Systems — Vol. 2, Issue 14 — June 26, 1984

AT&T unveils personal computer, data products and Information Systems Network

AT&T Information Systems left no doubt in anyone's mind today that it will be a major player in the computer marketplace.

In a multi-product announcement made at simultaneous press conferences in New York City, Chicago, Dallas, San Francisco, Washington and Atlanta, the company...

—Extended the sale of the 3B2 and 3B5 computers—and the AT&T personal computer interface—announced three months ago from a narrow market to all business customers;

—Entered the personal computer market by introducing a competitively priced, fast 16-bit machine that will be sold both by Information Systems sales people and retailers around the nation;

—Unveiled the Information Systems Network, a local area network that ties AT&T data and communications products, as well as many products produced by other vendors, into a single integrated system;

—Introduced a broad array of 80 new computer software applications for the AT&T PC and the 3B2 and 3B5 computers;

—Brought out a series of economical printers, protocol converters and coax eliminators that can be bought separately or as part of an AT&T PC or 3B package; and

—Detailed the most comprehensive support and service plan in the industry to back the AT&T PC and 3B computer line.

Using the new AT&T PC at Lincroft, NJ, are (l-r) Marketing and Sales' Dale Malik, Services' Rod Alberse (seated) and Product Management and Development's Bill Wong.

Introducing the new products in New York City were Information Systems Chairman Chuck Marshall, Marketing and Sales division President Bob Casale, and Product Management and Development division President Frank Vigilante. On hand to host the other press conferences were region Sales and Services vice presidents.

"With the introduction of the AT&T PC, we've brought the idea of the 16-bit personal computer up to date," said Vigilante at the New York conference, which was televised via AT&T's newest satellite, Telstar 301, to the other press conference sites. "The new AT&T PC offers users a number of built-in advantages. It operates faster than our competitors' PCs, with better resolution and graphics—and it's ready right now at sales sites and retail stores across the country."

(Continued on page 4)

FIGURE 16.7. Reprinted courtesy of AT&T.

Stick it to 'em!

Thomas Watson, Bell System pioneer inventor, might be very surprised if he saw a bumper sticker displaying his name. However, he'd probably be proud if he knew the bumper sticker drew attention to our recent product announcements, including the AT&T personal computer, and our commitment to success in the Information Age. "Watson, watch us now!" will be the attention-getting slogan in our advertising for the new AT&T PC. Communicate the spirit of the marketing campaign by displaying the bumper sticker enclosed in this issue. Placing a bumper sticker on a Services employee's car are Jenny Jenkins and George Dohrmann.

FIGURE 16.8. Reprinted courtesy of AT&T.

bumper sticker campaign had the effect of making employees a part of the PR effort and amplifying AT&T's message of excitement and innovation in technology.

Bulletin Boards. Bulletin boards have been a part of most people's lives since they were in elementary school. They still play an important role in keeping members of an organization apprised of developments and news in the organization. Keeping bulletin boards current and graphically interesting is vital if they are to attract interest.

Kiosks, Exhibits, Displays. Extensions of bulletin boards, these free-standing structures use signs and graphics to draw people to the information contained in fliers and brochures available at the display and on charts that may be part of it. As with bulletin boards, messages on these types of structures ought to be brief, since they only are meant to attract passers-by. Any detailed information should be available in a form people can take with them.

CAMPAIGNS

Shifting the conditions in the U.S. economy have forced many firms to lay off employees or ask them to take a salary reduction so that all could keep their jobs. Let's look at an example of how a firm might use public relations tools to convince an internal public—its employees—to agree to terms of employment that are far from perfect.

Here is the firm's choice of tools:

1. An announcement is delivered to each employee at work, stating that the

200-person company is facing a desperate financial situation and that an outside accounting firm has devised a plan whereby all employees could remain on the job if they agreed to a 15 percent wage cut and no salary increases for two years. Attached to the two-page announcement is a detailed 10-page report explaining how the accountants arrived at their conclusions. If the employees reject the proposal, a 20 percent reduction in staff will follow.
2. Extra copies of the announcement and the plan are posted, page by page, on bulletin boards all over the building.
3. All the employees are invited to hear the company's executive officer explain the situation and the plan at a gathering in the company auditorium. Microphones are placed in the aisles so that employees can ask questions of the CEO and other managers. Afterward, the CEO addresses the local press to explain the company's crisis.
4. Kiosks with brightly colored signs are erected at each entrance on every floor of the building. These kiosks contain information about when and where the vote on the proposal is to take place.
5. The employee newspaper, a biweekly, reprints both the announcement and the 10-page report and solicits comments and articles from employees.

Here are the results:

1. The divided work force communicated more often and with more intensity than ever before. Employees circulated their own fliers and posted their own announcements on bulletin boards and kiosks, along with those of the company.
2. Response to the house organ's invitation to submit written comments about the decision facing the employees was overwhelming. Letters poured in, and the paper's staff printed a special section to accommodate the volume.
3. Voting was relatively orderly on the day of the vote. The proposal passed.
4. The company called a press conference to announce the outcome and publicly expressed gratitude to its employees. All employees and their spouses were invited to a simple reception in the company cafeteria the next night. Within a week, bumper stickers carrying the company's logo and the slogan "We *All* Work Together" were given to the employees.

The information campaign saw participation by both management and the rank and file. What made that possible was a sharing of internal communication resources.

SUMMARY

Public relations writers have a major impact on the information published and broadcast by the media every day. Though they are usually invisible to readers and viewers, they have suggested stories, answered reporters' questions and clarified the information sought by them. They've arranged interviews for reporters and recommended new angles and approaches for their stories. Public relations writers use the same journalistic writing and stylistic techniques as journalists, with a difference in focus: Public relations writers cover a single organization, its products and ideas, whereas journalists cover a wide range of organizations and have no allegiance to any of them.

PR professionals choose the type of communication tools they use—news releases, brochures, speeches, PSAs and articles—based on the issue at hand and the audience they want to reach. A Coca-Cola executive's speech to a business luncheon forum about new products will work well with his adult audience, but it would bore a group of teen-age Coke drinkers. Better to hit them with Coke T-shirts and bumper stickers in conjunction with a radio promotion. And the newspaper reporter who couldn't get to the luncheon and isn't interested in a T-shirt will best be served by a comprehensive media kit that notes that executive X made such a speech and radio station Y is participating in this promotion, giving away shirts and stickers.

The internal relations specialist designs projects to bring information to publics already familiar with the organization and its goals. The objective is to sustain teamwork and foster confidence in the organization and to encourage productivity by employees.

In sum, in public relations, the message should be tailored to the audience. And the clarity of that message begins with good writing and good *human* relations.

EXERCISES

1. You are given this information:

   A student group wants polling places on campus so that they don't have to go off campus to vote. Many students without cars find it difficult to vote because they're without transportation to polling areas.

   A rally in front of City Hall is announced, organized by Students for Participatory Democracy. Chair: Jeanne Prentice, 447-3256. Rally: 3 p.m. Friday, Sept. 15.

   Number of eligible student voters at the university: 2,500.

   On the basis of these details, write the following:
   a. A news release

b. A 20-second PSA

c. A bumper sticker slogan

2. Write a public service announcement for the cancer dance-a-thon described in this chapter. It is being held at your university this weekend, and the name of the chairman is David Thompson. Write a 15-second and a 30-second version.

3. On separate sheets, write an opening statement David Thompson can make at the kickoff of the dance-a-thon. It should be no more than two typewritten pages, double-spaced.

4. On separate sheets, write a feature story about the dance-a-thon that you'll attempt to place in area media as a follow-up to the event and to prepare for next year's dance-a-thon. Be sure to use these facts:

176 students participated in the event—as dancers and as staff

$90,000 was raised, including a $10,000 anonymous donation

Quotes from David Thompson's opening statement

Mills' Beverage Outlet donated 2,000 cans of soda pop; Silver's Grocery donated 1,000 bags of potato chips; Bob's Burgers supplied one meal per day per dancer; Hal's Sporting Goods donated 10 pairs of aerobic and running shoes to dancers who won dance contests

Next year's dance-a-thon: Nov. 28

Here are some quotations:

Naomi Lowe, dancer: "I never had so much fun in my life. It was so worthwhile! I could just hug and kiss everyone!"

John Martin, Naomi's partner: "We danced 42 hours, man. I thought I was gonna pass out. But I kept thinking about those people dyin', man, and it kept me goin'."

Brendan McQuilken: "My knees really hurt after 15 hours. I had to drop out."

Latonya Williams: "I danced in the dance-a-thon last year, but I lasted only 20 hours. This year, I finished. I'm so proud, I can't tell you."

5. Rewrite this statement* in acceptable news release form.

   The following statement was made today by Dr. Charles F. Fogarty, executive vice president of Texas Gulf Sulphur Company, in regard to the company's drilling operations near Timmins, Ontario, Canada. Dr. Fogarty said:

   During the past few days, the exploration activities of Texas Gulf Sulphur in the area of Timmins, Ontario, have been widely reported in the press, coupled with rumors of a substantial copper discovery there. These reports exaggerate the scale of operations and mention plans and statistics of size and grade of ore that are without factual basis and have evidently originated by speculation of people not connected with TGS.

   The facts are as follows. TGS has been exploring in the Timmins area for six years as part of its overall search in Canada and elsewhere for various minerals — lead, copper, zinc, etc. During the course of this work, in Timmins as well as in eastern Canada, TGS has conducted exploration entirely on its own, without participation by others. Numerous prospects have been investigated by geophysical means, and a large number of selected ones have been core-drilled. These cores are sent to the United States for assay and detailed examination as a matter of routine and on advice of expert Canadian legal counsel. No inferences as to grade can be drawn from this procedure.

   Most of the areas drilled in eastern Canada have revealed either barren pyrite or graphite without value; a few have resulted in discoveries of small or marginal sulphide ore bodies.

   Recent drilling on one property near Timmins has led to preliminary indications that more drilling would be required for proper evaluation of this prospect. The drilling done to date has not been conclusive, but the statements made by many outside quarters are unreliable and include information and figures that are not available to TGS.

   The work done to date has not been sufficient to reach definite conclusions, and any statement as to size and grade of ore would be premature and possibly misleading. When we have progressed to the point where reasonable and logical conclusions can be made, TGS will issue a definite statement to its stockholders and to the public in order to clarify the Timmins project.

* Reprinted by permission of Texasgulf Inc.

6. Write a short article on a staff promotion. Remember that you are writing the story to publicize the company as well as the individual. Use these facts:

Name:	Jaimie B. Garrett
Experience:	15 years as a registered nurse, associate administrator with ABC Home Health Services of LaGrange, Ga., (your firm) for two years
Promotion:	Garrett has been promoted to chief administrator.
New duties:	Supervise a 22-person staff providing home health care in 10 counties
Experience outside ABC:	Director of education for a community hospital in Hartwell, Ga.; head nurse at St. Joseph's Mercy Hospital, Athens, Ga.; 10 years as charge nurse at Crawford W. Long Hospital, Atlanta
Education:	Took nursing degree at Virginia Intermont College, Bristol, Va.
Firm's address:	860 King St. Phone: 555–4740.
Counties covered by ABC:	Clarke, Jackson, Madison, Elbert, Oconee, Walton, Oglethorpe, Morgan, Greene, Barrow
Target market:	Every market served by the firm

CHAPTER 17

WRITING FOR THE MASS MEDIA

Having received instruction in writing for a wide variety of media areas, you may want to review those areas to set them in your mind. One way of leaving that impression is to examine how one news event was treated by the various media: the settlement of the United Airlines pilots' strike.

THE *WASHINGTON POST* COVERS THE STRIKE SETTLEMENT

The *Washington Post* presented its newspaper readers with a comprehensive and complex summary news lead that included a brief history of the strike as well as what was expected of the settlement.

United Airlines Prepares to Resume Full Service*

Process Expected to Take at Least a Week

By PETER PERL
Washington Post Staff Writer

United Airlines, grounded 29 days by a bitter pilots' strike that canceled 85 percent of its flights, geared up yesterday to resume service to all 50 states in a back-to-work process expected to take more than a week and to prompt continued court challenges and strong union protests.

United, the nation's largest air carrier, won important labor-cost concessions during the strike that ended midnight Friday with both sides claiming partial victories in the divisive walkout by 5,000 pilots and the 8,000 flight attendants who supported them.

Full service of 1,500 daily flights to 149 cities and 10 foreign destinations will resume about the end

---

* "United Airlines Prepares to Resume Full Service," by Peter Perl, 6/16/85, *The Washington Post*. Copyright © 1985 The Washington Post Company. Reprinted by permission of the publisher.

of the month, United said, although pilots and flight attendants are to begin returning to work today.

A United spokesman said a promotional plan to be unveiled Monday probably will include price reductions designed to lure passengers back into United's "friendly skies."

But officials of the Air Line Pilots Association (ALPA) and the Association of Flight Attendants (AFA) said yesterday that it will take considerable time for the friendliness to return to United, whose labor-management relations were previously regarded as among the industry's best.

"The company has bought itself a period of chaos," said AFA spokesman Mark Bigelow. "We tried to negotiate an orderly back-to-work agreement that would have provided normalcy, but they chose chaos."

ALPA's United chairman, pilot Roger Hall, said the company used "punitive and vindictive" tactics in an attempt to "break the union."

United Airlines Chairman Richard J. Ferris called the settlement "a good solution to some complex and difficult issues."

In obtaining pay cuts of more than 50 percent for newly hired pilots, United will gain momentum for its international expansion plans and will influence wages throughout the industry, airline analysts said.

But United's victory could prove costly by further souring labor relations, spokesmen for both sides said. And United's plans could be changed by the U.S. District Court.

The unions have vowed to fight vigorously against proposed seniority rules that would award higher-paying jobs and choice of home bases to union members who crossed picket lines.

The back-to-work plan by United would give "super-seniority" to 2,000 AFA members and 260 ALPA pilots who worked during the strike, which began May 17. United would "rebid" jobs, giving nonstrikers first choice and possibly causing future layoffs or involuntary transfers of strikers. Those factors were so important to the unions that they prolonged the strike by three weeks after economic matters were settled May 24.

The 260 pilots who crossed union picket lines could receive raises of as much as $60,000 per year because they would be given first choice in flying larger planes at salaries of as much as $150,000, compared with the $90,000 average pay for United captains. Similarly, the 2,000 flight attendants who worked throughout the strike could get first choice in picking the longer, higher-paying routes and the more desirable home bases.

Ferris said the company insisted on back-to-work agreements that would "back its promises to employees. We said we would never forsake those who kept the airline flying." But U.S. District Judge Nicholas J. Bua is to begin hearing union complaints Monday that such seniority changes violate union contracts.

The unions' solidarity and management's pledge to reward employes who broke with the unions became the powerful issues of the nationwide strike, with both sides refusing to back down and, instead, deferring to the court. The court will also decide the fate of the 570 new pilots who sided with the union after completing their training. The company is refusing to hire them.

ALPA, once regarded as among the most successful unions, has seen its power greatly eroded because airline deregulation spawned dozens of lower-wage, nonunion airlines and prompted unionized firms to demand deep cuts in the name of remaining competitive.

In United's case, the three-year contract sets up a "two-tier" pay scale in which new pilots are hired at $21,600 and progress after five years to $27,792. Fifth-year pilots now earn $60,456.

Hall said the union is "alive and well," noting that ALPA was able to keep almost its entire membership on strike and in limiting the two-tier system to five years — after which negotiators and arbitrators are to decide how long to continue it.

Current pilots will get 9.5 percent raises over three years.

The two tiers are important to United because it expects to hire many new pilots as part of its plan to acquire Pan American's Pacific routes in a $750 million international expansion, said Lee Howard, executive vice president of Airline Economics Inc., a consulting firm.

"This was crucial to United" because of its nonunion competitors and unionized rivals with two-tier wage systems, including American, Republic, Piedmont and Frontier, Howard said.

THE WALL STREET JOURNAL COVERS THE STRIKE SETTLEMENT

Because *The Wall Street Journal* is a newspaper primarily concerned with financial news, its lead stressed the financial results of the settlement. Succeeding paragraphs stressed other anticipated financial developments. Accompanying this major news story is a sidebar on the Transportation Department's willingness to expedite United Airlines' application to buy Pan American World Airways' Pacific division. The history and problems of the strike came toward the end of the story.

United Air Sets Expansion Plans As Strike Ends*

By HARLAN S. BYRNE
Staff Reporter of *The Wall Street Journal*

CHICAGO — United Airlines said it plans to begin a major long-range expansion this fall and to launch a short-term marketing blitz to regain traffic lost during the 29-day pilots' strike that ended Friday night.

"We've got a lot of growth plans and we can't wait to get started," said Richard J. Ferris, chairman and chief executive officer of United and its parent, UAL Inc. His comments came Saturday, after the United Master Executive Council of the Air Line Pilots Association ratified a settlement that ended the walkout by 5,000 pilots.

Mr. Ferris said the expansion, which United had delayed until it got sharply lower pay scales for new pilots, would begin in September when United gets back 10 of 25 Boeing 737s. United purchased the planes from Frontier Airlines and leased them back to Frontier; it expects the remaining 15 aircraft to be returned by next May. United also recently acquired from St. Louis-based McDonnell Douglas Corp. five MD-82s, of which three are out on short-term lease. The carrier currently has a fleet of 320 aircraft.

Mr. Ferris said United expects in the next three years to add 1,000 pilots at the new lower pay scales agreed to with the pilots' union. In addition, United is considering new

---

* Reprinted by permission of *The Wall Street Journal*. © Dow Jones & Company, Inc., 1985. All rights reserved.

aircraft purchases. It already has on order, subject to cancellation, 20 Boeing Co. 767 aircraft at a cost of more than $1 billion, for delivery beginning in 1987. United has an option to substitute for those 767s other aircraft made by Seattle-based Boeing, and the carrier recently said it was negotiating further aircraft purchases with Boeing and McDonnell Douglas.

James Hartigan, president of United, said the carrier expects to return by July 1 to its full daily schedule of 1,550 flights, serving 159 cities in all 50 states. The nation's largest airline has been flying only about 14% of its schedule as a result of the strike.

John Zeeman, executive vice president, marketing, predicted United has a "good chance" of recapturing its market share — about 15% in the U.S. — in 30 to 60 days. Mr. Zeeman plans today to unveil details of an aggressive marketing effort to win back traffic.

In resuming full service, United will seek to avoid touching off a fare war while launching brief promotions Mr. Zeeman said.

"We can't be sure how our major competitors will react, but we think they have so much business, they won't see any need, at this point anyway, to try to match everything we try," he said.

For frequent fliers, United is planning extra mileage credits and other inducements. It also plans to give double credits to fliers paying full fare. For vacationers, United will remove or ease some restrictions on deeply discounted fares, such as requiring shorter advance-purchase periods, he said. Mr. Zeeman said United will offer plans for travel agents to earn bigger bonuses and more free passes based on a point system that rewards the highest number of points for full-fare tickets sold.

Mr. Zeeman and other United officials are aware of the stiff competition United faces both in

---

Agency to Speed Hearings On United Air's Purchase
By a *Wall Street Journal* Staff Reporter

WASHINGTON — The Transportation Department said it will expedite hearings on United Airlines' application to buy Pan American World Airways' Pacific division for $750 million and will make a preliminary decision by Oct. 7.

The department said an administrative law judge will hold a hearing this summer and make a final decision on the purchase by Oct. 31.

The inquiry will focus on whether the Pan Am purchase by Chicago-based UAL Inc.'s main unit would significantly hurt competition. But it won't examine competing applications for New York-based Pan Am's Pacific route authority or for new route opportunities recently negotiated with Japan, the agency said.

---

recouping traffic lost by the strike and in expanding. United faces increasing competition from such financially strong major rivals as Dallas-based American Airlines, Atlanta-based Delta Air Lines and Minneapolis-based Northwest Airlines. In addition, the plan for Houston-based Texas Air Corp. to acquire Trans World Airlines also poses a major new threat for United. Texas Air's Continental Airlines unit, a low-cost, low-fare carrier, is expected to intensify pressure on United through New York-based TWA's strong international routes. United already considers Continental one of its strongest competitors. . . .

United on average normally boards more than 120,000 passengers a day, in contrast to the 25,000 a day it boarded during the strike.

United had expanded capacity barely 1% this year before the strike, while major rivals had expanded capacity 10% or more in the same period.

While United basically got what it wanted, and both sides seemed relieved that the strike was ended, the dispute left hard feelings. The pilots' union said it will press a lawsuit on back-to-work issues that it put aside at the bargaining table in the interest of ending the strike.

The pilots' union's main protest concerns what it calls super-seniority, or United giving non-striking pilots a chance to jump ahead of striking pilots in being considered for assignments and promotions. The union also wants job protection for some 500 United-trained pilot applicants who refused to go to work during the strike.

The controversial move to replace striking pilots apparently has been defused: United has ended the hiring and intends to lower about 100 hired under the plan to the rank of second officer and to the bottom of seniority list. But it has guaranteed their pay at the level at which they were hired.

The way for the pilots' ratification of the labor agreement was cleared by a move by the Association of Flight Attendants, which had supported the strike, to return to work without a contract. But the flight attendants have filed suit in federal district court here challenging United's position on seniority issues.

As reported previously, the United contract with the pilots union provides 40% less pay, on average, for newly hired pilots for the first five years. After five years, pay scales for new hires will be subject to arbitration if negotiations fail. All pilots will get raises of 9½% over the four-year life of the contract.

ASSOCIATED PRESS COVERS THE STRIKE FOR ITS NEWSPAPERS

Like the majority of the newspapers throughout the country, *The St. Louis Post-Dispatch* carried a wire-service story of the strike settlement. This Associated Press story, filed in the Chicago bureau, focused more on the human aspects of the strike. A union official, Patty Friend, is also quoted to the effect that United Airlines had threatened "savage reprisals" against union members who stayed off the job. United Airlines officials refused to comment on her remarks.

United Pilots End Their Strike

CHICAGO (AP) — Striking United Airlines pilots and the flight attendants who honored their picket lines have agreed to return to work, ending a bitter 29-day walkout against the nation's largest air carrier.

A 27-member master executive council of the Air Line Pilots Association approved a settlement shortly before midnight Friday, said Capt. Bob Lamote, a spokesman for the pilots' union.

"We are ready to go back to work," said Steve Crews, a union spokesman. "For the pilots, it's a matter of putting on uniforms."

A vote of the union's rank and file was not necessary to ratify the agreement.

Joe Hopkins, a United spokesman, said the company was "satisfied with the contract agreement" and would resume service to all 50 states and its 10 foreign locations. The schedule for that resumption, he said, would be announced on Monday.

"Our goal is to maintain our integrity and reliability," said Hopkins. "We will not be rushed. We want to come back in an orderly manner."

United has been operating about 14 percent of its pre-strike service of 1,550 daily flights since 5,000 pilots walked out May 17.

A few hours before the pilots settlement was announced, United flight attendants said they would return to work without a formal back-to-work agreement. The pilots had delayed final agreement on a settlement until the Association of Flight Attendants agreed to return to work.

Patty Friend, an official of the flight attendants' union, said at a news conference that the attendants would return without a back-to-work agreement because the company had threatened "savage reprisals" against union members who stayed off the job.

"We will vigorously litigate and arbitrate the terms and conditions of our return to work," said Friend, whose union represents about 10,000 United employees.

United spokesman Chuck Novak said the company would have no comment on her remarks.

When the strike began, the major obstacle in the dispute was the airline's proposal for a two-tier pay system under which newly hired pilots would be paid less than veterans. But the economic issues were settled May 24, leaving only back-to-work issues unresolved.

On Wednesday, both sides agreed to let a federal judge decide the back-to-work issues, which include the fate of 570 pilots newly trained by United who honored picket lines and the seniority of strikebreakers, said Capt. John LeRoy, a spokesman for the union.

U.S. District Judge Nicholas Bua has scheduled a hearing for Monday.

The lead for the AP story filed from Rosemont, Ill., stressed the same elements but in a different way. Here is the lead of that story:

By F. N. D'ALESSIO
ROSEMONT, Ill. (AP) — United Airlines and the company's pilots said yesterday they got what they wanted in a new contract agreement, but a pilots' union leader said the strike's bitterness will linger.

The 5,000 striking pilots agreed late Friday to end the walkout, which began May 17. United officials predicted yesterday it would take three to four weeks to restore full service to all 50 states and 10 foreign destinations served by the nation's largest air carrier.

ASSOCIATED PRESS RADIO SERVICE COVERS THE STRIKE SETTLEMENT

To keep radio newscasts from sounding the same throughout the day, various elements were stressed at different times in the radio story the Associated Press sent out over the wires.

An early news headline story on June 15 read like this:

UNITED AIRLINES SAYS IT WILL ANNOUNCE PLANS FOR

> RESUMING FLIGHTS MONDAY. THE CARRIERS' PILOTS HAVE VOTED TO END THE 29-DAY WALKOUT THAT FORCED THE CARRIER TO CUT ITS OPERATIONS.

The next day, a different element was played up in the early-morning wire:

> BOTH UNITED AIRLINES AND ITS UNION SAY THEY GOT WHAT THEY WANTED IN A NEW CONTRACT REACHED AFTER A 29-DAY STRIKE. HOWEVER, A LEADER OF THE PILOTS' UNION SAYS THERE WILL BE A LINGERING BITTERNESS FROM THE WORK STOPPAGE.

A longer item stressed still a different element:

> UNITED AIRLINES OFFICIALS SAY IT'LL TAKE UP TO A MONTH TO RESTORE FULL SERVICE AFTER A 29-DAY STRIKE BY ITS PILOTS. BUT THERE'S DISAGREEMENT OVER WHETHER HARD FEELINGS WILL EVAPORATE AS QUICKLY. UNITED SAYS IT EXPECTS NO RANCOR IN THE COCKPIT. BUT A PILOTS' UNION LEADER SAYS THINGS'LL BE DIFFERENT NOW, MAINLY BECAUSE OF WHAT HE CALLS THE COMPANY'S "PUNITIVE AND VINDICTIVE" ATTITUDE TOWARD FLIGHT ATTENDANTS WHO SUPPORTED THE JOB ACTION.

Throughout the day, AP varied those lead elements to provide their clients with fresh news.

CBS EVENING NEWS COVERS THE STRIKE SETTLEMENT

After Dan Rather introduced the strike settlement agreement, he switched to CBS Correspondent Ned Potter in Chicago for answers to some of the questions Rather had posed in his introduction.

CBS covered major elements in the strike with taped quotes from an Air Line Pilots Association spokesman, Mel Hoagland; a labor expert, Paul Grant; an airline passenger; and a flight attendant, Karen Reynolds. All were led into their quotes by Ned Potter. Here is a transcript* of their comments:

RATHER: United Airlines and its 5,000-member pilots' association today reached tentative agreement on the almost four-week-old strike against the nation's largest air carrier. Which side came out ahead? What was the effect on passengers? Those questions are addressed in Ned Potter's report.

NED POTTER: The negotiators said they had agreed on all the so-called back-to-work issues that had kept the pilots on the picket lines. All that remained was ratification by the union leadership.

MEL HOAGLAND (Air Line Pilots Association): The time frame, it— it could be as quick as two or three days. And I would hope that that's how it works out.

POTTER: Winners and losers, labor experts said—

---
* Reprinted with permission of CBS News Inc.

PAUL GRANT (Loyola University): We haven't seen all the details yet, but apparently I— I think on balance the airline was successful.

POTTER: The back-to-work issues are what caused the talks to break down three weeks ago, but several sources say United had already gotten the major point it wanted, an agreement that pilots hired in the future would have a lower wage scale until they reach the rank of captain, something that only happens with about 20 years' seniority. Analysts say this two-tier wage system may be the wave of the future. United has always been seen as generous with its workers, but it's played tough during this strike, and the strikers weren't even able to cause that much trouble for passengers.

MAN: The other airlines have picked up the over— overcapacity, and I've been flying them quite a bit.

POTTER: Near Los Angeles, strikers and their supporters were feeling very upbeat.

KAREN REYNOLDS (flight attendant): I mean, we've got it now and we are united. (Laughing)

POTTER: But nobody's saying how quickly the airline can return to a normal schedule or how quickly any hard feelings will go away.

Ned Potter, CBS News, Chicago.

PUBLIC RELATIONS TREATMENT OF THE STRIKE SETTLEMENT

The Corporate Communications division of United Airlines, under the direction of Kay Lund, released this story* on the settlement:

```
FOR IMMEDIATE RELEASE
   CHICAGO, June [16]-United Airlines and the Air Line
Pilots Association (ALPA) have reached agreement on a
new contract, ending the strike which began May 17 by
members of ALPA against the airline.
   United Chairman Dick Ferris expressed satisfaction
with the contract settlement. "From the very beginning
we said we needed an agreement that would make us cost-
competitive," he said.
   "We also said we needed an agreement that would
maintain the integrity of the company and back its
promises to employees. We said we'd never foresake those
who kept the airline flying," said Ferris.
   "We've achieved these objectives. This is a good
solution to some complex, difficult issues," he said.
"Now it is time to look to the future."
   ALPA's UAL Master Executive Council ratified the
tentative agreement which was reached early Wednesday
morning following lengthy bargaining sessions when both
parties accepted a federal mediator's proposal.

                         (more)
```

* Reprinted courtesy of United Airlines Corporation.

In the wake of the settlement, United turned its attention to rebuilding the airline and said it will be back to full strength in three to four weeks.

John R. Zeeman, executive vice president-marketing and planning, said the new contract with the company's approximately 5,000 pilots will allow United to compete effectively with its rivals and carry out its ambitious growth plans.

"We are eager to get this difficult period behind us and focus our energies on the future as we regain our momentum in the marketplace," he said.

United said that while it wanted to return the airline to full strength as soon as possible, its number one goal will be to maintain the integrity and reliability of the operation.

"We will not be rushed," said Zeeman. "We want to come back in an orderly manner that guarantees our customers a quality product."

United's major hubs of Chicago, Denver and San Francisco will continue as priorities-along with the State of Hawaii-as the buildup of service continues over the next few weeks.

"United airplanes will be back in every single city served by United prior to May 17 when the pilots went on strike, and United will be back in all 50 states," said Zeeman.

United will return to the marketplace as an aggressive, strong competitor. Added Zeeman: "There is a good chance we can recapture our market share in 30-60 days."

He said United is poised for substantial growth and added: "We also look forward to government approval of our recent acquisition of Pan Am's Pacific Division which will make United a major international airline."

David R. Pringle, senior vice president-human resources and United's chief negotiator, also said he was pleased the dispute had been resolved and elaborated on the terms of the contract which had been negotiated over a 14-month period.

Regarding the contract itself, Pringle said that when the strike began the only unresolved issue was the new-hire progression scale.

"Within one week of the strike," Pringle said, "both United and ALPA agreed to virtually the same new-hire scale that was proposed by the company prior to the work stoppage."

"New-hire rates for years one through five of the new contract range from 34 [to] 50 percent less than current rates," he said. "The number of classifications of first and second officers were substantially reduced."

"And, rates after the fifth year will be subject to negotiation or arbitration under specific guidelines.

(more)

Merger with incumbent pilots will occur in the ranks of captain, which typically is reached after 18 to 20 years of service."

Pringle said the negotiations bogged down on five issues in the back-to-work agreement after agreement was achieved on the new-hire scale.

"United refused ALPA's demands to assert bargaining rights for management personnel, flight attendants and pilot applicants, on the basis these groups were outside of ALPA's legal bargaining jurisdiction," Pringle said.

"The two remaining issues included the salary structure of fleet-qualified permanent replacements hired by United after the strike began and the company's right to rebid the airline during the strike with working pilots."

"Union demands to represent management pilots, flight attendants and pilot applicants were dropped from the back-to-work agreement."

ALPA is continuing its suit previously filed in Federal District Court for claims regarding pilot applicants, salaries for fleet-qualified pilots hired during the strike and the system rebid.

United negotiated with the Association of Flight Attendants (AFA) on back-to-work terms for those flight attendants who withheld their services during the strike. AFA is the legal representative for United's flight attendants.

During the strike, United continued to operate approximately 15 percent of its pre-strike levels using management pilots and pilots who crossed the picket line. This represented approximately 225 flights a day.

Ferris said he regretted any inconvenience and hardship which the strike caused United's customers—as well as approximately 100 cities where United temporarily suspended service.

"We pledge to be back bigger and better than ever. One positive aspect of the strike was that we uncovered a new spirit at United Airlines and a level of excellence that we do not intend to lose."

Prior to the strike, United was the nation's largest airline and the world's largest investor-owned carrier. It served 159 cities in all 50 states, Canada, Mexico, the Bahamas, Japan and Hong Kong. The airline normally operates 1,550 flights daily with a fleet of 320 aircraft.

The United-ALPA contract became amendable April 1, 1984. The agreement does not require rank-and-file ratification by the pilot membership.

The release is fairly complete. In the early paragraphs, it highlights United Chairman Dick Ferris's satisfaction with the settlement. The promotional aspect of this release is strongest in three of the last four paragraphs, where United emphasizes its regret about the strike, pledging "to be back bigger and better than ever" and mentioning that United Airlines is the "world's largest investor-owned carrier."

UNITED AIRLINES' ADVERTISING DEPARTMENT ANNOUNCES THE SETTLEMENT

United took out three full pages of advertising in major newspapers in Cleveland and Chicago and two-page ads in Los Angeles and San Francisco. In the three-page advertisement, the first page (Figure 17.1) is a head-on picture of the nose of a giant jet and the words "We're back" at the top of the page. At the bottom are these words: "Turn page and take off. . . ." Across the top of the next

Figure 17.1. Reprinted courtesy of United Airlines Corporation.

Friendly skies are here again.

From Nashville we can take you to all these cities.

The largest airline in the land is coming back.

We can take you to over 45 cities from Nashville. Coast to Coast. And beyond.

And with United's 50 State Rebate, you can save money, too.

Fly any regularly scheduled United flight anywhere in the United States any time between July 1st and July 7th, 1985. Send a copy of your ticket, along with the form you will receive in-flight and United will send you a cash rebate. A check for 50% of the amount paid for your travel on United.

For information and reservations, call your Travel Agent. Or call United at 800-241-6522.

We're coming back. And friendly skies are here again.

You're not just flying, you're flying the friendly skies.

- Akron
- Albany
- Bangor
- Boise
- Boston
- Buffalo
- Burlington
- Chicago
- Cleveland
- Denver
- Des Moines
- Detroit
- Grand Rapids
- Honolulu
- Las Vegas
- Los Angeles
- Manchester
- Minneapolis/St. Paul
- Newark
- New York
- Oakland
- Omaha
- Ontario
- Phoenix
- Portland, ME
- Portland, OR
- Providence
- Reno
- Rochester
- Sacramento
- Saginaw
- Salt Lake City
- San Diego
- San Francisco
- San Jose
- Seattle/Tacoma
- Spokane
- Syracuse
- Tokyo
- Toronto
- Tucson
- Vancouver, BC
- Youngstown

fly the friendly skies.

United

Figure 17.2. Reprinted courtesy of United Airlines Corporation.

two pages is this banner headline: "Friendly skies are here again." These pages are filled with an impressive array of major cities and flight times to and from them. At the lower right-hand corner of the two pages is the logo of United

SUMMARY

These examples of the ways in which different media were used to tell one story show the flexibility of the mass media. Events were depicted differently by journalists and by the writers representing the organizations involved. The news release contained solely United's point of view; the news stories contained many other voices, among them the striking pilots, the sympathetic flight attendants, the crusading union leaders, passengers who were affected by loss of service, officials of other airlines capitalizing on the strike and representatives of United's management.

The broadcast stories and interviews offered numerous brief accounts of developments and reactions to the strike and its settlement. The newspaper stories offered both broader and deeper treatment of the subject, using to full advantage a luxury the airwaves don't provide: space.

The large ads gave United an advantage over other forms of communication in grabbing its audience's attention and attempting to persuade them that the airline would soon be solidly back in business with service of pre-strike quality and capacity.

Each example shows how mass media writers use their tools to achieve their goals:

For journalists, the goal is to inform by presenting all sides of a story. The print-media journalist unravels and interprets complex details; the broadcast journalist summarizes and interprets by finding the most significant and vivid examples among the myriad details of a story.

The public relations writer uses facts to make the best case possible for the client's activity and helps journalists to understand specialized information. The advertising copywriter employs writing skills to arouse interest in a product or point of view.

All are engaged, in different ways, in making a contribution to the information explosion that is continually shaping and changing the way we look at the world in which we live.

APPENDIX A

COPY AND REPORTING RULES

Most newspapers follow the general rules given here on copy preparation and style. Study them well and you'll be able to step from the classroom into a commercial newspaper newsroom without too much trouble.

Preparation of Copy for Newspapers
1. Type on a 65-space line. (Each typed line roughly equals two newsprint lines.)
2. Double-space.
3. Type your name, headline or slugline, and date at the top left of all pages.
4. Leave top third of the first page blank.
5. Type your byline flush left and immediately above the first line of your story:
   By INDIANA JONES
6. Type "(more)" at the bottom of each page if another page follows.
7. Use standard copy-editing symbols to make corrections.
8. Type or print corrections.
9. Never write on the back of a page.
10. Read and revise your story carefully after you think you have finished. Let the editor or adviser know of any material that may be libelous.

Guidelines for News Reporting
1. Accuracy in reporting facts is more important than anything else.
2. Completeness is vital. An incomplete story is a wastebasket item. In general, a reporter should answer these questions as completely as possible: exactly who, exactly where, exactly when, exactly what, exactly why, exactly how. Do not insert your opinion into the story.
3. Names make news. Check and double-check spelling of names.
4. Identify persons and places. Assume that your reader has never heard of Tech Aqua, Joe L. Evins Appalachian Center for Crafts, John Smith.
5. Do your assignment and look for stories you are not assigned.
6. Be sure that the story you are writing is not already assigned. Keep the weekly assignment sheet up to date by adding stories you are writing that are not listed on the sheet.
7. Before you start interviewing, find out all you can about a story or the person you're interviewing.
8. Use reference materials: dictionary, almanac, telephone directories, student handbooks, catalogs, newspaper morgue.
9. Learn to use the telephone. It is much quicker than waiting in an office. But cover your beat in person. (You should establish a regular meeting time with your major beat source.)

The Lead

1. Place the most imortant story element in the first line, if possible. The latest development is usually a key element. Use "what" leads unless there's an overriding reason not to do so.
2. The fact that someone spoke is usually not as important as what is said.
3. Keep the lead short. The Associated Press leads run 18 to 20 words. Most leads run about two typed lines and form one sentence. Leads that exceed three typed lines are definitely too long.
4. Place non-vital information in the second paragraph. Long titles, descriptions and addresses are often found in the second paragraph.
5. Study the leads in a good daily newspaper for good, and bad, examples.

Capitalization

1. Capitalize proper nouns but not common nouns.
2. Capitalize formal titles that come immediately before a name: President James Smith. Do not capitalize titles that follow a name; James Smith, president.
3. Capitalize *city, county, state* and *federal* when part of a title: Putnam County, Cookeville City Council.
4. Lowercase names of departments: history department, English department.
5. Capitalize names of schools and colleges: the College of Education.
6. Do not capitalize seasons of the year.
7. Capitalize highways: Interstate 40 [Use I-40 on second mention]; Highway 70.

Numerals

1. In general, spell out whole numbers below 10. Use figures for 10 and above. Note exceptions listed here.
2. In general, numerals that ordinarily appear in figures should be in figures—ages, dates, times, dimensions, speeds: Johnny Smith, 8; 1 percent; 3.9 percent; 8 mph; 2-foot line; $4; 2-to-1 ratio; 2-under-par score; three hours; 2 p.m.
3. Hyphenate combinations that work as a single adjective: the 5-foot-6-inch board; a 30-yard pass; a 4-foot snake.
4. Substitute the word *million* for five or six zeros: $2 million, $5.1 million.
5. Spell out amounts less than one with hyphens: four-fifths; one-third; 10½.
6. Scores: Tech defeated Western 4–3; Tech scored a 4–3 victory.
7. Height: Jay Joyce [6–11] and Don Foy [6–10].
8. Records: Tech has a 12–3 mark. Austin Peay [14–13] and Kentucky [19–7] are in the tournament.

Abbreviations

1. In names, abbreviate only Mr., Mrs., Ms., Dr., Rev., Gov., Sen., Rep., Sr. and Jr.
2. It is James Smith Jr. [no comma].
3. Spell out names of most organizations when used first time. Use abbreviations thereafter: Air Line Pilots Association, ALPA. Do not spell out CIA, FBI, NATO and other well-known abbreviations.
4. Spell out United States unless used as an adjective: U.S. dollar.
5. Use Ph.D., M.A., B.A. only after a person's name.
6. Use *mph* for *miles per hour* [no caps, no periods]. Use *a.m.* and *p.m.*
7. Do not use postal abbreviations for states. Do not abbreviate Alaska, Hawaii, Idaho, Iowa, Maine, Ohio, Texas and Utah.
8. Abbreviate Ave., Blvd., and St. with a specific address; otherwise, spell it out: 406 Dixie Ave., Dixie Avenue. Do not abbreviate Drive, Circle, etc.

9. Spell out First through Ninth in street names: Eighth Street; 6 Eighth St.; North Dixie Avenue; 24 N. Dixie Ave.

Punctuation
1. A comma is not usually placed before the conjunction in a simple series: He would recommend Smith, Jones and Kirk.
2. Use commas to set off tag lines in direct quotes: Jones said, "You must move."
3. Commas and periods always go inside quotation marks: The movie I saw is "Be a Sport."
4. Commas set off states and countries: He is going from Rome, Ga., to Rome, Italy, next month.
5. Commas set off years in exact dates: Feb. 14, 1989, is the target date.
6. Place quotation marks around names of books, movies, operas, plays, poems, songs, television programs, lectures, speeches and works of art.
7. Do not place quotes around names of magazines or newspapers.

Time
1. Keep the order consistent—time, then day, then date: The party is 10 a.m. Monday, Dec. 4.
2. Use *Monday, Tuesday*, etc., for seven days before or after publication date. Use *tomorrow, today, tonight, this morning, yesterday* for times in relation to the day the paper appears.
3. Use Feb. 14, not Feb. 14th.

Sexism
1. Treat men and women alike. Use full name at first mention, last name only thereafter.
2. Avoid terms that imply gender unless gender is relevant: the position of camera operator [not cameraman], but the station's sole anchorwoman.
3. Avoid using a masculine pronoun to refer to a generic noun ["The average homeowner pays his taxes . . ."]; to rectify, recast the sentence or pluralize the noun: On the average, homeowners pay their taxes. . . .

APPENDIX B

Words Commonly Used and Abused: A List to Aid Spelling and Usage

absence
absent
absolutely
accept (receive)
access (entry)
accidentally
accommodate
accompanied
achieve
acknowledgment
acquaint
acquire
across
adapt (modify)
adequate
adherence
admirable
adolescent
adopt (take up)
advantageous
advice (n.)
advise (v.)
affect (v.)
aggravate
aggressive
agreeable
aisle
alien
allegedly
allies
allot (assign)

all right
already
altar (podium)
alter (change)
amateur
ambiguous
ambulance
analysis
analyze
angle
anxious
apologize
apparent
appreciate
appropriately
arduous
arguing
argument
arousing
arrangement
arriving
ascent (rise)
assent (agree)
assessment
athlete
attach
attendance
attitude
audience
authority
available

balance
bargain
basically
believable
benefited
bipartisan
boisterous
brilliant
burglar
business
campaign
canceled
cancellation
capital (city)
capitol (building)
career
careless
casualty
category
caucus
cautious
ceiling
cemetery
ceremony
certainly
character
chief
choose (select)
chose (selected)
circuit
cite (name)

clothes
coarse (rough)
coincidence
column
combated
commitment
committee
compel
competent
complement (adjunct)
compliment (remark)
concede
conceivable
condemn
conference
conferred
confident
conscience (n.)
conscious (adj.)
consequently
considerable
consistent
continuous
controlled
controversial
convenient
corporation
correspondence
council (group)
counsel (advice)
courageous
course (path)
courteous
criticism
criticize
curiosity
debt
decent (proper)
decision
defendant
definite
definition
delinquent
delivery
dependable
dependent
deplorable
descent (fall)
describe
description
despair
desperate
despise
destroy

deterred
develop
different
disagree
disappear
disapprove
discipline
discussed (talked about)
disgust (abhorrence)
dismissal
dissatisfied
dissent (objection)
distant
disturb
doubt
drowned
drunkenness
dyeing (coloring)
dying (expiring)
effect (n.)
elegant
eliminate
eloquent
embarrass
eminent (prominent)
emphasis
emphasize
encore
encouraging
enormity (horror)
enormousness (size)
ensure (guarantee)
equivalent
especially
evidence
exaggerate
except (exclude)
excess (surplus)
excitement
executive
exhilarate
existence
expel
experience
explanation
extraordinary
extremely
familiar
fantasies (n., pl.)
fantasize (v.)
farther (literal distance)
fascinating
favorite
feasible

field
finally
flexible
friend
friendliness
fundamentally
further (figurative distance)
gambling
generally
government
gracious
grief (n.)
grieve (v.)
guarantee
guard
guidance
handicapped
harass
hysterical
identical
ignorance
illegible
illiterate
illusion
immediate
imminent (impending)
imperative
implied (hinted)
inaugurate
incident
incongruous
incredible
independent
inevitable
inference (deduction)
influence
inherent
innocence
innocent
innocuous
inoculate
inseparable
insistent
insure (cover with insurance)
intelligent
intercede
interrupt
involvement
irrelevant
irresistible
irritable
its (of it)

it's (it is)
judgment
kidnapped
knowledge
knowledgeable
labor
laundry
lay (set)
laziness
legislative
legitimately
leisure
lie (recline)
liveliest
loneliness
loose (unattached)
lose (mislay)
losing
luxuries
lying
magnificent
maintenance
marriage
mechanic
medicine
merchandise
miner (worker)
minor (youngster)
minuscule
miscellaneous
mischievous
misconduct
mission
misspell
monopolize
moral (proper; lesson)
morale (spirit)
mortgage
muscle
muscular
mysterious
naturally
necessary
negotiate
neighbor
noticeable
nuisance
obedience
observant
obstacle
occasion
occurred
occurrence
omission

opportunity
organize
origin
outrageous
pamphlet
paragraph
parallel
paralysis
paralyze
patience
peaceful
peculiar
penetrate
perceive
perform
permanent
permit
persistent
personal (of a person)
personnel (employees)
perspiration
persuade
pertain
pervade
photograph
phrase
piece
political
portray
possess
possible
practically
precede
prefer
prejudice
presence
present
principal (chief)
principle (basis)
privilege
probable
proceed
prominent
prospective
protester
pursue
quality
quantity
quiet (silent)
quite (very)
radioactive
readily
recede
receipt

receive
recognize
recommend
reference
referred
regardless
relevant
reliable
relieve
reminisce
repentant
repetition
represent
resistence
responsible
revise
rhythm
ridicule
righteous
safety
scarcely
schedule
scholar
secretary
seize
sensitive
separate
several
severely
shield
significance
similar
simultaneous
sincerely
site (location)
solemn
sophomore
source
specifically
stationary (fixed)
stationery (paper)
stature
straight
subsequent
subtle
summary
supervise
supplement
suppose
suppress
susceptible
suspense
symbolize
systematically

tangible	tremendous	whether (if)
tentative	variable	who's (who is)
their (of them)	various	whose (of whom)
there (at that place)	vengeance	wield
they're (they are)	vigorous	worrisome
thief	violence	worshiper
tolerance	violent	wrist
tranquil	weather (atmospherics)	yacht
tranquillity	weight	yield
transferred	weird	

APPENDIX C

A COMMONSENSE APPROACH TO PUNCTUATION

No punctuation system is utterly foolproof. But this commonsense approach takes care of two archvillains, the comma and the semicolon, quite adequately. It also gives you something other than a bewildering array of punctuation rules to memorize. And who knows, this simple learning device may prove so interesting that you'll be moved to go to the freshman English handbook and study punctuation, by the rules.

This system is based on punctuating according to the way you read. After writing a sentence—simple, complex or compound—read it aloud. Wherever there is a natural pause, a punctuation mark is needed. All that remains is to determine which mark to use.

Since you all know what a question is, you need not concern yourselves with that mark. The same is true of a declarative sentence, so the period need not be considered. Exclamation marks usually fall into the same category as question marks. If a person yells "Fire!" or shouts, use an exclamation mark; otherwise, forget about it. Within a sentence, the vast majority of pauses in reading must be punctuated with a comma or a semicolon. Ninety-nine percent of all punctuation errors are comma or semicolon errors.

How can you be sure of using commas and semicolons properly to eliminate those punctuation errors? The answer is simple: Memorize the three instances in which the semicolon is used.

1. Use semicolons when independent clauses are not joined by conjunctions: He learned to box; she learned karate.
2. Use semicolons with independent clauses joined by conjunctions that have commas in the clauses: He learned to box as a lark, not caring whether he would use this skill later in life or even at all; however, she learned karate in preparation for life in the big city.
3. Use semicolons in series that already contain commas: They walked to the store and bought apples, oranges and carrots; milk, yogurt and cheese; and pork chops, a roast and a leg of mutton.

See if any of these instances apply to the natural pauses in your sentence reading. If they do, use a semicolon. If they don't, use a comma.

Other pauses may occur in sentences that are not resolved by the comma or semicolon. These may require a colon or a dash.

A colon points to what follows. In media writing it is usually used to introduce a series too long to be prefaced by a comma: Elected at the meeting were: Lisa Parnell, president; Joy Whitus, vice president; Mary Susan Moore, secretary-treasurer.

A dash marks a separation more intense than a comma—the sentence dashes off in another direction: Teresa Ashworth sat serenely behind her desk—scurrying around the makeup tables was Allison Collins. The dash can also be used to set off a parenthetical expression: The time for the meeting—2 o'clock to be exact—was set by Jim Herrin.

Follow these rules, and the vast majority of your punctuation problems will be solved.

APPENDIX D

COPY-EDITING MARKS

Copyreaders are responsible for the stories they edit. They ensure that the stories are accurate and free of libelous remarks. They cut out excessive wording and tie the stories up into neat little bundles with headlines as ribbons. These are the marks they use.

¶ ATLANTA (AP)—The organization	indent for paragraph
said Thursday. It was the first	paragraph
the last attempts. ⏋ ⎣ With this the president tried	no paragraph
the Jones Smith company is not	transpose
over a period of (sixty) or more years	use figures
there were (9) in the group.	spell it out
Ada, (Oklahoma) is the hometown	abbreviate
The (Ga) man was the guest of	don't abbreviate
prince edward said it was his	uppercase
as a result This will be	lowercase
the ac⌢cuser pointed to them	remove space
In⌊these times it is necessary	insert space
the order for the ~~later~~ devices (stet)	retain
The ruling ∧is a fine example	insert word
according to the ~~this~~ source	delete
according to the ~~this~~ source	delete
BF ⌐ By DONALD AMES ⌐	bold face, center
J.R. Thomas ⌉	flush right
⌈ J.R. Thomas	flush left
ˏ	insert comma

Copy-Editing Marks

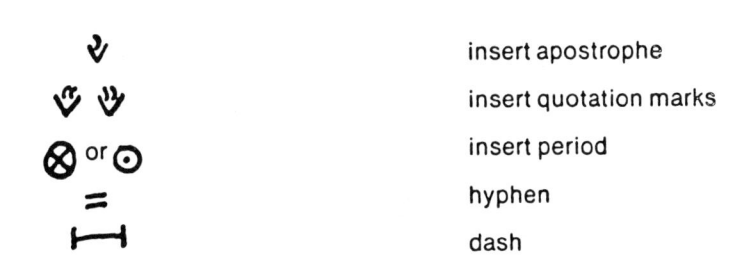

⋎	insert apostrophe
⋎ ⋎	insert quotation marks
⊗ or ⊙	insert period
=	hyphen
⊢⊣	dash

Reprinted with permission of the Associated Press.

INDEX

Accidents, 146–147
Accuracy, as a basic writing principle, 12, 13–14
Advertisements
 anatomy of, 396–401
 appeal to competence, 398–399
 appeal to standards of excellence, 399–401
 message elements of, 396
 problem-solving, 397–398
Advertising
 audience role in, 392–394, 401–403
 client role in, 392–394, 403
 copywriting elements of, 394–395
 goals of, 392
 impact of, 391
 setting objectives for, 392–394
 testing, 401–403
Aggressiveness, need for, 67–68
Agriculture, 155–156
Analysis of newspaper features, 291–294
Announcer-on-camera (AOC) television scripts, 271, 272–275
Annual reports, 423
Archiving information, 115–116
Assignment, newspaper features, 294
Aston, William A., 327
Attribution, 14, 143, 202–203. See also Quotes
Audiences. See also Leads
 differences in coverage and, 144–163
 importance of, 3–5
 for public relations, 414, 417–419, 430, 433–434
 radio, 233, 246
 reaction to reportorial reviews, 375
 role in advertising, 392–394, 401–403
 television news, 278

Background information. See Research
Baker, Russell, 367
Basic newspaper stories, 123–136
Beat
 assignment, 51–56
 behavior on, 53, 56–57
 business and labor as a, 66–67
 campus, 52–55
 city, 55–56
 courts as a, 56–59
 education as a, 64–66
 government and politics as a, 59–64
 major news, 56–67
 need for research on a, 53, 55–56
 newsworthiness and a, 53
 purpose of, 51
Behavior. See also Vigilance
 on a beat, 53, 56–57
 on interviews, 96–98
 reluctant news sources and, 71–73
Besuden, H. Carlisle, III, 155–156
Billboard news, 160–163
Births, 160
Blind spots, 9–11
Block method of organizing information, 113–114
Bombeck, Erma, 367
Brochures, 425
Bulletin boards, 432
Business
 as a beat, 66–67
 features, 330–331
 and labor, 151–152
Byrd, Ben, 159

Cabletext, 216, 222–223. See also Electronic journalism
Campaign(s)
 announcements, 429–430
 external public relations, 427–430
 fund raising, 427–429
 internal public relations, 432–433
 public relations, 427–430
 tools, 427
 types of, 430
Campus beat, 52–55
Canby, Vincent, 378
Carter, Lindy Keane, 425–426
Casale, Robert J., 419–423
Chandler, Russell, 153
Checklist for writing
 radio news, 238–240
 television news, 271
City beat, 55–56
Clients' role in advertising, 392–394, 403
Colley, Russell, 392
Color stories, 283
Columns, 365–368
Combination leads, 328–329
Complex stories
 cabletext and, 222–223
 for newspapers, 137–163, 443–448
Composing
 columns, 365–368
 for electronic journalism, 220–223
Comprehensive/complex newspaper stories, 137–163, 443–448

Comprehensive news leads, 236–238
Computer programming, 223
Conciseness, 220, 238
Confidentiality of sources, 70–71
Consumer testing, and advertising, 401
Conversational writing style, 238–240, 246
Copywriting, advertising, 394–395
County government, as a beat, 61–62
Courts, as a beat, 56–59
Coverage, audience differences and, 144–163
Creativity, 301–302, 329, 360, 379, 394
Credibility, 15–16
Crime, 148–149. See also Courts
Crowell, Craven, 150

Details, importance of, 293
Displays, and internal public relations, 432
Dow Jones News Retrieval, 217
Drafts, newspaper feature, 297–299
Dramatic leads, 326

Editorials, 363–365
Editors/editing
  computer programming and, 223
  copy, 18
  functions of, 124
  skills for electronic journalism, 218–220, 224
  television news tapes, 270
Education, as a beat, 64–66
Electronic journalism. See also Cabletext; Technology; Teletext; Videotex
  composing for, 220–223
  computer programming for, 223
  conciseness in, 220
  editors/editing and, 218–219, 224
  employment in, 213, 218
  5W + H and Significance questions in, 224
  format skills for, 218
  graphics for, 223
  impact of, 213–214
  information management and, 219
  leads in, 216–217
  news sense and, 219–220
  skills for, 217–223
  types of, 214–216
  writing guidelines for, 223–224
Employment, in electronic journalism, 213, 218
Engagements and weddings, 160–161
Essays, 368–374
Exhibits and internal public relations, 432
External public relations. See also Public relations
  annual reports and, 423

brochures and, 425
campaigns, 427–430
feature articles and, 425
media kits and, 423
news releases and, 415–417, 450–452
novelty items and, 426
public service announcements and, 425
speeches and statements and, 417–423
tools for, 414–426

Feature stories. See also Newspaper features
  business, 330–331
  compared to magazine articles, 326, 334–336
  personality profiles as, 332–337
  public relations as sources of, 425
  television news, 276–278
  travel and leisure, 331–332
Federal government, as a beat, 62–64
Fires, 147–148
5W + H and Significance questions
  differences in coverage and, 146
  electronic journalism skills and, 224
  leads, inverted pyramid, and, 125–129
  research and, 36
Follow-up stories, 140–142
Format
  for electronic journalism, 218
  for magazine articles, 345–347
  for reviews, 375–379
  for television news, 272
Form for persuasion/opinion writing, 361–365
Frederick, Elise, 56–57, 58–59

Gannett Co., 217
Gerstner, John, 326
Gill, Brendan, 378–379
Goodman, Ellen, 365–367
Government
  administrative side of, 63
  county, 61–62
  federal, 62–64
  offices as sources, 38–42
  pack journalism and, 63
  and politics, as a beat, 59–64
  records, 63–64
  secrecy in, 73–76
  state, 62–64
Graphics, and electronic journalism, 223

Hagen, Bill, 377–378
Hard news leads, 234–235
Harwood, William, 150
Headlines
  advertising, 394–395
  newspaper, 124

HIT (hook, idea, transition), 288–290, 300, 308, 326
Homework. *See* Research
House organs, 430, 432
How. *See* 5W + H and Significance questions
Howard, Carole, 414
Humorous opinion writing, 360

Identifiers, 239–240
Imagery, 206–208
Imagination, 5–6
Immediacy, in writing for radio, 238–239
Impact
　of electronic journalism, 213–214
　in newspaper features, 305–308
　writing for, 199–211
Information. *See also* News; Newsworthiness; Research; Stories
　archiving, 115–116
　block method of organizing, 113–114
　key words/quotes, and organizing, 114–115
　management in electronic journalism, 219
　need for, 58
　newspaper features and gathering of, 294–296
　organizing, 107–120
　outlines, as method of organizing, 108–113, 115
Informative opinion writing, 359
Internal public relations, 430–433. *See also* Public relations
Interpretations of news, 11–12
Interpretive opinion writing, 359–360
Interviews
　arranging and conducting, 93–98
　goals of, 98–99
　listening to answers in, 97–98
　news, 142–144
　as newspaper features, 295–296, 301–304
　putting people at ease in, 96–97
　question and answer, 301–302
　research and, 35, 95–96
　setting for, 98
　telephone, 94–95
Inverted pyramid, 124–128, 415

Journalism, compared to science, 14–15
Journalistic writing, and public relations, 433

Kael, Pauline, 377
Key words/quotes, 114–115
Keycom Electronic Publishing, 217
Kilby, Bill, 156
Kiosks, 432
Knight-Ridder Newspapers Inc., 217

Labor. *See* Business
Language, 206–208
Laws
　shield, 70–71
　sunshine, 73–76
Leads
　audiences and, 237
　combination, 328–329
　comprehensive (umbrella), 236–238
　definition of, 123
　dramatic, 326
　golden rules for, 128–129
　hard news, 234–235
　identifiers in, 239–240
　latest developments as, 243
　for magazine articles, 326–329, 347
　newspaper, 123–136
　for newspaper features, 288–290
　of news releases, 415–417, 425, 450–452
　no-nonsense, 327–328
　novelty/curiosity, 327
　for personality profiles, 332–333
　questions as, 327
　radio news, 233–238, 246
　salient-feature, 139
　sentence structure and, 199
　setting, 328
　simple, 124–128
　soft news, 233–234, 237
　for sports stories, 157
　story styles and, 137–142
　summary news, 137–138, 328, 443, 445, 447, 448
　suspended-interest, 139–140
　throwaway news, 235–236
　titles of magazine articles and, 329
　tone and, 289–290
Lewis, Anthony, 368
Libraries, 37–38, 44
Local news, 146–149
Logotypes, advertising, 395
Long, John, 153

Magazine articles
　format for, 345–347
　ideas for, 343
　leads for, 326–329, 347
　markets for, 343–345
　newspaper features and, 326, 334–336
　reader-interest plane and, 329–342
　specialization and, 325, 347
　steps for developing, 342–345
　titles of, 329
Major news beat, 56–67
Maslow (A.H.) hierarchy of needs, 393
Mass media. *See* Advertising; Magazine articles; Newspapers; Public relations; Radio news; Television news

Media kits, 423
Mill, John Stuart, 368
Motivational research, 403
Mulgrew, Tom, 154

Narrative hook. *See* Reader-interest plane
Neuharth, Allen H., 123
News. *See also* Information; Newsworthiness; Stories
   billboard, 160–163
   interpretations of, 11–12
   local, 146–149
   releases, 415–417, 425, 450–452
   sense, 219–220
   special-interest, 152–160
   stories and editorials, 363–364
   technical, 149–152
Newspaper features. *See also* Feature stories; News
   analysis of, 291–294
   assignment of, 294
   content of, 283–284
   details in, 293
   drafts of, 297–298
   impact in, 305–308
   interviews as, 295–296, 301–304
   leads for, 288–290
   outlines for, 296
   paragraphs in, 290–291, 293–294
   quotes in, 292, 300
   research and, 294–296
   rewriting, 299–301
   sidebars, 300–304
   sources for, 286–287
   structure of, 287–291
   style of, 293
   suspended-interest stories and, 287–294
   valleys and peaks of, 292–293
   writing, 294–301
Newspaper libraries, as sources, 44
Newspapers. *See also* Newspaper features
   basic stories for, 123–136
   columns for, 365–368
   comprehensive/complex stories for, 137–163, 443–448
   copy and reporting rules for, 457–459
   headlines in, 124
   inverted pyramid and, 124–128, 415
   leads for, 123–136
   sidebars and, 445, 446
   slugs in, 124
   stories for, compared to radio news stories, 242
   writing for, 199–211, 443–448, 455
Newsworthiness, 8–12, 53, 121–122, 414
No-nonsense leads, 327–328
Novelty/curiosity leads, 327
Novelty items, 426

Obituaries, 161–162
Objectives, advertising, 392–394
Objectivity, as a basic writing principle, 13–15
Observation, 5–8
Off-the-record sources, 72–73
Opinion writing
   composing the column, 365–368
   essays and, 368–374
   form and, 361–365
   humorous, 360
   informative, 359
   interpretive, 359–360
   opening paragraphs and, 361
   outlines and, 360–361
   persuasion and, 360–368
   preparation for, 359–361
   research and, 360
   reviews and, 375–379
   self-examination and, 360
   skills needed for, 359–361
   types of, 359–360
Outlines. *See also* Reader-interest plane
   creativity and, 360
   developing, 109–113
   of newspaper features, 296
   order in, 109
   for speeches and statements, 419
   for writing opinion, 360–361

Pack journalism, 63
Page, Susan, 333–334
Paragraphs. *See also* HIT; Reader-interest plane
   body, 290–291
   concluding, 293–294
   inverted pyramid and, 124–128, 415
   for magazine articles, 330–342
   opinion writing and opening, 361
   patterns of, 203–205
   triadic structure of, 203–205
Peaks and valleys approach, 292–293. *See also* Reader-interest plane
Perceptions, 11–12
Personality profiles, 332–337
Persuasive writing. *See* Advertising; External public relations; Internal public relations; Opinion writing; Public relations
Political and civic groups, as sources, 38
Politics. *See* Government
Porter, Andrew, 376
Prerecorded television scripts, 271
Primary news sources. *See* Beat
Private sources, 42–44
Professional groups, as sources, 42–43
Promotion writing. *See* Public relations
Pronunciation guides, 240
Public records, as sources, 39–42

Public relations. *See also* External public relations; Internal public relations
   audience for, 414, 417–419, 430, 433–434
   goals of, 413, 415, 434
   journalistic writing and, 433
   newsworthiness and, 414
   as sources of news, 413, 433
   writing for, 450–454, 455
Public service announcements, 425
Public sources of news, 37–42
Pyramid, inverted, 124–128, 415

Question-and-answer interviews, 301–302
Question leads, 327
Quotes, 143, 245, 246, 292, 300. *See also* Attribution

Radio news
   audience, 233, 246
   formula for, 243–245
   leads for, 233–238, 246
   media reporting and, 233, 238
   and newspaper stories, 242
   quotes in, 245, 246
   rewriting wire copy for, 241–243
   style for writing, 238–240, 246
   technical aspects of writing for, 244–245
   writing for, 238–240, 448–449, 455
Reader-interest plane
   business features and, 330–331
   charting, 337–342
   essays and, 369–374
   magazine articles and, 329–342
   personality profiles and, 332–337
   persuasive writing and, 361
   reviews and, 375–379
   travel and leisure features and, 331–332
Readership studies and advertising, 403
Reasoning, 7–8
Records, government, 63–64
Reed, W.A., 153–154
Reference sources, 44–45
Rejections, magazine article, 346–347
Religion, 153–155
Reluctant news sources, 71–76
Reportorial reviews, 375
Research. *See also* Information; Outlines
   advertising, 393
   background, 37–49
   beats and, 53, 55–56
   evaluating, 107–116
   5W + H and Significance questions and, 36
   importance of, 35, 58
   interviews and, 35, 95–96
   motivational, 403

   newspaper features and, 294–296
   opinion writing and, 360
   organizations as news sources, 43–44
   primary sources of, 35–36
   secondary sources of, 35
Reviews, 375–379
Rewriting
   drafts as, 297–299
   newspaper features, 299–301
   radio wire copy, 241–243
Rieland, Randy, 331–332
Rowan, Carl T., 367–368
Rozhon, Tracie, 328

Salient-feature leads, 139
Sarton, May, 369–370
Scripts, television, 270–278
   announcer-on-camera (AOC) and, 271, 272–275
   prerecorded, 271
   shooting, 398
   taped news events in segments, 271–275
Secondary sources, 35, 38
Secrecy
   in government, 73–76
   public records and, 39–42
Seigenthaler, John, 69–70
Self-examination, and opinion writing, 360
Sentence patterns, 199–203
Setting leads, 328
Shield laws, 70–71
Shooting scripts, 398
Sidebars, 283, 302–304, 445, 446
Signatures, advertising, 395
Skills
   for electronic journalism, 217–223
   for writing opinion, 359–361
Slogans, advertising, 395
Slugs, 124, 272
Smisson, Patti L., 151, 152
Soft news leads, 233–234, 237
Sound and television news, 270
Sources. *See also* Beat
   government offices as, 38–42
   libraries as, 37–38
   for magazine articles, 343
   of newspaper features, 286–287
   political and civic groups as, 38
   private, 42–44
   professional groups as, 42–43
   public, 37–42
   public relations as, 413, 433
   reference, 44–45
   reluctant news, 71–76
   research, 35, 38
   research organizations as, 43–44
   special-interest groups as, 43

Special-interest
  groups as news sources, 43
  news, 152–160
Specialization, and magazine articles, 325, 347
Speeches and statements, 417–423
Sports, 156–160
State government, as a beat, 62–64
Stoltz, Craig, 330–331
Stories. *See also* Feature stories; Interviews; Newspaper features
  color, 283
  comprehensive/complex newspaper, 137–163, 443–448
  developing, 243
  editorials and news, 363–364
  follow-up, 140–142, 243
  newspaper and radio, 242
  suspended-interest, 287–294
Storyboards, 397–398
Style
  inverted pyramid, 124–128, 415
  leads and, 137–142
  needs and, 3–5
  of newspaper features, 293
  of news releases, 415
  for radio, 238–240, 246
Subheads, advertising, 395
Subjectivity. *See* Objectivity, as a basic writing principle
Summary leads, 137–138, 328, 443, 445, 447, 448
Sunshine laws, 73–76
Suspended-interest
  leads, 139–140
  stories, 287–294

Tact, need for, 67–68
Tape editing, television news, 270
Taped television news event in segments, 271–275
Tape recorders, 95–96
Teamwork, need for, 16–18
Technical news, 149–152
Technology. *See also* Electronic journalism
  cabletext, 216, 222–223
  news, 213–232
  reporting about, 150–151
  teletext, 215–216, 221–222
  videotex, 214, 216, 217, 220–221
  writing and, 16–17, 45
Telephone interviews, 94–95
Teletext, 215–216, 221–222. *See also* Electronic journalism

Television news
  audiences, 278
  features for, 276–278
  format for, 272
  scripting, 270–278
  slugs for, 272
  techniques, 270–278
  TV talk and, 270
  VTR package and, 274–275
  writing for, 270, 271, 449–450, 455
Testing, advertising, 401–403
Text, advertising, 395
Theater testing, advertising, 402–403
Throwaway news leads, 235–236
Thurber, James, 370
Titles, magazine article, 329
Tone, 289–290
Travel and leisure features, 331–332
Triadic structure of paragraphs, 203–205
Tribune Co., 217

Umbrella leads, 236–238

Valleys and peaks, newspaper feature, 292–293. *See also* Reader-interest plane
Videotex, 214, 216, 217, 220–221. *See also* Electronic journalism
Vigilance, need for, 67–76
Visual image, and television news, 270
VTR package, 274–275

Weather, 162–163
Weddings, 160–161
Welles, Chris, 44–45, 66–67
What. *See* 5W + H and Significance questions
When. *See* 5W + H and Significance questions
Where. *See* 5W + H and Significance questions
White, E.B., 337–342
Who. *See* 5W + H and Significance questions
Why. *See* 5W + H and Significance questions
Wicker, Tom, 361–365
Wire copy, rewriting radio, 241–243
Witte, Scott, 328–329
Woody, Larry, 158–159
Writing principles, basic, 13–16

Yankelovich, Daniel, 328